CENSORED

The News That Didn't Make the News—and Why

The 1996 Project Censored Yearbook

CARL JENSEN & PROJECT CENSORED

INTRODUCTION BY WALTER CRONKITE

CARTOONS BY TOM TOMORROW

SEVEN STORIES PRESS

NEW YORK

Censored: the news that didn't make the news and why
ISSN 1074-5998

10 9 8 7 6 5 4 3 2 1

SEVEN STORIES PRESS
632 Broadway, Seventh Floor
New York, NY 10012

Designed by LaBreacht Design

DEDICATION

To George Seldes
Journalist, Author, Media Critic,
Muckraker, Censored Judge, and Friend.
America's Most Censored Journalist
November 19, 1890–July 2, 1995

Table of Contents

CENSORED

"The truth has always been
dangerous to the rule of the rogue,
the exploiter, the robber.
So the truth must be
ruthlessly suppressed."
—Eugene V. Debs

PREFACE

20 Years of Raking Muck, Raising Hell

This edition of CENSORED! *The News That Didn't Make The News—And Why* marks the 20th anniversary of Project Censored and my retirement from the project. Fortunately the project will continue in the very capable hands of my friend and colleague, Peter Phillips, an assistant professor of sociology at Sonoma State University.

The Censored Yearbook is published annually in response to a growing national demand for news and information not published nor broadcast by the mainstream media in America.

Originally self-published by Project Censored as a spiral bound resource book, the 1996 Project Censored Yearbook is published by Seven Stories Press of New York. As in the six previous Yearbooks (1990–1995), CENSORED! features the top 25 *Censored* stories of the year, background information about Project Censored, comments about the top 25 stories by the original authors and others, brief synopses of each of the stories, and a chapter on the top "junk food news" stories, with comments by the news ombudsmen who selected them.

This edition also includes a special introduction, "Let the Chips Fall Where They May" by Walter Cronkite; a déjà vu chapter of previously censored stories that finally have been "discovered" by the mainstream media; an updated eclectic chronology of censorship since 605 BC which attempts to put the issue of censorship into historical context; and a current censored resource guide to alternative media organizations, electronic and print alternative media, and selected mainstream media sources.

The Alternative Writer's Market has been updated and expanded. It provides brief information about publications that are open to the work of alternative journalists.

Chapter 3, Censored Books, provides a modest, but intriguing, insight into some of the books that failed to attract the attention of major media critics in 1995.

Also, as before, this edition contains complete reprints of the original top 10 *Censored* articles wherever possible. You'll be able to review the brief synopsis of the story, see what the author has to say about the subject, and then read the original article in its entirety.

The synopses, included in Chapter 2, are originally written by Project Censored researchers participating in a seminar in news media censorship offered by the Communication Studies Department at Sonoma State University, a member of the California State University system. They are then edited for style and clarity. The synopses are not meant to replace the original articles upon which they are based, but rather to briefly summarize the major thrust of a much longer article or, in some cases, a brochure or book.

CENSORED! *The News That Didn't Make The News And Why* is another effort by Project Censored to provide information about important issues the public should know. I hope you will learn more about issues that touch your life, your community, and, in a larger context, the global village of which we are all citizens.

THIS MODERN WORLD by TOM TOMORROW

I also hope that it will disturb you to discover that all this information was available to the press and that you will wonder why your local and national news media haven't already told you about these subjects.

I would like to invite you to become a news muckraker by joining Project Censored as a scout or source for stories that deserve more attention from the mainstream media. Please see the postscript for information on how to nominate stories for the "Best Censored News Stories of 1996."

Project Censored is flattered when we are referred to as a muckraking organization with goals similar to those who gave birth to the Golden Age of Muckraking from 1902 to 1912. However, we hasten to point out that the true muckrakers are the individual journalists who are responsible for the articles cited as censored stories.

Our role is to stimulate journalists, editors, producers, and publishers to support more muckraking investigative journalism. Unfortunately, despite a slight blip in the aftermath of Watergate, journalism has failed to fulfill its watchdog role as exemplified during the Golden Age of Muckraking.

Indeed, while the United States is without equal in terms of communications technology, it would appear that it has suffered a massive breakdown when it comes to communications content. While we may have a free press and the most sophisticated communications system in the world, unfortunately a free press and high technology do not guarantee a well-informed society.

As a society, we are exposed to more information now than ever before in history. And thanks to recent advances in communications technology followed by the current explosion in computer sciences, the average citizen today is exposed to more information, at a greater speed, from

throughout the world, than was available to our country's leaders not too many years ago. CNN viewers in Keokuk, Iowa, were probably more quickly informed of what was happening during recent events in the Balkans than the President of the United States was informed of events in Vietnam during that conflict.

Like the horse and buggy, the agricultural and industrial ages are far behind us; we are hurtling headlong into the cyberspace of the information age. All indicators support this thesis—from the diversity of information sources to the sophistication of communications technology to the amount of time people spend with the media.

The problem is not with the quantity of information available in our society, which sometimes reaches an overload level, but rather with the quality of that information.

For example, when something starts to go wrong in your personal life, there generally are some warning signals that alert you to the problem. If you are a rational person, you normally act upon that information in an effort to solve the problem.

So too, it is with a society. When a problem arises, there should be a warning signal—information—that alerts citizens that something is wrong which needs attention and resolution. An aware and informed populace could then influence its leaders to act upon that information in an effort to solve the problem. This, unfortunately, is not the case in the United States.

I suspect there are few people who do not believe that the United States has serious problems that need to be resolved if we are to succeed and survive in the future. Yet, how many of us are fully aware of the scope of these problems and how many of us have all the information we need to deal with them?

Despite the quantity of news and information being disseminated around the clock, you and some 250 million other Americans are not being told everything you have a need and right to know. And, without full information about the affairs of our society, we cannot function as good citizens.

It is not realistic to expect anything to change, in America or in your community, until enough people lean out their windows and shout: "I'm mad as hell and I'm not going to take it any more!"

But, for that to happen, we need someone out there raking muck and raising hell. This of course should be the role of a free press—but the media are failing us. Instead they have become the willing tools of the propagandists that Jacques Ellul warned us about in his 1965 book *Propaganda: The Formation of Men's Attitudes*—propagandists so skilled we are not even aware of being manipulated.

The point is that our primary sources of news and information are increasingly controlled by a very small group of men—confirming the thesis that an elite group has gained control over the information industry in the United States. As media scholar Ben Bagdikian points out in *The Media Monopoly*, his classic critique of corporate media control, fewer than 20 corporations now control most of the nation's mass media.

The next step in the information control process in America is to use this control to effectively exploit our minds. This, also, it seems, has been accomplished. The mind manipulators are well aware of the first principle of successful mind control—repetition.

To be successful, as Jacques Ellul wrote, propaganda must be continuous and lasting—continuous in that it must not leave any gaps, but must fill the citizen's whole day and all his days; lasting in that it must function over a long period of time.

Today's information industry learned this lesson well from Adolph Hitler who so successfully used propaganda in his quest for power. More than a half century ago Hitler said the masses take a long time to understand and remember, thus it is necessary to repeat the message time and time and time again. The public must be conditioned to accept the claims that are made...no matter how outrageous or false those claims might be.

The Madison Avenue propagandists use the same techniques to sell us products and services we don't need and often can't afford. Repetition is also the key to success on Madison Avenue. Unfortunately, we, as a society, appear to have been well-conditioned to accept any number of claims regardless of how detrimental they may be to our environment or to our own well-being.

Propaganda tends to transport the individual to a separate reality, a world lacking outside points of reference where you are continuously at the mercy of the propagandists. You must not be allowed time for meditation or reflection in which to see or define yourself as might occur when propaganda is not continuous. For if propaganda is not continuous, you might have a moment or two when you can emerge from its grip and realize you have been manipulated.

Finally, to assure complete compliance with the propagandistic techniques, to close the information control loop, to prevent you from finding external points of reference which might cause you to question the propagandists' messages, the information industry attempts to insulate you by trying to censor anything contradictory, any dissonant messages that might come in from the outside.

Since 1976, I have been conducting a national media research project which seeks to locate and publicize those dissonant messages, messages the media elite don't want the rest of us to know about.

PROJECT CENSORED LAUNCHED

Concerned about increasing social problems and apparent public apathy, I launched a national research effort in 1976, called Project Censored, to explore whether there really is a systematic omission of certain issues in our national news media. My concern was specifically stimulated by personal bewilderment over how the American people could elect Richard Nixon by a landslide more than four months after Watergate, one of the most sensational political crimes of the century. (For an insight into how the mass media failed the electorate in that election, see the 1972 Watergate reference in Chapter 6, "An Eclectic Chronology of Censorship from 605 B.C. to 1995.")

Project Censored is now an internationally renowned media research project in its 20th year. By exploring and publicizing stories of national importance on issues that have been overlooked or under-reported by the mainstream news media, the project seeks to stimulate journalists and editors to provide more mass media coverage of those issues. It also hopes to encourage the general public to seek out and demand more information on significant issues.

Since its start, the research effort has generated queries for more information about the project as well as about individual stories from journalists, scholars, and concerned people throughout the world. It has been described as a tip sheet for investigative television programs like "60 Minutes" and "20/20," as a distant early warning system for society's problems, and even as a "moral force" in American media, as cited by media columnist David Armstrong in the *American Journalism Review*, July 1983. The National Association for Education in Journalism and Mass Communication cited the project for "providing a new model for media criticism for journalism education."

Concerned with the increasing attempts at censorship in our public schools and on college campuses since the Supreme Court's 1988 Hazelwood decision, Project Censored is particularly interested in reaching journalism teachers, advisors, and students. Our objective is to offer stimulating resource materials to student journalists in an effort to broaden discussion, understanding, and response to the threat of news media self-censorship.

In response to the many tips and suggestions the Project receives concerning issues that might well be of interest to investigative journalists, we developed a "CENSORED TIPS" program. As news stories are received, they are summarized and sent out to media and journalism organizations who have the resources to investigate them. Some of the "tips" sent out in 1995 included information about the efforts by Congress to muzzle political lobbying by non-profit organizations, the Clinton administration's efforts to keep a nuclear war hole card, an incompetent federal judge who has manipulated a critical DDT pollution case, how the Pentagon mysteriously lost $33 billion, and how some of the S&L bailout money may go to the S&L industry rather than be used to help ease the budget deficit.

Project Censored Canada, launched with the support and counsel of Project Censored, is now in its third successful year. The Canadian Association of Journalists, located in Ottawa, Ontario, and the School of Communication at Simon Fraser University, in Burnaby, British Columbia, jointly initiated Project Censored Canada. They have now been joined by the Department of Communication Studies at the University of Windsor, in Windsor, Ontario. The project explores issues and events that do not receive the coverage they deserve in the Canadian media.

The Canadian effort originated with Bill Doskoch, a journalist with the *Leader-Post*, in Regina, Saskatchewan, and is coordinated by Dr. Bob Hackett, associate professor, and Donald Gutstein, lecturer, both at Simon Fraser University, and by Dr. Jim Winter, associate professor at the University of Windsor.

THE CENSORED RESEARCH PROCESS

Researchers who participate in the censorship seminar (taught each fall semester at Sonoma State University, in Rohnert Park, California) have reviewed thousands of stories over the past 20 years, stories that many Americans have not seen or heard about—but should have. The stories are nominated annually by journalists, scholars, librarians, and the general public from across the United States and abroad.

From the hundreds of articles submitted each year, the seminar researchers select the top 25 stories according to a number of criteria, including the amount of coverage the story received, the national or international importance of the issue, the reliability of the source, and the potential impact the story may have. Next, the top 25 *Censored* stories are submitted in synopsis form to a panel of judges who select the top ten stories of the year.

Some of the judges who have participated in the project in the past include Hodding Carter, Shirley Chisholm, Noam Chomsky, Hugh Downs, John Kenneth Galbraith, Charlayne Hunter-Gault, James J. Kilpatrick, Robert MacNeil, Mary McGrory, John McLaughlin, Jessica Mitford, Bill Moyers, George Seldes, Susan Sontag, Alvin Toffler, and Mike Wallace. This year's judges are cited later in the acknowledgments.

Before examining why some issues are overlooked (what we call "censored") and why other issues are over-covered (what we call "junk food news") we must define what we mean by censored.

WHAT IS CENSORSHIP?

Censorship has a long and scurrilous history which started at least two millennia before the invention of the printing press, as noted in the chronology found in Chapter 6.

A brief review of definitions offered by more traditional sources provides an insight into the problems surrounding the censorship issue. The definitions seem to be as varied and numerous as there are scholars, politicians, and lexicographers eager to address the subject.

When I started Project Censored in 1976, I developed an alternative definition of censorship. Rather than starting with the source of censorship as traditionally defined—with the obligation of an elite to protect the masses (the classic "we know what's best for the people and they're better off without this information" syndrome)—my definition focuses on the other end—with the failure of information to reach the people.

Expanding on this foundation, following is our alternative definition of censorship as originally offered in 1976:

First, we assume that real and meaningful public involvement in societal decisions is possible only if a wide array of ideas are allowed to compete daily in the media marketplace for public awareness, acceptance, and understanding.

Next, we realize that the mass media, particularly the network TV evening news programs, are the public's primary sources of information for what is happening in the world.

If, however, the public does not receive all the information it needs to make informed decisions, then some form of news blackout is taking place.

In brief, then, for the purposes of this project, censorship is defined as the suppression of information, whether purposeful or not, by any method—including bias, omission, under-reporting, or self-censorship—which prevents the public from fully knowing what is happening in the world.

In the final analysis, the greatest sin of censorship may well be the act of self-censorship. For while other forms of censorship may be seen, felt, and eventually exposed that which is censored at the source is never known. By the same token, those who censor incoming information by avoiding ideas not supportive of their own are doing themselves a great injustice. If you do not expose yourself to all truths, as well as the false-hoods that may come with them, you can never truly know the difference between right and wrong.

WHY ARE SOME ISSUES OVERLOOKED?

One of the questions often asked of Project Censored is why doesn't the press cover the issues raised by the research. The failure of the news media to cover critical and sometimes controversial issues consistently and comprehensively is not, as some say, a conspiracy on the part of the media elite. News is too diverse, fast-breaking, and unpredictable to be controlled by some sinister establishment media cabal.

However, there are a variety of factors operating that, when combined, lead to the systematic failure of the news media to fully inform the public. While it is not an overt form of censorship, such as the kind we observe in some other societies, it is nonetheless real and often equally dangerous.

The traditional explanations, or excuses, for censorship are plentiful. Sometimes a source for a story isn't considered to be reliable; other times the story doesn't have an easily identifiable "beginning, middle, and end;" some stories are considered to be "too complex" for the general public; on occasion, stories are ignored because they haven't been "blessed" by *The New York Times* or *The Washington Post*. (Reporters and editors at most of the other 1650 daily newspapers know their news judgment isn't going to be challenged when they produce and publish fashionable "follow-the-leader" stories, a practice which leads to the "pack" or "herd" phenomenon in journalism.)

Another major factor contributing to media self-censorship is that the story is considered potentially libelous. Long and costly jury trials, and occasional multimillion dollar judgments against the media, have produced a massive chilling effect on the press and replaced copy editors with copy attorneys.

Nonetheless, the bottom line explanation for much of the censorship that occurs in America's mainstream media is the media's own bottom line. Corporate media executives perceive their primary, and often sole, responsibility to be the need to maximize profits, not, as some would have it, to inform the public. Many of the stories cited by Project Censored are not in the best financial interests of publishers, owners, stockholders, or advertisers. Equally important, investigative journalism is more expensive than the "public stenography" school of journalism. And, of course, there is always the "don't rock the boat" mentality which pervades corporate media boardrooms and filters on down to the newsroom.

Real news is not repetitive, sensationalistic coverage of events such as the O.J. Simpson trial, or the super-hyped Windows 95, or Connie Chung's pink slip, or Hugh Grant's curbside dalliance, or anything at all about Michael Jackson. These are examples of what I call "Junk Food News" as described in Chapter 5.

By contrast, real news is objective and reliable information about important events that affect the lives and well-being of the public. The widespread dissemination of such information helps people become better informed, and a better informed public can elect politicians who are more responsive to its needs.

WOULD IT MAKE ANY DIFFERENCE?

Finally, there is yet another question that is often asked about the project. Would it really make any difference if the press were to provide more coverage of the kinds of stories cited by Project Censored?

The answer is very simple: yes. But first, we must address the issue of public apathy. Critics of Project Censored say that the media give the public what it wants, i.e. "junk food news," because people are not interested in reading about the issues raised by Project Censored. We counter this by suggesting that the public is not given the opportunity to read or see those stories in the mainstream media and thus, unfortunately, will read or watch what the mass media do offer.

We suggest that it is the media's responsibility, as watchdogs of society with the unique protection of the First Amendment, to explore, compile, and present information that people should be aware of in a way that will attract their attention and be relevant to their everyday lives. And, when the media do this, people will read and respond to the issues raised. There is, indeed, a genuine desire on the part of the public to know more about issues that truly affect them. Your interest in this book confirms that.

But then the question remains, would it make any difference if people were better informed?

Hunger in Africa was consistently nominated as a "censored" subject during the early 1980s. When I would ask journalists why they did not cover the tragedy unfolding there, they would say: "It is not news," or, "Everyone already knows about starving Africans," or "Nothing can be done about it anyway."

Early in 1984, an ABC-TV News correspondent in Rome came upon information that led him to believe that millions of lives were being threatened by drought and famine in Africa. He asked the home office in New York for permission to take his crew to Africa to get the story. The answer, based on costs, was no.

Later, a BBC television crew traveling through Ethiopia captured the stark reality of children starving to death. People throughout the world saw the coverage and responded. Overnight, it sparked a world-wide reaction that reportedly saved the lives of seven million Ethiopians. Indeed, the media can make a difference.

The press has the power to stimulate people to clean up the environment; to prevent nuclear proliferation; to force corrupt politicians out of office; to reduce poverty; to provide quality health care for all people; to create a truly equitable society; and, as we have seen, to literally save the lives of millions of human beings.

And this is why we must look to, prod, and support a free, open, and aggressive press. We have a free press in the United States guaranteed by the First Amendment and we have the best communications technology in the world. Now let us seek a more responsible and responsive press—a press that truly earns its First Amendment rights. Indeed, a press not afraid to do a little muckraking. Then, and only then, will we all have the information we need to build a more enlightened and responsive society.

—Carl Jensen
Cotati, California

Acknowledgments

We must first acknowledge the substantial contribution made to journalism by George Seldes, the most censored journalist in American history. George was a good friend, a mentor, and a former Project Censored judge. He died July 2, 1995, at the age of 104. We all will miss him.

The next acknowledgment must go to all our *Censored* colleagues who contribute to the success of Project Censored by sending us stories as nominations. We receive some 700 nominations annually from journalists, educators, librarians, and many others who are concerned with the public's right to know. We truly are grateful to all of you who bring those stories to our attention.

Another group critical to the success of the project are the Sonoma State University students who participate as *Censored* researchers in the annual Project Censored seminar. It is their responsibility to analyze the hundreds of nominations received in order to determine whether they qualify as censored stories of the year. Following are the SSU students who evaluated the *Censored* nominations of 1995:

PROJECT CENSORED RESEARCHERS OF 1995

Greg Downing, Tina Duccini, Marcie Goyer, Kristi Hogue,
Brad Hood, Stephanie Horner, Dylan Humphrey, Doug Huston,
Pia C. Jensen, Vanessa Mann, Jon Merwitzer, Amy Niesen,
Stephanie Prather, Fritz Rollins, Mary Jo Thayer, Mike Thomas,
Justin Twergo, Tami Ward, Nikki Washburn, Lysa Wayne

Many other groups and individuals contribute to the success of Project Censored, not the least of which are the publications, mostly from the alternative media, that publicize the annual results, and the many radio and television news and talk show hosts who discuss the *Censored* stories each year.

A special thanks goes to Bill Doskoch, of the Canadian Association of Journalists, Bob Hackett and Don Gutstein, of Simon Fraser University, and Jim Winter, of the University of Windsor, in Canada.

We also wish to acknowledge the support we receive from Sonoma State University including its president, Ruben Armiñana; Alan Murray, Director of Entrepreneurial Services; Mark Resmer, Associate Vice President for Information Technology; and Brian Wilson, a systems specialist with the Computer and Information Science Department, who has wrought miracles to ease our trip into cyberspace.

There are five organizations that deserve special recognition. The interest, encouragement, and financial support from the C.S. Fund, of Freestone, California; Anita Roddick and the Body Shop Foundation, of England; the John D. and Catherine T. MacArthur Foundation, of Chicago; the Angelina Fund, of New York; and the Threshold Foundation, of San Francisco, contribute significantly to the successful outreach of Project Censored.

Also, if it were not for support from these foundations, we would not have an assistant director, Mark Lowenthal, who helps me run the Project, nor a research associate, Amy S. Cohen, working with us. Among many other activities, Mark and Amy are responsible for responding to the thousands of letters and phone calls we receive from people throughout the country and abroad each year. Mark is the tireless performer on the many radio and television talk shows that tell the *Censored* story. Amy compiled and updated this year's resource guide and Alternative Writer's Market and is in charge of the *Censored* outreach program which is designed to serve journalism professors and students across the country. I'm also grateful to both Mark and Amy for the time they spent reviewing and editing this manuscript. Tina Duccini, majoring in rhetoric and political science at the University of California, Berkeley, served as a research associate this year and also coordinated the "Censored Tips" program.

I am indebted to my publisher Dan Simon, at Seven Stories Press, in New York, for having the faith and fortitude to take on a subject that many conglomerate publishers rejected. Special thanks are also due to

Cynthia Cameros for her careful editing and to Cindy LaBreacht who designed the book. I would also like to acknowledge that the interest and planning of Brian Donoghue at the Learning Alliance have been instrumental to the success of the Censored Awards Ceremony.

I want to especially thank my wife, Sandra Scott Jensen, for the many hours she spent reviewing early versions of this document and for all the support and encouragement she has given me and Project Censored since its start in 1976. She also is retiring this year.

WALTER CRONKITE
"LET THE CHIPS FALL WHERE THEY MAY"

I am grateful to Walter Cronkite, former managing editor and anchor of the CBS Evening News, for the introduction. Cronkite, who earned his title as the "most trusted man in America," discusses the many pressures on journalists to present a story one way or another and the absolute need for journalists to tell it the way they see it and let the chips fall where they may.

TOM TOMORROW—THE CARTOONIST

Tom Tomorrow's comic strip, "This Modern World," appears in more than 90 newspapers across the country. He now has two critically acclaimed, and publicly adored books—*Greetings From This Modern World* and *Tune In Tomorrow*—available from St. Martin's Press. To communicate with Tom, write him at POB 170515, San Francisco, CA 94117, or, by E-mail: tomorrow@well.com.

PROJECT CENSORED JUDGES OF 1995

One of the most difficult challenges of Project Censored is to select the "Ten Best Censored" stories from among the 25 top nominations. This responsibility falls on our distinguished national panel of judges who volunteer their efforts. Perhaps one of the greatest tributes to the project is that some of our judges, identified with asterisks, have participated in Project Censored every year since selecting the first group of *Censored* stories in 1976. (Ben Bagdikian sequestered himself in the years he also was a *Censored* author.) We are deeply indebted to the following judges who selected the top ten Censored stories of 1995.

DR. DONNA ALLEN, founding editor of *Media Report to Women*

BEN BAGDIKIAN,* professor emeritus, Graduate School of Journalism, UC-Berkeley

RICHARD BARNET, senior fellow, Institute for Policy Studies

JEFFREY A. CHESTER, executive director, The Center for Media Education

SUSAN FALUDI, journalist/author

GEORGE GERBNER, professor of communication and dean emeritus, Annenberg School of Communications, University of Pennsylvania

SUT JHALLY, professor of communications, and executive director, The Media Education Foundation, University of Massachusetts

NICHOLAS JOHNSON,* professor, College of Law, University of Iowa

RHODA KARPATKIN, president, Consumers Union, nonprofit publisher of *Consumer Reports*

CHARLES L. KLOTZER, editor, *St. Louis Journalism Review*

JUDITH KRUG, director, Office for Intellectual Freedom, American Library Association

FRANCES MOORE LAPPÉ, co-founder and co-director, Center for Living Democracy

WILLIAM LUTZ, professor, English, Rutgers University

JULIANNE MALVEAUX, Ph.D., economist and columnist, King Features and Pacifica radio

JACK L. NELSON,* professor, Graduate School of Education, Rutgers University

MICHAEL PARENTI, Ph.D, author and lecturer

HERBERT I. SCHILLER, professor emeritus of communication, University of California, San Diego

SHEILA RABB WEIDENFELD,* president, D.C. Productions, Ltd.

INTRODUCTION

LET THE CHIPS FALL WHERE THEY MAY
by Walter Cronkite

A quarter of a century ago I testified before the United States Senate Subcommittee on Constitutional Rights. I discussed our guarantees of free press and free speech, limitations on free press, and the role of the First Amendment. Much of what I said then is valid today, and some even more so.

First, I pointed out, it is assumed that we want a free press. Such is synonymous with democracy. There are few who would argue otherwise. However, I dare say there is scarcely a public figure anywhere who has not at one time or another, and perhaps more frequently than not, railed at his or her treatment by the press.

The media are from time to time, and not always without reason, considered untrustworthy, disloyal, unkind, disobedient, sullen, cowardly, dirty and irreverent. This is as it should be. To be trustworthy in one person's eyes, may be not to warrant trust in another's. While individuals or journals may at one time or another place their loyalty at the feet of one person or ideology, it is the very strength of a free press that not all reporters and journals will so do. In this diversity is the strength of the free press, and since the nation's founding it has been so perceived by those who love democracy.

The free press provides as can no other system that communication between government and the people so essential to a democracy's functioning. Not to be overlooked, although too frequently it is, is the press' role in providing intra-government communication. We hardly need to belabor the point that our system surely would fail if Congress' knowledge of the workings of the Executive Branch was limited to that which the Executive wished it to know. And vice versa. What is true of the federal government also is true on the level of state and local governments.

Down through our history, particularly at times of national stress, there have been calls for bringing the press to heel. From time to time, sometimes with the press participating, searches have been mounted to find means of imposing "responsibility" on the press. There have been suggestions for government panels, bodies of concerned citizens, councils of self-judges from the press itself. There are some distinguished journalists who believe that a press council of some kind might work, and, if it did, would be desirable. But all of these suggestions, whether from within or without the press, have, with the rarest of exceptions, one thing in common: They stress the voluntary, non-enforceable nature of any such moderator. Almost universally the belief is sustained that nothing should inhibit the basic freedom of press as guaranteed by the Constitution's First Amendment.

One explanation for the need of such councils is the alleged prejudice and bias of journalists. Well, we journalists are biased and we are prejudiced. We are human beings. There is not a person who can truthfully say that he or she does not harbor strong sentiments pro and con on some if not all the issues of the day.

Yet, if there is any single hallmark of the professionalism we claim— indeed, that distinguishing characteristic that makes us professionals and not mere craftsmen—is that we have learned, in our journalism schools and in practice, to recognize the symptoms of personal opinion and to seek to avoid them in reporting the day's news. None of us succeeds in this difficult task in all instances, but we know the assignment and the pitfalls and, I submit, we succeed, far, far more often than we fail or that our critics would acknowledge.

Nonetheless, we are far from perfect. There is a fair portion of what we do that is not done well. There are things we are not doing which we ought to do and critics like Project Censored are often there to point them out to us. There are challenges we have not fully met. We are a long way from perfection. But that is not the point. How could we be improved by outside monitors without destroying the independence which is so essential to a free press?

One criticism that we receive with increasing frequency in these days of mega-media-mergers is that a handful of us determine what will be on the evening news broadcasts, or, for that matter, in the *New York Times* or *Washington Post* or *Wall Street Journal*.

Indeed, it is a handful of us with this awesome power—power that not one of us underestimates or takes lightly. It is a strongly editorial power. With each item we report we can and do seek factual honesty, fairness and balance. But we must decide which news items out of hundreds available we are going to expose that day. And those available to us already have been culled and re-culled by persons far outside our control. Your local newspaper decides each day which of the events of its area it will cover. The local *Associated Press* representative decides which of those items will go onto his or her wire. A regional relay editor decides which of the items on the regional wire shall go on to New York, or Washington, or Los Angeles. And we decide which of those items remaining are to go on the air. In the case of television, the decision frequently involves which items can be illustrated—which we freely acknowledge gives the item far greater impact than the paragraph recited by the broadcaster.

Many factors go into the decisions we make, so many and so complex that it would be hopeless to attempt to detail them here.

Only a handful of professional journalists make these significant judgments on the news of the day, and it is a lot of power for a few men. But what would be the alternative? We would never get on the air or go to press if we attempted to submit each judgment to a committee of Congressmen, bureaucrats, sociologists, teachers, policemen, union leaders, religious leaders. Nor can we go to a plebiscite for each decision.

Impossible would be the position of the journalists working under such conditions. For each piece of potentially controversial reporting (and there is scarcely any topic, including the weather, that is not controversial) the journalist would presumably have to go to management for approval to broadcast. Or, since this would be impractical, they would ignore the item and fill the broadcast with something less likely to involve the company in lengthy review by non-professional and frequently politically-biased critics.

News gathering and dissemination cannot be accomplished without fear or favor, the only way it counts, if the reporter or editor constantly must be looking over his or her shoulder for those who would have the story reflect their standards of right and wrong, of fairness and bias.

If journalism were ever brought to that state by the courts, or Congress, or anybody else exercising a right to question the judgment of its practitioners, then it ceases to be a virile seeker of the truth and becomes a pallid conduit for that propaganda which is palatable to the majority of the people, or the Congress, or the administration of the moment.

Now despite the law's promise of a legally-unrestrained press there are certain limitations to press freedom.

When a medium depends on advertising revenue, there may develop a certain tendency to not unnecessarily offend the paying customer. The larger the medium and the more diverse its sources of advertising revenue, however, the less likely it is to be subject to such pressures.

Another limitation on press freedom may stem from the profit-making nature of most media. The owners of profit-making enterprises are likely to be members, also, of the economic and social elite—the establishment. This is a complaint heard often today and there is some validity to it.

Again on the human side, there is a weakness in the fabric of freedom that is part of the make-up of the journalists themselves, and their editors and publishers.

It takes courage in this business—raw physical courage at times, but more often the courage to face social ostracism for reporting the unpleasant and disagreeable, for reporting the world as it is, rather than the way one's peer group might believe it to be. Freedom of press and speech is meaningless unless it is exercised, even when bravery is required to do so.

Other limitations on press freedom are imposed by the government itself despite the very clear wording of the First Amendment that there shall be "no law abridging the freedom of speech or of the press."

The government limits freedom of information through secrecy, the almost uncontrolled use of the document classification privilege. It limits freedom also by limiting access to news sources. The government limits freedom when it, as the courts have from time to time, forces revelation of reporters' sources, a process which can cut off valuable, perhaps unique, springs of information. And there is what I consider to be the greatest threat to freedom of information: the government licensing of broadcasting.

In addition to these threats to press freedom there is what is turning out to be a war of considerable duration between conservative theory and the First Amendment. This dates back to the Nixon-Agnew conspiracy that had as its objective the destruction of the press' credibility. Their brilliant concept was that they could raise their own credibility by lowering ours.

They planted the seeds of suspicion of the press, the harvest from which we are still reaping. Since then, encouraged by that suspicion and in the belief that they have at least a complacent public, succeeding administrations dare these extraordinary measures to surround the government with a secrecy that surely the founding fathers never intended.

But simultaneously, fed by perhaps the same reading of public opinion, there is another danger to our freedom of speech and press—one that comes from within. Faced with what is perceived to be increasing public criticism and the danger of devastating law suits, publishers and broadcasters may, understandably, take the course of timidity and caution and withdraw their support from aggressive and fearless news departments.

There is no question that the view from the newsroom and the executive suite is, and should remain, quite different. The front office has one overriding priority—to stay in business. With the concomitant second priority of returning an adequate dividend on investment. No matter how devoted it may be to a third objective of public service, management understands that this clearly should not be permitted to infringe on the second priority of making a profit and must never be permitted to threaten the first priority of staying in business.

Thus we have a built-in dichotomy and an ever present threat to the integrity of the newsroom.

There always have been courageous broadcasters who believe so deeply in their role as news disseminators that they permit, even encourage, their newsrooms to skate dangerously close to those priorities of profit and survival. Indeed, some have even found greater profit in their reputation for public service that an aggressive news staff can assure. But other timid broadcasters always have kept a tight leash on their newsrooms to avoid any possible danger of offending any segment of the population or risking costly legal attack.

It is questionable that the latter fulfill their obligation to the majority of the people who are now getting most of their news from television. That obligation simply cannot be discharged unless the news department aggressively seeks out and exposes dishonest public servants, cheating manufacturers and merchants, or dangerously incompetent doctors and lawyers.

And if newspapers and broadcast stations are afraid to do that, if they feel they have lost legal protection and popular support in doing that, if they fear that the cost of courage to pursue this sacred obligation is too high— then what value is a First Amendment. What value is freedom unused?

Again, I concede that we make mistakes. We leave undone some things we should do, and do some things we might better have left undone. And this is where media watchdog groups, such as Project Censored, play an important role by alerting us to things we might do better and stories we might have missed.

But we must continue doing what we have been doing— reporting the news as best we can, hewing as nearly as can mortal man to the objectivity which is the hallmark of the professional journalist, and letting the chips fall where they may.

CENSORED

"[ABC News is] a fantastic organization that has
these brands—*Nightline, World News Tonight
with Peter Jennings, 20/20, Prime Time Live.*
These are not new, but they're not old.
They're adolescent, healthy brands. I don't know
where they go. But they've got to go somewhere."
—Michael Eisner, Walt Disney CEO

CHAPTER 1

U.S. Censorship in 1995

There were a number of significant events that concerned media censorship in 1995, not the least of which occurred on December 12 when the U.S. Senate defeated a proposed constitutional amendment to ban desecration of the U.S. flag by three votes. However, the good news might be temporary since the House previously passed a similar proposal in June and 49 of the 50 states have petitioned Congress for the amendment. Senator Orrin Hatch (R-Utah) promised it would be back in 1996. If passed, the amendment would overturn the 1989 U.S. Supreme Court ruling that burning the flag is a form of free speech protected under the First Amendment.

Another major Congressional issue in 1995 was the legislative bill aptly called the Telecommunications Deregulation Bill. While the battle between long distance and local telephone companies and politicians' concern with obscenity received widespread media coverage during the year, the bill's most dangerous provisions did not. These are the ones that eliminate anti-trust regulations and permit unparalleled concentration of the nation's media. Not surprisingly, this issue is the number one *Censored* story of 1995 and is discussed in Chapter 2.

Ironically, the concentration of media owners was well underway even before the telecommunications bill encouraged it further. Following are some of the newspapers that folded or were merged in 1995: *El Daily News* (the Spanish newspaper started by the *New York Daily News*); *San Diego Hoy* (the only Spanish-language daily newspaper in San Diego); *The Providence* (R.I.) *Evening Bulletin* (founded in 1863 to provide late-breaking Civil War news); the 85-year-old *Baltimore Evening Sun* (H.L. Mencken's paper); the 110-year-old *Houston Post* (source of the #3 *Censored* story of 1990); the *Lincoln Journal* folded into the *Lincoln Star* (leaving Nebraska's capital with just one daily newspaper, the *Lincoln Journal Star*, for the first time in more than a century); *The Milwaukee Journal* (folded into the *Milwaukee Journal Sentinel*); *The Mitford Citizen* (a 100-year-old Connecticut newspaper); *New York Newsday* (the feisty ten-year-old competitor in New York's tabloid wars that won three Pulitzer Prizes in its short life span); the 102-year-old *Westerly* (R.I.) *Sun* (the last Sunday afternoon paper in America) moved to morning publication; and finally, on a personal note, *The Arcata Union* (the 109-year-old northern California weekly newspaper where I started my journalism career) was shut down without having time to publish its own obituary.

Gene Roberts, managing editor of *The New York Times* and one of the most respected journalists in America, warned his colleagues of the dangers of media concentration at the 1995 convention of the Society of Professional Journalists, as reported in *Quill* (November/December 1995). "Year after year, newspapers have become concentrated into fewer and fewer organizations. Those organizations have become more and more centralized, less and less concerned about the flow of information to the

public and more and more occupied with the flow of profits to the central corporation," Roberts said.

However, as newspapers go out of business and politicians plot to make buyouts even easier in the future, the big debate in journalism circles was around a non-issue called "public" or "civic" journalism. Although there seems to be no agreed-upon definition of public journalism, essentially it seems to call for active involvement of newspapers, editors, and journalists in public or community affairs. One has to wonder how the press can maintain its watchdog role if it is part of the group it is supposed to be watching.

Following are a few other "suicidal tendencies" in journalism today. A national survey of 50 local television newscasts by the Rocky Mountain Media Watch, a Denver-based nonprofit group, revealed what many viewers already knew: local TV news focuses on crime, disasters, sensational visuals, weather, sports, promotions, and ads—to the exclusion of real news. Despite criticism, journalists compromise themselves and the profession by becoming money-making celebrities on TV talk and lecture circuits. The Society of Professional Journalists spent more than two years discussing a proposed new code of ethics without coming to an agreement. It may be time to stop discussing it and to start enforcing the existing code. In addition, in a little known profit-driven technological innovation, newspapers are starting to move to a narrower paper roll which results in a smaller news hole.

Finally, studies and reports reveal the public is less trusting of the mainstream media than ever before. And a national viewer-opinion poll revealed the most trusted man in television news is still Walter Cronkite, more than ten years after his retirement.

Meanwhile, *USA Today* reported (9/12/95) that Don Hewitt, executive producer of "60 Minutes," the nation's leading investigative television news magazine, said he was worried about getting enough stories for the fall season. Mr. Hewitt could do worse than to review the top 25 *Censored* stories cited herein. Or he might get some clues from the following state of the nation review.

While the media are intent on devouring one another and politicians are piling up their mud for an election year, the nation's pulse seems to be weakening. Following are some of the symptoms of an unhealthy society:

New studies show that rather than being an egalitarian society, the United States has become the most economically stratified industrial nation in the world with the wealthiest one percent of U.S. households owning nearly 40 percent of the nation's wealth. (*The New York Times*, 4/17/95)

The United States is still the world's largest debtor nation with the net debtor position worsening by 24.9 percent in the past year. (Associated Press, 6/29/95)

There are more poor working families in the United States today than there were in 1975 and their situation will only worsen if Congress restrains spending on tax relief, child care, Medicaid and food stamps. (Associated Press, 7/11/95)

The number of Americans behind bars, on probation, or on parole climbed to a record 5.1 million in 1994. (*Los Angeles Times*, 8/28/95)

Although corporate profits are greater than they have been at the end of any post-World War II recovery, the majority of American workers' incomes fell or were stagnant from 1989 to 1995. (Scripps Howard News Service, 9/4/95)

While the nation's economy has improved significantly, its quality of life has declined according to an index of social health that tracks how well U.S. society is doing in 16 areas, including infant mortality, drug abuse, unemployment, access to affordable housing, and the gap between rich and poor. (Associated Press, 10/16/96)

The income gap between rich and poor was wider in the United States during the 1980s than in any other large industrialized country in the world. (*The New York Times*, 10/27/95)

While the stock market skyrocketed to record levels in 1995, with the total value of securities traded on the New York Exchange reaching $6 trillion and the Dow Jones industrial average closing at 69 new highs, the paychecks of American workers rose by just 2.7 percent, the smallest annual increase on record. (*The New York Times*, 11/1/95)

In the mid-70s, the ratio of average pay for large-company CEOs to their workers was 41 to 1, or $326,000 to $8,000. In 1994, it was 187 to 1, or $3.7 million to $20,000. (*USA Today*, 11/15/95)

During the 1950s, corporations paid 31 percent of the federal government's general fund tax collections; now they pay 15 percent. If corporations paid taxes at the same rate they did in the 1950s, the U.S. Treasury would collect an extra $250 billion a year—and there would be no federal deficit. (Molly Ivins, *Ft. Worth Star-Telegram*, 11/30/95)

Not surprisingly, yet another poll found that the unbridled optimism that once characterized American society has been replaced by a sense of economic desperation and gloom about the future, as reported by the Newhouse News Service (5/4/95).

Given all this, some observers wonder why there has been so little public protest on issues that are central to many people's lives. Explanations offered suggest that advocacy groups may be increasingly subsidized and therefore increasingly co-opted; or that the momentum has shifted from liberal advocacy groups to conservative ones; or that the nature of advocacy has changed from mass protests to focus groups, paid TV ads, E-mail, and faxes coordinated by Washington attorneys; or that the sheer scope of the battle—over Medicare, Medicaid, legal services, and welfare—is overwhelming. Oddly enough the pundits ignore the failure of the mass media to put these issues on the national agenda with the same intensity and consistency the media provided the O.J. Simpson trial.

There was one event in 1995 that should have provided a wake-up call to all Americans but didn't. In August, the bodies of 68 human beings were dumped into a 160-foot-long mass grave in Chicago. Most of them were poor elderly people who died alone and unknown during the heat spell in Chicago. There was some media coverage, some concerns raised, and some memorials held, but then they were forgotten in their deaths as they had been in their lives. Let us never forget that this mass burial did not occur in some impoverished Third World nation, but here, in the United States, the richest nation in the world.

The traditional hallmark of a responsible press is that it should afflict the comfortable and comfort the afflicted; it would seem that today's press has turned that measure on its head.

IMPACT OF THE OKLAHOMA CITY BOMBING—The terrorist bombing of the Alfred P. Murrah Federal Building in Oklahoma City on April 19 produced some immediate repercussions not the least of which was a strong anti-terrorist bill hastily introduced in Congress. Seven weeks after the bombing and after just four days of debate, the U.S. Senate passed the bill by a vote of 91-8. Both liberals and conservatives felt the bill posed a threat to constitutional rights. Fortunately it fell prey to political maneuvering in the House Judiciary Committee where it remained as the year ended.

The terrorist bombing also drew the attention of the national news media to increasing right-wing militia activity in the United States. However, it was another story the mainstream media were late in recognizing. In 1991, at the request of a producer at "60 Minutes" for possible story ideas, Project Censored sent along some articles about the growth of the militia movement. In September 1991, we received a response from the producer explaining why CBS News wasn't interested in the militia story, saying in part: "I don't think it is a story for us. Some of the documentation on how these militias view their role is pretty startling. However, the chance that they will be 'called up' and able to put their theories into practice seems quite remote. Therefore, the story seems to lack a sense of urgency."

MEDIA MERGER MANIA—Ted Turner is by far the unanimous choice for the media-merger-mania "hypocrite of the year" award. While attending cable TV's annual Western Show convention in Anaheim in

THIS MODERN WORLD   by TOM TOMORROW

OVER THE PAST FEW YEARS, AN UGLY SIDE OF AMERICA HAS GROWN INCREASINGLY VOCAL... THINLY-VEILED HATRED AND BILE HAVE COME TO DOMINATE MUCH OF THE NATIONAL DISCOURSE... SELF-STYLED PATRIOTS HAVE WRAPPED THEMSELVES IN THE FLAG WHILE BELITTLING THE VERY VIRTUES OF COMPASSION AND TOLERANCE FOR WHICH THAT FLAG STANDS... AND NOW IT APPEARS THAT A FEW SICK AND TWISTED INDIVIDUALS HAVE TAKEN IT ALL MUCH TOO FAR...

Home-grown terrorism

THE FIRST SUSPECT ARRESTED WAS REPORTEDLY A MEMBER OF A "CITIZEN'S MILITIA"...OFTEN LINKED TO WHITE SUPREMACIST ORGANIZATIONS, THESE PARAMILITARY GROUPS HAVE BEGUN TO POP UP IN BACKWOODS SETTINGS ACROSS THE COUNTRY--STOCKPILING WEAPONS AND EXCHANGING BIZARRE, PARANOID FANTASIES ABOUT ZIONIST CONSPIRACIES AND SECRET WORLD GOVERNMENTS...

late November, he warned of the potential control the corporate media giants would have due to recent mergers.

"It would be a very, very sad day if we just had four or five great big companies controlling all the programming and all the pipelines in the country," Turner opined.

This, of course is what media merger critic Ben Bagdikian has been saying for more than a decade. Turner came to the same conclusion just after merging Turner Broadcasting System with Time-Warner Inc. to form the world's largest news and entertainment corporation. What is wrong with this picture?

In reality, the Turner/Time-Warner marriage was just one of three blockbuster media mergers announced in 1995, a record-breaking year for corporate mergers in many industries. By December 28, as reported by the Associated Press, there had been 8,773 deals worth $466.34 billion, eclipsing the $347 billion of 1994.

But the three mega-media mergers that captured the public's attention in 1995 were Time-Warner/Turner, Disney/Capital Cities-ABC, and CBS/Westinghouse. It was as if the media giants couldn't wait for passage of the telecommunications bill, which was expected to open the floodgates for media mergers with its deregulating provisions.

The blockbuster media mergers started on July 31 when the Walt Disney Co. announced it would buy Capital Cities/ABC for $19 billion. The merger would make Disney the world's largest information and entertainment corporation. Michael Eisner, chairman of Disney, said the deal, the second-largest in American business history, would help Disney compete in TV programming, cable, and foreign enterprises. It also inspired him to make the comment about news "brands" at the head of this chapter.

The news ink reporting Disney's takeover was hardly dry when Westinghouse Electric announced on August 1 it was buying CBS for more than $5.4 billion. Joining CBS radio and TV networks and broadcast-programming operations with Westinghouse's Group W broadcasting subsidiary, makes Westinghouse the nation's largest broadcast company. Karl Grossman, a communications professor at State University of New York at Old Westbury and a longtime source of *Censored* stories dealing with nuclear issues, pointed out that Westinghouse and General Electric (NBC's parent company) "are the Coke and Pepsi of nuclear power" and we now have two of the four major networks owned by the nuclear industry.

The media-merger hat trick was complete on September 22 when Time Warner Inc. and Turner Broadcasting System announced they would merge in a stock deal worth $7.5 billion following a well-publicized five-week courtship. With projected revenues of $19.8 billion, the new corporation would become the world's largest communications company, outranking Disney which had claimed the title less than two months earlier. This merger also introduced a new player in the game: Michael Milken, the convicted felon and former junk bond king. He could receive up to $50 million dollars for his role as media consultant to Ted Turner.

While the big three got most of the media-merger press in 1995, there were a number of other media buyouts and consolidations. According to the Bloomberg Business News report of January 1, 1996, media and telecommunications mergers in 1995 exceeded $61.6 billion.

In late January, the Times Mirror Co. sold its cable TV operations for $2.3 billion to Cox Enterprises. The merged company, Cox Communications Inc., became the nation's third-largest cable system.

In another cable deal in early February, Time Warner announced it was buying Cablevision Industries Inc. for about $2.5 billion. The purchase gives Time Warner a total of 11.5 million cable subscribers permitting it to vie with Tele-Communications Inc. (TCI) for the title of the nation's largest cable TV operator. TCI reportedly had from 11 to 11.65 million subscribers.

In mid-April, the Seagram Co., a Montreal-based liquor distributor, bought into the Hollywood power game by buying 80 percent of MCA Inc. which brought America "Jurassic Park" and "Jaws" for $5.7 billion.

In a $2 billion deal, MCI Communications Corp. and Rupert Murdoch's News Corp. formed a joint venture on May 10 to produce television, movies, publications and provide broadband network and direct broadcast capabilities anywhere in the world.

In mid-May, Microsoft Corp. and NBC announced an alliance to develop content for computer networks, CD-ROMs, interactive television and traditional broadcast media.

On June 3, *Editor & Publisher* announced the reporting staffs for the morning *Indianapolis Star* and the afternoon *Indianapolis News* would be combined, thereby ending 92 years of news competition in Indianapolis.

On July 24, Gannett Co. Inc., the nation's largest newspaper publisher, announced it was expanding its broadcasting properties by buying Multimedia Inc. for $1.7 billion. Multimedia will bring Gannett several TV and radio stations, cable franchises, and talk shows including Donahue, Sally Jessy Raphael, and Rush Limbaugh.

Also in late July, Viacom Inc. said it would sell its cable system to Tele-Communications Inc. for about $2.25 billion. The deal brings TCI an additional 1.2 million subscribers making it, once again, the unchallenged leader in the cable industry.

In August, Thomson Newspapers, which owns 142 dailies in North America, agreed to sell 12 small U.S. dailies to Canadian publisher Conrad Black's Hollinger Inc. The deal includes newspapers in the South, Midwest, and Northeast, with a total circulation of 114,000.

On August 28, Knight-Ridder Inc., the nation's second largest newspaper group, bought Lesher Communications Inc. in Northern California for $360 million. The deal, which includes four dailies in the San Francisco Bay Area, gives Knight-Ridder a major presence in the area where it already owns the *San Jose Mercury News*.

John Morton, newspaper analyst with Lynch, Jones & Ryan, noted, in the October issue of the *American Journalism Review*, that the Lesher sale, along with that of the *Raleigh News & Observer*, and the *Berkshire Eagle* in Pittsfield, Massachusetts, are examples of family dynasties increasingly being taken over by newspaper chains.

Lake Havasu City, Arizona, joined the growing ranks of one newspaper cities on September 1 when *The Daily Herald* and *Today's Daily News* merged as *Today's News-Herald*.

On October 23, wire services reported that convicted junk bond king Michael Milken and media mogul Rupert Murdoch, head of News Corp., joined forces to buy half ownership of Premiere Radio Networks Inc., a Southern California radio programming syndicator.

In a development that should concern supporters of public television in the United States, the Public Broadcasting System announced on November 6 that it was teaming up with *Reader's Digest* to develop family-oriented programs and spinoff products. The Reader's Digest Association, known for its strong conservative values, is one of the six corporations that gross more than half of all book revenues.

By the end of the year, there were a number of analysts predicting additional mergers and buyouts in 1996. One of the most widely publicized—and most heatedly denied—stories had the Hearst Corporation buying the *San Francisco Chronicle* and closing down Hearst's afternoon paper, the *San Francisco Examiner*. One of the priciest speculations had General Electric buying Time Warner-Turner, or, alternatively, selling its NBC division.

Finally, it appears that news buffs will soon have more than one 24-hour news network to turn to. On November 28, Rupert Murdoch announced that his News Corp. would start a 24-hour, all-news TV network to compete with Ted Turner's 15-year-old CNN, a channel he said had veered left. In the manner of mighty media magnates, Turner responded, "I'm looking forward to squishing Rupert like a bug." On December 5, ABC News announced its plans for an all-news channel. And on December 11, NBC announced it would have its Microsoft-NBC (MSNBC Cable) round-the-clock news service running by late 1996.

INFORMATION HIGHWAY TRAFFIC REPORT—For the past two years we've reported the official opening of the Information Superhighway was delayed pending passage of the Telecommunications Deregulation Bill. Now, perhaps the best thing we can say about the information highway in 1995 is that Congress threw up a lot of roadblocks for the telecommunications bill and it ended up in a house committee as the year ended. The worst thing that might be said is it appears the censors will have their way with the bill when it is finally enacted.

THIS MODERN WORLD by TOM TOMORROW

The Computer Decency Act, sponsored by Sen. Jim Exon, (D-Neb), would hold the Internet to the same obscenity standards as broadcast media and deprive it of the same First Amendment protections given newspapers and magazines.

While the highway hasn't officially opened, it's already attracting a lot of traffic. The Internet and on-line services proved to be sources of information for thousands during disasters such as the bombing in Oklahoma City and the earthquake in Los Angeles. Others turn to it for current information on events such as the assassination of Israeli Prime Minister Yitzhak Rabin. Cyberspace columnist Kris Jensen said, "Reasons for going on-line can be a basic human need to share the weight of a tragedy, plain curiosity or distrust of traditional news sources."

Not wanting to be left at the starting gate, eight of the nation's largest newspaper chains formed a national network of on-line newspaper services called New Century Network. Services will include news, features, sports information, ticket services, home shopping, and guides to community, entertainment, and other events. Founders of the network include Advance Publications, Cox Newspapers, Gannett, Hearst, Knight-Ridder, Times Mirror, Tribune Co. and the Washington Post Co.

A new on-line service was formed by the merger of News Corp.'s Delphi Internet Service Corp. and MCI's electronic-mail service, World Wide Web site and FYI on-line services. It will be competing with CompuServe, America Online, Prodigy, and Microsoft.

Meanwhile, the world's seven leading industrial nations—Britain, Canada, France, Germany, Italy, Japan, and the United States—agreed to remove the roadblocks from the international information superhighway in an effort to develop a Global Information Society. The Group of Seven

(G-7) approved 11 pilot projects to promote international cooperation in developing and using new technologies.

Nonetheless, in the largest case of mass censorship involving the Internet, on December 28, the world's second-largest on-line computer service, CompuServe, blocked access to more than 200 computer newsgroups on orders of a German federal prosecutor who said the newsgroups were indecent and offensive. On January 4, the Associated Press reported that CompuServe hopes to restore access to the newsgroups everywhere except in regions where objections are raised.

CENSORSHIP ON CAMPUS—Censors at public schools were more successful this past year than at any time during the 13 years the People for the American Way (PAW) have been observing public school censorship. According to a report from PAW, there were 338 direct attempts to censor school materials during the 1994-95 school year. And, sadly, fifty percent of them were successful. The most frequent causes for censorship were sexual content, objectionable language and religion. Objections to "promoting" homosexuality also showed a 50 percent increase from the prior year. Calls to the Student Press Law Center (SPLC) continue to increase, rising from 548 in 1988 to 1,402 in the 1994-95 school year. Mark Goodman, executive director of SPLC, said the topics being censored today (generally any stories dealing with sexuality) are about the same as those censored when the SPLC started in 1974-75; however, he pointed out, the topic most often censored is "anything perceived as critical of school policies or officials."

Meanwhile, the fight to restore freedoms taken away from student journalists by the U.S. Supreme Court's 1988 *Hazelwood School District v. Kuhlmeier* decision stalled in three states—Missouri, Nebraska, and Oregon. States that have passed anti-*Hazelwood* laws are Arkansas, California, Colorado, Kansas, Iowa, and Massachusetts.

The political correctness movement on campuses suffered a well-deserved defeat when a Superior Court judge in California's Santa Clara County ruled that a Stanford University regulation banning "hate speech" was based on the content of speech and thus unconstitutional. He also upheld a state law guaranteeing freedom of speech for private university students. Sheldon Steinbach, general counsel for the American Council on Education, which represents 1,700 colleges and universities, said the Stanford decision "is the final nail in the coffin of speech codes."

Finally, the Spring 1995 issue of *Democratic Culture* carried a warning for teachers across the country—Reed Irvine's Accuracy in Academia is back! Originally founded in 1985 to expose "liberal bias" in college classrooms, Accuracy in Academia (AIA) quietly faded away after being ridiculed in the *Doonesbury* comic strip and the media for its efforts to have students spy on professors. Now, according to *Democratic Culture*, AIA is preparing to revive its spying plan. "In 1995, Peter LaBarbera wrote a letter to distributors of the AIA newspaper. 'As the new Executive Director of AIA, I will rededicate *Campus Report* to the cutting edge, nononsense investigative journalism that first characterized its debut in 1985. In that regard, I will focus on stories that **expose the teachings of individual professors in their classroom**—so that at least radical instructors know that there is someone out there scrutinizing what they teach.'" (bold in original)

MISCELLANEOUS MEDIA GAFFES OF 1995—Symptoms of an ailing institution:

The top media gaffe-of-the-year awards go to ABC-News, *The New York Times*, the *Washington Post*, and CBS-News.

ABC-News issued the most publicized retraction in media history on August 21 when it apologized to the Philip Morris Co. and R.J. Reynolds Tobacco Co. for allegations the network made on its "Day One" program in 1994 about the ways they control nicotine levels in cigarettes. In return, the tobacco companies dropped their $10 billion libel suits. *The Nation* spoke for many free speech advocates (9/11/95) when it said, "ABC's apology to Philip Morris/R.J. Reynolds for a nicotine-spiking exposé on its news show 'Day One' was not only an appalling cave-in, it was a disaster for investigative reporting." Reese Cleghorn, president of *American Journalism Review*, said the apology is devastating to ABC's credibility and "shows us how ominous the corporatization of the news has become."

The *Washington Post* and *The New York Times* jointly published a 35,000-word manifesto written by the so-called Unabomber who threatened "to send a bomb to an unspecified destination with intent to kill" if they didn't. The Unabomber already had killed three people and injured 23 with 16 mail bombs since 1978. Both papers said they published the tract, which urged a revolution against "the industrial-technological" system, at the request of Attorney General Janet Reno "for public safety reasons." *The Progressive* commented (November 1995), "It's disgraceful that the nation's two leading newspapers caved in to the Unabomber and agreed to publish his 35,000-word manifesto." *The American Editor* reported (October 1995) that William Serrin, chair of the journalism department at New York University and former *New York Times* reporter, told the *Washington Post*, "I think it's disgraceful, absolutely disgraceful. You're giving your paper over to a murderer and letting the government dictate what you put in your paper. Suddenly, because of a request of the Attorney General, you cave in."

"60 Minutes," the nation's premiere television news magazine, pulled an interview scheduled for November 12 with a former Brown & Williamson Tobacco Co. executive who was critical of the industry, on the advice of its attorneys. CBS News said it didn't broadcast the interview because "CBS management told us we couldn't do that," because of fears of a lawsuit. Joan Konner, dean of the Graduate School of Journalism at Columbia University, told *The New York Times*, "The conflict of interest between business and journalism was naked on the stage. I felt very bad for the '60 Minutes' crew because they're great journalists, but they were embarrassed and it showed." Walter Cronkite, dean of American television journalists and former CBS News anchor, said, "Those who permit such pressure to be exerted clearly are thinking purely of their pocketbooks and that alone—not of the people's right to know or necessity to know—and I abhor it."

In a revealing follow-up to the "60 Minutes" cancellation, on December 3, the *Washington Post* reported that Loews Corp., which owns CBS-TV, purchased six cigarette brands from Brown & Williamson. Loews added the six new brands to its subsidiary, Lorillard Tobacco. A Brown & Williamson spokesperson said the sale of its brands had nothing to do with the broadcast. Nonetheless, Rep. Henry Waxman, (D-Los Angeles), a tobacco foe,

THIS MODERN WORLD   by TOM TOMORROW

told the *Post*, "There's a troubling appearance of impropriety. I think the public needs to know more about the terms and conditions of the sale."

Other media gaffes of 1995: NBC censored a segment about militant opponents of abortion during a "TV Nation" special produced by Michael Moore; on CBS-TV's "Eye to Eye" program, interviewer Connie Chung sandbags Newt Gingrich's mother Kathleen pressuring her for an answer, "Why don't you just whisper it to me, just between you and me"—which was then broadcast; *The New York Times* violated one of journalism's sacred rules when it printed comments by Hillary Rodham Clinton made "off the record" at a luncheon with ten other journalists who honored the pledge; the shocking photo of Nicole Brown Simpson's bruised and swollen face on the front page of the *National Enquirer* was, in fact, a "computer recreation."

Rupert Murdoch's publishing house HarperCollins offers little-known author but high profile Speaker of the House Newt Gingrich a $4.5 million advance to write two books (later reduced to $1 by Gingrich when obvious conflict of interest issues were raised); the Internet carried a story with an AP byline and a Vatican City dateline describing a press conference in which the Vatican announced that Microsoft Inc. agreed to acquire the Roman Catholic Church for "an unspecified number" of Microsoft shares (the story later proved groundless); WCPO-TV, the CBS affiliate in Cincinnati, fired investigative reporters Corky Johnson and Karl Idsvoog for complaining when a story they were working on about campaign contributions to Ohio judges was spiked.

Mike Wallace, known for his ambush interviews on "60 Minutes," taped an interview with another journalist without her knowledge and in violation of basic journalistic practice after assuring her she wouldn't appear on

camera; *SmartMoney* financial columnist James J. Cramer touted two stocks he happened to have a stake in; author Martin Amis plagiarized quotations from *Entertainment Weekly* for a profile he was writing for *The New Yorker*; several days after appearing on the Jenny Jones talk show, an interviewee was slain by the man he admitted secretly admiring; Mark Hornung resigned as editorial page editor of the *Chicago Sun-Times* after admitting he plagiarized a *Washington Post* editorial in a column.

Miramax Films, a subsidiary of Disney, caved in to pressure from the Catholic League and changed the national release date of a movie about priests that was scheduled to open on Good Friday; "Eye To Eye With Connie Chung" persuaded Tonya Harding's mother, LaVona Golden, to wear a hidden microphone to tape their conversations during Harding's Olympic training in 1994; CBS was criticized for skipping the memorial service for the Oklahoma City bombing victims to broadcast the Greater Greensboro (N.C.) golf open instead; weatherman Sean Boyd was fired by his boss at KMJ Radio, in Fresno, for refusing to change his weather forecast which predicted a chance of rain for the KMJ-sponsored "Dittohead Picnic and Politically Incorrect Barbecue" honoring Rush Limbaugh.

John Harwood, of *The Wall Street Journal*, was expected to win election to the congressional press gallery's prestigious Standing Committee of Correspondents—but didn't—after he urged journalists to disclose their "outside income" (income earned from speeches and sources other than their day jobs); Sam Donaldson, ABC news co-anchor of "Prime Time Live," was upset by media criticism because he crusaded on the air against farm subsidies while accepting nearly $100,000 in federal sheep and mohair subsidies on the 18,000 acres he owns in Hondo, New Mexico; reporters from *USA Today* and "Court TV" were kicked out of the O.J. Simpson trial courtroom by Judge Lance Ito for "constant whispering;" several quotes highly critical of current 49er quarterback Steve Young and 49ers management by former quarterback Joe Montana were changed in a *Sports Illustrated* article after pressure from Montana's wife and his agent; United Nations officials ordered at least 70 changes or deletions in the UN's 50th anniversary book, including the names of many countries and all references to the Dalai Lama.

CBS stood by its sports analyst Ben Wright after he reportedly made some disparaging remarks about lesbian golfers during McDonald's LPGA Championship tournament; an article about the importance of alternative weeklies and media watchdog groups like FAIR in keeping the corporate media more honest was dropped at the last minute from an issue of Gannett's *Media Studies Journal* on media criticism; *The International Herald Tribune*, which is owned by *The New York Times* and the *Washington Post*, was ordered to pay $678,000 in damages for an opinion article which reportedly libeled three of Singapore's top political leaders.

When 60 million viewers tuned in to the Diane Sawyer interview with Michael Jackson on ABC's "Prime Time Live," they didn't know the concessions ABC made to Jackson to get the interview included commercial time worth up to $1.5 million, in exchange for rights to his future videos; a Wal-Mart store pulled a popular T-shirt, which said, "Someday a woman will be President," from its shelves saying it was offensive to some shoppers; *Editor & Publisher* reported that the Seattle *Post-Intelligencer* rejected a CompuServe advertisement that criticized Microsoft Network, a pet project of hometown favorite Bill Gates; Time Warner sold its 50 percent stake in controversial Los Angeles-based Interscope Records, thereby abandoning its "gangsta-rap" business after months of pressure from politicians and media watchdog groups.

After asking if "talk-radio is going to talk only about what big money wants discussed," ABC Radio Network talk show host Jim Hightower got his answer on September 22 when the network canceled his show; after lavishly promoting "The First Interview with O.J. Simpson," a "Dateline NBC Exclusive!," NBC was left with egg on its face after Simpson didn't show up; Ted Turner's Cable News Network refused to air a commercial sponsored by long-distance telephone companies that opposed the telecommunications bill which is supported by Turner; the *Omaha World-Herald* delayed and then softened a negative article about University of Nebraska football players after Nebraska football coach Tom Osborne lobbied its editors to kill the story.

Checkbook journalism got a boost when ABC News reportedly paid $1 million for exclusive North American rights to the hour-long BBC special on Princess Diana that aired November 24; in late December, National Public Radio made an on-air apology for a humorist's remark on the return of Christ, after the Christian Coalition complained that the comment was anti-Christian; and, finally, the media waited until December 27 to tell the public that the television industry's plan to convert to a digital transmission system will make obsolete all 220 million television sets now operating—including the nine million television sets sold during the December 1995 holiday season.

THIS MODERN WORLD

by TOM TOMORROW

LET ME READ YOU SOME-THING, BIFF: "A NEWSPAPER MUST AT ALL TIMES ANTAG-ONIZE THE SELFISH INTER-ESTS OF THAT VERY CLASS WHICH FURNISHES THE LARGER PART OF A NEWS-PAPER'S INCOME..."

"THE PRESS IN THIS COUN-TRY IS...SO THOROUGHLY DOMINATED BY THE WEALTHY FEW...THAT IT CANNOT BE DEPENDED UPON TO GIVE THE GREAT MASS OF THE PEOPLE THAT CORRECT INFORMA-TION CONCERNING POLITI-CAL, ECONOMICAL AND SOCIAL SUBJECTS--"

"--WHICH IT IS NECESSARY THAT THE MASS OF PEOPLE SHALL HAVE IN ORDER THAT THEY VOTE...IN THE BEST WAY TO PROTECT THEMSELVES FROM THE BRUTAL FORCE AND CHI-CANERY OF THE RULING AND EMPLOYING CLASSES."

WHO ARE YOU QUOT-ING, SPAR-KY? SOME LEFT-WING *WACKO*?

ACTUALLY, BIFF, THAT WAS WRITTEN AT THE TURN OF THE CENTURY BY E.W. SCRIPPS, FOUNDER OF THE FIRST MODERN NEWS-PAPER CHAIN.

WELL, HE WOULDN'T GET VERY FAR IN JOURNALISM *TODAY* WITH AN ATTITUDE LIKE THAT.

NO, I SUPPOSE HE *WOULDN'T...*

web: http://www.well.com/user/tomorrow .... Email: tomorrow@well.com .... Email: tomorrow@well.com

TOM TOMORROW©1-10-96

CENSORED

"And you will
know the truth,
and the truth will
make you free."
—Jesus

CHAPTER 2

The Top 25 Censored News Stories of 1995

In this chapter we provide a detailed analysis of each of the top 25 *Censored* stories of 1995. In each case we start with the publication source and author of the original article (or articles). A brief synopsis by the Sonoma State University *Censored* researcher of the nominated article follows. We conclude with comments about the issue and article, in most cases by the author of the original source article. Readers also can contact source publications and/or organizations by referring to the Resource Guide, Appendix A, for information. An asterisk (*) after an article title indicates it is reprinted in Appendix D, "*Censored* Reprints." Following the top 25 stories are comments about this year's nominations by some of our *Censored* judges; a comparison of the top ten *Censored* stories with the top ten *biggest* stories cited by the Associated Press and the top ten television news stories reported by the Tyndall Report on television coverage; and a brief description of the subjects and categories of *Censored* stories of 1995.

1 CENSORED

Telecommunications Deregulation: Closing Up America's "Marketplace of Ideas"

Source:
CONSUMER PROJECT ON
TECHNOLOGY
Date: 7/14/95
Title: "Federal
  Telecommunications
  Legislation: Impact on Media
  Concentration," an Internet
  Newsletter*
Authors: Ralph Nader, James Love,
  and Andrew Saindon

SYNOPSIS: America's "marketplace of ideas," upon which our democracy rests, began shutting its doors in the summer of 1995. The harbinger of the bad news for the public was aptly titled the Telecommunications Deregulation Bill, which moved through both houses of Congress. As the name implies, the bill eliminates virtually all regulation of the United States communication industry.

As tends to be the case with most anti-consumer legislation, the bill stealthily moved under the guise of "encouraging competition"—but will, in reality, have the opposite effect of creating huge new concentrations of media power.

The most troubling aspect of the bill allows easing—and outright elimination—of current antitrust regulations. In what *The New York Times* described as "a dazzling display of political influence," the nation's broadcast networks scored big in the House version of the bill by successfully getting the limits on ownership eased so that any individual company can control

THIS MODERN WORLD — by TOM TOMORROW

television stations serving up to 50 percent of the country. The Senate version of the bill provides for a more modest 35 percent coverage.

The legislation also dismantles current regulations which limit the number of radio stations that can be owned by a single company. Currently no one single company can own more than 40 stations.

It also would lift the current FCC ban on joint ownership of a broadcast radio or TV license and a newspaper in the same market—allowing a single company to have 100 percent control over the three primary sources of news in a community.

Consumer advocate Ralph Nader warned, "Congress is moving the law in the wrong direction, toward greater concentration and fewer choices for consumers, all under the guise of 'greater competition.' Laws and rules that limit cross-ownership and concentration not only enhance competition, a putative goal of the new legisla-tion, but they also serve important non-economic goals, by promoting a greater diversity of program-ming, and enhancing opportuni-ties for local ownership." Nader also said the predictable result of placing even greater power in the hands of fewer giant media moguls will be less diversity, more pre-packaged programming, and fewer checks on political power. "That these provisions are being included in legislation that is being sold as pro-competitive is particularly galling."

Also galling was the major media's almost complete and utter avoidance of the "monopoly owner-ship" factor in their reporting of the bill's progress in Congress. The threat to the nation's "marketplace of ideas" from mega-media monop-olies has been a nomination to Project Censored several times in the past.

SSU Censored Researcher:
Justin Twergo

CONSIDER THAT **NBC** IS ALREADY OWNED BY **GENERAL ELECTRIC**--AND THAT **WESTINGHOUSE** PLANS TO BUY **CBS**...WHICH MEANS THAT TWO OF THE THREE MAJOR NETWORKS WILL NOW BE OWNED BY CORPORATIONS WHICH ARE HEAVILY INVOLVED IN **NUCLEAR POWER** AND **DEFENSE CONTRACTING**...

THAT COULDN'T **POSSIBLY** AFFECT THE INTEGRITY OF THEIR NEWS DIVISIONS!

HEAVENS NO! I'M SURE THERE WILL BE **MANY** HARD-HITTING EXPOSÉS OF PENTAGON OVERSPENDING AND THE HAZARDS OF NUCLEAR WASTE!

IT IS ALSO WORTH CONSIDERING THE PROBABLE **REASON** FOR THIS MERGER-MANIA-- CORP-ORATE AMERICA'S DESIRE TO EXPLOIT THE POORLY UNDERSTOOD, LARGELY HYPOTHETICAL--BUT UNDENIABLY FORTHCOMING-- **INFORMATION HIGHWAY**...OR INFORMATION **SHOPPING MALL**, AS THE CASE MAY BE...

GOSH, BIFF-- THERE ARE JUST SO MANY **CHOICES!**

YES--I CAN'T DECIDE IF I'D RATHER VISIT THE **CHEVRON WEB SITE**--OR DOWNLOAD THE LATEST **PEPSI INFOMERCIAL!**

COMMENTS: Speaking for the authors, James Love thought that "local newspapers did a poor job of explaining the nature of the concentration and cross-ownership issues, particularly cross-ownership issues such as the possible ownership of local newspapers, broadcast licenses and the telephone company." He continued, "Network television was owned by firms that had much at stake in the legislation, and aside from 'Nightline's' show with Tom Shales, I did not see the type of reporting that seemed appropriate, given the issues. However, the general question of the appropriateness of several mergers, ABC/Disney, CBS/Westinghouse or Turner /Time-Warner, did seem to get a fair amount of play, but without much emphasis on the legislative debates. *The New York Times* had a couple of very good editorials on the legislative proposals, but the news reporting on the issue, from the *Times* or the *Washington Post*, did not dwell much on the concentration issue, aside from the occasional reporting of a Presidential veto on this issue. I must say that the cross-ownership questions were rarely addressed, even though they are extremely important, and relevant to the newspaper industry. For example, no one in the media would even acknowledge that there was a debate over cross-ownership for wireless spectrum, such as satellite or PCS licenses."

Love felt if the public were better informed about the issue, it might bring about some reforms in the opposite direction of the legislation. "Instead of encouraging greater concentration and more monopoly power," he suggested, "we might see policies that promote greater diversity and more competition. That would benefit the public in a number of ways.

"The interests which benefit the most from the lack of debate over policies about concentration and cross-ownership are the large corporations which own telecommunications and media businesses, as well as some players who want a chance to sell their firms to the larger players. Newspapers benefit, because they would be allowed to purchase broadcast licenses. Cable and telephone companies benefit, because both would have greater freedom to enter into new deals, and both want the opportunity to acquire the new wireless spectrum that could someday offer troublesome competition. Broadcast license holders would be easier to sell and acquire, and they would have more opportunities to develop greater market power in local markets."

Love concluded it would be helpful if the press could generate greater interest in the media concentration decisions being made by

Congress and the FCC for the future of telecommunications in the U.S.

2 CENSORED

The Budget Does Not Have to be Balanced on the Backs of the Poor

Source:
PUBLIC CITIZEN
Date: July/August 1995
Title: "Cut Corporate Welfare: Not Medicare"*
Author: John Canham-Clyne

SYNOPSIS: Congress could go a long way toward balancing the budget by 2002 without slashing Medicare, Medicaid, education, and social welfare. In fact, the Washington-based Center for the Study of Responsive Law has identified 153 federal programs that benefit wealthy corporations but cost taxpayers $167.2 billion annually. For comparative purposes, federal support for food stamps, housing aid, and child nutrition costs $50 billion a year.

An analysis by *Public Citizen* reveals how Congress could balance the budget by cutting "aid to dependent corporations." The federal budget and tax codes are rife with huge subsidies to business—the sums involved make traditional "pork barrel" spending look like chicken feed.

Public Citizen President Joan Claybrook said the budget axe misses the subsidies for the wealthiest and most powerful U.S. corporations. "The proposed $250 billion, or 15 percent cut in Medicare, demands serious sacrifice from the more than 80 percent of seniors with incomes below $25,000—yet big corporations on the public dole are not asked to sacrifice at all."

Following are some examples of corporate welfare that escape the Congressional budget axe:

Direct Subsidies: Under the Market Promotion Program, the U.S. Department of Agriculture in 1993 gave $75 million for overseas product advertising, including $500,000 to advertise Campbell's soup and $10 million to promote beer, wine, and liquor.

Indirect Subsidies: The Forest Service, for example, spends $100 million annually building more than 340,000 miles of access roads through national forests to assist timber companies' logging operations.

Bailouts: From Lockheed and Chrysler to the S&L industry, the bigger the failure, the more likely Uncle Sam will save it. The most recent example is the so-called "Mexican peso bailout"—more of a bailout for American banks, Wall

Street, and wealthy individuals who made bad investments in Mexican bonds.

Below Market and Guaranteed Loans: The federal government loans businesses money at below-market interest rates, or offers the credit of the U.S. government as a guarantee to a lender if a business opportunity should go sour.

Insurance: Limiting the liability of certain businesses is a nuclear time bomb; the Price-Anderson Act makes it likely that almost the entire cost of a Chernobyl-style nuclear catastrophe would be shifted to taxpayers or the victims.

Tax Expenditures: The largest of all corporate welfare programs are specially targeted tax loopholes and provisions in the tax code. Citizens for Tax Justice identified $412 billion in potential savings over five years by closing just 10 tax loopholes.

Trade Barriers: For example, U.S. government trade quotas on imported sugar cost the taxpayer virtually nothing but cost consumers over $1.4 billion a year in higher sugar prices.

Giveaways of Government Intellectual Property for Private Use: Tens of millions of dollars annually fund research contracts to develop new drugs, aircraft for NASA, and weapons systems for the Department of Defense.

SSU Censored Researcher:
Tina Duccini

COMMENTS: Author John Canham-Clyne notes that while "corporate welfare" was largely ignored in the past, it recently received substantial coverage and now "the budget debate opened a window for occasional presentation of the issue as a source of alternative budgetary savings." However, Canham-Clyne continued, "It has not reached the same level of assumption as has the false notion that the budget absolutely cannot be balanced without slashing so-called entitlements. The media generally operate from a corporate conservative framework which assumes that taxes cannot be raised, the military cannot be seriously cut, and that 'entitlements' are therefore the only significant source of budgetary savings. This framework congealed over the past two decades, and because ideas like 'corporate welfare' were not discussed seriously for so long, the new conservative congressional majority was able to seize the high ground and dominate the budget debate.

"Thus, corporate welfare issues were presented in the media as a sort of quirky alternative, but reporters do not feel comfortable saying or writing without attribution that 'Congress could easily save $100 billion a year simply by cutting corporate subsidies,' as they do saying 'if Medicare and Medicaid aren't brought under control, they'll consume almost the entire federal budget by the year 2050.' The latter statement is a nonsensical idea, and doesn't lead logically to the conclusion that Medicare benefits need to be cut, but by accepting the assumption, the media have facilitated the asserted solution."

If the public were better informed about the scope of corporate welfare, Canham-Clyne said, it "would understand better how the political economy functions: that the 'free market' is not the solution to every problem; that corporate CEOs who advocate 'free market' solutions don't really mean what they say because their businesses generally benefit from federal subsidy; that the budget can be balanced without unduly burdening the poor, the young, the elderly; that our society is dominated by a very small number of wealthy individuals and large corporations; that our politics are driven by the selfish concerns of the creditor class; and that the policy wonks and pundits who appear on our television screens often haven't the faintest idea what they're talking about or else knowingly assert ideology as economic fact."

Canham-Clyne said that the primary beneficiaries of the limited coverage given this issue are "multinational corporations, and the politicians and alleged intellectuals they purchase."

"There's no line item in the budget entitled 'corporate welfare,' which makes getting rid of it extremely difficult," he continued. "A number of ad hoc coalitions have arisen around specific groups of corporate welfare issues, including mineral rights on public lands, white elephant nuclear reactors, timber roads, and so forth. However, there were relatively few victories in Congress this session, despite the supposed fervor for fiscal responsibility. Notably, funding for the Gas Turbine Modular Helium Reactor, a useless technology that benefits a single company, was eliminated in both the House and Senate Energy Appropriations bills. However, the mother lode has yet to be mined, and the assault on working families and the poor continues while corporations and the wealthy continue to stuff themselves at the public trough largely unscathed by congressional and media outrage."

3 CENSORED

Child Labor in the U.S. Is Worse Today Than During the 1930s

Source:
SOUTHERN EXPOSURE
Date: Fall/Winter 1995
Title: "Working in Harm's Way,"*
Author: Ron Nixon

SYNOPSIS: Every day, children across America are working in environments detrimental to their social and educational development, their health and even their lives.

In 1992, a National Institute of Occupational Safety and Health (NIOSH) report found that 670 youths aged 16 to 17 were killed on the job from 1980 to 1989. Seventy percent of these deaths and injuries involved violations of state labor laws and the Fair Labor Standards Act (FLSA), the federal law which prohibits youths under 18 from working in hazardous occupations. A second NIOSH report found that more than 64,100 children went to the emergency room for work-related injuries in 1992.

These numbers are a conservative estimate since even the best figures underestimate the number of working children by 25 to 30 percent. As of yet, there is no comprehensive national data collection system that accurately tracks the number of working youth, nor their occupation, where they work, or how many are injured or killed on the job.

Of the estimated five million youth in the work force, thousands are injured, even killed, because several barriers continue to prevent them from being adequately protected in the workplace.

A patchwork of inefficient data collection systems fails to monitor the total number, much less the well-being, of youth in the workplace. Enforcement of the FLSA is lax. Cultural beliefs about the worth of work for children are strong. And, various PACs lobby successfully to keep child labor laws from being strengthened, and, in many cases, to weaken existing laws.

"Child labor today is at a point where violations are greater than at any point during the 1930s," said Jeffrey Newman of the National Child Labor Coalition, an advocacy group founded in 1904.

Violations are occurring today on farms and businesses around the country. Farm owners beat the system by allowing their entire family, including the children, to work under one person's social security number or by hiring a farm contractor who, on the books, counts as only one employee (while the contractors then hire whomever they wish).

Businesses aren't worried about the child labor violations they commit because the laws are rarely enforced. One report found the average business could expect to be inspected once every 50 years or so. Inspectors spend only about five percent of their time looking into child labor problems.

Even when companies are inspected and violations are found, the maximum penalty of $10,000 per violation is rarely enforced.

Lobbying efforts by various business trade organizations are making congressional reform nearly impossible. In the nation's capital, money talks, and both the National Restaurant Association (NRA) and the Food Marketing Institute (FMI), representing areas where many child labor violations occur, speak persuasively with their generous contributions to potential supporters of their agenda.

The restaurant industry alone has given $1.3 million to Republican candidates in recent years; House Speaker Newt Gingrich has been a favorite of both the NRA and the FMI. Since 1991, Gingrich has received more than $27,000 from both PACs.

SSU Censored Researcher: Marcie Goyer

COMMENTS: Author Ron Nixon confirmed that the story of children who are abused, injured, and even killed on the job received almost no attention in the major media last year. "CBS ran a story on agriculture workers that featured a small part on child labor in agriculture," Nixon noted. "But other than that particular story, the mainstream press did little on child labor. Part of the reason is that child labor is viewed as an old story. However, as we found, no one had ever bothered to look at the barriers that prevent children from being injured in the workplace. Coverage of the topic was always: 'children are being injured; what can we do to educate them and the parents about workplace dangers.' No one ever focused on the data gaps, lack of enforcement, cultural myths about the value of work for children, and most of all, the political opposition to strengthening the child labor laws.

"The public would benefit from wider exposure of this story because it would allow parents to know about the conditions their children may be working in and would inform the general public of the abuses—namely injuries and deaths of working children in the name of profit. As far as migrant children are concerned, it would also show the American public the price we pay for our agricultural products.

"Those who benefit most from the lack of coverage of this topic are the industries that employ the most youth: the restaurant, grocery, agricultural, and garment industries. The restaurant and grocery industries, which employ 35 percent of all working children, gave nearly a half-million dollars to congressmen who sit on the committees that oversee child labor laws. In return, the House of Representatives recently passed a bill that would allow youth under 18 to operate dangerous machinery. However, there has been no press coverage.

"Along with the National Child Labor Coalition, we sent copies of the child labor story and a computer-assisted story on the campaign contributions from the grocery and restaurant industries to the Washington press just before the hearings on the latest child labor bill. Not one paper picked up the story. Only the *Multinational Monitor* and the *Corporate Crime Reporter* reported the results. We are currently compiling a list of all injuries, deaths, and violations of child labor laws in each state from a variety of sources that will give us a clearer picture of just how bad the problems are."

4 CENSORED

The Privatization of the Internet

Source:
THE NATION
Date: 7/3/95
Title: "Keeping On-Line Speech Free: Street Corners in Cyberspace,"*
Author: Andrew L. Shapiro

SYNOPSIS: You may not have noticed, but the Internet, one of the hottest news stories of 1995, was essentially sold last year. The federal government has been gradually transferring the backbone of the U.S. portion of the global computer network to companies such as IBM and MCI as part of a larger plan to privatize cyberspace. But the crucial step was taken on April 30, when the National Science Foundation shut down its part of the Internet, which began in the 1970s as a Defense Department communications tool. And that left the corporate giants in charge.

Remarkably, this buyout of cyberspace has garnered almost no protest or media attention, in contrast to every other development in cyberspace such as the Communications Decency Act, and cyberporn. What hasn't been discussed is the public's right to free speech in cyberspace. What is obvious is that speech in cyberspace will not be free if we allow big business to control every square inch of the Net.

Given the First Amendment and the history of our past victories in fighting for freedom of expression, it should be clear how important public forums in cyberspace could be—as a way of keeping on-line debate robust and as a direct remedy for the dwindling number of free speech spaces in our physical environment.

There already are warning signs about efforts to limit on-line debate. In 1990, the Prodigy on-line service started something of a revolt among some of its members when it decided to raise rates for those sending large volumes of e-mail. When some subscribers protested, Prodigy not only read and censored their messages, but it summarily dismissed the dissenting members from the service.

There are at least three fundamental ways that speech in cyberspace already is less free than speech in a traditional public forum:

First, cyberspeech is expensive, both in terms of initial outlay for hardware and recurring on-line charges. For millions of Americans, this is no small obstacle, especially when one considers the additional cost of minimal computer literacy.

Second, speech on the Net is subject to the whim of private censors who are not accountable to the First Amendment. Commercial on-line services, such as America Online and Compuserve, like Prodigy, have their own codes of decency and monitors to enforce them.

Third, speech in cyberspace can be shut out by unwilling listeners too easily. With high-tech filters, Net users can exclude all material from a specific person or about a certain topic, enabling them to steer clear of "objectionable" views, particularly marginal political views, very easily.

If cyberspace is deprived of true public forums, we'll get a lot of what we're already used to: endless home shopping, mindless entertainment and dissent-free talk. If people can avoid the unpalatable issues that might arise in these forums, going on-line will become just another way for elites to escape the very non-virtual realities of injustice in our world. As the "wired" life grows exponentially in the coming years, we'll all be better off if we can find that classic free speech street corner in cyberspace.

As the Supreme Court said in *Turner Broadcasting v. FCC* (1994), "Assuring that the public has access to a multiplicity of information sources is a governmental purpose of the highest order, for it promotes values central to the First Amendment."

SSU Censored Researcher:
Fritz Rollins

COMMENTS: The main subject, according to investigative author Andrew L. Shapiro, is "how the rapid corporatization of cyberspace, with the assistance and acquiescence of government, is squeezing out public spaces on-line that are truly dedicated to freedom of expression." Shapiro points out that his piece urges, "in contradiction to the libertarian bent of most writing in defense of free speech on the Internet, that government take an active role in safeguarding the virtual public forum.

"This is a topic which has not received sufficient, if any, exposure in the mass media. While there has been endless coverage of cyberporn and the Exon Bill's attempt to thwart obscenity on the Internet, and of myriad other cyberspace-related issues, I've seen little out there on this specific subject. Of course, there have been relevant straight news pieces on huge new on-line services (e.g., the Microsoft Network) and on mergers (e.g., Murdoch's News Corp. buying the independent Delphi on-line service).

"People are seeking critical analysis of the emerging information technologies, but most of what they're getting is off-the-cuff and not very thoughtful or just straight out of the P.R. releases of the big hardware, software, and Internet gateway companies. I don't think many people realize what an oppor-tunity may be passing them by—to have a potentially inexpensive, democratizing, grass-roots form of communication and information-gathering at their fingertips. When it comes to the Internet, most folks assume that government is the enemy of free speech because of irresponsible legislation like the Exon Bill. What they don't realize is that corporate-owned cyberspace will probably be a lot more stifling, since private on-line services who censor Net users are totally unaccountable under the First Amendment, which only protects citizens from government regulation of speech."

Shapiro said it was easy to point out whose interests are being served by the limited coverage given the corporatization of cyberspace: "The private on-line services that are gobbling up the Net, like America Online, Compuserve, Prodigy, etc. It's also not surprising that most of these services are now owned by, or in partnerships with, bigger media conglomerates that own most of the mass media that has failed to cover the privatization of cyberspace."

As for recent developments, Shapiro warns, "the conglomeration of on-line services continues, advertising is starting to dominate the World Wide Web, Web site addresses are now being auctioned instead of given away, and there is generally less room for the freewheeling, open chat that was more typical of the earlier cyberspace incarnations like Usenet."

5 CENSORED

U.S. Pushes Nuclear Pact But Spends Billions to Add Bang to Nukes

Sources:
WASHINGTON POST
Dates: 5/1/95 and 5/28/95
Titles: "U.S. Seeks Arms Ingredient As It Pushes Nuclear Pact" and "House Bill Would Order Nuclear Reactor As New Source of Tritium"*
Author: Thomas W. Lippman

SYNOPSIS: Even as the United States urges the rest of the world to indefinitely extend a treaty requiring signatories to work toward elimination of nuclear weapons, the U.S. Department of Energy is planning a multibillion-dollar project to resume production of tritium—a radioactive gas used to enhance the explosive power of nuclear warheads.

Apparently the only decision not yet made as the year drew to a close was what kind of facility the department plans to build and where it plans to build it.

The choice is between a huge particle accelerator, using theoretically workable but untested technology, and a nuclear reactor, which would be the first reactor ordered in the U.S. since the 1979 Three Mile Island nuclear accident.

Either choice involves immense political, financial, environmental and national security risks, yet the American public is little aware of the enormity of the decision to be made.

Many officials in the Clinton administration are averse to nuclear power and do not want the federal government to sponsor construction of a reactor. But many career staff members in the Energy Department and the Pentagon have long supported the nuclear industry and favor the reactor method of producing the tritium needed for the weapons program.

While Energy Secretary Hazel O'Leary has pledged to begin work on a new facility to produce tritium in the next fiscal budget, she has been under intense congressional pressure to choose the reactor option and to build it at the Energy Department's Savannah River, S.C., weapons plant where all of the tritium for the nation's nuclear arsenal has been produced.

O'Leary's choice appears to be between investing billions of federal dollars in a particle accelerator or accepting a proposal from a nuclear industry consortium to use mostly private funds to construct a reactor.

In late May, the *Washington Post* reported the House committee had approved legislation requiring the Energy Department to begin development next year of a nuclear reactor that would produce tritium for the nation's nuclear warheads, generate electricity, and burn plutonium as fuel. Meanwhile, the National Security Committee tacked the provision onto the defense authorization bill.

While the bureaucrats' and politicians' argument has been limited to two choices—either the accelerator or the nuclear reactor—the American public deserves to be made aware of the issues surrounding this critical decision.

Further, the public should be made aware that there is a third option: *not* to produce the tritium needed to add more bang to America's nuclear warheads.

SSU Censored Researcher: Tina Duccini

COMMENTS: Author Thomas Lippman said the nuclear issue did not receive sufficient coverage by the mass media but wondered, "What would you expect? It is a complex, somewhat arcane subject." Nonetheless, he continued, "The public should be aware that while the Cold War is over, the arms race isn't. The public should realize that billions of dollars are spent creating and marketing nuclear weapons." Lippman added he'll "leave it up to the public whether that's a good idea or not."

Lippman suggests the "lack of coverage results from the difficulty of the subject matter and a lack of sex appeal. No one was covering up or suppressing this information." Lippman said the published articles resulted from: 1) his former experience in covering the Energy Department, including the nuclear weapons plants and labs, and his current experience in covering the State Department and foreign policy, which give him sources in nonproliferation and nuclear communities; and 2) the "willingness of the *Washington Post* to give news space to difficult, complex subjects."

6 CENSORED

Radical Plan From Newt Gingrich's Think Tank to Gut FDA

Source:
MOTHER JONES
Date: September/October 1995
Title: "Agency Under Attack"*
Author: Leslie Weiss

SYNOPSIS: The Food and Drug Administration (FDA), sometimes criticized in the past for being too cozy with corporations, is now under attack for exactly the opposite reason. A powerful bloc of critics in the drug industry has joined hands with the Republican Congress and together they are pushing to overhaul the FDA. These critics claim the FDA is too tough on drug companies, unnecessarily inhibits innovation, and delays approval of new drugs and medical devices.

Leading the charge in Congress is Speaker of the House Newt Gingrich, who has labeled the FDA the "number one job killer" in the country, and called its head, David Kessler, "a bully and a thug." Gingrich's Progress & Freedom Foundation has a radical plan to privatize much of the FDA supervision of drugs and medical devices.

If enacted, the Progress & Freedom Foundation's plan will place responsibility for drug development, testing, and review in the hands of private firms hired by the drug companies themselves, while retaining a weakened FDA to rubber-stamp their recommendations. Additionally, the plan limits the liability of drug companies that sell dangerous drugs to the public.

Under the plan, government-licensed firms called DCBs (drug or device certifying bodies) would be retained by drug companies to develop, test, and review new products. According to the proposal, "competition between firms would inevitably produce a lower-cost, faster, and higher-quality development and approval process."

FDA spokesperson Jim O'Hara charged, "What this report proposes is dismantling many of the safeguards that protect the public from drugs and devices that are unsafe or just don't work. This is basically a proposal that says public health and safety are commodities for the marketplace."

Though drug testing and review would be privatized under the plan, the FDA would still exist and would theoretically have the final say on new products. However, the report states there would be "a strong presumption that private certification decisions would not be overturned without substantial cause." Further, the FDA would not be authorized to request additional testing or data, and it would "have to exercise its veto within a fixed time period (e.g. 90 days) after which the drug or device would automatically receive FDA approval."

The Progress & Freedom Foundation plan also limits the drug company's liability should a patient be injured or killed by a dangerous drug or medical device. According to the plan, a victim could not sue for punitive damages if the manufacturer of the product could show it met regulatory standards (no matter how weakened they were) during development and testing.

Dr. Sidney Wolfe, director of Public Citizen's Health Research Group, says the plan to limit corporate liability is "hypocrisy at the very least." Even some in the drug industry feel it goes too far.

Not surprisingly, the foundation has financial backing from some of the biggest names in the pharmaceutical industry, including Bristol-Myers Squibb Co., Eli Lilly & Co., and Marion Merell Dow. Another drug manufacturer, Glaxo, has given an undisclosed amount to the foundation, in addition to contributions of approximately $325,000 to the Republican Party and Republican candidates. As a whole, the drug industry contributed more than $1.6 million to the Republican Party in the 1993-94 election cycle.

SSU Censored Researcher: Tina Duccini

COMMENTS: Author Leslie Weiss said the plan to strip the FDA of its power did not receive sufficient coverage in the mass media. "Once I learned of the Progress & Freedom Foundation's (PFF) proposal to gut the FDA, I was surprised at the lack of coverage it received. When PFF released the report, it received coverage only in the *Wall Street Journal* (and then, of course, in *Mother Jones*)."

When asked why the general public should know more about this issue, Weiss said, "For most of us, reliance on therapeutic drugs and devices for healing is second nature. We expect quality and depend on the FDA to ensure it. Our lives depend on it. Any discussion of altering the safeguards that protect us from potentially dangerous drugs or medical devices must take place in a public forum; otherwise, we risk falling victim—financially and physically—to what easily could become an unregulated industry."

Weiss charged, "Drug and medical device producers, with their well-financed lobbying armies, are the only beneficiaries of limited media coverage on this subject. Reduced safety regulations and clinical testing periods reduce their costs by millions of dollars. So does reducing liability regulation."

7 CENSORED

Russia Injects Earth With Nuke Waste

Source:
THE NEW YORK TIMES
Date: 11/21/94
Title: "Poison in the Earth:
A special report; Nuclear Roulette for Russia: Burying Uncontained Waste," *
Author: William J. Broad

SYNOPSIS: For more than three decades, the Soviet Union and now Russia secretly pumped billions of gallons of atomic waste directly into the earth and, according to Russian scientists, the practice continues today.

The scientists said Moscow had injected about half of all the nuclear waste it ever produced into the ground at three widely dispersed sites, all thoroughly wet and all near major rivers. The three sites are at Dimitrovgrad near the Volga River, Tomsk near the Ob River, and Krasnoyarsk on the Yenisei River. The Volga flows into the Caspian Sea and the Ob and Yenisei flow into the Arctic Ocean.

The injections violate the accepted rules of nuclear waste disposal, which require it to be isolated in impermeable containers for thousands of years. The Russian scientists claim the practice is safe because the wastes have been injected under layers of shale and clay, which in theory cut them off from the Earth's surface.

But the wastes at one site already have leaked beyond the expected range and "spread a great distance," the Russians said. They did not say whether the distance was meters or kilometers or whether the poisons had reached the surface.

They began injecting the waste as a way to avoid the kind of surface-storage disasters that began to plague them in the 1950s. But by any measure, the injections were one of the Cold War's darkest secrets.

The amount of radioactivity injected by the Russians is up to three billion curies. By comparison, the accident at the Chernobyl nuclear power plant released about 50 million curies of radiation, mostly in short-lived isotopes that decayed in a few months. The accident at Three Mile Island discharged about 50 curies. The injected wastes include cesium-137, with a half life of 30 years, and strontium-90, with a half life of 28 years and a bad reputation because it binds readily with human bones.

The Russians are now working with the U.S. Department of Energy to try to better predict how far and fast the radioactive waste is likely to spread through aquifers.

At best, the Russian waste may stay underground long enough to be rendered largely harmless by the process of radioactive decay.

At worst, it might leak to the surface and produce regional calamities in Russia and areas downstream along the rivers. If the radioactivity spreads through the world's oceans, experts say, it might prompt a global rise in birth defects and cancer deaths.

At the least, the media should be reporting what progress is being made by the Department of Energy to monitor this potentially horrendous disaster.

SSU Censored Researcher:
Vanessa Mann

COMMENTS: Given the potential scope of this radioactive waste disaster, relatively little media attention appeared following the original *New York Times* story on November 21, 1994, by William J. Broad. The original *Times* story was picked up by the Memphis *Commercial Appeal*, the *Santa Cruz Sentinel*, and the Greenwire on 11/21/95.

On November 22, the *Minneapolis Star Tribune* editorialized, "If there is a silver lining in the horrifying disclosure of irresponsible underground radioactive waste disposal in Russia, it is that the world now knows at least something about what happened. When the Cold War was hot, much information—that Russian nuclear installations pumped billions of gallons of radioactive waste into underground rock formations—remained the deepest state secret."

Most interestingly, and not covered elsewhere, the *Star Tribune* revealed that the nuclear engineers at Hanford, Washington, and Oak Ridge, Tennessee, experimented with subsurface disposal also, although on a much smaller scale and at lower concentrations than that of the Russian scientists.

A news database search indicated there were no follow-up stories on these revelations throughout 1995.

However, by the end of the year, there were indications that Russia was making some attempts to deal with its radioactive waste problem. On December 19, 1995, the Greenwire reported that Russia and Norway signed an agreement on December 15 to work together on nuclear waste disposal, including spent nuclear fuel dumped by Russia; on December 31, Reuters reported a joint venture by Japan and the United States to build a radioactive liquid waste storage and reprocessing plant in Russia.

William J. Broad, author of the original article in *The New York Times*, declined to respond to our questionnaire attempting to follow-up on his story.

8 CENSORED

Medical Fraud Costs the Nation $100 Billion Annually— Or More

Source:
MOTHER JONES
Date: March/April 1995
Title: "Medscam"*
Author: L.J. Davis

SYNOPSIS: The United States' $1 trillion annual health bill is 14 percent of the gross domestic product, making the medical industry the largest business in the land.

Of this sum, a staggering amount is stolen. According to the National Health Care Anti-Fraud Association, the yearly swag totals between $31-$53 billion; according to the authoritative General Accounting Office, the annual take is $100 billion; according to other investigators the amount is as high as $250 billion. In fact, an extensive *Mother Jones* investigation discovered that no one really knows how much money is stolen from the medical system every year—and, possibly even worse, no one has any way of finding out.

Although Medicare and Medicaid were created in 1965, no specialized police force was established until 1978, giving the bad guys, according to Bill Whatley Jr., president of the National Associ–ation of Medicaid Fraud Control Units, "a 13-year head start, and we never caught up. The people who put this program together didn't believe that the [health care providers] in the program would commit fraud, because medicine was such a high calling."

Unfortunately, such optimism was misplaced; it did not take health care providers long before they developed a series of medscam techniques including the following:

Upcoding: a doctor performs one medical procedure and charges the insurer for another (more profitable) one;

Unbundling: the whole is some-times worth less than the sum of its parts. A wheelchair broken down into its components—a wheel here, a seat there—with a separate bill for each, can mean bigger profits;

Pharmacy Fraud: a corrupt phar-macist, often abetted by a physician and a patient, dispenses a generic drug rather than a brand-name drug and pockets the difference;

Psychiatric Schemes: in the 1980s, the nation experienced an "epidemic" of clinical depression, as hospital chains filled their beds with teenagers, the overweight, and substance abusers;

Home Health Care: this includes overbilling, billing for services not rendered, kickbacks, the use of untrained (i.e. inexpensive) per-sonnel, and the delivery of unnec-essary equipment;

Ghost Patients: there are doctors who continue to treat patients after they're dead and doctors who work more than 24 hours a day.

Social Security is another area rife with fraud, costing billions of dollars. The Social Security Ad-ministration (SSA) runs a $1.4 bil-lion program that pays drunks and junkies to remain drunks and junkies. As long as the substance abusers continue to abuse sub-stances, they receive a federal payday every month; if they go straight, the checks stop. In a number of documented instances, the SSA provided the wherewithal that enabled abusers to drink or overdose themselves to death.

The irony of all this is that prosecuting medical insurance fraud is one of the government's few profit centers, returning about $72 for every taxpayer dollar spent; even allowing for the usual bureaucratic exaggeration, the monies recovered are substantial—to say nothing of the money that is saved when a fraudulent practitioner is removed from circulation.

SSU Censored Researcher:
Vanessa Mann

COMMENTS: Investigative author L.J. Davis felt the story was "reported, if at all, anecdotally and poorly, but not systematically. It made the news, for example, when National Medical Enterprises (NME), a centi-million-dollar hospital chain, was raided by the FBI in one of the largest operations in recent history, but no attempt was made to discover if NME was symptomatic of a larger phenomenon—which it was. This is typical, I have found."

The general public would benefit from wider exposure of the medical fraud story since it would "discover how grossly its tax and insurance money is ripped off," Davis said. "And, it might occur to the public that if medical fraud were halted, the nation could afford just about any kind of health system it could think of."

Davis charged that corrupt healthcare providers and medical equipment companies benefit most obviously from the limited coverage given medical fraud. "Of these, easily the greatest beneficiaries are the private, for-profit hospital chains, a form of company unknown in this country until the creation of Medicare—and whose obsession with the bottom line has allowed, and often actively encouraged, massive fraud."

THIS MODERN WORLD   by TOM TOMORROW

Davis concluded, "After 30 years in the business, the editorial mind remains something of a mystery to me. For example, I brought the story of AIDS fraud and quackery to another magazine, which shall remain nameless. Because of editorial agendas, quackery—a great tragedy—vanished entirely. The story concentrated on home health-care fraud, an important story, but not the whole story. At another magazine, I proposed a story on how the hospital chains are migrating into managed care—and the rich opportunity for a whole new fraud. 'How do I know you're right?', said the editor. In a related event, Joe Sharkey produced a splendid book, *Bedlam*, on psychiatric fraud. It sank without a trace."

9 CENSORED

U.S. Chemical Industry Fights for Toxic Ozone-Killing Pesticide

Source:
EARTH ISLAND JOURNAL
Date: Summer 1995
Title: "Campaign Against Methyl
    Bromide: Ozone-Killing
    Pesticide Opposed"*
Author: Anne Schonfield

SYNOPSIS: Methyl bromide is a pesticide that is at least 50 times more destructive to the ozone layer, atom for atom, than chlorofluorocarbons (CFCs), yet America's chemical industry is fighting to prevent it from being banned.

In 1992, the United Nations estimated that bromine atoms released into the upper atmosphere are

responsible for five-to-ten percent of global ozone depletion, a share that is expected to increase to 15 percent by the year 2000.

In 1994, the UN listed elimination of methyl bromide (MB) as the most significant remaining approach (after phase-out of CFCs and halons) to reducing ozone depletion. UN scientists conclude that eliminating MB emissions from agricultural, structural, and industrial activities by the year 2001 would achieve a 13 percent reduction in ozone-depleting chemicals reaching the atmosphere over the next 50 years.

MB also is extremely toxic and can cause acute and chronic health effects. Farmworkers, pesticide applicators, and people living or working where MB is used can suffer poisoning, neurological damage and reproductive harm. The chemical is so toxic to humans and animals that the Environmental Protection Agency (EPA) classifies it as a Category 1 acute toxin, the most deadly group of substances.

For 60 years, MB has been used to kill pests in soils and buildings, and on agricultural products. In 1991, the U.S. accounted for nearly 40 percent of the pesticide's world-wide use. Soil fumigation to sterilize soil before planting crops is by far the largest use of MB in the U.S. Worldwide, most MB is used for luxury and export crops, like tomatoes, strawberries, peppers, tobacco and nursery crops.

Under the Clean Air Act, the EPA has mandated a halt to MB production in, and import to, the U.S. in 2001—but manufacturers and agricultural users have mounted a formidable campaign to delay the ban. Because no gradual phaseout is required, methyl bromide can be used without major restrictions until 2001. Since the act does not prohibit the use of existing stocks after 2001, application of the pesticide can continue as long as stockpiled supplies last.

The Methyl Bromide Global Coalition (MBGC)—a group of eight international MB users and producers—has launched a multi-million-dollar lobbying campaign to keep the product on the market. A leaked document from the Methyl Bromide Working Group, which includes Ethyl Corp. and Great Lakes Chemical Corp., the country's major MB producers, ignores reports of record ozone depletion, and states, "If we continue to work together, we stand an increasingly good chance of being able to use methyl bromide well beyond the year 2001."

While some nations are actively fighting a phaseout, other countries have already banned or vigorously regulated MB. In 1992, the Netherlands eliminated all soil fumigation using MB, and other countries, including Denmark, Germany, and Switzerland, are planning similar actions.

SSU Censored Researcher:
Brad Hood

COMMENTS: Despite press releases to nearly 400 journalists, follow-up calls to many of them, and the distribution of 2,500 briefing kits, the methyl bromide issue received limited coverage in some local newspapers and no coverage by network TV, the news weeklies, or major dailies, according to investigative writer Anne Schonfield. In general, she added, "New scientific reports about continuing ozone depletion, and methyl bromide in particular, received little media attention in the U.S. (while in Canada, for example, ozone depletion and UV-B exposure are regularly covered in weather reports on TV). Down under, in Australia, Chile and New Zealand, coverage is also common.

"Methyl bromide is a classic illustration of the interconnected hazards caused by synthetic pesticides. This invisible, odorless gas is extremely dangerous to farm workers, to people who live or work near where it is used and those who re-enter fumigated structures, causing health problems ranging from mild irritation to death. If Americans knew more about methyl bromide, they would think twice about buying conventionally-grown strawberries and Florida tomatoes (which are almost universally produced with methyl bromide) and other crops that may look wholesome but are actually harming farmworkers and killing the soil.

"Moreover, methyl bromide is destroying the ozone layer. It is this global impact, well-documented by international science panels, that should be generating media coverage. However, Americans seem to believe that ozone depletion has been taken care of since many countries have banned CFCs, the most well-known ozone depletors. In fact, ozone depletion continues to worsen every year and is expected to peak around 1998.

"The producers of methyl bromide (primarily Great Lakes Chemical and Albemarle Corporation in the U.S. and Dead Sea Bromine in Israel) certainly benefit from the lack of exposure on this issue (interestingly, both U.S.-based companies have production facilities in Arkansas), as do the specialized companies that inject the chemical into the soil (such as Trical in California). The producers and major users are actively debunking the science of ozone depletion and point to their investments in alternatives (not surprisingly, they're focused on chemical alternatives rather than those that will not produce fat agrichemical corporate profits)."

Schonfield adds that there is a coalition of 17 consumer, health, environmental justice and labor groups, called the Methyl Bromide Alternatives Network, working to increase media attention and public awareness of methyl bromide. The coalition ranges from big organizations like Friends of the Earth and NRDC to farmworker self-help groups, black southern farm co-ops and labor unions. But despite numerous press releases, petitions, editorial calls and wide distribution of briefing kits, "it has been very difficult to get more than occasional media attention to this issue (usually from freelancers), and it has not been picked up by wire services, papers of record, or the networks."

On December 10, 1995, *The New York Times* reported that more than 100 governments agreed to phase out developed countries' production of methyl bromide. The agreement called for the manufacture of methyl bromide to be cut by 25 percent by 2001, 50 percent by 2005, and 100 percent by 2010. It also noted that parties to the accord will meet in 1996 to consider allowing exemptions for "critical agricultural use."

10 CENSORED

The Broken Promises of NAFTA

Sources:
COVERT/ACTION QUARTERLY
Date: Fall 1995
Title: "NAFTA's Corporate Con Artists"*
Authors: Sarah Anderson and Kristyne Peter

MOTHER JONES
Date: January/February 1995
Title: "A Giant Spraying Sound"*
Author: Esther Schrader

SYNOPSIS: The promises of prosperity that the North American Free Trade Agreement (NAFTA) would bring the USA and Mexico were most loudly proclaimed by USA*NAFTA, a pro-NAFTA business coalition. The USA*NAFTA coalition promised that the free trade pact would be all things to all people. It would improve the environment, reduce illegal immigration by raising Mexican wages, deter international drug trafficking, and most importantly, create a net increase in high-paying U.S. jobs.

Now, some two years after the agreement became law, USA*–

NAFTA's own members are blatantly breaking the coalition's grand promises. Many of the firms—that only a short time ago were extolling the benefits of NAFTA for U.S. workers and communities—have cut jobs, moved plants to Mexico, or continued to violate labor rights and environmental regulations in Mexico.

An analysis by the Institute for Policy Studies revealed how the original promises are being broken in Mexico: while the standard of living may be better for the wealthy, there's been a 30 percent increase in the number of Mexicans emigrating to the U.S.; the peso devaluation of December 1994 cut the value of their wages by as much as 40 percent (making them far less able to buy U.S. goods today than they were before NAFTA); interest rates on credit cards climbed above 100 percent; retail sales in Mexico's three largest cities have dropped by nearly 25 percent.

The continuing economic crisis in Mexico is expected to cause the loss of two million jobs in 1995, and economic desperation is blamed for the 30 percent increase in arrests by U.S. border patrols between January and May 1995.

NAFTA's promises to U.S. workers also have been broken: the Department of Labor's NAFTA Transitional Adjustment Assistance program reported that 35,000 U.S. workers qualified for retraining between January 1, 1994, and July 10, 1995, because of jobs lost to NAFTA. A University of Maryland study estimates that more than 150,000 U.S. jobs were cut in 1994 as a result of increased consumer imports from Mexico. And since the peso devaluation in December 1994, the U.S. trade surplus with Mexico has turned into a deficit expanding from $885 million in May 1994 to $6.9 billion a year later, wiping out any basis for claiming that NAFTA is a net job creator for U.S. workers.

And, finally, an investigative piece by *Mother Jones* revealed that the environmental impact of NAFTA has been as severe as the economic impact. While government officials promised that NAFTA would reduce the level of pesticides coating Mexico's fields, this hasn't occurred.

The competition that NAFTA has set off between growers may actually increase the amount of pesticides used on Mexican crops. In fact, since NAFTA, Mexican growers are spraying more toxic pesticides on fruits, vegetables, and workers. Responsibility for pesticide use lies not only with Mexican growers but also with their U.S. agribusiness partners. The *Mother Jones* investigation also revealed that these companies, which supply capital to more than 40 percent of large-scale agribusiness in Mexico, distribute produce that has been sprayed with pesticides not permitted for use in the United States.

SSU Censored Researcher:
Pia C. Jensen

COMMENTS: Sarah Anderson, co-author of the *CovertAction Quarterly* article with Kristyne Peter, notes the general theme of the article is "the hypocrisy of pro-NAFTA U.S. corporations which, less than two years into the agreement, are already confirming the fears of NAFTA critics. It looks at the broader range of NAFTA's impact, and attempts to raise awareness of the links between workers and communities on both sides of the border. The worse things get in Mexico, the worse things will get in the United States, but the mainstream media seem to have missed that point.

"The general public could benefit from an increased awareness of how free trade leads to downward pressure on labor and environmental conditions on both sides of the border. If U.S. citizens begin to see their fates as being linked to those of workers in Mexico and other low-wage countries, they will begin to redirect their frustrations away from Mexican workers and immigrants and toward the real culprits—the corporations that are pitting workers and communities against each other in a race to the bottom. I also hope that this article will help increase the already growing concern about the excessive influence of corporations over our political system. The vast majority of people who worked in opposition to NAFTA came away from that battle convinced that the first step towards achieving more socially responsible economic and trade policies is to get money out of politics.

"Clearly, it is the corporate con artists who are benefiting from the lack of media coverage of this issue. While the leaders of these corporations were eager to appear in the media before the vote on NAFTA

to promote what they claimed would be its numerous benefits for the U.S. public, they are now noticeably absent from the limelight.

"Pat Buchanan, as the only presidential candidate talking about free trade, has become the most prominent NAFTA critic. Unfortunately, Buchanan's racist views leave the impression that anyone who is opposed to the agreement is also a nationalist and a protectionist. The mainstream media have reinforced the false impression that the debate on trade has only two sides (free trade vs. protectionist). There are many who believe that trade can be beneficial, but want to ensure that these benefits are reaped by the greater public, not just the corporate CEOs. Buchanan's virtual monopoly of the trade issue makes it imperative that those who promote an internationalist approach to trade policy try even harder to get this view into the mainstream media."

Esther Schrader, author of the *Mother Jones* article, said she was not surprised the subject of her article—the investigation into Mexican worker deaths associated with pesticides—was not undertaken by anyone else. However, she was disturbed the subject did not surface in major media during the NAFTA debate, where concern over pesticides was limited to fears about their effect on U.S. consumers eating fruit and vegetables. Never in the NAFTA debate did the frightening effect of pesticides on Mexican workers in the field receive major media coverage.

Schrader notes, "In the most callous sense, U.S. residents are not at all affected by improving conditions for Mexican workers. But if the tremendous harms suffered by Mexican workers in the fields every day were taken up by the mass media, the U.S. government might feel compelled to exert pressure on its Mexican counterparts to enforce their own laws. With the establish-

ment last year of the NAFTA environmental commission, Mexican officials can now be censured for their failure to adhere to their own laws. All that is lacking is desire on the part of U.S. officials.

"Of course Mexican agribusiness and the Mexican government, both interested in increasing exports to the U.S., benefit from the limited coverage given the abuse of pesticides on Mexican farms. But powerful U.S. agribusiness would also be harmed by closer attention to this subject, since U.S. growers are the powerful owners of many Mexican agribusiness operations."

Schrader concludes, "It is a shame that the environmental commission set up under NAFTA does not take up this issue and other similar abuses. Until Americans are dying, I doubt they will."

The revelations concerning NAFTA's broken promises cited in the original source articles by *Covert/Action Quarterly* and *Mother Jones* were confirmed January 12, 1996, when the *Washington Post* reported that, "During 1995, the Mexican economy shrank by six percent and lost more than one million jobs as it sank into its deepest recession in 60 years. The value of the peso dropped nearly 60 percent, the annual inflation rate exceeded 50 percent, tens of billions of dollars in capital fled the country, and Mexicans complained of a rise in violent crime." Further,

the *Post* added, "As a result, illegal border crossings rose substantially last year. Across the entire 2,000-mile border, apprehensions were up 92 percent from a year earlier, INS officials said."

11 CENSORED

Giant Oil Companies Owe U.S. More Than $1.5 Billion

Source:
PROJECT ON GOVERNMENT OVERSIGHT REPORTS
Date: April 1995
Title: "Department of Interior Looks the Other Way: The Government's Slick Deal for the Oil Industry"
Author: Project on Government Oversight (POGO), Danielle Brian

SYNOPSIS: Seven of the largest oil companies in the United States—Texaco, Shell, Mobil, ARCO, Chevron, Exxon, and Unocal—owe the federal government more than $1.5 billion in uncollected royalties, interest, and penalties, according to a well-documented report by the Project on Government Oversight (POGO). POGO is a non-partisan, non-profit organization that investigates conflicts of interest and abuse in government.

POGO also obtained a draft of a Department of Interior (DOI) Inspector General report which concludes that over a four year period, royalties alone "may have been underpaid by as much as $29.5 million from 1990 through 1993 and may continue to be underpaid as long as pipelines continue to operate as private carriers."

The big oil companies, with the exception of Exxon, operate the largest pipelines with the state of California. These pipelines cross federal land in one or more places which by federal law requires them to be operated as common carriers (common carriers allow small oil company crude to be transported for free). Instead, they are operated as private carriers. This monopoly forces smaller oil companies to pay higher rates in order to move their crude oil from the wells to the refinery. Also, the largest oil companies have been artificially suppressing the price of their crude in order to avoid high royalties as mandated under the Mineral Leasing Act.

Surprisingly, the DOI, the agency responsible for collecting these royalties, is a willing partner of the oil companies in this extraordinary corporate welfare program. In addition to the forthcoming Inspector General report, DOI has ignored: U.S. Department of Commerce comments about the problem; a DOI Office of Policy Analysis that calls for the Department to determine the amount of royalties due (including interest and criminal penalties, if any), and to initiate collection procedures; and the DOI Minerals Management Service conclusion that "we should pursue potential Federal royalty underpayments."

Beyond the obvious impact of losing more than $1.5 billion that is owed to the federal treasury, this sweetheart deal with the oil industry has even more direct harm. By federal law, one half of all money collected by the federal government from oil royalties is to be returned directly to the state from which the oil has been pumped. In California, the law requires that such funds be credited to the State School Fund. This means that the California school system, which is in serious financial trouble, has been bilked out of nearly $750 million.

To date, the Department of the Interior has failed to collect these funds and the nation's press has taken scant notice of this classic example of corporate welfare.

SSU Censored Researcher:
Fritz Rollins

COMMENTS: Author Danielle Brian acknowledged that while there was some limited media coverage of the issue, there was no significant follow-up. "ABC Evening News ran a piece on this story and a short follow-up that focused on an individual bureaucrat," Brian said. "No other networks touched it. The *Washington Post* and the *L.A. Times* both ran stories in their Business Sections. The Cox wire service ran an article that resulted in a number of small town newspapers picking up the story. However, none of these outlets were willing to do any follow-up, despite the fact that we received sensational new documents after the original stories ran. In fact, the *L.A. Times* ran two 'Letters to the Editor' attacking POGO and the story. While they did identify one of the authors as representing the oil industry, they did not identify the other as recently having represented an oil industry association. Needless to say, the *L.A. Times* refused to run our response, despite our ability to prove the letters were inaccurate and misleading."

Brian believes the general public would benefit from wider exposure of this subject because "it is only through public exposure, as is usually true, that the government's acquiescence to the oil industry will stop. Until the mass media cover this story aggressively, we will not be able to stop this form of corporate welfare. Furthermore, more media attention would not only energize the Administration, but it would also motivate Congress—

which up to this point has dropped the ball as well."

Clearly, Brian continues, the oil industry benefits from the lack of media coverage. "Of course they are not interested in having to pay back $1.5 billion to the federal government. In addition, the Department of Interior bureaucrats, whose interest is to protect the status quo, also benefit from the lack of coverage of the subject. Not only is it easier to continue doing business as usual, but no one wants to admit they have allowed such a massive fraud to take place against the government."

After the POGO report was released, the organization received leaked internal e-mail messages that revealed the Department of Interior's efforts to cut a deal with industry, Brian added. "The Department was asking for industry's support of DOI's reorganization plan. In exchange DOI was offering to shorten the Statute of Limitations so that the oil industry could no longer be prosecuted for withholding royalty payments. Even though we actively worked with those journalists who had already covered the story, as well as a number of other major media outlets including the *Wall Street Journal* and *Time Magazine*, no one, other than the trade press, ran any further stories."

12 CENSORED

180,000 Patients Die Annually from Treatment in Hospitals

Sources:
HEALTH LETTER
Date: August 1995
Title: "Hospital Errors"
Author: Excerpted from ABC
    "Nightline" (7/4/95) transcript

NEWSDAY
Date: 7/17/95
Title: "No mortality rate stats for
    hospitals"
Author: Thomas Maier

SYNOPSIS: More people are killed or seriously injured in U.S. hospitals annually than from airline and automobile accidents combined.

An estimated 1.3 million people a year receive some kind of injury related to treatment at hospitals, and 180,000 of those people die.

About half of these deaths— 80,000 to 90,000 of them—are preventable, the result of negligence, such as prescribing the wrong medicine, receiving the wrong dose of medication, or adverse drug interactions.

The first in-depth look at how often such drug errors occur was published in the July 5, 1995, issue of the *Journal of the American Medical Association* (JAMA).

The JAMA report revealed that there were 6.5 drug complications for every 100 admissions to the hospital. The major problems were in four areas: the wrong drug or the wrong dose; incorrect copies of the drug order; pharmacies dispensing the wrong drug order; and nurses administering the drug to the wrong patient. While most patients survive these drug errors, some people, like Betsy Lehman, a health writer from Chicago, and Vincent Gargano, a postal worker from Chicago, died from incorrect and fatal doses of anti-cancer drugs.

Most hospitals lack systems which could automatically double-check individual decisions. Two hospitals in Boston—Massachusetts General and Brigham and Women's—have just instituted such a system to catch mistakes before patients suffer from them. Other hospitals say such systems are too expensive.

But Dr. Sidney Wolfe, Director of the Public Citizen's Health Research Group, pointed out that "Several billion dollars a year are being wasted treating preventable adverse drug reactions."

Given the extent of injuries and deaths from hospital errors, one must wonder why the American public isn't more aware of this problem.

Unfortunately, hospitals are not adequately regulated and there is little to no public accountability in America's health care system. (The #8 *Censored* story of 1993, "America's Deadly Doctors," pointed out how the medical profession fails to report its incompetent physicians.)

Both written and verbal queries about hospitals made to the Joint Commission on Accreditation of Health Organizations have gone unanswered, according to Wolfe. "For instance," Wolfe pointed out, "we don't have a list of the 40 percent of hospitals who did not pass the test, in terms of quality review over surgery and medicine. But I think the more important point is that this should be a public function. Why is the airline industry, with a much better crash record than hospitals, a public function? Why does the public demand, when a crash occurs or when pilots get licensed, that we look at what's going on? We don't have those kinds of data."

Compounding the problem, in 1995 the Clinton administration quietly killed the formerly-required yearly report comparing hospitals' death rates for Medicare patients, replacing it with less confrontational "systems-oriented" analyses that concentrate on how hospitals generally can perform better. The new reporting requirements do not publicly identify local institutions or their performance, including mortality rates.

SSU Censored Researcher:
Nikki Washburn

COMMENTS: Sidney Wolfe, editor of the *Health Letter* and participant in the ABC "Nightline" program excerpted in the above-cited article, suggested that most of the coverage of this issue was in the form of local examples—the *Boston Globe* reporter killed by an overdose of cancer drugs; a Tampa hospital cutting off the wrong leg/arthroscoping the wrong knee, etc. "The 'Nightline' piece was one of the only, if not the only, national media stories about the causes or solutions to the problem of 80,000 people killed in American hospitals annually.

"The solution to hospital (or doctor-office) errors will not occur as long as the problem is portrayed as specific to certain places. Especially in light of increasing trends of understaffing hospitals, they are once again becoming places where too many people go to die. Hospital trustees (and patients) cannot exercise their ability to improve conditions in their hospitals unless the scope of this problem is known.

Wolfe said that organized medicine and organized hospitals/HMOs are most likely to benefit from the limited coverage; they can simply pretend that this is just a few bad apples and that the basket is mainly okay.

Wolfe also noted that the *Health Letter* will publish "13,000+ Questionable Doctors," the fourth version of their report naming those physicians disciplined by federal or state authorities, in early 1996. And, he concluded, "Much more vigilance concerning *all* doctors and hospitals is needed."

Thomas Maier, author of the *Newsday* article, said, "Each year, an estimated 180,000 Americans die from injuries caused in their hospitals—the same place where most people probably think they are safest. Yet as this *Newsday* story exposed, the only public method of keeping track of death rates in hospitals in the U.S. was quietly killed in 1995. *Newsday's* story, which received no attention from the national media, highlighted how the Clinton Administration reneged on its promise to provide consumers with 'report cards' on local hospital performance, and instead dismantled the only federal barometer of that performance.

"Before these yearly reports were eliminated, the results of death rates in local hospitals often drew large headlines in the press. Hospitals, doctors and administrators often objected to the yearly tests—including Clinton's new appointee to the same agency that wound up killing the studies.

"What happened here is a classic example of how the government lied to the press and no one ever followed up. Yet, the consequences are extremely important to anyone who enters a hospital in this country. With more information about death rates instead of less, patients could make intelligent decisions about where to go when they are sick, and policy-makers could take action to improve hospitals where performance appears to be poor.

"Clearly, the medical community lobbied hard for the elimination of the death rates studies and the creation of a new 'systems-oriented' review where the results are never made public. Hospital administrators get a private briefing about the problems found in their institutions. But the public which pays millions for the studies never does."

Maier also noted that *Newsday* has worked hard on behalf of the public's right to know. "*Newsday* has pushed hard to make government mortality rate studies available to the public," Maier said. "Three years ago, *Newsday* won a lawsuit which forced New York state officials to make public its death rate statistics on cardiac by-pass surgery."

13 CENSORED

Congress Wants to Take the Money and Run

Source:
COMMON CAUSE MAGAZINE
Date: Summer 1995
Title: "Take the Money and Run"
Author: Vicki Kemper

SYNOPSIS: At a time when voters are more disgusted than ever by the big-money business of political campaigns, it's nice to know that there is a "cop" on the beat. The "cop" is the Federal Election Commission (FEC). Its job is to ensure that all money that goes into and comes out of campaign war chests is legal and accounted for, and ultimately that the nation will never again be rocked by a Watergate-scale political scandal financed by secret slush funds.

And voters need such a cop to watch Congress. Just last year, the overworked and much maligned FEC watchdog agency collected a record $1.7 million in civil penalties for illegal campaign financing activities.

However, the FEC's hard work isn't appreciated by everyone. It has had an on-going battle, as far back as 1986, with budget cuts. Most recently, the 1994 election results threaten to weaken the agency for years to come. The Republicans, who won control of the House, took just over a month to quietly approve a series of actions that could cripple the FEC.

First, the House Appropriations Committee voted to strip the FEC of almost $2.8 million, roughly 20 percent of what's left of its budget for the current fiscal year. Then, the House Oversight Committee rejected the FEC's budget request for the 1996 fiscal year, authorizing almost $4.2 million less than the agency said it needed.

Few believe the budget cuts are unrelated to recent FEC enforcement actions, although it probably was just a coincidence that the Oversight Committee acted precisely one day before the most-hated of regulations ever declared by the FEC—rules that bar candidates from using campaign funds for vacations, cars, meals, and other personal expenses—took effect on April 5, 1995.

"We don't think that the FEC should be micro-managing our campaigns," said House Appropriations Chair Bob Livingston (R-La.), an agency opponent who now controls its purse strings. Livingston, who adamantly opposes the personal use rules, tried to slash the FEC's budget last year—precisely so it wouldn't have the funds to regulate and enforce campaign spending.

While the House Republicans have been attacking the FEC's budget, there's been an explosion in the number of campaigns for Congress and the presidency which ultimately create an increased work load for the FEC.

Since 1990, the number of federal candidates has increased 34 percent; the amount of money raised and spent is up 54 percent; the number of campaign-related complaints filed with the FEC has increased 45 percent; and the number of information requests is up 17 percent.

It's ironic that the same Congress that loudly calls for tougher anti-crime measures is working to disempower the agency charged with policing its own campaign activities.

SSU Censored Researcher: Tami Ward

COMMENTS: Vicki Kemper, investigative writer for *Common Cause Magazine*, said that except for a piece by syndicated columnist David Broder, who contacted her for background information, the subject received virtually no attention in the mass media as far as she knew.

Kemper feels strongly about the public's need to be aware of how elected officials are abusing their power to stay in office and spending their campaign money as they please. "Of course," Kemper continued, "part of what was behind the House's actions against the FEC is an attempt to make sure the public does *not* know how candidates use their campaign funds. As serious students of campaign spending reports know, for years many candidates have used their campaign accounts as personal slush funds, financing meals, travel, clothing, country club dues and more. The key instigators of the investigation of the FEC and the budget cuts were acting in part out of pique over recent regulations designed to restrict the personal use of campaign funds. Voters need to know the extent to which their elected officials are abusing their offices, the extent to which they feel entitled to do so, and the lengths to which they're willing to go to maintain those privileges."

Kemper had a warning for voters in 1996: "Voters also need to be aware that candidates running for office in 1996 will likely be able to get away with more monkey business than ever because of the constraints placed on the FEC by the very people it's supposed to monitor."

Kemper noted that limited coverage of this subject benefits "everyone who runs for federal office and wants to get away with something. Most of all, it benefits incumbents who are running for reelection."

"I submitted op-eds on the subject to the *New York Times*, the *Washington Post* and the *Post's* Sunday opinion sections (where I've had pieces published before) with no results," Kemper said. An editor of the *Post's* 'Outlook' section explained their rejection of the piece this way: They'd been running too many articles on budget cuts to federal programs. Clearly they'd missed the point."

The Fall 1995 issue of *Common Cause Magazine* published a follow-up report which revealed that the investigation of the FEC by its congressional opponents "turned up no smoking guns." In fact, the House Appropriations Committee's staff report concluded that "the disclosure and audit side of the FEC, including personnel, appears to be well-managed."

14 CENSORED

The Gulf War Syndrome Cover-Up

Source:
COVERT/ACTION QUARTERLY
Date: Summer 1995

Title: "Gulf War Syndrome
    Covered Up: Chemical and
    Biological Agents Exposed"
Author: Dennis Bernstein

SYNOPSIS: While the Pentagon denies that U.S. soldiers were exposed to chemical and biological warfare agents during the Gulf War, its own records contradict the official line. Now, four years after the war's end, tens of thousands of Gulf War personnel have come down with one or more of a number of disabling and life-threatening medical conditions collectively known as Gulf War Syndrome.

The syndrome's cause is unclear, but veterans and researchers have focused on the elements of a toxic chemical soup in the war zone that included insecticides, pesticides, various preventive medicines given experimentally to GIs, and smoke from the burning oil fields of Iraq and Kuwait. There also is reliable evidence that one of its causes is exposure to low levels of chemical and biological warfare (CBW) agents during the war.

According to a variety of sources, including recently declassified Marine Corps battlefield *Command Chronologies* and *After Action Reports*, widespread exposure to CBW agents occurred when U.S.-led forces bombed Iraqi chemical facilities, and during direct attacks by the Iraqis.

Despite Pentagon denials, evidence of CBW exposure during the war is abundant and mounting. In response to a Freedom of Information Act request by the Gulf War Veterans of Georgia, in January the Pentagon released 11 pages of previously classified Nuclear, Biological, and Chemical Incident (NBC) logs. The NBC log excerpts, which cover only seven days of the war, document dozens of chemical incidents. They also reveal chemical injuries to U.S. GIs, discoveries of Iraqi chemical munitions dumps, fallout from allied bombing of Iraqi chemical supply dumps, and chemical attacks on Saudi Arabia.

The recently released Marine Corps battlefield reports also confirm scores of CBW incidents during the ground war including the use of anthrax and Lewicite, a chemical nerve agent. Army documents strongly support contentions that CBW agents were present in the Gulf: "Conclusions: Clearly, chemical warfare agents were detected and confirmed" during the war. "It cannot be ruled out that [CBW agents] could have contributed to the illness in susceptible individuals."

Reports from VA doctors contradict the Pentagon line while numerous reports from the field also cite the presence of CBW agents. In addition, Iraqi documents captured by U.S. and British forces further bolster the information in the NBC logs and the on-the-scene accounts, as do reliable reports by U.S., British, and Czech chemical weapons specialists deployed in Iraq and Kuwait after the war.

Given the abundance of evidence, one must wonder why the U.S. continues to deny CBW exposure. First, to admit that CBW exposures occurred means the military must admit its inability to protect U.S. forces from CBW agents. Next is the embarrassing history of U.S. government and corporate cooperation with Iraq in the 1980s. With the active support of two presidents and many U.S. officials, U.S. and Western European companies sold the technology to Iraq that may now be making tens of thousands of soldiers and civilians ill.

And there always is the military bureaucracy's natural instinct to cover itself in the face of any problem or scandal. Finally, the cover-up is being compounded by evidence that the military has harassed and mistreated Gulf veterans who have reported ill-effects.

SSU Censored Researcher:
Dylan Humphrey

COMMENTS: Investigative journalist Dennis Bernstein said, "While certain aspects of this story, such as the large number of birth defects suffered by the off-spring of

Gulf Vets, have received some reasonable amount of coverage in the mainstream media, key elements of the story have been ignored. Most egregious among them is a massive and ongoing cover-up led by the current director of central intelligence, John Deutch, formerly the number two man at the Defense Department, and a self-proclaimed Gulf War information point man. Indeed, thousands of documents and hundreds of interviews with soldiers and various experts in five countries pointing to the widespread presence of chemical and biological warfare agents in the Gulf during the war with Iraq have been set aside and ignored in the face of a few limp denials by Deutch.

"The real story here, besides the fact that hundreds of thousands of people are suffering worldwide because of the stonewalling on crucial information needed for proper diagnosis and treatment, is the undeniable reality that major U.S. and European corporations with the help of key Reaganites including major support from George Bush, made the very technology available that Iraq needed to create its chemical and biological arsenal.

"Hundreds of thousands of Middle-Easterners and U.S. troops and civilians remain in jeopardy of being exposed to the deadly warfare agents that are still being produced by U.S. and European corporations and distributed world wide at great profit. I believe more reliable information about the continuing dangers of exposure to the toxic chemistry and the role key U.S. corporations have played in this deadly situation could make it more difficult for such tragedies to be repeated. It would also make the Pentagon and the DOD more responsive to the needs of so many Gulf Vets, active duty soldiers and their families who continue to be told that their serious medical conditions are psychological in nature!"

Bernstein said he recently learned through further investigation that the very same chemical alarms that were triggered in Iraq during the war by the thousands— and which the Pentagon has repeatedly claimed to be a faulty and unreliable measure of the presence of deadly warfare agents on the battlefield—are still being purchased and deployed by the military in the Gulf. "There also are reliable reports coming out of Iraq and Kuwait that thousands of children are suffering and dying from exposure to the deadly toxins during the war," Bernstein added.

On November 8, 1995, the Department of Veterans Affairs announced it is launching another new study of health complaints by veterans of the Gulf War.

15 CENSORED

The Rebirth of Slavery in the Dark Heart of Sudan

Source:
THE BOSTON PHOENIX
Date: 6/30/95
Title: "Africa's Invisible Slaves:
Human bondage resurfaces in
the dark heart of Sudan"
Author: Tim Sandler

SYNOPSIS: From mass murder in Rwanda to mass starvation in Somalia, Africa's horrors continue to shake the world's sensibilities. Yet, despite heightened attention to Africa's troubles, its largest country, Sudan, still harbors the continent's darkest secret: the rebirth of slavery.

In the last several years, pure chattel slavery—the use of people as property—has quietly re-emerged as a social institution in Sudan. And as a participant in this slave trade, Sudan's government has good reason to make sure it remains a secret.

In an area that Sudan's Muslim-fundamentalist government has declared off-limits to outsiders, stories of modern-day slavery are rampant. Despite the government's denial of slavery, throughout the vast southern region of Sudan, where the Arab world meets black Africa, the resurgence of systematic slavery is as evident as the bloated stomachs of the malnourished children. Lashing marks, branding scars, and permanent injuries on freed and escaped slaves offer vivid corroboration of their accounts of human bondage.

Sudan's Muslim-fundamentalist regime has turned the 12-year-old north/south civil war into a government-sponsored jihad against Christians, animists, and even modern Muslims. Sudan is now high on the U.S. State Department's list of terrorist governments and the motivation for the State Department's warning against travel in Sudan by foreigners is clear.

While the number of slaves in Sudan is easily in the thousands, a more precise figure is difficult to calculate. A U.N. special investigator reported in 1994 that in the past several years tens of thousands of black Christians and animists had been abducted from southern Sudan and the Nuba Mountains and brought to the north.

Thousands of young boys are routinely rounded up by the government forces and taken to cultural-cleansing camps where they are beaten, renamed, forced to convert to Islam, and often compelled to fight on the front lines against their own people in the south.

Slaves in southern Sudan are sometimes sold openly in "cattle markets," a term that illustrates the value Arab traders place on the humans exchanged there. Women and children are sold for as little as 200 to 300 Sudanese pounds in the Nuba Mountains area.

An accurate estimate of the number of slaves in Sudan is hampered by the government's placement of severe limitations on travel into the country. Officially-sanctioned travel outside the Khartoum area is rare, and all foreigners are supposed to register with police.

Unfortunately, slave labor is not limited to the Sudan, nor even Africa. The Anti-Slavery Society, of Australia, charged that between 104 million and 146 million children—some as young as four—are forced to work in appalling conditions to make consumer products for Western nations (Associated Press, 9/19/95). The Society said that the children, with an estimated 73 million to 115 million of them in India alone, are making car parts, jewelry, clothing, toys, food, fireworks, chemicals and other goods in sweatshops. Other nations cited by the group as tolerating forced child labor were Pakistan, Nepal, Philippines, China, Bangladesh, Indonesia, Thailand, and Sri Lanka.

SSU Censored Researcher:
Justin Twergo

COMMENTS: *Boston Phoenix* writer Tim Sandler reported that the mass media virtually ignored the resurgence of slavery in Sudan. "I say ignored because a good many of the major news outlets, including network television, are now aware of the situation (the *Phoenix* sent its story to many of them). Still, there has been no follow-up."

"Given America's history of slavery," Sandler continued, "it would be difficult to imagine that wider exposure to modern-day slavery in Sudan would not be greeted with widespread outrage. Outrage often translates to action, and public exposure could well prompt U.S. political leaders to take meaningful measures to address the problem.

"Clearly, the general silence about Sudan's slavery allows the Sudanese government, which is involved in the slave trade, to continue to do so with impunity. Indeed, Sudanese government officials continue to assert there is no such thing as slavery in their country."

Sandler notes that this is a politically thorny issue "because you have black Muslims participating in the enslavement of black animists and Christians. Unlike the black-and-white dynamic of South Africa in the 1970s and '80s, there is a less apparent racial divide. In the U.S., that creates a significant political dilemma for political leaders who may have both Muslim and Christian constituencies."

16 CENSORED

Fiberglass— The Carcinogen that's Deadly and Everywhere

Sources:
RACHEL'S ENVIRONMENT & HEALTH WEEKLY #444
Date: 6/1/95
Title: "A Carcinogen That's Everywhere"
Author: Peter Montague

IN THESE TIMES
Date: 8/21/95
Title: "Fiberglass, the Asbestos of the 90's"
Author: Joel Bleifuss

SYNOPSIS: A World War I era shortage of asbestos, once valued for its thermal insulation and fire resistant properties, spurred the first full-scale production of fiberglass in the United States. Unfortunately, man-made glass fibers have been found to share another characteristic with naturally-occurring asbestos fibers: they can cause lung cancer when inhaled.

According to the *American Journal of Industrial Medicine*, asbestos will have killed 300,000 Americans by the end of this century. As it was phased out, fiberglass production has steadily increased. More than 30,000 commercial products now contain fiberglass. Uses include thermal insulation, acoustic insulation, fireproofing and various applications in automotive components. Fiberglass insulation is present in 90 percent of American homes.

In the early 1970s, a body of evidence linking these ubiquitous fibers to lung disease began to accumulate. In a series of papers published from 1969 to 1977, the National Cancer Institute determined that tiny glass fibers were "potent carcinogens" in laboratory rats and that "it is unlikely that different mechanisms are operative in man." Specifically noted was the cancerous potential of fibrous glass in the pleura of lab animals. The pleura is the outer casing of the lungs; in humans, cancer of the pleura is called mesothelioma and it is caused by asbestos fibers.

The finding that fiberglass causes diseases similar to asbestos was chilling news in the early 1970s and an additional 25 years of research has only confirmed the earlier warnings. In 1990, members of the U.S. National Toxicology Program

(NTP), who represent ten federal health agencies, stated unanimously: "Fiberglass may reasonably be anticipated to be a carcinogen" in humans. NTP was preparing to include fiberglass in its 1992 *Seventh Annual Report on Carcinogens* when politics intervened. Although fiberglass industry lobbying delayed publication of NTP's conclusions for two years, the report was sent to Congress in June 1994.

Following the report, Health and Human Services finally determined that fiberglass should be listed as a substance "for which there is limited evidence of carcinogenicity in humans and/or sufficient evidence of carcinogenicity in experimental animals." Yet the news made scarcely a ripple in the national media. *In These Times* learned from a source who asked to remain anonymous that ABC news executives bowed to industry pressure not to air a "20/20" investigation on the dangers of fiberglass. What coverage there was played down any threat to public health. Frank Swoboda and Maryann Haggerty in the *Washington Post* reported as fact the assertion of Public Health Service spokesman Bill Grigg that there is no data "that would indicate there's any problem that would involve any consumer or worker." Grigg ignored six epidemiological studies that showed otherwise.

Robert Horowitz, chairman of Victims of Fiberglass, said, "The arguments from industry are the same arguments that we've seen time and time again. It doesn't matter what the substance is. Whether it is DDT or cigarettes or asbestos, industry says, 'You can't prove beyond a shadow of a doubt that we are killing you.' But do we have to wait for that absolute scientific proof before we do something? Breathing in microscopic shards of glass could not possibly be good for you."

SSU Censored Researcher: Mike Thomas

COMMENTS: Author Peter Montague, of the Environmental Research Foundation, said the subject received almost no media attention, "even after the U.S. National Toxicology Program (NTP) declared in June 1994 that fiberglass is 'reasonably anticipated to be a carcinogen.' This story should have been on every television set and in every newspaper. Unfortunately it was hardly covered at all. Part of the responsibility lies with government officials because they chose to minimize the importance of their own announcement. It seems to me, their purpose was most likely to protect the interest of the $2 billion-per-year fiberglass industry.

"Fiberglass is pervasive in our society—90 percent of all homes are now insulated with it—and it will cause many cancers in the coming decades. It should be banned for the same reasons that asbestos has been banned. Of particular importance is the finding that fiberglass is now found everywhere in the environment. Forty years ago one could not measure fiberglass in the ambient air. Today fiberglass can be measured in the air on remote mountain tops in California. Since fiberglass is 'reasonably anticipated to be a carcinogen,' the public needs to know the facts about fiberglass, so that public health policy can evolve through informed debate."

The National Toxicology Program (NTP) first proposed to list fiberglass as a probable carcinogen in its *Seventh Annual (1993) Report on Carcinogens*. "In response," Montague said, "the North American Insulation Manufacturers Association (NAIMA) hired a former member of President Clinton's transition team to lobby Donna Shalala, Secretary of Health and Human Services. After receiving a letter from NAIMA's lobbyist, Secretary Shalala postponed the publication of the NTP report and called for an unprecedented review of NTP's decision on fiberglass. Furthermore, NAIMA threatened to take legal action if the NTP listed fiberglass as a probable carcinogen. NAIMA has four members: CertainTeed Corp.; Owens-Corning Fiber Glass Corp; Knauf Fiber Glass GMBH; and Schuller International, Inc. (formerly Manville Co.).

"Donna Shalala eventually accepted NTP's classification of fiberglass as a probable carcinogen but her agency downplayed the announcement of the NTP report and particularly downplayed the importance of declaring fiberglass a probable human carcinogen. The interests of the four corporations that comprise NAIMA are uniquely served by Secretary Shalala's spin on the issue, and by the scant news coverage."

Montague concludes that while the debate over the hazards of fiberglass continues to rage, "five billion pounds of new fiberglass are being added each year to the world's growing inventory of this poison. As a result, our children will be breathing a few fibers of fiberglass with every breath they take, no matter where on earth they take it. This cannot be good news."

Joel Bleifuss, author of the *In These Times* article, charged that the "potential threat to human health from fiberglass has received virtually no exposure in the mass media, with the exception of some very poor reporting in the *Washington Post*." While some journalists were very interested in the subject, no major coverage resulted. For example, a reporter for a major television news program explored this story and invested a lot of time researching the subject. But the story was finally rejected by the executive producer after the reporter concluded that fiberglass was more harmful than the industry admits. Bleifuss acknowledged that his concern about press freedom at a network news show is "more disturbing to me as a journalist than is the fact that a story about a public health threat was canned by a major network news executive."

Bleifuss feels the fiberglass issue is a subject in dire need of public exposure. "Virtually every homeowner I know has at some time in their life installed fiberglass without a respirator. I have done so several times. Further, I believe that exposure of the issue would help curtail the dangerous practice of insulating houses with blown fiberglass particles."

The politically powerful fiberglass industry is clearly benefiting from the limited coverage given this subject, according to Bleifuss who adds, "Dow Corning, which is particularly influential, is doing all it can to prevent fiberglass from becoming another asbestos-like scandal."

In These Times published two letters concerning Bleifuss' article in its November 13, 1995, issue. In one, Robert Horowitz, cited above in the synopsis, notes that formaldehyde, a known carcinogen, is used in manufacturing fiberglass insulation and believes it deserves further study. In the other, Catherine I. Imus, communications director for the North American Insulation Manufacturers Association, said, "...in the most recently completed review of the available scientific evidence regarding fiberglass, researchers at the Harvard School of Public Health concluded that 'taken together, the data indicate that among those occupationally exposed, glass fibers do not appear to increase the risk of respiratory system cancer.'"

Bleifuss responded that the review failed to examine published work by scientists whose research has shown fiberglass to be carcinogenic. And he points out, "This glaring omission is perhaps explained by the fact that the Harvard study was supported by a grant from the North American Insulation Manufacturers Association."

17 CENSORED

Small Arms Wreak Major Worldwide Havoc

Sources:
CHRISTIAN SCIENCE
    MONITOR
Date: 4/5/95
Title: "Boom in the Trade of Small
    Arms Fuels World's Ethnic and
    Regional Rivalries"
Author: Jonathan S. Landay

FOREIGN AFFAIRS
Date: September 1994
Title: "Arming Genocide
    in Rwanda"
Authors: Stephen D. Goose and
    Frank Smyth

SYNOPSIS: Rwanda is just one example of what can happen when small arms and light weapons are sold to a country plagued by ethnic, religious, or nationalist strife. In today's wars, such weapons are responsible for most of the killings of civilians and combatants. They are used more often in human rights abuses and other violations of international law than major weapons systems.

In the post-Cold War era, in which the profit motive has replaced East-West concerns as the main stimulus behind weapons sales, ex-Warsaw Pact and NATO nations are dumping their arsenals on the open market. Prices for some weapons, such as Soviet-designed Kalashnikov AKM automatic rifles (commonly known as AK-47s), have fallen below cost. Many Third World countries, such as China, Egypt, and South Africa, also have stepped up sales of light weapons and small arms. More than a dozen nations that were importers of small arms 15 years ago now manufacture and export them. But most of this trade remains unknown. Unlike major conventional weapons systems, governments rarely disclose the details of transfers of light weapons and small arms.

The resulting impact of such transfers are apparent. Small arms and light weapons have flooded nations like Rwanda, Sudan, Somalia, and Bosnia-Herzegovina, not only fanning warfare, but also undermining international efforts to embargo arms and to compel parties to respect human rights. They have helped to undermine peacekeeping efforts and allowed heavily armed militias to challenge U.N. and U.S. troops. They raise the cost of relief assistance paid by countries like the United States. Yet the international community has no viable mechanism to monitor the transfer of light and small weapons, and neither the United Nations nor the Clinton administration has demonstrated the leadership required to control that trade.

It is increasingly clear that the proliferation of light weapons endangers not only internal, but also regional and international stability.

The largest conventional arms exporter in the world is the United States. The Clinton administration has trumpeted the increased threat of the spread of weapons of mass destruction as the foremost danger facing the U.S. Yet it has issued hardly a word on conventional arms except to assert their importance to U.S. defense manufacturers. The Senate Appropriations Subcommittee of Foreign Operations reports, "Regrettably, the evidence clearly indicates that the Administration has sought to promote arms sales, rather than to reduce them."

While the vast majority of the U.S. major weapons transfers are public, most of its transfers of light weapons and small arms are not. No regular reporting is made to Congress in either classified or unclassified form. Many sales are private commercial transactions, and attempts to get detailed data on them through the Freedom of Information Act are routinely denied on proprietary grounds.

The United States, as the world's number one arms merchant (the #4 *Censored* story of 1992), should take the lead in proposing new ways to control the flow of light weapons and small arms. An administration that is struggling to deal with crises in Rwanda, Bosnia, Somalia, and elsewhere should recognize its own need to check this type of proliferation and stop shooting itself in the foot.

SSU Censored Researcher:
Tina Duccini

COMMENTS: Jonathan S. Landay, author of the *Christian Science Monitor* article, said the subject did not receive mainstream media attention, although it is a subject that is of increasing concern on Capitol Hill. "I believe the public would be horrified if it was aware of the way U.S. tax dollars are spent to promote sales of light arms. Also, President Clinton campaigned on a promise to reduce U.S. arms exports. In fact, he has done the opposite, formally authorizing U.S. embassies to promote arms deals." Landay said the government benefits from higher arms sales abroad since "the earnings from foreign sales allow U.S. weapons manufacturers to reduce their prices to the Pentagon." He also added, "Obviously, U.S. arms makers also benefit."

Frank Smyth, co-author of the article in *Foreign Affairs*, felt that the issue of arming Rwanda did receive considerable newspaper exposure in the United States, Europe, and Africa, but received little attention in U.S. newsweeklies or on network television. "One explanation for this," Smyth said, "is that there was no American angle, as France, Egypt and South Africa were the main suppliers of arms. Another is that the issue of small arms transfers is simply too complex to fit into a superficial outlet.

"The U.S. public would benefit from wider exposure of this issue by understanding that outside powers like France helped fan the flames of Rwanda's civil war," Smyth said. "On a wider scale, the international public would benefit by understanding that there is now a world glut in small arms—fueled by countries as diverse as Russia, South Africa, and the United States—and they are gravitating to some of the world's worst conflicts such as Sudan.

"In the United States, no specific interests have worked to limit the coverage of arming Rwanda," Smyth said. "On the contrary, perhaps because France and not the United States was the main target of our criticism, establishment outlets including *The New York Times* and *Foreign Affairs* welcomed this story. One question which remains is why didn't this story receive more attention in France. Most of the major papers there reported our charges, but few gave it as much space or attention, for example, as *The International Herald Tribune*, a U.S.-controlled publication. I personally see parallels—in both the stories and the way they were covered—between the U.S. role in El Salvador in the 1980s and France's role in Rwanda in the 1990s."

18 CENSORED

Scientific Support for Needle Exchange Programs Suppressed

Sources:
IN THESE TIMES
Date: 1/9/95
Title: "Political Science"
Author: Shawn Neidorf

WASHINGTON POST
Date: 2/16/95
Title: "Reports Back Needle Exchange Programs"
Author: John Schwartz

SYNOPSIS: After reviewing a massive study on the effectiveness of intravenous needle-exchange programs to curtail the spread of disease, including AIDS, the Centers for Disease Control and Prevention (CDC) recommended that a ban on federal funding for such programs be lifted. But no action has been taken and the review itself has been suppressed.

The 700-page California study, originally released in October 1993, found it was "likely" that needle-exchange programs (NEPs) decrease the rate of new HIV infections, while finding "no evidence" that the programs increase drug use in the communities they serve.

CDC scientists were asked by their parent agency, the Public Health Service, to review the California study's methodology, findings, and conclusions. That review, which has yet to be made public, determined that the federal funding ban (in effect since 1988) "should be lifted to allow communities and states to use federal funds to support NEPs as components of comprehensive HIV prevention programs."

A second review of the California study was ordered by the Department of Health and Human Services in 1994. While making no specific recommendations, this second analysis also concluded that the study demonstrates more clearly than any previous research that use of NEPs is associated with decreases in blood-borne infections.

Nonetheless, the Clinton administration has taken no action on the issue. Dr. Peter Lurie, the lead researcher for the California study, suggests that the potential political consequences of advocating a controversial program account for the inaction. The release of the review would be significant, Lurie contends, because it would be the first document in which a government health agency publicly endorsed needle-exchange programs to prevent transmission of AIDS.

Regarding the legal and philosophical obstacles which apparently block federal involvement in the activation of NEPs, Lurie said the failure of the government to release the report is inexcusable. "The federal government is playing politics with the lives of drug users, their sex partners and their children," he said, adding, "Delay, delay, delay, delay—people are dying."

Meanwhile, the Administration hesitates to ruffle conservative feathers, and scientific credibility for NEPs remains under wraps while grim statistics keep piling up.

A quarter of all adult AIDS cases reported to the CDC through June 1994 were traced to the sharing of needles. Either sharing a needle or having sex with someone who did accounted for nearly 75 percent of all cases in women.

Since the original study, others, including one by the National Academy of Sciences, have confirmed that NEPs greatly reduce the spread of the virus that causes AIDS while not encouraging more illicit drug use.

SSU Censored Researcher: Mike Thomas

COMMENTS: Shawn Neidorf, author of the *In These Times* article, said that while several of the largest U.S. dailies have covered needle exchange and the suppression of the study, the coverage has changed nothing, at least on the federal level. "The problem is that one story or one editorial in a particular paper isn't going to do it," Neidorf explained. "To make a difference—to be 'sufficient'—extensive coverage has to do several things:

"First, it has to remind the post-Watergate, post-Iran-Contra public that it's wrong—unacceptable—for the government to keep this information secret. Second, it has to make it clear to readers why needle exchange should matter to them. They need to know that they can contract HIV from injection drug use, even if they're not using. All members of the 'general population' have to do is have unprotected sex with a user or someone who has had unprotected sex with a user. Third—and this is essential—reporters need to demand specifics from the public health officials and hold them accountable for their statements. Just what type of evidence do they need before they'll acknowledge the efficacy of needle exchange?

"The general public is going to pay for AIDS, in one way or another. Drug users who share needles, their sex partners and the future sex partners of their sex partners, and all of their children are at risk for contracting HIV. Those who don't contract it will pay for it financially. A few years ago, Dr. Fred Hellinger estimated that it costs about $119,000 to care for one person with HIV until he or she dies. He estimated that the cost could jump by as much as 48 percent by 1995. Injection drug users don't have the health insurance that many gay men did. Their bills are going to be the public's. Personally, I'd rather pay for a needle exchange program. The median cost to run one is about $169,000 a year, according to Dr. Peter Lurie's study—a great deal if each program prevents only two HIV infections a year. I think most taxpayers would appreciate that efficiency, even if they hate drug users on principle."

Neidorf identified three groups that benefit from the lack of coverage given the subject: "Politicians with an uncompromising allegiance to the War on Drugs; politicians who would back needle exchange if they weren't afraid of the 'you-coddled-drug-users' backlash at reelection time; and public health officials who know the data, but are afraid for their careers to act on it."

John Schwartz, author of the needle exchange article in the *Washington Post*, said, "Needle exchange programs get a great deal of attention—not only because they are part of the broad spectrum of AIDS programs, but also because such programs tend to generate controversy wherever they are started. What *wasn't* covered was the government's own conclusions that the programs are effective—

because the government wasn't releasing those reports."

"There are a number of obstacles to getting effective needle programs implemented," Schwartz said. "Even if the Administration decided to take a hard stand in favor of such programs, a tangle of conflicting legal restrictions on the programs would make it very difficult to pass and implement them. If people had enough information to see this as a public health issue and not a political issue, lives could be saved."

Schwartz noted that he was neither an AIDS activist nor a full-time AIDS reporter, and added, "This was simply a story about common sense needlessly tangled up in politics—the kind of story that no reporter could screw up. I'm glad to have gotten a chance to work on it."

19 CENSORED

Solving the Nuclear Waste Problem With Taxpayers' Dollars

Source:
THE WORKBOOK
Date: Fall 1995
Title: "Where Is Nuclear Waste Going—Or Staying?"
Author: Don Hancock

SYNOPSIS: After years of effort and millions of dollars spent on campaign contributions and highly-paid lobbyists, the nuclear power industry expects Congress to pass legislation that will free the industry of its responsibility for storing commercial spent nuclear waste. The proposed legislation, H.R. 1020—also known as the "industry bill"—will require that all accumulated wastes—estimated to be about 36,000 metric tons by the end of 1997—be moved to Nevada, beginning in 1998.

The problem is that for the past three administrations, the Department of Energy (DOE) has consistently maintained that a nuclear waste repository cannot be opened until at least 2010. That is the projected date to open Yucca Mountain, Nevada, the only site being investigated. In 1995, DOE issued a formal decision that there is no legal requirement that the federal government begin accepting spent fuel in 1998 because a repository will not be available and because the federal government does not currently have authority to provide an interim storage facility.

This has not deterred the nuclear power industry from pushing H.R. 1020. The bill, sponsored by Rep. Fred Upton (R-Mich.), would require the federal government to open a spent fuel storage facility in Nevada by the 1998 date. And it would impose fines and penalties for missing that deadline. More than 15 utilities filed a lawsuit in 1994, asking the court to require DOE to begin taking their wastes in 1998. The fines and penalties would be a new federal government cost, never included in any previous budget—and would, in essence, be a new tax.

The utilities do not seem to be concerned that such a storage facility could not be sited and constructed by the 1998 date if it were to meet existing health, safety, and environmental protection laws—and probably not even if all environmental laws were waived.

But the impossible deadline is not the only onerous aspect of H.R. 1020: Provisions of H.R. 1020 would also require Congress—rather than the Environmental Protection Agency (EPA)—to establish radiation protection requirements for a potential site at about 25 times higher than that allowed by current EPA disposal standards.

It would require DOE to develop—without full public participation and judicial review—a "multi-purpose cask" to be used for storage, transport, and disposal of radioactive spent fuel. It would force construction of a new railroad line from throughout the country to the Nevada Site at a cost of more than $1 billion and would eliminate existing environmental restrictions on such a railroad.

The bill would also guarantee that the fee for spent fuel genera-tion would not be raised without an act of Congress, no matter how much the waste program would cost.

The nuclear industry insists that whatever form the final legislation takes, it must require the opening of a storage facility in Nevada by 1998; the development of a trans-portation system; continuing work on the Yucca Mountain repository; and protection against any large fee increases.

Not mentioned anywhere are the risks to millions of people along highways and railroads in 43 states carrying the highly radioactive spent fuel. Possibly most impor-tant, beyond the unknown financial costs of the project, fundamental principles of constitutional rights will be compromised if the rush to meet the 1998 date proceeds.

SSU Censored Researcher:
Kristi Hogue

COMMENTS: Investigative author Don Hancock reported there was very little coverage of this issue, in part because it's a seemingly never-ending story. "Also, the nuclear power industry, which is promoting a quick-fix bailout, has no interest in the mainstream media covering its plans because they would not be well-received by much of the public. The story is complicated and includes governments, corpora-tions, as well as affected citizens.

The nuclear waste will be with us for literally thousands of generations, so there is not an apparent solution."

Nonetheless, Hancock feels it is important for people to know about the issue since, "They would gain a better understanding of the importance of nuclear waste to present and future generations. They would gain a better understanding of the current congressional discussion about the issue and how any decisions can have a significant effect on taxpayers and the general public, not just on citizens of the currently targeted states—Nevada and New Mexico. As a result, they could become more involved in decisions, whether they live close to nuclear power plants, along transportation routes to waste sites, or in the targeted states."

Benefiting from the lack of coverage of the issue, Hancock said, are "the nuclear industry executives and the public officials who support them, since their plans are not exposed to public scrutiny."

Hancock added, "Citizen activists in various states have banded together in the Nuclear Waste Citizens Coalition to become a more effective force in Washington, D.C. and to educate and involve citizens nationally regarding the important issues being decided, including the risks of transportation of spent fuel throughout the nation."

20 CENSORED

ABC Spikes New Tobacco Exposé When Sued for Libel

Source:
THE VILLAGE VOICE
Date: 9/12/95
Title: "Up In Smoke"
Author: James Ledbetter

SYNOPSIS: In 1993, ABC's "Turning Point" hired Frank and Martin Koughan, an Emmy Award-winning documentary team, to do a broad survey of the tobacco merchants' *annus horribilis* that followed the Environmental Protection Agency's classification of second-hand smoke as a carcinogen, and the Clinton Administration's proposal to support health care reform by heavily taxing cigarettes.

The final cut, reported by ABC's Meredith Vieira, was a tough, well-narrated takeout on the business responsible for the nation's largest health problem. It focused on the marketing and manufacturing of tobacco products here and abroad, and broke some new ground.

Martin Koughan said the film "was passed on and approved by ABC's editorial and law departments," and was scheduled to run in late March or early April 1994.

It didn't. On March 24, Koughan said he got a call from "Turning Point" senior (now executive) producer Betsy West, who told him that he was going to have to "rework" the film.

Coincidentally, March 24 also was the day that Phillip Morris filed a $10 billion libel suit against Capital Cities/ABC for two "Day One" reports on tobacco-doctoring (which prompted the network to cough up an abject apology in August 1995).

What happened next is in dispute. Koughan says there was a dispute about meeting schedules and that ABC never showed up for a planned session to discuss revisions. West says that Koughan "was absolutely uncooperative in making the story better" adding that ABC executives had never signed off on the show. West also swears, "I know this suit is not the reason it didn't air." Paul Friedman, ABC's executive vice president, also said the lawsuit "didn't even enter my mind" when he killed the segment.

Eventually, Koughan was told that the film would not be used. In a settlement agreement, his production company was paid for its work, but ABC owns all rights to the film. Thus, although ABC has spent some $500,000 on the project, the network has no plans to air it, nor can it be broadcast anywhere else.

There are at least two segments of "Tobacco Under Fire" that would have been network scoops. One details how the American tobacco industry is moving production overseas. The documentary claims that American tobacco companies are developing and distributing seeds to be grown in Brazil, Malawi, Guatemala, and Argentina, where tobacco farming costs about half of what it costs here, and where, unlike Kentucky or the Carolinas, there are no regulations about acreage, volume, or pricing. The film predicts that this shift will ultimately undermine American tobacco farmers, who are some of the industry's most powerful lobbyists.

Second, the film claims that during the Reagan and Bush Administrations, the U.S. Trade Representative's office spent an inordinate amount of time threatening trade sanctions against Asian countries that had stalled at letting American tobacco companies advertise. This extraordinary charge came from Reagan's own surgeon general C. Everett Koop, who said "If these trade policies were known right now, they'd be condemned by the American people."

Unfortunately, most Americans will not hear about the trade policies or the other tobacco company transgressions because ABC censored the documentary.

SSU Censored Researcher:
Stephanie Horner

COMMENTS: Investigative author James Ledbetter said the "subject received precious little attention—it was covered in the *New York Daily News* in 1994 and the *Washington Post* in passing. I believe, however, I am the only one who wrote about the *actual content* of 'The Turning Point' segment."

Ledbetter feels the public would benefit from greater exposure of this issue since "It would gain insight into the realities of tobacco's aggressive overseas marketing; and it points out how difficult it is for network television to criticize tobacco companies."

Those who benefit from the lack of media coverage given this issue, according to Ledbetter, include, "tobacco companies, ABC executives, and the Bush Administration."

Ledbetter concluded, "Obviously, in light of the canned '60 Minutes' story, it is one more chapter in the sorry recent history of networks caving in to powerful interests."

21 CENSORED

The New 3R's: Reading, Writing, and Reloading

Source:
MOTHER JONES
Date: January/February 1995
Title: "Why Johnny Can Shoot"
Authors: Susan Glick and Josh
    Sugarmann

SYNOPSIS: If all goes as expected, by 1999 more than 26 million students will have been exposed to a marketing program that will entice them to buy guns and persuade them to argue against gun control.

The marketing program, a partnership between the government and the gun industry, is designed by the industry's leading trade association—the National Shooting Sports Foundation (NSSF).

The program is paid for in large part by federal tax dollars.

In 1993, the NSSF received nearly $230,000 from the U.S. Fish and Wildlife Service (USFWS) to update and expand three videos on hunting and wildlife management. The videos, for grades 4 through 12, are free to public and private schools with enrollments of at least 300 students.

The NSSF made the link between schools and increased firearm sales crystal clear in a 1993 issue of *S.H.O.T. Business*, its industry publication. A columnist tells dealers and manufacturers, "There's a way to help ensure that new faces and pocketbooks will continue to patronize your business: Use the schools....Every decade there is a whole new crop of shining new faces taking their place in society as adults....Will [they] be for or against a local ordinance proposal to ban those bad semiautos? Will they vote for or against even allowing a 'gun store' in town? ....How else would you get these potential customers and future leaders together?....Schools are an opportunity. Grasp it."

The NSSF proposal, submitted and approved under the Bush Administration, noted it would "make the initial offering to the largest schools....This strategy reaches students in large cities and suburban areas where approval of hunting is lowest"—and support for gun control strongest.

Among the more than 1,100 NSSF members which include America's leading gun manufacturers, many of whom actively target youth, are Remington Arms, Colt's Manufacturing, Smith & Wesson, Feather Industries, and Taurus.

The issue is not hunting, but whether any industry should, with federal funds, use public schools to increase the sale of its product and to build a political base.

The U.S. Fish and Wildlife Service acknowledges the program's benefits to the gun industry. USFWS spokesperson Craig Rieben said, "They've got a product. They're looking for a market."

Rieben says the USFWS sees no need to review the grant guidelines. And as it targets other niche markets, the firearms industry is banking on USFWS' "see no evil" attitude. Potential new USFWS grantees include an NSSF-linked program designed to increase gun sales to women.

SSU Censored Researcher: Stephanie Prather

COMMENTS: The authors, Susan Glick and Josh Sugarmann, reported, "While some notable print media and columnists took interest in the story, the story did not receive broader media coverage, especially television, for two reasons. The first was that most television reporters wanted the story to be simpler than it was. The Violence Policy Center obtained publications issued by the National Shooting Sports Foundation (NSSF), the firearms industry's trade association, which clearly stated that the organization was working to use the schools to increase firearms sales to children and youth and that these videos were a key tool. The videos themselves, however, did not come right out and say 'go buy guns, kids' but worked to soften up youth attitudes towards hunting and firearms as a means to this end. The insidious nature of the videos was too complex for many broadcast outlets who couldn't put the two pieces (the videos and the print statements) together but focused solely on the videos. The most notable practitioner of this superficial thinking was NBC's 'Dateline,' which pulled a story on the study at the last minute (a fact they neglected to tell us, but did tell the NSSF). Although we explained the story to a myriad of 'Dateline' producers in painful, repetitive detail, none of them ever quite got it. Of course, after the story was pulled, 'Datelines' inability to grasp it was cited as 'proof' by the NSSF to other media outlets that the story was not worth reporting. The second factor was that even though the NSSF said that they had nothing to hide regarding the program, the organization refused to make the list of schools that had received it readily available. This dramatically limited the opportunity for local and regional coverage.

"Most Americans would probably agree that the firearms industry should not be allowed to try and increase the sale of their products through America's school systems—especially with federal tax dollars. Greater publicity about the program would allow parents and educators to identify where the program is being used and make schools aware of the video's true intent. It would also focus attention on the firearms industry's marketing program to children and youth and raise the question of whether in tight budgetary times the federal government should be subsidizing America's gun industry."

The authors say that the obvious beneficiary of the lack of coverage given this issue is America's firearms industry. They note that the industry, "in the wake of slumping handgun sales among the primary market of men, has focused its attention on women and children. One of the gun industry's greatest triumphs has been its ability to shield itself from public scrutiny and to have people think of it as something other than an 'industry' possessing the same profit motive and marketing needs as any other."

22 CENSORED

There May Be A Cure—Up There in the Rain Forest

Source:
PITTSBURGH POST-GAZETTE
Date: 1/4/95
Title: "Cures lure druggists to rain forest"
Author: Dan Wagner

SYNOPSIS: Scientists in the United States are exhilarated because, after years of scavenging the Asian rain forests for magic bullets, they are now beginning to turn up promising leads in the search for medical treatments from trees and plants.

Environmentalists are excited by the prospect that important pharmaceutical discoveries could provide a financial incentive to preserve rain forests that one day may provide a cure for AIDS, various cancers, Alzheimer's disease, or diabetes. If any of these new "discoveries" of rain-forest plants for Western medicine are to ever come to fruition, the world's major pharmaceutical companies will have to cooperate.

However, with tropical forests vanishing at an alarming rate, sci-entists fear that with every tree that disappears, so might the cure for AIDS or cancer.

In fact, if the current rate of logging in rain forests continues, all but a few samples of the world's forests will be gone by the year 2040. However, the devastation continues; on 8/28/95, wire services reported that negotiations were underway to log 3.7 million acres of Cambodia's dwindling forest cover.

In the search for natural cures, rain forests are considered the most promising natural environments for research because of the vast diversity of life that they shelter. More than half of the world's estimated 250,000 species of plants live in tropical forests, yet less than ten percent have ever been tested for their ability to cure disease. Many of the species remain unknown to science, and few have been diagnosed for their full medicinal potential. However, Amazonian Indians use hundreds of local plants to treat everything from herpes sores to lung diseases. Many of these medical conditions are still not sufficiently treated and cured by modern drugs.

In the past 30 years, many pharmaceutical researchers have shied away from the natural laboratory of the rain forest and have instead concentrated on synthetic chemistry as a source of medicines. While we should not underestimate the success of synthetic drugs, we must realize that not everything can be made in a chemistry laboratory. There is a great potential for natural products to be the source of new drugs. Even now, 25 percent of all pharmaceutical drugs in the United States come from plant-derived compounds. The National Cancer Institute, one of the largest plant-research facilities in the world, screens more than 40,000 natural substances each year for cancer, anti-tumor or AIDS use.

With the erosion of our environment and the vanishing culture of native peoples, it is a race against the clock to preserve the biological and cultural diversity that remains in the rain forests. The mass media need to spread the word that clear-cutting rain forests no longer is just about the trees, it's about people, culture, ethics, and perhaps even life-saving medical discoveries.

SSU Censored Researcher:
Tami Ward

COMMENTS: Other than the primary source cited above, there were few news stories concerning the impact of clear-cutting on possible pharmaceutical discoveries in the rain forests in 1995.

Most notably, among newspapers, the San Diego Union-Tribune (7/5/95) reported on the efforts of a local resident who created Project Green Genes, a business venture designed to collect plant materials for DNA preservation, and a Los Angeles Times report (9/24/95) on environmentalists protesting Suriname's plan to allow loggers at its rain forest.

However, the international edition of Time Magazine (10/30/95) featured an in-depth article on worldwide environmental issues focusing on the issue. The cover article, by Edward O. Wilson, a leading advocate of global conservation and the Pellegrino University Professor at Harvard, revealed that "more than 40 percent of all prescriptions dispensed by pharmacies in the U.S. are substances originally extracted from plants, animals, fungi and microorganisms." He pointed out that less than one percent of all species and organisms have been examined for natural products that might lead to new medicines. The article also mentioned that the United States is one of the few nations that did not sign the Convention on Biological Diversity, signed by 156 nations and the European Union at the 1992 Earth Summit in Rio de Janeiro.

Ironically, one of the most informative articles published in 1995 about the potential cures to be found in the world's rain forests was published in a trade publication, Chemical Marketing Reporter, on September 18.

23 |CENSORED|

Dioxin: Still Deadly After All These Years (and All That Hype)

Source:
EARTH ISLAND JOURNAL
Date: Spring 1995
Title: "EPA Study Reveals Dioxin Dangers"
Author: Stephen Lester

SYNOPSIS: When the Environmental Protection Agency's (EPA) long awaited "reassessment" of the health effects of dioxin was finally released in draft form in September 1994, it indicated that dioxin's health impacts were worse than previously reported. The preliminary EPA study confirmed what grassroots activists have feared: dioxin, a by-product of chemical processes that use chlorine, does irreparable damage to the human body.

Yet, for a full year, these findings have gone almost unnoticed by the mass media. These are the same media that widely publicized a 1991 report by The Centers for Disease Control that found dioxin was less harmful than previously suspected and subsequently led the EPA to consider a "reassessment."

These were upbeat dioxin stories on how we've been confused once again by experts who can't seem to agree on anything. There was even an "NBC Nightly News" mention (8/15/91) of how folks from the contaminated, condemned, and evacuated Times Beach area along the Mississippi River, were wondering if it might be okay to go home again.

But the recent unpublicized EPA report found that dioxin levels 100 times lower than those associated with developing cancer may cause severe reproductive and developmental effects, and disrupt regulatory hormones in industrial workers and laboratory animals.

Ninety percent of dioxin enters the human body through the food chain. Dioxin particles produced by industrial processes and waste lodge in soil, settle on plants, and contaminate water systems. People then eat fish, meat, and produce that contain low but hazardous dioxin levels. The report details how dioxin and dioxin-like chemicals damage the body by "attaching" to specific receptor sites in cell tissues. When hormones and enzymes are displaced, certain normal cell functions cannot be carried out. The report clearly suggests that, despite earlier reports, no amount of exposure to dioxin is safe.

Dioxin is created as a by-product of the manufacturing

process by chemical companies; plastics producers; makers of rubber, dyes and pesticides; pulp and paper mills that use chlorine bleaches; and incinerator plants.

The report does not mention corporate producers of dioxin, such as Dow or Monsanto, who stand to lose if the EPA clamps down on dioxin releases. For years, these companies have orchestrated a political and scientific campaign to confuse the public and create a bureaucratic stalemate.

Corporations could face billion-dollar lawsuits for health and environmental damage caused by dioxin exposures. But they stand to save millions of dollars if they can settle pending lawsuits before the EPA reassessment is finalized, because the final report would give complainants greater evidence that dioxin is hazardous.

The Virginia-based Citizens Clearinghouse for Hazardous Waste has called for an immediate halt to the incineration of hazardous waste and a phaseout of chlorinated organic compounds in all industrial production. Greenpeace's Zero Dioxin campaign argues that processes that create dioxin must either be altered so that no dioxin is produced, or banned.

SSU Censored Researcher: Mary Jo Thayer

COMMENTS: The significance of the recent findings of the health dangers of dioxin received very little attention from the mainstream press, according to investigative author Stephen Lester. "To my knowledge, there was no TV coverage, no coverage by the news weeklies and only minor coverage by several major newspapers. Given that dioxin is the most potent carcinogen for the general population ever tested; that we know that dioxin is coming from incinerators, paper mills and chemical processing plants; and that it is getting into dairy products, meat, fish and breast milk, you'd think that the issue would have received more than the cursory attention of the chemical trade press and one day of 'here's EPA's newest report' in the *Washington Post* and *New York Times*."

Lester warned that dioxin is the DDT of the '90s. "It is persistent, pervasive and showing up in the bodies of people all over the world. It differs from DDT in that the main concern with DDT was its carcinogenicity. With dioxin, not only is it a potent carcinogen, but its non-cancer causing effects (infertility, depressed immune response, endometriosis, loss of sex drive, diabetes) occur at very low levels, levels already found in the general population. These and other non-cancer effects may prove to be more important than dioxin's ability to cause cancer. We have to know what dioxin is, where it is coming from, and how it's hurting us before we can do anything about it. And, we need to know that we can do something about it. Not lifestyle changes, but saving our lives."

Lester charges corporate America is benefiting from the limited media coverage given dioxin. "More specifically, the chemical and paper industry that does not want to alter its production practices to eliminate the chemicals (largely chlorine) that generate dioxin as a by-product of production. Industry says that we need more studies and they hire high powered public relations firms to argue their points and deluge the mainstream media with issues designed to confuse and defuse the press's interest. Government is reluctant to act and finds it easiest to do nothing but study and study and study and study ..."

The organization Lester works for, the Citizens Clearinghouse for Hazardous Waste, has begun a campaign to educate the American public about the dangers of dioxin. "We have written several additional articles for our newsletter, prepared 'campaign kits,' sent copies to grassroots environmental organizations and to the mainstream press. We have written and published a book—*Dying from Dioxin* (South End Press, 1995)—and have begun efforts to create alliances with organizations across the country to educate people and begin to eliminate dioxin exposures. Still, there has been very little media interest and coverage of this story."

24 CENSORED

U.S. Trails Most Developed Nations in Maternal Health Ranking

Sources:
SAN FRANCISCO CHRONICLE
Date: 7/25/95
Title: "Deadly Differences in
    Prenatal Care"
Author: Ramon G. McLeod

THE NEW YORK TIMES
Date: 7/26/95
Title: "In a Ranking of Maternal
    Health, U.S. Trails Most
    Developed Nations"
Author: Philip J. Hilts

SYNOPSIS: An estimated 1.3 million women die worldwide every year from complications of pregnancy and childbirth, according to a report from Population Action International, a think tank in Washington, D.C.

The problem results from a deadly confluence of economic and social factors related to pregnancy and childbirth, most associated with a lack of prenatal care and medical personnel, according to the researchers.

The study reviewed data in ten categories of maternal health and gave each of the 118 countries surveyed a score based on its performance in those categories. Areas rated included the number of women who die during childbirth, teenage pregnancy, contraceptive use, prenatal care, and availability of safe abortions.

The countries with the best overall rankings were, in order, Italy, Denmark, Norway, Sweden, and Belgium. Ranked the worst were Mali, Congo, Somalia, Angola, and Zaire. In the latter three countries, the average woman has more than six babies in her lifetime, and maternal death rates range from 600 to 1,000 per 100,000 births.

The study shows that the chance of dying from pregnancy or childbirth varies dramatically in different parts of the world, from 1 in 7 in Mali to about 1 in 17,000 in Italy.

The rate in the United States is 1 in 5,669 and the U.S. was ranked 18th. The U.S. did not rank higher among the developed nations largely because of teenage pregnancies—its rate is about six times that of European nations—and a relatively low rate of contraceptive use.

Although it still fell in the study's "very low risk" group of countries, the United States ranked behind such emerging countries as Taiwan and Singapore.

Dr. Shanti R. Conly, Director of Policy Research for Population Action International, warned that the U.S. "is likely to drop even farther if this Congress continues as it has started." A proposal to end public contraceptive services in the U.S. has been approved in committee, she said.

Although an important factor affecting the ranking is a country's relative wealth, according to Dr. Conly, some quite poor countries have worked on women's health issues and ranked well, while other nations of great wealth scored relatively poorly.

SSU Censored Researcher:
Doug Huston

COMMENTS: Ramon G. McLeod, author of the *San Francisco Chronicle* article, said the subject of "prenatal care of women in the Third World, and even in industrial states, is hardly one that gets much attention in the media. It just isn't the kind of subject matter that grabs a lot of journalists, male or female. The reason, I think, is that most U.S. editors and writers don't see it as an issue that affects Americans much. The reality is that it affects us both directly and indirectly.

"High maternal death rates are almost always found in countries with unstable populations. When women are healthier they have healthier, and fewer babies. So while the average American reader may not care about whether a mother in Kenya survives childbirth, she may care a great deal about the impact of high population growth on the environment and immigration pressures. And if she cares about these issues she may be more willing to support the funding increases needed to help other women survive their childbirths."

McLeod feels the only ones who benefit from the lack of coverage are those that "don't want to spend any money on overseas development or who may somehow believe that improving maternal health equals abortion, which it doesn't."

25 CENSORED

E. Coli— Now A National Epidemic—Kills 500 Americans Annually

Source:
ABC-NEWS 20/20 Transcript #1538
Date: 9/22/95
Title: "Always, Always Well Done"
Author: Reported by Arnold Diaz

SYNOPSIS: Most Americans first became familiar with E. coli several years ago when four children died from eating hamburgers at Jack In the Box restaurants. What millions of people don't know is that there have been dozens of outbreaks since then and many hundreds of people have died. The problem has not been resolved, but rather has worsened.

E. coli 0157H7 has now become so widespread it is being called an epidemic. Official estimates reveal that E. coli is killing as many as 500 people a year and causing another 20,000 people to become sick.

The deadly E. coli, first discovered in hamburger in 1982, has increased significantly over the past decade. It's found in the intestines and feces of some cattle and is sometimes accidentally transferred onto the meat during the slaughtering process. With steaks and roasts, E. coli isn't considered much of a problem because it lies on the surface and is easily killed during cooking. But when the meat is ground up, the bacteria on the surface can get mixed into the middle of the hamburger where it's much harder to cook out.

E. coli is not in every hamburger, but it could be in any hamburger. With an estimated one out of every 1,000 hamburgers containing this organism, this should be a matter of concern for most Americans. Americans eat more than 20 billion hamburgers a year, so millions of raw hamburgers may be contaminated.

Consumers can protect themselves from deadly situations by making certain that their hamburgers are always cooked well-done. Experts say that if the middle of a hamburger reaches 155 degrees Fahrenheit, the E. coli will be killed. The government and the meat industry are trying to get the word out on some ways individuals can protect themselves, but given the continuing growth of the epidemic, they haven't been too successful so far.

According to American Meat Institute scientist Janet Collins Williams, the industry has tried to reach the public through brochures they've sent to grocery stores and by applying safe handling labels now required on all meat packages. However, others believe that more attention-grabbing labels and detailed information should be used and that the United States Department of Agriculture inspection practices should be tightened.

Meanwhile, since the prevalence of E. coli is increasing, the media should make the public aware that there is an epidemic underway and that one of America's favorite foods—hamburgers—can kill them.

While the source of this story is a television news magazine, researchers found little follow-up in the print media.

SSU Censored Researcher:
Marcie Goyer

COMMENTS: Despite the alarming "20/20" report on September 22 that E. coli kills as many as 500 people a year and that the prevalence of the virulent bacterium is increasing, a news database search revealed no press reports of such an epidemic by the end of the year. Among the E. coli stories cited, two reported an E. coli epidemic in Russia; one was a general overview on infectious diseases, including E. coli; a *Los Angeles Times* article featured a viral epidemiologist who tracked diseases, including E. coli, for the Centers for Disease Control and Prevention (CDC); a *USA Today* item in a news round-up noted a warning to boil water in a Wilmington, Delaware, neighborhood, where E. coli had been found; and a series of *Kansas City Star* articles reporting nine persons had been stricken by E. coli bacteria in Kansas.

During the same period of time, the Federal News Service reported statements by two medical scientists warning of the dangers of virulent bacterium including E. coli. And a trade magazine, *Food Chemical News*, reported on September 25, that Dr. Anne Schuchat, a medical epidemiologist at CDC, said, "it looks like there's an epidemic" of E.

coli 0157H7 infections because reporting has been mandated in most states and health departments recognize the importance of alerting public officials to an outbreak. Finally, on January 7, 1996, *USA Weekend* noted there were 1,420 cases of E. coli bacteria infections reported by the Centers for Disease Control in 1994.

There were no news reports that either supported the "20/20" report or challenged it. If 500 Americans were dying annually from E. coli and the disease is spreading, this surely would seem to warrant more press attention. "20/20" representatives declined to respond to our questionnaire attempting to follow-up on this story.

COMMENTS BY PROJECT CENSORED JUDGES

Following are reflections on this year's *Censored* selections by some of the judges who helped select the top ten stories of 1995:

DONNA ALLEN, founding editor of *Media Report to Women* and a *Censored* judge since 1980, said, "It is good to see the inclusion of stories about the media—the Telecommunications Deregulation Bill and Privatizing the Internet, for two examples. Only a few people own the means—the television networks—of reaching 98.6 percent of the public 24 hours a day, seven days a week. We must return freedom of the press (including its modern electronic forms of 'press' dissemination) to its original intent as a citizen right—not a property right.

"Those with this essential information—in all 25 of these stories and, in fact, also the 700 from which these were selected—should have equal means of communicating it to the public as do wealthy owners of mass media. Thank you, Project Censored, for continuing to focus the public's attention on the need to democratize media, so all this information can be heard and be taken into account in the nation's decision-making. Access to the majority of the public is political power and in a democracy it must be equal. Thank you all for helping in the long task ahead of restoring freedom of the press as a citizen right for all of us and for getting this kind of information out to the public."

BEN BAGDIKIAN, former dean, Graduate School of Journalism, University of California, Berkeley, and a *Censored* judge since 1976, said, "A typical case of the media downplaying a story in which it has a vested interest is the meager coverage of the telecommunications bill that is startling in its direction to encourage monopolies in all the major media, particularly in broadcasting and cable. The Congress is moving toward a real possibility that three or four companies may control all the stations in markets that have 60 or 100 AM and FM radio stations.

"This comes at a time when the Congress has also removed the earlier FCC requirements that all stations holding a license must promise and perform some public service, non-commercial broadcasting, including information on issues facing its community. The downplaying of these issues by all media not only flows from the growing control of many kinds of media—newspapers and broadcasting—by one corporation, but also letting an entire generation remain uninformed of the fact that the air waves belong to the public, not the broadcasters, and that every station holds its license on condition of serving 'the public interest, convenience, and necessity.'"

RICHARD BARNET, senior fellow, Institute for Policy Studies, said he "thought the list was strong this year. All the nominations were important stories that did not receive the attention they deserve."

JEFFREY A. CHESTER, executive director of the Center for Media Education, said, "This year's nominees reveal that the mainstream media continue to ignore stories which are of critical importance to all citizens."

SUSAN FALUDI, journalist/author, felt, "This year's nominations are especially troubling for two reasons. First, they highlight the media's failure to cover itself. While the press has always worn blinders when it comes to observing its own backyard, such blindness now poses a real danger because that backyard has become so vast and powerful. The media's monopolization, consolidation into an info-entertainment-database industry, and enormous global reach all make up the big story of the late 20th century—and we barely covered it.

"Also disturbing are the many signs on this list that the media have failed to investigate the supposedly much-covered story of the year: the GOP Congressional campaign for a balanced budget. Whether it's Gingrich, et al.'s, systematic effort to strip and privatize federal agencies or the government's failure to make real cuts in the budget which ignored corporate fat (like the $1.5 billion oil companies owe the government), the media appear to have missed it, preoccupied instead with the many passing 'lifestyle' stories of Capitol Hill."

GEORGE GERBNER, founder and chair, The Cultural Environment Movement, said, "The principal censorship today is the *imposition* of a marketing formula that demands the selection of 'news' that fits the fantasy of the television world. When one of every three or four TV news stories is crime and violence, how can there be a balanced perspective in the news?"

SUT JHALLY, professor of communication and executive director of The Media Education Foundation, University of Massachusetts, said, "The stories offered for selection this year continue the pattern of the post-cold war era with the focus shifting much more to national stories from international ones. It is unclear what is responsible for this shift of focus, as the demise of the eastern-bloc dictatorships does not mean that American and corporate global strategic interests have ceased to exist and therefore there are fewer stories to uncover at this level. Military, political, economic, and cultural power continues to be exercised against the peoples of the world by governments and businesses. As such, the selection of stories offered for consideration says as much about the perspective of journalists, mainstream and alternative, as it does about the state of the world.

"As invaluable as the focus of Project Censored is, I think it may be a good time to expand the notion of what constitutes a 'censored' story. As it presently stands, to qualify requires that a story or report *exist* in the first place—that it have some visibility, however slight. The question then becomes one of its under-reporting. But there are other stories, so under-reported that they fail even to materialize as one small story—so censored as to be rendered invisible. Perhaps in addition to the list of the 10 most censored stories, a procedure could be established for highlighting every year one story that remained invisible but that should have been discussed in the media."

NICHOLAS JOHNSON, professor, College of Law, University of Iowa, had the students in one of his law classes rank the top 25 nominations; their top 10 list: 1. Balancing the Budget; 2. New 3R's—Reading, Writing, Reloading; 3. Adding Bang to Nukes; 4. Russia's Nuke Waste; 5. Chemical Industry's Ozone-Killing Pesticide; 6. ABC-TV Spikes Tobacco Exposé; 7. Needle Exchange Programs; 8. Child Labor in U.S.; 9. Patients Die from Treatment in Hospitals; 10. Small Arms Wreak Worldwide Havoc.

RHODA H. KARPATKIN, president of the Consumers Union, nonprofit publisher of *Consumer Reports*, said, "At least half of this year's nominations involve health-related articles: reports on dangerous substances, quality of care, legislative policy, maternal health, medical fraud, and the power of the tobacco companies to stifle major news media.

"Why so many? The collection uncovers some sad truths. Our health care delivery system is dysfunctional for a very large number of our people, especially when it comes to its major victims, the poor. And our hard-won health, safety, and environmental protections don't go far enough and even those are under assault.

"The role of a free press is to help citizens discern what is precious in our society, and to inform them about matters that affect their interests. In addition, the media must clearly present the facts when important public interests need advancement or are under attack. They should tell us what is involved, who is responsible, and who the winners and losers are. That's an arduous task but the major media clearly have the resources and mission to pursue it.

"Sadly, most of the nominees in this year's group do not come from major media. If any of their editors read this book—and they should—I hope they ask themselves if they've done all they should to cover the news people need in the way it ought to be covered. The alternative press outlets that researched and developed most of these stories typically have far fewer resources, but they have great investigative zeal, and for that, they are to be commended."

CHARLES L. KLOTZER, editor, *St. Louis Journalism Review*, said, "It is always difficult to select the 10 least reported from the 25 nominations. While all of the listings deserve wide exposure, missing among them is the cause of the malaise which currently besets the American scene and has not been widely covered. U.S. corporations were unable to convince the American public to abandon federal environmental, safety, labor, health and similar legislation. Thus business began attacking the root cause of their discomfort: the Government, Washington, DC, the National Bureaucracy, etc. Once government is weakened, deprived of much funding, enforcement of laws which cut into corporate profits will also be weakened if not totally abolished. This effort has been amazingly successful. The anti-government drive has infiltrated all strata of American society and threatens to undo legislative achievements of the last half century."

JUDITH KRUG, director, Office for Intellectual Freedom, American Library Association, noted, "It's becoming more difficult every year to select the top 10 "censored" stories. They all deserve substantially more press. The fact that this project continues is a serious indictment of the U.S. press."

FRANCES MOORE LAPPÉ, co-director of the Center for Living Democracy, said, "The great underreported story of the 90s is the media itself. Seventy-one percent of the American people see the media as standing in the way of our solving our public problems. More Americans blame the media for our problems than blame Clinton or the Republicans.

"But media concentration continues; and the range of views expressed and issues covered narrows. The media become more and more a vehicle for selling rather than a forum for free exchange of ideas, so essential to public problem solving. Media become increasingly disconnected from the towns and cities in which they operate, as they are answerable to fewer and fewer distant owners.

"By the fact of their limited exposure, all these stories, of course, reflect the problem. But I thought it was important to select those stories that specifically highlight the media itself—media deregulation and an example of the power of large corporations to silence the media.

"Despite the dominant trend, a small but significant number of media outlets are recreating themselves as members of the communities in which they operate, becoming facilitators of dialogue and problem solving without become partisans. This is another censored story! You see very little news of the emergence of what is called 'civic' or 'public' journalism, but which is actually the very old notion of journalism as a key contributor in public problem-solving in a democracy." (As noted in Chapter 1, the author, with all due respect, takes exception to this point.)

WILLIAM LUTZ, professor of English at Rutgers University, said, "The old adage—'What you don't know can't hurt you'—is wrong, dead wrong. What you don't know can get you killed. Hiding vital information is an old trick used by the powerful to control and manipulate others. While exposing the hidden news won't necessarily improve our lot, it will improve our chances for making better, more informed decisions. As the nominations show yet again, there are plenty of people up to no good, and we can't even begin to fight them if we don't know about them and what they're up to. More than ever, Project Censored serves a vital, essential need to keep information flowing."

JACK NELSON, a professor in the Graduate School of Education at Rutgers University, and a *Censored* judge since 1976, commented specifically on several stories and the process. "1. The slavery story is simply startling, and should be (have been) more publicized to arouse the vigilance needed to stop such inhumanity; 2. It was a toss-up for #2 between the story on Congress (to be expected, alas) which needs continuing surveillance, and the child labor story which is appalling and relatively unknown; 3. It is always hard to pick the top 10, as in the 'most wanted' lists, when there is so much unreported or reporter-ignored criminal and unethical behavior that decreases human civilization. We need such lists, but each story deserves public review."

MICHAEL PARENTI, Ph.D., author and lecturer, said he "tended to give greatest weight to stories about the destruction of the environment by corporate profiteering and government complicity. The ecological crisis threatens to reach the point of no return. All other issues become nothing more than rearranging the chairs on the Titanic if we don't stop the war being waged against the planet itself.

"Also, stories about the more brutal side of the political economy (war on the poor; child labor; NAFTA) seem especially important in this era of corporate global domination and the growing impoverishment of the many by the few.

"Several of the stories I nominated combined important questions of political economy, the power of wealth, inequality, public policy, and the environment.

"Some of the stories I did not nominate seemed important enough, but they had been reported in the *New York Times, Washington Post, Christian Science Monitor,* ABC or other national media. So it seemed less easy to make a case that they were kept from the U.S. public, though I understand that a one-shot appearance in some outlet does not mean they got all the coverage they deserved and does amount to a kind of suppression.

"Also stories about the control of the communication universe itself (concentration of the media; privatization of the Internet) strike a cord in me.

"Some of the stories (U.S. maternal health ranking; E. coli; hand guns) seemed too limited in scope or relatively 'mild,' as compared to the even more horrendous ones—which doesn't mean they are not important. It is all relative."

HERBERT I. SCHILLER, professor emeritus of communication, University of California, San Diego, said, "The stories are important but I am distressed that foreign policy issues and U.S. foreign policy in particular (with the exception of NAFTA) is left uncovered. The continuing deprivations of transnational corporate forces are ignored. Even the pressure exerted on France and Chirac to reverse social policies goes unremarked. These are areas deserving full attention. A recent article on Indonesia and the activities there of a U.S. transnational company raises scandalous issues."

SHEILA RABB WEIDENFELD, president of D.C. Productions, Ltd., and a founding member of the *Censored* panel of judges in 1976, said, "That these stories and many others have received a second chance is a tribute to Project Censored. For the past 20 years, the Project has focused attention on big stories that have not gotten the exposure they deserve. The Project was created because some stories, like O.J. Simpson, are over-reported while others, like this year's crop which included 'The Gulf War Syndrome Cover-Up,' '180,000 Patients Die Annually from Treatment in Hospitals,' and 'Fiberglass—the Carcinogen that is Deadly and Everywhere,' are under-reported."

COMPARING PROJECT CENSORED WITH THE ASSOCIATED PRESS

Following is a comparison of Project Censored's top ten *Censored* stories of 1995, as selected by our judges, with the Associated Press's top ten news stories of the year, as selected by AP newspaper and broadcast news executives across the country.

PROJECT CENSORED	ASSOCIATED PRESS
1. Telecommunications Bill	1. Oklahoma Bombing
2. Biased Balanced Budget	2. The Balkans Conflict
3. Child Labor in U.S.A..	3. O.J. Simpson Case
4. Privatization of Internet	4. Rabin's Assassination
5. Adding Bang to Nukes	5. Kobe, Japan Earthquake
6.Radical GOP Plan to Gut FDA	6. Contract with America
7.Russia's Nuke Waste	7. Tokyo Subway Gassing
8.Medical Fraud	8. USAF Pilot Scott O'Grady
9. Ozone Killing Pesticide	9. Chicago Heatwave
10. Broken Promises of NAFTA	10. Susan Smith Life Sentence

Once again, the most immediate distinction between the two lists is that no single story appears on both lists. But perhaps the most important distinction between the two lists is that while something can be still be done about the issues raised by Project Censored, little if anything can be done about most of the stories on the Associated Press' top ten list.

The primary responsibility of the press should be that of a watchdog that issues a warning signal when something is going wrong in society. The *Censored* top ten list warns of social, corporate, political, and environmental problems that need to be addressed.

For example, the telecommunications story warns about the threat to an open marketplace of ideas that might occur if the bill's onerous deregulation provisions take effect; the budget story notes that it is not necessary to balance the budget on the backs of the poor but that it could be balanced merely by cutting "aid to dependent corporations;" and the child labor story alerts an unaware public to the hazardous working conditions endured by many young people today.

On the other hand, AP's top ten list reports, on the whole, natural or man-made disasters or events that have occurred when little can be done about them now. Also, unlike the *Censored* list, the AP's top ten includes individuals—O.J. Simpson, Prime Minister Yitzak Rabin, Scott O'Grady, and Susan Smith—while the *Censored* list cites no individuals. The sensationalization of personalities, such as O.J. Simpson, which also was AP's #1 news story of 1994, does not qualify as real news. However, Simpson did make the top spot in Project Censored's "junk food news" lists in both 1994 and 1995.

While Simpson only ranked as the #3 top news story in 1995 according to the Associated Press, he was the runaway winner for the number one spot in television news in 1995, according to the Tyndall Report's year-end summary. The Tyndall Report, produced by Andrew Tyndall, monitors the time given each subject on the ABC, CBS, and NBC evening news broadcasts throughout the year.

Following are top ten television news stories of the year and the number of minutes devoted to each, as recorded by the Tyndall Report: 1. O.J. Simpson trial (1673 minutes); 2. Yugoslavia wars: Bosnia fighting (1292); 3. Oklahoma City bombing (546); 4. Federal budget balancing dispute (467); 5. Medicare budget faces cutbacks (193); 6. 104th Congress convenes (186); 7. Russia-Chechen separatist fighting (156); 8. Poverty: welfare reform proposals (155); 9. NYSE-NASDAQ action (145); 10. Israel-PLO peace plan (127).

As Tyndall points out, it is interesting to note that while the Republican Congress ranked #6 in terms of TV news time in 1995, the President and White House, normally the networks' busiest beat, didn't even make the top 10 television coverage list.

Another interesting comparison this year is the NAFTA story which ranked #10 on the *Censored* list but doesn't appear on AP's list. The promises of NAFTA were AP's #7 top news story of 1993; the broken promises of NAFTA made Project Censored's top 10 list in 1995.

Overall, comparing this year's two lists of stories should make it abundantly clear why it is time for news editors and directors to invest more time and funds in investigative reporting and less in merely covering disasters after they happen or reporting self-serving comments spoken at press conferences.

THE CENSORED SUBJECTS OF 1995

Continuing a trend started last year, health issues dominated the list in 1995, accounting for nearly a third of the top 25 *Censored* stories. In fact, the total of eight health-oriented stories was the largest number of health issues to make the top 25 list since the Project started in 1976. One possible explanation is that the aging boomer generation, including its alternative journalists, is becoming more concerned with health problems.

Another trend which began last year and continued is the emphasis on domestic issues versus international issues. As noted in the judges' comments cited earlier, Herbert Schiller is concerned with the lack of coverage given foreign policy issues. However, while there were no international issues cited last year, there were three on the list this year—NAFTA, the Sudan, and small arms in Rwanda.

Another judge, Sut Jhally, also commented on the shift toward national stories from international ones. Jhally rightly points out that the end of the Cold War does not mean the end of U.S. and corporate strategic interests overseas. The impact of these interests on the rest of the world surely are deserving of alternative as well as mainstream media attention.

Finally, as several judges noted, this year, for the first time since 1992, we had specific media issues on the list. The top-ranked *Censored* story of the year, the Telecommunications Deregulation Bill which will determine the diversity of, and access to, the marketplace of ideas in the future, might well be one of the most important *Censored* issues we have cited to date. Similarly, it is hoped that the added exposure given the #4 story, "Privatization of the Internet," will slow the rush toward the commercialization of this public service.

Following are the top 25 stories of 1995 separated by category.

HEALTH
   # 3—Child Labor in the United States
   # 8—Medical Fraud Costs the Nation Billions
   # 12—180,000 Patients Die Annually From Treatment in Hospitals
   # 16—Fiberglass—the Deadly Carcinogen is Everywhere
   # 18—Scientific Support for Needle Exchange Suppressed
   # 22—Health Cures in Rain Forests
   # 24—U.S. Trails in Maternal Health Ranking
   # 25—E. Coli is a National Epidemic
ENVIRONMENT
   # 7—Russia Injects Earth with Nuke Waste
   # 9—Chemical Industry and its Ozone-Killing Pesticide
   # 19—Solving Nuclear Waste with Taxpayers' Dollars
   # 23—Dioxin—Still a Deadly Health Threat
POLITICS
   # 2—Balancing the Budget on the Backs of the Poor
   # 6—Radical GOP Plan to Gut the FDA
   # 13—Congress Wants to Take the Money and Run
INTERNATIONAL
   # 10—The Broken Promises of NAFTA
   # 15—Rebirth of Slavery in the Sudan
   # 17—Small Arms Wreak Major Worldwide Havoc
MEDIA
   # 1—Telecommunications Deregulation Bill
   # 4—Privatization of the Internet
MILITARY
   # 5—U.S. Pushes Nuclear Pact But Adds Bang to Nukes
   # 14—Gulf War Syndrome Cover-Up
CORPORATE
   # 11—Oil Companies Owe U.S. More Than $1.5 Billion
   # 20—ABC-TV Spikes Tobacco Exposé
EDUCATION
   # 21—New 3R's—Reading, Writing, and Reloading

CENSORED

"As good almost kill a man as kill a good book:
who kills a man kills a reasonable creature,
God's image; but he who destroys
a good book kills reason itself."
—John Milton

CHAPTER 3

Top Censored Books of 1995

Nineteen-ninety-five was a terrific year for the sale of non-fiction books by mainstream booksellers. Oddly enough, however, much of the year's book-selling success could be attributed to just two authors/subjects—neither of whom were widely known for their literary talents—Newt Gingrich and O.J. Simpson, both authors and subjects of this year's best-sellers.

Gingrich's book deal with HarperCollins, which is owned by Rupert Murdoch, came under considerable criticism when it was discovered that Gingrich signed a $4.5 million advance at a time when Murdoch was lobbying Congress on legislation affecting his business interests. Bowing to pressure, Gingrich turned down the offer and took a $1 advance, plus royalties, instead. *To Renew America*, which outlined his political philosophy, shot to the top of the best-seller lists.

Altogether, it was reported that at one time there were nearly a dozen books by or about Newt Gingrich in the works at America's publishers.

The other most popular author/subject, O.J. Simpson, made the best-seller list with *I Want To Tell You*, a collection of mail he received while in jail and his responses. Among other books stemming from the O.J. Simpson trial published in 1995, at least two of them also made the best-seller lists: *Raging Heart* by Sheila Weller and *Nicole Brown Simpson: The Private Diary of a Life Interrupted* by Faye Resnick.

After the trial ended and the year drew to a close, there were reports of publishers scrambling to make deals with jurors, and defense and prosecution attorneys. Some of the reported deals included Marcia Clark with an advance of $4.2 million, Johnnie Cochran with an advance reported to be between $3 million and $4.3 million, and Robert Shapiro with an advance of $1.5 million.

Looking at these and other books by non-authors that suddenly rocket to the top of the best-seller lists, one must wonder how credible the "best-seller" lists are. Book Passage, a large independent bookstore in Corte Madera, California, raised this issue in a copy of its "Book Passage News & Reviews," No. 2, 1995.

The problem, they suggest, starts when a publisher pays millions of dollars for a celebrity biography or political memoir and then has to sell enough books to recoup the advance. The usual solution, according to Book Passage, is the bandwagon effect: "The publisher pulls out all the stops to get the book on the bestseller lists. And the quickest way to do this is to pay the chains and the warehouse clubs enough promotional money to get their cooperation: Get them to order large quantities of the book with the understanding that they'll report it as a bestseller."

Then, national newspapers, such as *The New York Times*, compile the lists by merely calling selected retailers and asking them what they're selling. They "weigh" the responses, giving more votes to chainstores like Barnes & Noble and K-Mart's Borders stores. This, of course, assumes that a sampling of the big retailers' reports will provide an accurate account of overall sales.

Who wins from all this manipulation of best-selling book lists? Most obviously, the chain bookstores and the warehouse clubs, the big publishers, and the celebrity or politician authors.

And who loses is just about everyone else, as Book Passage points out. "Small publishers lose because they can't afford to play the game. Book buyers lose, because publishers manipulate their buying habits. Independent booksellers lose, because they don't get the promotional subsidies that publishers pay to their chain store competitors. Other authors lose, because their books don't make it to the front of the chain stores or the top of national bestseller lists unless their publisher has paid for such position."

We might also point out that the country loses since the public is further distracted by the self-serving discourse of the Gingriches and Simpsons. As a result, important issues, such as those cited in books in this chapter, seldom reach the front of the bookstores or the best-seller lists.

Further compounding the problem is the growing concentration of media ownership in America which includes the publishing industry. *The Media Monopoly*, by Ben Bagdikian, reveals that while there are some 2,500 companies that publish one or more books a year, the industry is dominated by just six corporations that gross more than half of all book revenues.

The six companies (and some of their subsidiaries) are: Paramount Communications (Macmillan, Simon & Schuster, Ginn & Company); Harcourt Brace Jovanovich (Academic Press); Time Warner (Little, Brown; Scott, Foresman); Bertelsmann, A.G. (Doubleday, Bantam Books); Reader's Digest Association (Condensed Books); and Newhouse (Random House).

An example of the impact of megamedia power on the public's right to know was provided by a *New York Times* report (9/27/95). It seems that a group of publishers, including HarperCollins, were preparing to bid on a memoir by Harry Wu, the prominent Chinese-American human rights advocate. According to the *Times*, "just before the bids were to be submitted on the book (to be written with William Novak), HarperCollins called to say that they had been instructed not to bid, people in the publishing industry said. HarperCollins is owned by Rupert Murdoch's News Corporation, which has a television programming deal in China."

In recent years, as the number of book publishers decreased and the chain bookstores grew more powerful, Project Censored started receiving more and more nominations of books as censored stories. As a result, we now publish a chapter dealing solely with books.

As with our criteria for other censored issues, we limit our nominations to non-fiction books that have been published, but have not received the media exposure they deserve. Also, while we recognize the censorship of many classic books, we limit the nominations to recently published non-fiction books exploring critical issues.

The American Library Association's Office for Intellectual Freedom publishes its bimonthly *Newsletter on Intellectual Freedom*, which regularly features books, including classics, that are "Targets of the Censor" at libraries, public schools, and universities. The *Newsletter*, cited in Appendix A, The CENSORED! Resource Guide, is available by subscription.

Another vital organization involved in the fight against book censorship is the National Coalition Against Censorship (NCAC) which defends "Books In Trouble" through daily work with people on the frontlines in local communities. NCAC also is cited in Appendix A.

Nominations cited in this year's compilation of *Censored* books are drawn from two basic sources: a Project Censored survey of publishers cited in the *Alternative Publishers of Books in North America*, a catalog compiled by Byron Anderson, Project Coordinator for Alternatives in Print, at Northern Illinois University Libraries, DeKalb, Illinois; and from books nominated directly to Project Censored by authors, publishers, librarians, educators, and the general public. (The catalog of alternative publishers is available from CRISES Press, 1716 SW Williston Road, Gainesville, Florida, 32608, 904/335-2200.)

We plan to include an expanded selection of censored books in next year's *Censored* Yearbook; if you know of any books that should be included, please write CENSORED BOOKS, Project Censored, Sonoma State University, Rohnert Park, CA 94928, for a listing application.

In most cases, in the listing of books that follows, the information concerning the book and author has been provided by the publisher; in some cases, the information has been excerpted from a review. In addition to basic information about the book—its price, availability, length, etc.—we have included a brief description of the book's subject, some information about the author, and a description explaining why the publisher feels it is important for the public to know about the book.

AGAINST EMPIRE
by Michael Parenti

SUBJECT: This book provides a study of present day United States imperialism at home and abroad. *Against Empire* also is a history of resistance, struggle, and achievement and offers compelling alternatives for progressive change. Michael Parenti exposes the ruthless agenda and hidden costs of the U.S. empire. He documents the pretexts and lies used to justify violent intervention and maldevelopment abroad and demonstrates how the conversion to a global economy is a victory of finance capital over democracy.

AUTHOR: Michael Parenti is a noted political analyst, lecturer, and author of such recent books as *Democracy for the Few; The Sword and the Dollar; Inventing Reality: The Politics of the News Media;* and *Land of Idols: Political Mythology in America.* He received his Ph.D. in political science from Yale University in 1962 and has taught at a number of universities.

IMPORTANCE: The publisher says that this book provides a number of important perspectives that are never discussed by the dominant media. It explains to the reader how civil society is impoverished by policies that benefit rich and powerful transnational corporations and the national security state. Hard-won gains made by ordinary people are swept away.

AVAILABLE: Directly from the publisher or by phone: 415/362-8193. Pbk: ISBN 087286-2984; price: $12.95; 224 pages.

PUBLISHER:
CITY LIGHTS
261 Columbus Avenue
San Francisco, CA 94133
Tel: 415/362-1901
Fax: 415/362-4921

ANGELS DON'T PLAY THIS HAARP: Advances in Tesla Technology
by Jeane Manning and
Dr. Nick Begich

SUBJECT: This book is about a new system for waging environmental and geophysical warfare. The U.S. government has a new ground-based "Star Wars" weapon which is being tested in the remote bush country of Alaska. This new system manipulates the environment in a way which can: disrupt human mental processes; jam all global communications systems; change weather patterns over large areas; interfere with wildlife migration patterns; negatively affect your health; and potentially will have an adverse impact on the earth's upper atmosphere. The U.S. military calls its zapper HAARP—High-fre-quency Active Auroral Research Program. But it is not about the Northern Lights. HAARP also was the #9 *Censored* story of 1994.

AUTHORS: Jeane Manning is an experienced magazine journalist, reporter for daily newspapers and former editor of a community newspaper. Her upcoming book, *The Coming Energy Revolution* (Avery Publishing Group, New York, 1996), is based on a decade of researching non-conventional electrical energy technologies. Born in Cordova, Alaska, and now living in Vancouver, Canada, she has tracked HAARP with deep interest. Dr. Nick Begich, past-president of the Alaska Federation of Teachers and the Anchorage Council of Education, has been pursuing independent research in the sciences and politics for most of his adult life. He received his doctorate in traditional medicine from The Open International University for Complementary Medicines in November 1994 and wrote the first major story on the HAARP project, published in *Nexus*, October 1994.

IMPORTANCE: This book deals with a secret and revolutionary weapons system which has the potential of affecting every living person on earth. It could weaken or destroy the upper layers of the atmosphere in a way which allows harmful radiation to enter the earth's atmosphere. The story discloses the use of this system as a "nonlethal" weapon which can be used to disrupt human mental functions, blow electronic circuits, alter weather patterns, and kill people. These effects are created using invisible radio-frequency radiations.

AVAILABLE: Through the publisher's order department: phone 907/249-9111 or fax 907/696-1277. Pbk: ISBN 0-9648812-0-9; price: $14.95; 230 pages.

PUBLISHER:
EARTHPULSE PRESS
c/o Begich
P.O. Box 201393
Anchorage, AK 99520
Tel: 907/249-9111
Fax: 907/696-1277

BREAKFAST OF BIODIVERSITY: The Truth About Rain Forest Destruction
by John Vandermeer and Ivette Perfecto

SUBJECT: This book will help readers fully understand the root causes of a global environmental crisis, most visible with the vanishing of the rain forests. In this hard-hitting, scrupulously researched book, ecologists John Vandermeer and Ivette Perfecto look beyond simplistic, blame-the-victim explanations to show exactly why biodiversity is in such jeopardy around the world and what steps must be taken to slow the ravaging of rain forests.

AUTHORS: John Vandermeer is the Alfred Thurneau Professor of Biology at the University of Michigan. Ivette Perfecto is Associate Professor of the School of Natural Resources and the Environment, University of Michigan. Both are longtime rain forest researchers/activists.

IMPORTANCE: The authors acknowledge there are many books about specific causes of the disappearance of the rain forest, but point out their analysis is multifaceted, focusing on the "web of causality," and provides a solution that addresses the root causes. Larry Lohmann, co-editor of *The Struggle for Land & the Fate of the Forests*, says, in "this clear-sighted book...linking economics, politics, sociology and the most up-to-date work in rain forest biology, Vandermeer and Perfecto help bring into focus a realistic and fruitful vision: one which places land security and ecological agriculture at its center, and in which 'nature conservation' is both constantly being redefined by, and becomes the consequence of, grassroots struggles for democracy."

AVAILABLE: Through independent bookstores or by mail order: 800/274-7826, Subterranean Company, Box 160, 265 S. 5th Street, Monroe, OR 97456. Pbk: ISBN 0-935028-66-8; price: $16.95; 200 pages.

PUBLISHER:
FOOD FIRST BOOKS
398 60th Street
Oakland, CA 94618
Tel: 510/654-4400
Fax: 510/654-4551

CENSORSHIP: A Threat to Reading, Learning, Thinking
Edited by John S. Simmons

SUBJECT: *Censorship: A Threat to Reading, Learning, Thinking* offers thought-provoking perspectives from experts in the field of education on the methods used by protesters to remove books and materials from classrooms and libraries. The authors clearly outline the rationales behind censors' motivations—from the struggle of the religious right to preserve a particular morality and worldview to the need for all groups to have their voices heard. The authors also examine important censorship cases and explain how they affect teaching and learning. They detail how teachers, administrators, and school library media specialists can prepare for and fight attacks with specific plans of action.

EDITOR: John S. Simmons, professor of English Education and Reading at Florida State University, Tallahassee, Florida, has served on The National Council of Teachers of English and The International Reading Association

Joint Task Force on Intellectual Freedom.

IMPORTANCE: It is vital for all teachers, administrators, media specialists, parents, and concerned citizens to understand the pervasiveness of censorship in schools and the ways to prepare for challenges from censors. Only with this knowledge can we fight censorship and stop the threat to students' right to read, learn, and think.

AVAILABLE: Directly from the publisher, P.O. Box 8139, Newark, DE 19714-8139, or 800/336-READ, ext. 266. Pbk: ISBN 0-87207-123-5; price: $18.00 ($12.50 to members of the International Reading Association); 256 pages.

PUBLISHER:
INTERNATIONAL READING ASSOCIATION
800 Barksdale Road
Newark, DE 19714-8139
Tel: 302/731-1600
Fax: 302/731-1057

A CULTURE OF CENSORSHIP: Secrecy and Intellectual Repression in South Africa
by Christopher Merrett

SUBJECT: One of the major historical problems South Africans take with them into a democratic future is a lack of openness and accountability in public affairs, derivative of the censorship implicit in a history of colonialism and apartheid. This book defines censorship broadly and traces its development during the twentieth century, up to the election in April 1994 of South Africa's first democratic government. Reflecting a concern about the continuing influence of censorship as part of the legacy of apartheid, the book examines different facets of the problem at the moment of political transition in South Africa, suggesting ways in which they might be approached.

AUTHOR: Christopher Merrett, Deputy University Librarian, University of Natal (Pieter–maritzburg), holds degrees from the Universities of Oxford, Sheffield, and Natal. In 1991 he was awarded the John Phillip Immroth Memorial Award for Intellectual Freedom by the American Library Association's Intellectual Freedom Round Table.

IMPORTANCE: This book alerts the reading public to a particular threat posed by censorship in a particular place, and in doing so illuminates certain features of censorship that threaten persons in all places. Censorship, which has manifested itself in a variety of ways ranging from book banning to violence, is an integral part of the history of South Africa. Many aspects of this institution remain embedded in the fabric of South African life and constitute a threat to the transparency and participation required of an emergent demo-

cratic society. A major concern is that the politicians of the "new" South Africa will inherit a range of repressive measures from the old.

AVAILABLE: Directly from the publisher or Ingram Book Distributors. Pbk: ISBN 0-86554-455-7; price: $18.95; 296 pages.

PUBLISHER:
MERCER UNIVERSITY PRESS
With David Philip and University of Natal Press
6316 Peake Road
Macon, GA 31210-3960
Tel: 912/752-2880
Fax: 912/752-2264

THE DOCTORS' CASE AGAINST THE PILL: 25th Anniversary Updated Edition
by Barbara Seaman

SUBJECT: This book was first published in 1969 and set off a chain reaction of events that led directly to the flourishing of the women's health movement in the early 1970s. *The Doctors' Case* unearthed some of the best kept secrets in women's health at the time and warned women about the dangers of the contraceptive pill. Considered the definitive statement on modern birth-control technologies, this updated anniversary edition includes new, up-to-date chapters on the dangers of Norplant and the risks women on the pill face today.

AUTHOR: Barbara Seaman is cofounder of the National Women's Health Network, a trustee of the National Council on Women's Health, chair of the advisory board of the Coalition for Family Justice, and founding member of New York Women's Forum. A contributing editor to *Ms. Magazine*, she is the author of numerous articles and books including *Free and Female*, *Women and the Crisis in Sex Hormones*, and a biography of novelist Jacqueline Susann called *Lovely Me*. Gloria Steinem saluted Barbara Seaman as "the first prophet of the women's health movement."

IMPORTANCE: The new edition of *The Doctors' Case* brings an important issue and Barbara Seaman back into focus after years of censorship and blacklisting. The original edition was almost not published due to a campaign by groups with vested interests in the issue including pill manufacturers. Even now, 25 years later, the author reports she has been the victim of blacklisting efforts.

AVAILABLE: At some major bookstores or directly from the publisher by phone: 800/266-5592 Hbk: ISBN 089993-181-5; price: $24.95; Pbk: ISBN 089993-182-5; price $14.95; 258 pages.

PUBLISHER:
HUNTER HOUSE
P.O. Box 2914
Alameda, CA 94501-0914

Tel: 510/865-5282
Fax: 510/865-4295

EXTREMISM IN AMERICA: A Reader

Edited by Lyman Tower Sargent

SUBJECT: This reader is a collection of primary sources that document the existence and persistence of radical movements in the U.S. Essays include William L. Pierce's "Program for Survival," R. G. Butler's "Twelve Foundation Stones to Establish a State for Our Aryan Racial Nation," and George E. Pittam's "If This Be Rebellion." Selections include descriptions of how to organize an anti-government community, utilize propaganda to attract new members, and launch paramilitary operations. The book is divided into thematic chapters, covering topics such as taxes and welfare, race, communism and anti-communism, and gender relations.

AUTHOR: Lyman Tower Sargent is Professor of Political Science at the University of Missouri, St. Louis. He is the author of *Contemporary Political Ideologies: A Comparative Analysis* and *Contemporary Political Ideologies: A Reader*.

IMPORTANCE: The publisher notes that the tragedy in Oklahoma City brought to light the dark side of American politics. Timothy J.

McVeigh has come to symbolize the right-wing paramilitary revolutionary, trying to wrest control from an intrusive federal government. Although it would be comforting to think that what happened in Oklahoma is an isolated incident, the forces that shaped McVeigh can be found throughout America and throughout American history. *Extremism in America* documents these forces and paints a vivid and powerful portrait of life and thought on the political fringe.

AVAILABLE: At bookstores everywhere. Hbk: ISBN 0-8147-7978-6; price: $55.00; Pbk: ISBN 0-8147-8011-3; price: $17.95; 385 pages.

PUBLISHER:
NEW YORK UNIVERSITY PRESS
70 Washington Square South
New York, NY 10012
Tel: 212/998-2575
Fax: 212/995-3833

FBI SECRETS:
An Agent's Exposé
by M. Wesley Swearingen

SUBJECT: A former FBI agent recounts the shocking details of the FBI's clandestine wars against political freedom in the United States. As a participant in countless covert FBI operations, former agent M. Wesley Swearingen describes the FBI's campaigns against political dissidence, from harassment to orchestrated assassinations. Swearingen records his participation in campaigns against Communists and Moslems, Weathermen, Black Panthers, and United Slaves. The material uncovered in *FBI SECRETS*, according to former Special Agent William W. Turner, should be enough to "trigger a Bureaugate."

AUTHOR: M. Wesley Swearingen was an FBI agent for 25 years and since his retirement has been instrumental in documenting FBI harassment against political dissidents.

IMPORTANCE: This is the first insider's account of the FBI's COINTELPRO era. Readers interested in domestic repression or U.S. history more generally, will find invaluable primary source material in this historic exposé. Ward Churchill, author of *The COINTELPRO Papers* and the introduction to *FBI SECRETS*, says the book "represents a giant step toward lifting the shroud of secrecy under which the FBI has sought to conceal its true malignancy."

AVAILABLE: From the publisher and at bookstores. Pbk: ISBN 0-89608-501-5; price: $13.00; Hbk: ISBN 0-89608-502-3; price: $30.00; 180 pages.

PUBLISHER:
SOUTH END PRESS
116 Saint Botolph Street
Boston, MA 02115

Tel: 617/266-0629
Fax: 617/266-1595

HAITI: Dangerous Crossroads, NACLA

Editors: Mark Fried, Pierre LaRamée, Deirdre McFadyen, and Fred Rosen

SUBJECT: *HAITI: Dangerous Crossroads* is the first book to analyze Haiti after the U.S. occupation. It provides the background and context needed to understand the ongoing crisis in this current post-Cold War hot spot. It is a succinct history and up-to-date analysis of the tragic betrayal of Haitian democracy. Starting with the 19th century War of Independence, through the Duvalier dynasty, the election of Aristide, the coup, and the current intervention, this volume traces Haiti's tireless efforts to bring about democracy—and the equally tireless efforts of those determined to squash it.

AUTHOR: The North American Congress on Latin America (NACLA) is an independent non-profit research organization founded in 1966 which monitors activities in Latin America and the Caribbean.

IMPORTANCE: This book gathers together the most reliable information and most comprehensive analysis of Haiti that the U.S. Left has to offer. The Haitian crisis has its roots in colonial times, came of age in the era of gun-boat diplomacy, and exemplified Cold War policy. Its denouement today is paradigmatic of the New World Order. It is therefore essential reading not only for those wanting a deeper understanding of Haiti, but also for anyone trying to grasp the complexities of post-Cold War geopolitics.

AVAILABLE: At independent bookstores or directly from the publisher: 800/533-8478. Hbk: ISBN 0-89608-506-6; price: $35.00; Pbk: ISBN 0-89608-505-8; price: $15.00; 200 pages.

PUBLISHER:
SOUTH END PRESS
116 Saint Botolph Street
Boston, MA 02115
Tel: 617/266-0629
Fax: 617/266-1595

THE HITE REPORT ON THE FAMILY: Growing Up Under Patriarchy

by Shere Hite

SUBJECT: This controversial book will cause you to rethink your childhood, your relationships, and quite possibly your life. It is a powerful and original analysis of the changing shape of private life. Listening carefully to the real stories of real people, Hite developed a new framework for understanding growing up. It provides theoretical legitimacy to all of the infinite ways that we live as "families," whether as single parents, as same-sex parents, in traditional family groups, or alone. The fact that this book was originally withheld from publication by its U.S. publisher suggests that the backlash against feminism is far from over.

AUTHOR: Shere Hite has two degrees in history, is a member of a number of professional and scholarly associations, and is the author of *The Hite Report on Female Sexuality*, *The Hite Report on Men and Male Sexuality*, and *Women and Love: A Cultural Revolution in Progress*. Her books have been translated into 13 languages and have sold millions of copies around the world.

IMPORTANCE: Hite challenges established views, arguing that the family is not collapsing but being democratized. She lights the way to understanding change in the family as the constructive result of choice—not as a moral crisis, but as a successful evolution toward private democracy.

AVAILABLE: At bookstores everywhere and directly from the publisher: 800/788-3123. Hbk: ISBN 0-8021-1570-5; price: $22.00; 424 pages.

PUBLISHER:
GROVE/ATLANTIC
841 Broadway
New York, NY 10003
Tel: 212/614-7865
Fax: 212/614-7886

IN SERVICE OF THE WILD: Restoring and Reinhabiting Damaged Land
by Stephanie Mills

SUBJECT: This book presents a challenging and effective answer to the crisis of environmental degradation. In *In Service of the Wild*, Stephanie Mills lends her intelligent and highly personable voice to the rapidly emerging field of land restoration. Mills describes a passionate grassroots effort peopled by some of our most creative thinkers, like scientist/activists Nina Leopold Bradley and Steve Packard who lead a prairie restoration effort in Chicago that involves hundreds of volunteers. It has also created a rich new lode of botanical, zoological, and geological knowledge. She tells stories of northern California bioregionalists exerting themselves in cold water and heated community meetings; inventing ways to save endangered indigenous salmon; and of a visionary community in south India working to replant and regenerate 2,500 acres of blasted earth.

AUTHOR: Stephanie Mills has been a highly visible participant in the ecology movement since her memorable vow made in a 1969 commencement speech at Mills College that she would never have children due to the world's overpopulation and other environmental ills. She is the author/editor of *In Praise of Nature* and author of

Whatever Happened to Ecology? as well as a prolific writer and speaker on issues of overpopulation and bioregionalism.

IMPORTANCE: Bioregionalism and the land restoration movement are rapidly-growing volunteer movements, involving skills available to anyone, which may restore the vitality of the earth. Yet this grassroots effort is portrayed by the media as the actions of the naive and fanatic, rather than as life-affirming, responsible, and necessary. *In Service of the Wild* highlights the necessity of land restoration as well as the inspiring results of this relatively new attitude toward the land and its ecology.

AVAILABLE: At bookstores everywhere. Hbk: ISBN 0-8070-8543-0; price: $23.00; 237 pages.

PUBLISHER:
Beacon Press
25 Beacon Street
Boston, MA 02108-2892
Tel: 617/742-2110, ext. 552
Fax: 617/723-3097

LEASING THE IVORY TOWER: The Corporate Takeover of Academia
by Lawrence C. Soley

SUBJECT: The author charges that the real story about academe today is not "political correctness" but about university physics and engineering departments being seduced by Pentagon contracts; biology and chemistry departments being wooed by drug companies and biotech firms; and computer science departments in bed with Big Blue and a few high-tech chip makers. The book reveals how corporate investments have dramatically changed the mission of higher education; have led universities to attend to the interests of their well-heeled patrons, rather than those of students.

AUTHOR: Lawrence C. Soley has taught at the University of Alabama, University of Georgia, Penn State, and the City University of New York; he currently teaches at Marquette University in Milwaukee. His previous books include *The News Shapers, Radio Warfare*, and *Clandestine Radio Broadcasting.*

IMPORTANCE: This book provides the dirty details about what is really happening on university campuses nationwide, including Columbia, Yale, Harvard, MIT, Michigan State, Johns Hopkins, University of Arizona, Catholic University, Brigham Young, and the University of California. Impassioned, outraged, and meticulously documented, this book exposes the growing corporate threats to the future of intellectual inquiry and civil society itself.

AVAILABLE: From the publisher and at bookstores. Pbk: ISBN 0-89608-503-1; price: $13.00; Hbk: ISBN 0-89608-504-x; price: $30.00.

PUBLISHER:
SOUTH END PRESS
116 St. Botolph Street
Boston, MA 02115
Tel: 617/266-0629
Fax: 617/266-1595

MAKING LOVE VISIBLE: In Celebration of Gay and Lesbian Families
by Geoff Manasse and Jean Swallow

SUBJECT: This book portrays a new kind of family in America formed by gays and lesbians. The authors went throughout the country, talking with gay men and lesbians; those with children and without; young and old; with mixed families and blended families; chosen families, broken and healed families. In a photojournalistic-essay style, the chapters are organized around family life events, including birth and a birthday celebration, Grammy visiting, a wedding, working together, a retirement dinner, quiet moments at home, Christmas at home, getting ready for a dinner for friends, preparing for death and living through mourning.

AUTHORS: Photos by Geoff Manasse have appeared in *National Geographic*, *Newsweek*, *Infoworld*, on calendars and in galleries. He is the winner of the 1992 Northwest Design Awards' Award of Excellence for Photography and the 1980 Cowles Award for feature photography awarded by the *Associated Press*.

IMPORTANCE: The publisher believes that the majority of Americans have a false and damaging idea of the family life of their gay and lesbian neighbors—either believing they don't have children, have all been ostracized or thrown out by their own families, or live lonely, singular lives punctuated with episodes of constantly changing lovers—in essence, that they are unable to create loving familial bonds. This book puts a human face on families of all kinds, and by hearing from mothers, fathers, sisters, children, loving families of friends of gays/lesbians, readers can sweep away the cobwebs created by inaccurate media images and doomsday religious groups that seek to make invisible the familial bonds that bind us all—gay or straight. In this way, the publishers hope to dissolve the "us v. them" mentality, break the myths, and replace prejudice with loving understanding.

AVAILABLE: At bookstores or directly from the publisher. Pbk: ISBN 0-89594-7781; price: $18.95; 176 pages.

PUBLISHER:
THE CROSSING PRESS
P.O. Box 1048
Freedom, CA 95019
Tel: 408/722-0711
Fax: 408/722-2749

THE MARK:
A War Correspondent's Memoir of Vietnam and Cambodia
by Jacques Leslie

SUBJECT: *The Mark* starts with the author's "tour of duty" in Saigon, a wild city choked with poverty, prostitution, corruption, American soldiers looking for trouble—and the journalists who were both observers and participants in the chaotic scene. It describes a complex and fascinating time and place: Indochina in the 1970s, a flashpoint for what was supposed to be the showdown between Communism and democracy—and what turned into a vicious war between an arrogant and out-of-touch American command and its largely corrupt allies on the one side, and a dedicated and ruthless indigenous force on the other. The author describes some of the members of a select crew of journalists—people like Sydney Schanberg, Peter Arnett, and Gloria Emerson, people who shaped our understanding of the war in Vietnam.

AUTHOR: Jacques Leslie was born in Los Angeles in 1947. Shortly after graduating from Yale, he went to Vietnam for the *Los Angeles Times*. By the end of his two-year tour in Indochina, Leslie experienced the collapse of both the American-supported regimes in Vietnam and Cambodia and was the first American journalist to cross the front lines and report on the Viet Cong from their point of view. He was awarded the Overseas Press Club Citation (1973) and the Sigma Delta Chi Correspondence Society Distinguished Service Award for Best Foreign Correspondence (1973).

IMPORTANCE: *The Mark* is an exploration of the inner workings of journalism and an inside look at the people and institutions supplying the news during the Vietnam War. It is an effort to identify the source of the author's "mark"—the obsession that many journalists develop with violence and personal danger, the feeling that they are most alive when in a war zone.

AVAILABLE: At bookstores or directly from the publisher: 800/626-4848. Hbk: ISBN 1-56858-024-X; price: $22.00; 356 pages.

PUBLISHER:
FOUR WALLS EIGHT WINDOWS
39 West 14th Street, Room 503
New York, NY 10011
Tel: 212/206-8965
Fax: 212/206-8799

MARKETING MADNESS: A Survival Guide for a Consumer Society

by Michael F. Jacobson and Laurie Ann Mazur

SUBJECT: *Marketing Madness* conveys the extraordinary extent to which commercialism has penetrated practically every corner of our lives. Well-documented, this heavily illustrated book gives a devastating critique of how advertising's ceaseless attack undermines our health, steals our time and money, distorts our values, destroys the environment and makes pawns of the press. The publisher adds that the book has received little media coverage—perhaps because of the book's critique of advertising.

AUTHORS: Michael F. Jacobson, a consumer advocate for more than 20 years, founded the Center for the Study of Commercialism and is executive director of the Center for Science in the Public Interest. Jacobson also is author of *What Are We Feeding Our Kids*, *The Complete Eater's Digest and Nutrition Scoreboard*, and *The Fast-Food Guide*. Laurie Ann Mazur is a writer with expertise in environmental and social justice issues. She has written extensively for foundations and non-profit organizations, including the Ford Foundation, the Rockefeller Family Fund, and the Pew Charitable Trusts.

IMPORTANCE: *Marketing Madness* is an invaluable self-defense guide in the war against commercialism. It offers a broad menu of reforms to be undertaken by individuals, schools, businesses, and government. It will be of use to everyone from parents' groups concerned about children's increasing materialism to feminists outraged by the use of women's bodies in advertising.

AVAILABLE: At local bookstores or directly from the publisher: 800/456-1995. Hbk: ISBN 0-8133-1980-3, price: $59.95; Pbk: ISBN 0-8133-1981-1, price: $18.95; 264 pages.

PUBLISHER:
WESTVIEW PRESS
5500 Central Avenue
Boulder, CO 80301-2877
Tel: 800/456-1995
Fax: 303/449-3356

OF "SLUTS" AND "BASTARDS": A Feminist Decodes the Child Welfare System

by Louise Armstrong

SUBJECT: This book provides a scathing analysis of Republican proposals for child welfare and explodes some widely accepted myths about welfare mothers. One myth suggests that "Driven by sheer greed to bilk the government of a whopping three percent of its budget (this rhetoric goes), these young women have more and more babies just so they can continue to live nearly $5,000 a year below the poverty line." And when they try the patience of the fathers, the Victorian Super Pops take them away to be raised in orphanages—reminiscent of the way authoritarian and abusive males often punish women, by threatening to take away, or even harm, the children.

AUTHOR: Louise Armstrong made her debut as a wry and forceful feminist social critic with publication of *Kiss Daddy Goodnight* in 1978—the ground-breaking book on incest. Since then her investigative journalism has followed the issue of society's will to individualize, medicalize, and trivialize all forms of violence against women and children.

IMPORTANCE: The publisher says that this book provides a clear picture of what's really going on with the welfare system. According to Barbara Ehrenreich, "This book should spark outrage and immediate action."

AVAILABLE: Directly from the publisher or at local alternative bookstores; Hbk: ISBN 1-56751-067-1; price: $29.95; Pbk: ISBN 1-56751-066-3; price: $18.95; 334 pages.

PUBLISHER:
COMMON COURAGE PRESS
P.O. Box 702
Monroe, ME 04951
Tel: 207/525-0900
Fax: 207/525-3068

OUR VOICES/OUR LIVES:
Stories of Women from Central America and the Caribbean
Edited by Margaret Randall

SUBJECT: Margaret Randall captures the voices of women in struggle, from Cuba to Chile, from El Salvador to Belize, in this series of previously unpublished interviews. Revealing the wisdom and tenacity of women fighting in revolutions, the book addresses the role of women in Cuba's ongoing struggles; gay and lesbian culture in Nicaragua and the international movement; the social and religious issues facing Central American women; and the author's pilgrimage to the general cemetery in Santiago, Chile, 20 years after the bloodiest takeover in contemporary Latin American history.

AUTHOR: Margaret Randall is the author of more than 60 books including *Sandino's Daughters*. Famous for fighting the Immigration and Naturalization Service for the right to retain her U.S. citizenship, she has lived for 23 years in Mexico, Cuba, and Nicaragua. She now lives in New Mexico.

IMPORTANCE: "What serves as connective tissue and can be heard throughout like some common energy source, are the voices of women. Women speak of their experience. They reveal a time of dramatic change and project the future from a particularly 20th century ability to theorize out of practice"—Margaret Randall.

AVAILABLE: Directly from the publisher by mail or telephone: 800/497-3207. Hbk: ISBN 1-56751-047-7; price: $29.95; Pbk: ISBN 1-56751-046-9; price: $12.95; 213 pages.

PUBLISHER:
COMMON COURAGE PRESS
P.O. Box 702
Monroe, ME 04951
Tel: 207/525-0900
Fax: 207/525-3068

THE SECRET VIETNAM WAR: The United States Air Force in Thailand, 1961-1975
by Jeffrey D. Glasser

SUBJECT: Throughout the war in Vietnam, few people realized the U.S. Air Force's combat raids were carried out by units stationed in Thailand. The U.S. Air Force operated from seven primary bases in Thailand where nearly 300,000 servicemen were stationed. Through extensive research, including previously classified government documents and interviews with airmen who flew the missions, a detailed history of Air Force operations in Thailand emerges. The primary focus is on the units, their missions, and the aircraft involved. The plight of those who flew from the Thai bases only to be captured is also thoroughly examined with a discussion of the POW/MIA issue.

AUTHOR: Jeffrey D. Glasser served two tours of duty with the U.S. Air Force in Thailand. He is currently a television engineer and lives in Columbus, Ohio.

IMPORTANCE: Though much has been written about the Vietnam War in the past 20 years, there has been little coverage of this subject. The Thai-based aircrews were most likely to be captured and imprisoned by the North Vietnamese. This is the first time that this important subject has been fully documented.

AVAILABLE: Directly from the publisher: 800/253-2187. Hbk: ISBN 0-7864-0084-6; price: $48.00; 287 pages.

PUBLISHER:
McFARLAND & COMPANY, INC.
Box 611
Jefferson, NC 28640
Tel: 910/246-4460
Fax: 910/246-5018

TOP HEAVY:
A Study of the Increasing Inequality of Wealth in America
by Edward N. Wolff

SUBJECT: This Twentieth Century Fund report suggests that the U.S. might be changing from a land of opportunity to a land of inequality as a result of distribution of wealth that is more unequal than in what used to be perceived as the class-ridden societies of Europe. While previous studies have shown an income gap, this one uses wealth instead of income—because it is a more meaningful measure—and finds an even larger gap. Not since 1922-29 (just before the Great Depression) has the wealth gap in the U.S. been so vast. Today, the top one percent of Americans hold 39 percent of the total household wealth, a five percent increase since 1983. During the same period, the share held by the bottom 40 percent declined, and all gains accrued to the top 20 percent.

AUTHOR: Edward N. Wolff is a professor of economics at New York University, where he has taught since 1974. He holds a Ph.D. from Yale University and his principal research areas are productivity growth and the distribution of income and wealth. The Twentieth Century Fund is a non-profit foundation created in 1919 to analyze public policy issues.

IMPORTANCE: The wealth distribution trend in the U.S. proves the "trickle-down" policies of the 1980s helped the rich and no one else. Public awareness is important for generating policies aimed at a distribution that is of benefit to our entire society.

AVAILABLE: Through the Twentieth Century Fund's distributor: 800/275-1447 (in Washington, DC, call 797-6258). Pbk: ISBN 0-87078-360-2; price: $9.95; 93 pages.

PUBLISHER:
THE TWENTIETH CENTURY FUND
41 E. 70th Street
New York, NY 10021
Tel: 212/452-7723
Fax: 212/535-7534

TOXIC SLUDGE IS GOOD FOR YOU: Lies, Damn Lies and the Public Relations Industry
by John Stauber and Sheldon Rampton

SUBJECT: This blistering and often hilarious exposé reveals the hidden underside of America's homegrown, private-sector ministries of propaganda. A century ago, "public relations" was the domain of carnival hawkers and circus advance men. Today it subsidizes "scientific" and "public affairs" front groups and uses satellite feeds, sophisticated polling, and its own TV crews to created biased "reporting" that is often broadcast verbatim as news to an unsuspecting public.

AUTHORS: John Stauber, executive director of the Center for Media and Democracy, has been a grassroots activist since the 1960s and is the editor of *PR Watch*. Sheldon Rampton is associate editor of *PR Watch* and the author of *Friends in Deed: The Story of U.S. Nicaraguan Sister Cities*.

IMPORTANCE: This comprehensive overview shows how the multi-billion dollar PR industry is helping corporations and the federal government manipulate the institutions of democracy, including the use of PR firms by a "torturers' lobby" in Washington to convert taxpayers' dollars into foreign aid money for repressive dictatorships. The book concludes with practical guidelines to help citizens recognize PR in the news and examples of effective citizen campaigns to counteract well-financed corporate PR aimed at subverting the public interest.

AVAILABLE: At good bookstores or directly from the publisher. Hbk: ISBN 1-56751-061-2; price: $29.95. Pbk: ISBN 1-56751-060-4; price: $16.95; 240 pages.

PUBLISHER:
COMMON COURAGE PRESS
PO Box 702
Monroe, ME 04951
Tel: 207/525-0900
Fax: 207/525-3068

THE WAY THINGS AREN'T:
Rush Limbaugh's Reign of Error
by Steven Rendall, Jim Naureckas, and Jeff Cohen, FAIR

SUBJECT: In *The Way Things Aren't*, the media watch group FAIR has caught more than 100 of Rush Limbaugh's most blatant misstatements, exaggerations, and lies. In sections pitting "Limbaugh versus Reality," FAIR exposes Limbaugh's finely-honed ability to distort the truth. Other features include "Limbaugh versus Limbaugh" (with glaring examples of Limbaugh contradicting himself); silly photographs; acerbic cartoons by Garry Trudeau and Tom Tomorrow; and an introduction by Molly Ivins. A final section offers suggestions for holding Limbaugh accountable and a postcard to mail to him directly.

AUTHORS: Founded in 1986, FAIR (Fairness & Accuracy In Reporting) is an independent non-profit media watch group challenging media bias and censorship and focusing public attention on the narrow corporate ownership of the press. Steven Rendall is FAIR's senior analyst; Jim Naureckas is editor of *EXTRA!* and the *EXTRA! Update* newsletter; Jeff Cohen is FAIR's executive director and a syndicated columnist.

IMPORTANCE: *The Way Things Aren't* documents the incredible pattern of disregard for facts and truth that are the hallmark of Limbaugh's shows and books ... and is the first trade book to call Limbaugh a liar. Behind its lighthearted cover, this book is a serious critique of a dangerous media demagogue about whom the American public should be informed.

AVAILABLE: In bookstores nationwide; direct from W.W. Norton (distributor for The New Press): 800/233-4830; and through FAIR. Pbk: ISBN: 1-56584-260-x; price: $6.95; 128 pages.

PUBLISHER:
THE NEW PRESS
450 West 41st Street, 6th Floor
New York, NY 10036
Tel: 212/629-8802
Fax: 212/268-6349; 212/629-8617

WHOLE LIFE ECONOMICS:
Revaluing Daily Life
by Barbara Brandt

SUBJECT: *Whole Life Economics* opens the door to personal and societal recovery from deadly addictions to money, overwork, and short-term gain. Well-researched, free of economic jargon, and full of working examples, this book describes how many people are quietly yet vigorously building a new economy. This economic system is more socially just, personally fulfilling, and respectful of communities and the environment than the conventionally recognized economy. *Whole Life Economics* challenges the dominance of corporations, values women's work and other invisible forms of production, and charts the steps to an emerging economics of empowerment that is as much or more about caring for children, planting gardens and helping friends, as it is about counting money and using up the earth's natural resources.

AUTHOR: Barbara Brandt is a long-time organizer and social-change activist who integrates environmental, community, economic, and gender issues with personal and societal concerns.

IMPORTANCE: *Whole Life Economics* reminds readers that everyone, every day, should help create the economy with their hearts, minds, and hands. It helps readers see and honor the tremendous value of the economically invisible work done by women and marginalized groups.

AVAILABLE: At most bookstores or directly from the publisher: 800/333-9093. Hbk: ISBN 086571-265-4; price: $39.95; Pbk: ISBN 086571-266-2; price: $14.95; 224 pages.

PUBLISHER:
NEW SOCIETY PUBLISHERS
4527 Springfield Avenue
Philadelphia, PA 19143
Tel: 215/382-6543
Fax: 215/222-1993

"It was déjà vu
all over again."
—Yogi Berra

CHAPTER 4

Censored Déjà Vu of 1995

Project Censored annually sounds an alarm on disturbing social, environmental, economic, political, and other issues that may emerge in the alternative media but do not attract the attention of the mass media. If the mass media were to bring early national attention to these problems, we as a nation would be better able to resolve them before they get out of control. Unfortunately, too often the warnings issued by America's alternative press go unheeded.

HARVEST OF SHAME: One such example is the story of the plight of migrant farm workers. This story was dramatically told by Edward R. Murrow on CBS-TV in 1960 on the day after Thanksgiving when Americans were still stuffed from their traditional bountiful meal.

The controversial documentary, "Harvest of Shame," was one in the award-winning "CBS Reports" series that investigated and exposed critical social issues. The slave-like working conditions in the fields horrified the public. Other CBS documentaries that created public debate and captured the attention of politicians at the time included *The Selling of the Pentagon* and *Hunger in America*.

The quality of reporting represented by "CBS Reports" was a major reason CBS became known as the "Tiffany Network" of television. Unfortunately, as noted by Alexander Kendrick in *Prime Time: The Life of Edward R. Murrow*, (1969), "The controversy over 'Harvest of Shame' coincided with a kind of phasing-out of CBS public affairs programs ... by James Aubrey, the television network president who had ... dedicated himself to making more money than ever for CBS." Aubrey's rationalization was that they cost too much.

In an almost unnoticed "déjà vu," on July 20, 1995, CBS's Dan Rather presented "Legacy of Shame," a hard-hitting modern-day sequel to "Harvest of Shame." As USA Today television reviewer Matt Roush noted, "It's surely troubling that this particular field of nightmares is still there to be tilled by enterprising journalists." Indeed, the only apparent difference from the earlier exposé was the lack of follow-up by other media and the subsequent lack of impact on either the public or politicians.

On the other hand, each year we *do* find issues that were cited by Project Censored in the past that have finally attracted the attention of the national news media and been put on the national news agenda. One such issue in 1995 was Guatemala.

GUATEMALA: The #15 Censored story of 1988 asked "What's Happening in Guatemala?" and answered with a report of "world- class" human rights atrocities that had been occurring there, without the press noticing, for at least 30 years—since the CIA overthrew the democratic Arbenz government in the late 1950s. Nonetheless, U.S. support of the oppressive regime continued unabated.

In 1989, the #5 Censored story charged there was "Guatemalan Blood on U.S. Hands." It revealed how the Bush administration strengthened ties with the oppressive Guatemalan military at the same time that human rights violations by the army rose sharply. One example cited was that of Sister Diana Ortiz, a U.S. citizen working as a teacher in Guatemala, who was kidnapped, beaten, tortured, and sexually molested by three men, one of whom was a uniformed Guatemalan police officer.

But it wasn't until March and April of 1995 that the media confirmed the full, horrifying story of what happened to thousands of Guatemalans with the support of the United States. As *New York Times* columnist Anthony Lewis pointed out (4/10/95), "The Guatemalan killings publicized here in recent weeks ... were just two of hundreds of atrocities committed by Guatemalan security forces, which are by all odds the most murderous and criminal in the Western Hemisphere."

On March 11, wire services reported the Clinton administration was suspending the last of its military aid to Guatemala, more than seven years after the atrocities were revealed in the alternative press. On April 13, Tim Weiner, an investigative journalist with *The New York Times*, reported that a federal judge ordered an ex-Guatemalan general to pay $47.5 million to Sister Diana Ortiz and eight Guatemalans who were terrorized by the Guatemalan military in the 1980s. On July 26, Weiner also reported that an internal CIA investigation into the agency's conduct in Guatemala concluded that CIA officers covered up their clandestine Guatemalan activities. On October 7, the *Associated Press* reported Guatemalan soldiers had massacred ten peasants endangering peace talks then underway. Altogether, the 34-year civil war, the longest in Central America, has claimed more than 100,000 lives and created at least 45,000 refugees. And much of the tragedy was supported by U.S. taxpayer dollars.

OTHER DÉJÀ VU STORIES OF 1995

ACID RAIN CAUSES WIDESPREAD DEATHS IN CHINA—The #8 *Censored* story of 1977 warned of the ecological damage in the U.S. resulting from acid rain caused, in part, by coal burning. A "déjà vu" update in the 1995 *Censored* Yearbook revealed that acid rain warnings

were being ignored in Mexico with the construction of two massive coal-fired power plants. Now it appears China is paying the penalty for also ignoring the dangers of acid rain, according to a report in *Toward Freedom* (December 1994). At least six Chinese cities are badly hit by acid rain that wreaks havoc on crops and vegetation, damages anything made of metal, and has even more serious effects on people. Government health data shows that chronic lung disease linked to fine airborne sulphur dioxide, spread by acid rain, was the country's leading cause of death—accounting for 26 percent of all fatalities.

GROWING GLOBAL THREAT OF TB ACKNOWLEDGED—Researchers warned that an estimated 90 million new cases of tuberculosis could cause 30 million deaths by the year 2,000 in an article published in the *Journal of the American Medical Association* (1/18/95). In June the World Health Organization reported TB was the leading cause of death worldwide among people infected with HIV. And in July, BBC World Television broadcast a documentary titled "TB: The Forgotten Plague." "The Return of Tuberculosis" was the #8 *Censored* story of 1994.

NO SURPRISE TO NO IRAQGATE COVER-UP—The #5 *Censored* story of 1992, "Iraqgate," warned of the massive efforts being made to interfere in the investigation of the secret sale of military materials to Iraq by the Reagan/Bush administrations. Unfortunately those efforts proved successful: On January 23, 1995, the U.S. Department of Justice issued a 200-page report that concluded there was no cover-up and that the U.S. did not illegally arm Iraq.

THE BOOK IS CLOSED ON SOMALIA—On February 28, the U.S. Marines went ashore in Somalia to protect the final withdrawal of U.N. forces after a 26-month failed effort called Operation Restore Hope. The mission, launched by President Bush in December 1992, cost $2 billion and the lives of 140 American and U.N. peacekeepers and did little permanent good. "Why Are We Really In Somalia?" was the #2 *Censored* story of 1993.

SPERM COUNTS CONTINUE TO DROP DRAMATICALLY—The #7 *Censored* story of 1978 warned of male sterility caused by pesticides. Subsequent studies throughout the world confirmed a reduction in sperm count due to exposure to pesticides. On February 2, the *Associated Press* reported a French study that found sperm counts of donors at a Paris sperm bank had dropped by one-third over the past two decades. The AP's lead paragraph: "Men's sperm counts seem to be falling, and no one knows why."

EPA AGREES TO BAN CARCINOGENIC PESTICIDES—After a six-year legal battle over carcinogens in processed food, the EPA has agreed to ban, within two years, the use of pesticides that leave cancer-causing residues in any of an array of food products, including ketchup, raisins, ground spices, flour, cocoa and syrup (*McClatchy News Service*, 2/8/95). The 1958 Delaney Clause, the subject of the #20 *Censored* story of 1994, called for a zero-tolerance on carcinogenic additives in processed foods. It is targeted for elimination by current congressional Republicans.

RETURN TO THE TORRIJOS/NORIEGA DAYS IN PANAMA—The #6 *Censored* story of 1990 suggested that what really happened when America invaded Panama was a far different story than what was reported in the press—partially due to the "success" of the Reagan-created press pool coverage. *The New York Times* reported on February 9 that five years after the American invasion it is now business as usual in Panama. The Democratic Revolutionary Party (PRD), founded by General Omar Torrijos as the political arm of the Panamanian military and inherited by Noriega, "is back in power and intent on settling old scores."

CORPORATE WELFARE BECOMES BUGABOO OF 1995—The #4 *Censored* story of 1993 charged that the real welfare cheats in America were not ordinary people struggling to get by, but America's biggest corporations which were the largest recipients of taxpayer handouts. The term "corporate welfare" finally became popularized in 1995. The *San Francisco Chronicle* called for Washington to "Cut Corporate Welfare, Not Food for Children" (2/27/95); *The New York Times* reported how business giants were on "corporate" welfare (3/7/95); *USA Today* editorialized to "End corporate welfare" (4/20/95); and the *Los Angeles Times* concluded (5/23/95) that while the term corporate welfare has replaced "subsidies," it may be just as hard to end.

ALTERNATIVE MEDICINE FINALLY GETS SOME RESPECT—The #20 *Censored* story of 1990 reported how the Food and Drug Administration and the American Medical Association ignored alternative medicine and suppressed new cancer treatments. On March 2, the National Institutes of Health Office of Alternative Medicine, which was established in 1991, issued a 420-page report titled "Alternative Medicine: Expanding Medical Horizons." It details alternative approaches to healing, including meditation, support groups, herbs, chiropractic manipulation, diet, as well as unproved biological agents such as shark cartilage.

TAXPAYERS FUND MERGER OF WORLD'S LARGEST DEFENSE COMPANY—Despite exposure of a secret Pentagon plan to subsidize defense contractor mergers (the #3 Censored story of 1994), the Martin Marietta Corporation and the Lockheed Corporation merged in mid-March to form the world's largest defense firm. An estimated 17,000 to 30,000 employees could lose their jobs. Unfortunately they won't benefit from the $92 million, a third of which was paid by taxpayers, in compensation given 460 top executives who were also laid off. The lucky beneficiaries include presidential candidate Lamar Alexander, who received $236,000, Melvin Laird, former Secretary of Defense, who got $427,000, and former Martin Marietta Chairman Norman Augustine, who received $8.2 million.

AMERICA'S CHICKEN SHIT SOLUTION TO RADIOACTIVE WASTE— The #3 Censored story of 1981 warned how America was being buried by radioactive waste. On April 4, the Associated Press (AP) reported that the Energy Department estimates that the cleanup of radioactive waste in America will take more than four decades and will cost up to $350 billion. Even then, hundreds of acres with buried debris would be cordoned off from the public and many other areas would be suitable only for limited use. However, on May 6, the AP revealed that raising chickens on radioactive land would be cheaper than cleaning up the sites, according to researchers at the Savannah River Ecology Laboratory. Chickens foraging in contaminated areas would be taken to a processing plant off the site and fed uncontaminated food; the radioactive material would pass from their systems, and, in about ten days, the meat and the eggs would be fit for human consumption. However, there was no explanation as to how to dispose of the radioactive manure.

TRAINING TERRORISTS IS AN OLD STORY IN U.S.—On April 4, The New York Times published a feature article exposing the School of the Americas, the elite U.S. Army academy at Fort Benning, Georgia, which some say teaches professionalism to Latin American soldiers while others accuse it of training terrorists and assassins. Its graduates include Panama's Manuel Noriega, El Salvador's Roberto D'Aubuisson, as well as members of notorious death squads throughout Latin America and in Haiti. The #6 *Censored* story of 1981 revealed how terrorists were being trained at Camp Libertad, Florida, a similar training site established earlier.

PHYSICIAN, HEAL THYSELF—As scare stories of medical malpractice by doctors and hospitals make the news, there were increased calls for more physician reviews and for stronger penalties for irresponsible doctors. Indeed, state medical boards disciplined 3,685 physicians in 1994, ll.8 percent more than the prior year (*Associated Press*, 4/6/95). The #8 *Censored* story of 1993, "America's Deadly Doctors," revealed that 5 to 10 percent of doctors—some 30,000 to 60,000—could be hazardous to your health.

DEADLY VIRUS SPREAD FROM ANIMALS TO MAN—The *Associated Press* reported (4/7/95) a highly virulent new mystery virus that jumps from animals to humans. It killed 14 horses and a horse trainer in Australia. The #25 *Censored* story of 1994 discussed another disease that jumped from animals to humans—the "Mad Cow Disease", which had originated in England and then spread to North America.

NATION'S DRUG CZAR REPEATS HIMSELF—In 1994, White House drug czar Lee Brown made the "déjà vu" listing by conceding the fight against drugs is "not getting any better." Our #4 *Censored* story of 1989 charged that the "government's war on drugs is more hype than reality." On May 13, 1995, the drug czar once again admitted his drug war is getting nowhere, according to the *Cox News Service*. And by July 10, the *Washington Post* "revealed" the U.S. is losing the war on drugs.

RAPES, BEATINGS, DEATHS ARE NOT NEW ALONG THE BORDER— On April 12, the *Associated Press* reported that Border Patrol agents routinely abuse people attempting to enter the U.S. from Mexico and the victims are ignored. The #18 *Censored* story of 1988 revealed how Hispanic women attempting to enter the U.S. illegally were victims of blackmail, battery, and rape, and were unable to report the crimes.

UNIVERSITY OF ARIZONA TELESCOPE PROJECT UNDER THE GUN AGAIN—Wire services reported (4/25/95) another setback for the construction of a powerful telescope on Mount Graham by the University of

Arizona. University officials now say further delays could kill the $60 million project. The #25 Censored story of 1992 revealed how the University, along with the Defense Department, the Vatican, and others involved in the international project, were threatening a sacred Native American site with the massive observatory.

U.S. LIED ABOUT DEATH SQUADS TO SUPPORT REAGAN'S WARS IN CENTRAL AMERICA—On June 12, following a 14-month investigation, the *Baltimore Sun* revealed the CIA and State Department collaborated with a secret Honduran military unit despite knowing it was kidnapping, torturing and executing its own people. Classified documents and interviews revealed U.S. officials deliberately misled Congress and the public to keep up public support for the Reagan administration's wars in Central America. Fearing for their careers or lives, U.S. and Honduran participants had kept silent until now. Central American death squads were the subjects of *Censored* stories #4 and #21 in 1984.

MOZAMBIQUE REFUGEES FINALLY RETURNING HOME—The *San Francisco Chronicle* Foreign Service reported on May 26 that 1.6 million Mozambican refugees had voluntarily gone back to their homeland from camps in Malawi, South Africa, Tanzania, Zambia, Zimbabwe and Swaziland. The #3 *Censored* story of 1989 revealed how the United States supported "one of the most brutal holocausts since WWII." During the long civil conflict in Mozambique, which officially ended in October 1992, more than one million people died, nearly four million refugees were driven from their homes, and there was an estimated $15 billion in damages.

NORPLANT HIT BY AVALANCHE OF SUITS—On May 28, *The New York Times* reported that Norplant, the controversial birth-control device implanted just under the skin, is the target of an avalanche of lawsuits. Wyeth-Ayerst Laboratories, producers of Norplant, said bad publicity and negative word-of-mouth have driven sales down from about 800 a day to about 60. Norplant was the target of the #17 *Censored* story of 1992.

MILITARY TOXIC WASTE BILL FINALLY HAS TO BE PAID—Over the years there have been many warnings about the eventual cost of cleaning up toxic waste at military bases, including *Censored* story #2, "Military Toxic Wastes," in 1985, and #14, "Military's Toxic Legacy to America," in 1990. Now the warnings can't be ignored any longer. The *McClatchy News*

Service reported on May 29 that the McClellan Air Force Base in California is the most polluted base in America and that taxpayers will have to pay the bill, which will hit at least $700 million.

15-YEAR-OLD WARNING ABOUT PBS FULFILLED—The #25 *Censored* story of 1980 warned the "Public Broadcasting System Goes Commercial." On June 7, the *Washington Post* reported, "'Barney & Friends' and other PBS programs may soon carry what public TV has always disdained— aggressive 30-second pitches by corporate sponsors of national programs."

GEORGIA FLOODS REVEAL POTENTIAL FOR DAM DISASTERS— "NBC Dateline" reported on June 27 that 200 dams burst during the fatal Georgia floods and some 1,800 dams nationwide were now in danger of collapse. The #8 *Censored* story of 1978 warned that of the 49,422 large dams counted by the Corps of Engineers in a national inventory, about 39,000 have never been inspected by state or federal engineers. It was estimated that, in any given year, 25 to 30 of the nation's dams may break.

NURSING HOMES FINALLY GET NEW RULES—The *Scripps-Howard News Service* reported that new regulations intended to clean up nursing homes took effect on July 1. These provided sanctions which had been lacking in the nursing home reform plan approved by Congress in 1987. The #9 *Censored* story of 1984 revealed how Ronald Reagan's close friend, Charles Wick, also director of the U.S. Information Agency, operated a nursing home in California which, according to one inspector, had the "worst nursing home conditions" ever seen in California. ABC-TV News investigated and filmed the story. Just before the final edit, it was killed, reportedly after a call directly from the White House to ABC.

HUMAN RIGHTS VIOLATIONS IN U.S. PRISONS ARE NOT NEWS IN U.S. BUT CHINESE VIOLATIONS ARE—Human rights violations in Chinese prisons were widely publicized in the U.S. press following the imprisonment in China and release of Chinese-American activist Harry Wu. However, in 1979, when a panel of seven international jurists conducted a nationwide investigation of U.S. prison conditions and the judicial system— and found the U.S. guilty of systematic violations of human rights—the press was not interested. It was the #3 *Censored* story of 1979. On July 3, 1995, *The Nation* reported that a Human Rights Watch investigation of more than 20 prisons and jails in the United States revealed extensive abuses of the U.N.'s minimum standards for the treatment of prisoners.

MISTAKEN AIDS VIRUS DIAGNOSIS RESULTS IN $4.1 MILLION AWARD—The July 10 issue of *New York Native* reported that a man who said he underwent nearly seven years of experimental drug treatment after mistakenly being diagnosed as having the AIDS virus was awarded $4.1 million in damages by a federal jury. The dangers of "false positive" HIV antibody tests was the #16 *Censored* story of 1994. On August 10, the Food and Drug Administration ordered the American Red Cross and other blood centers to start using a new test to screen for the AIDS virus according to the *Associated Press*.

BENEFITS OR DANGERS OF ESTROGEN REPLACEMENT THERAPY STILL UNRESOLVED—The #20 *Censored* story of 1977 warned about the dangers of estrogen replacement therapy. On July 12, the *Associated Press* reported a new study that indicated that taking estrogen would not increase the risk of breast cancer. Less than a month earlier, another study reported it *would* increase the risk. Lead authors of both studies say more research is needed.

FDA FINALLY CONCLUDES THAT NICOTINE IS A DRUG—The danger of smoking tobacco has been a *Censored* subject a number of times over the years (1979, 1980, 1984, 1985) and most recently the subject of a major "déjà vu" update in the 1995 *Censored* Yearbook. On July 13, the Food and Drug Administration concluded, for the first time, that nicotine is a drug that should be regulated and proposed initial steps for regulating tobacco products. Also on July 13, the *San Francisco Examiner* reported that the American Medical Association, concerned about the addictive properties of nicotine, recommended no one under 21 be allowed to smoke and that all tobacco exports be banned.

U.S. FINALLY ACKNOWLEDGES HUMAN RIGHTS CONCERNS IN EAST TIMOR—*The Nation* reported on July 17 that the Commander in Chief of U.S. Pacific forces privately told Congressional officials the time has come for Indonesia to get out of East Timor. Many may think it is past time for the U.S. to stop supporting Indonesia: the slaughter in East Timor was the #7 *Censored* story in 1979 and the #3 *Censored* story in 1985.

KILLING FIELDS REVISITED—The #6 *Censored* story of 1977 reported the execution, starvation, and torture by the Khmer Rouge in Cambodia, which led to more than 1.2 million deaths. It became known as the site of the "killing fields." On July 19, *Reuters* reported the discovery of a Khmer Rouge "killing field" near Phnom Penh which may turn out to be the biggest execution site in Cambodia.

WORLDWIDE OCEAN FISHING PACT SIGNED—The *Washington Post* reported on August 4 that after three years of talks, the nations of the world have agreed for the first time on a treaty to regulate fishing on the high seas. While some environmental groups say the pact does not go far enough, others are more optimistic, saying there is no longer free-for-all fishing on the high seas. "60 Billion Pounds of Fish Wasted Annually" was the #7 *Censored* story of 1994.

"DIRTY WARS" STILL HAUNT LATIN AMERICA—The "dirty wars" of Latin America were cited by Project Censored as undercovered issues starting in 1980 with the #1 *Censored* story about distorted press reports from El Salvador. Knight-Ridder Newspapers reported on August 10 that ghosts of those wars are still haunting the region. In some areas, such as Honduras, military forces are retaking power, while in others, such as El Salvador, elected leaders are forming "truth commissions" to respond to the public's demand to know the truth of past abuses.

UNOCAL LEAVES ITS MESS IN CALIFORNIA—Unocal sold all its crude oil and natural gas holdings in California to Torch Energy Advisors Inc., a Houston company, for $500 million. It plans to focus its efforts on the expanding markets of Asia and in the Gulf of Mexico. The *Associated Press* story that reported the sale on August 31 did not mention Unocal was responsible for the cover-up of what might be the largest oil spill in California history, the subject of the #12 *Censored* story of 1994. Unocal also was the company involved in the 1969 Santa Barbara oil spill disaster.

SUPER SECRET SPY COURT MAINTAINS PERFECT RECORD—The September issue of the *Secrecy & Government Bulletin* reports the secretive Foreign Intelligence Surveillance Court approved 576 government applications for domestic electronic surveillance of suspected foreign agents in 1994, up from 509 approvals in 1993. Since its inception in 1978, it has approved a total of 8,130 surveillance actions without a single denial. The extraordinary perfect record of our super-secret spy court was the subject of the #2 *Censored* story of 1982.

OSHA HASN'T STAFF TO SAVE WORKERS' LIVES—The *Associated Press* reported (9/5/95) that 75 percent of the U.S. work sites where accidents claimed the lives of 1,835 and injured thousands had not been inspected by the Occupational Safety and Health Administration (OSHA) in recent years. One reason OSHA did not make the inspections was a shortage of inspectors. The #19 *Censored* story of 1983 revealed how the Reagan administration cut OSHA's staff by 23 percent and appointed officials who are easy on enforcement.

FEMA STRAIGHTENS OUT UNDER CLINTON ADMINISTRATION— The once highly criticized Federal Emergency Management Agency (FEMA) was the subject of the #9 *Censored* story of 1984, which revealed how Edwin Meese, Ronald Reagan's attorney general, redirected FEMA to combat terrorism, and the #11 *Censored* story of 1989, titled "FEMA: The 'Emergency Management' Agency That Failed." On September 10, the *New Orleans Times-Picayune* reported FEMA has "undergone a dramatic transformation under the Clinton administration." FEMA was cited for its quick and effective response when Hurricane Luis hit Puerto Rico and the Virgin Islands in early September.

STILL NO SIGNIFICANT PROGRESS IN THE FIGHT AGAINST CANCER—The #2 *Censored* story of 1977 revealed that, despite billions of dollars in research, the chance for an American to survive cancer has not increased more than one percent since the late 1940s. In September 1995, the *Congressional Quarterly* reported the cancer death rate is rising and cancer is now expected to become the nation's leading cause of death in less than a decade, despite the costly campaign to find cures and treatments. The #11 *Censored* story of 1977 warned about the environmental causes of cancer, specifically the chemical carcinogen problem.

ORGANIC FARMING CAN BE PROFITABLE—USA TODAY reported (9/19/95) a new study that revealed organic farming can be just as profitable as using chemicals. The #2 *Censored* story of 1978 reported that

"Successful multi-million dollar organic farms in Switzerland and the U.S. have proven there is an economically feasible alternative to farming with potentially dangerous agricultural chemical pesticides."

PRESIDENT APOLOGIZES FOR HUMAN RADIATION TESTS—The #6 *Censored* story of 1994 discussed a 1947 AEC memo that revealed why human radiation experiments were censored. On August 18, the *Albuquerque Tribune* reported the U.S. Energy Department had conducted 435 human radiation experiments involving 16,000 people, including tests on aborted fetuses, infants, pregnant and nursing women, prisoners and institutionalized children and adults, according to Energy Secretary Hazel O'Leary. Then on October 4, the *Los Angeles Times* reported that President Bill Clinton apologized to the survivors and families of those who unknowingly were subjects of government-sponsored radiation experiments. He also ordered his cabinet to devise a system of relief, including financial compensation. Finally, on December 26, the *Cincinnati Enquirer* reported that the Department of Energy spent more than $22 million researching Cold War human radiation experiments in the past two years. An attorney for radiation victims said the amount of money already spent could have settled all the claims.

YOUR PERSONAL MEDICAL RECORDS MAY BE AVAILABLE TO ANYONE—In 1978, the #15 *Censored* story warned how the Medical Information Bureau (MIB), which gathers data from insurance companies, had files on 15 million Americans and was adding about 400,000 new names a year. On October 9, *USA Today* warned its readers, "Lack of medical privacy enough to make you sick." It told how advancing computer technology is spreading your most private medical and credit reports, farther and wider. The potential dangers of such "open records" was reported 10/24/94 by the *Associated Press*. A St. Paul, Minnesota, man was denied life insurance because he lives with a partner who has AIDS. While he tested negatively for the HIV virus, he had been reported to the Medical Information Bureau which provides insurance companies with individuals' health information.

CALIFORNIA ADOPTS FLUORIDATION DESPITE POTENTIAL HAZARDS—Despite fluoridation warnings raised by a public health report from the U.S. Department of Health and Human Services cited in the #22 *Censored* story of 1991, California Governor Pete Wilson signed a bill on October 9 that requires most California communities to add the tooth-decay-fighting fluoride agent to their drinking water (*San Francisco Chronicle*, 10/10/95).

OZONE-HOLE IS A REALITY NOT A MYTH—Researchers who conducted pioneering studies of ozone layer depletion were awarded the 1995 Nobel Prizes in chemistry and physics by the Royal Swedish Academy of Sciences, as reported in *USA Today* (10/12/95). This professional honor helped silence critics who questioned whether there was such a phenomenon. The Clinton administration's retreat on the ozone crisis was the #5 *Censored* story of 1994. An earlier *Censored* story, #4 in 1990, revealed how NASA space shuttles help destroy the ozone shield. *Military and the Environment*, a newsletter published by the Pacific Studies Center and San Francisco State University, reported in December 1994 that while NASA plays down the environmental impact of its solid rocket motors, stratospheric ozone reactive chemicals generated by space launches do have an impact.

PENTAGON FINALLY WILL PROBE ITS COLD WAR ARMS SPENDING SPREE—The #1 *Censored* story of 1984, titled "Soviet Military Build-up Myth," revealed CIA estimates of Soviet military spending were found to be highly inflated, leading to exorbitant U.S. military expenditures. A "déjà vu" update on "The Costly Myth of the Big Red Scare," in the 1993 *Censored* Yearbook, noted that CIA Director Robert Gates admitted CIA intelligence data had been "cooked" to portray the Soviet economy as stronger than it was. Finally, on November 2, 1995, the *Associated Press* reported the Pentagon was reviewing billions of dollars in arms purchases that may have been based on bogus estimates of Soviet strength during the Cold War.

NRC APPROVES LAST COMMERCIAL NUCLEAR POWER PLANT STILL BEING BUILT—Despite ongoing concerns about safety that delayed its start-up for 23 years, the Watts Bar nuclear power plant in Tennessee received approval for its low-power permit from the Nuclear Regulatory Commission on November 9 (*Associated Press*, 11/10/95). Critics say Watts Bar is unsafe because it was built so long ago. It is only the third plant to receive an operating license in this decade. The hazards of nuclear reactors dominated Project Censored's early years, starting in 1976 when it was the #6 *Censored* story of the year.

CHLAMYDIA NOW NATION'S MOST COMMON BACTERIAL SEXUAL INFECTION—With more than 4 million new cases annually, chlamydia has surpassed gonorrhea as the most common bacterial infection spread through sexual contact (*San Francisco Examiner*, 11/12/95). Chlamydia was the #20 *Censored* story of 1984 which warned that it was causing sterility in up to 100,000 women annually. Ironically, chlamydia can be cured by a single dose of antibiotics.

CUBAN EPIDEMIC FINALLY DISCOVERED BY U.S. NEWS MEDIA— On November 21, the *Los Angeles Times* reported a study, published in the *New England Journal of Medicine*, that announced the cause of a Cuban epidemic. The lead read: "It was the largest epidemic of its kind in history. From November 1991 through the summer of 1993, the bizarre neurological disorder struck more than 50,000 people in Cuba, frightening and mystifying the bereft island nation." It noted that most victims became partially blind. The cause: "Tens of thousands of Cubans were not getting quite enough to eat." The *L.A. Times* article reported that the study didn't mention the impact of the U.S. embargo on food supplies "chiefly because U.S. government researchers aren't allowed to criticize federal policy. The #15 *Censored* story of 1993 was titled "Thousands of Cubans Losing Their Sight Because of Malnutrition."

NATIVE AMERICAN SUICIDE RATE ATTRACTS MEDIA ATTENTION— The #20 *Censored* story of 1989, "The Indian Problem," tried to alert the nation to the oppression and exploitation of Native Americans. On November 26, wire services reported statistics that show American Indians commit suicide at a rate three times higher than the suicide rate for the general population of the U.S. and up to 10 times higher on some reservations. The deep despair that drives people to end their lives reportedly is often caused by poverty, unemployment, and alcoholism.

THE SKY IS FALLING! THE SKY IS FALLING!—The failure of the mass media to inform the public of the potential dangers of astropollution and space fall-out was the #22 Censored story of 1978. In a front page story on November 29, 1995, *USA Today* warned its readers that a 2,000 pound falling Chinese satellite, big enough to survive re-entry, may crash on a big city somewhere on earth in 1996.

U.S. TURNS TO PSYCHICS FOR HELP WITH GOVERNMENT SPYING—
On November 29, the Associated Press announced that the U.S. secretly used psychics in an unsuccessful attempt to hunt down Libyan leader Moammar Gadhafi, find plutonium in North Korea, and help drug enforcement agencies. The 20-year-old ESP spying program, code-named "Stargate," received $20 million from the military's secretive "black budget," the subject of the #7 *Censored* story in 1990, and the #10 story in 1992.

HAITIAN PARAMILITARY LEADER ON CIA PAYROLL—The #10 *Censored* story of 1993 revealed that some of Haiti's high military officials involved in the coup which ousted President Jean-Bertrand Aristide were on the CIA payroll. On December 3, *The New York Times* reported that Emmanuel "Toto" Constant, the former leader of Haiti's most feared right-wing paramilitary group, confirmed he was a paid agent of the CIA.

"ONE FLEW OVER THE CUCKOO'S NEST"—AGAIN!—The return of electroshock, the form of psychiatric therapy born in the age of lobotomies and made famous in "One Flew Over the Cuckoo's Nest," was the #24 *Censored* story of 1990. On December 6-7, *USA Today*, in a major two-part exposé, warned its readers that electroshock treatment is on the rise and that patients often aren't warned of the full danger of the treatment.

751 MILLION POUNDS OF EDIBLE FISH DUMPED OFF ALASKA—
The Alaska Department of Fish and Game reported that a record 751 million pounds of edible fish, enough for 50 million meals, was dumped by the fishing fleet off Alaska, according to the Associated Press on December 8. The #7 *Censored* story of 1994 revealed that the world's fishing fleets waste about 60 billion pounds of fish and seafood worldwide every year.

BIG BROTHER IS WATCHING YOU—The unpublicized threat to personal privacy in the electronic age was the subject of four *Censored* stories dating back to 1978 when the #15 story warned how the Medical Information Bureau collected, and shared, intimate details about the private lives of American citizens. *USA Today* addressed the same issue on October 9, as cited earlier, and again on December 19 when it asked its readers, "PRIVACY: Do You Have Any Left?," in a major front page story.

CENSORED

"O.J. Simpson, Whitewater, Michael Jackson,
Lyle and Erik Menendez, the Royal Family...
WHO THE HELL CARES?"
—The Humanist

CHAPTER 5

The Junk Food
News Stories of 1995

The flip side of the "best censored *news* stories" research project is the compilation of the "*junk food news* stories" of the year. This annual analysis was developed in 1984 in response to criticism from some editors that I wasn't exploring media censorship but rather I was just another frustrated academic criticizing editorial news judgment.

Editors and news directors said it was more a difference of opinion as to what information is important to publish or broadcast and not a case of censorship. They pointed out, quite rightly, that they have a finite amount of valuable time and space for the news and that it is their responsibility to determine which stories are the most critical ones for the public to know about and therefore most deserving of publication or broadcast.

This appeared to be a legitimate criticism, so I decided to review the stories that editors and news directors consider to be most important and worthy of filling their valuable time and space. It was in the course of this review that I found a journalistic phenomenon which I call "Junk Food News." The typical junk food news diet consists of sensationalized, personalized, and homogenized inconsequential trivia which is served up to the public on a daily basis. While it may not be nourishing for the public, it is cheap to produce and profitable for media owners.

No reader should be surprised to learn that the subject that easily outranked all others for the dubious "junk food news" honors in 1995 was O.J. Simpson. Simpson now becomes the only subject to be cited as the top "junk food news" story in more than one year.

Despite some critics who claim the media only give the public what it wants, the O.J. experience says more about the failure of the press than about the taste of the public. If indeed the news media reported only what they think the public wants, there would be no need for professional journalists—or the First Amendment, for that matter.

Have you noticed that the media say they give the public what it wants while the public says it doesn't want what it's getting from the media? *The Quill* (November/December 1995) reported a national poll by Hearst Broadcasting that asked the public what it would like to hear *less* about on news programs. O.J. Simpson was the runaway "winner" with 62 percent while Michael Jackson, President Bill Clinton, and Newt Gingrich tied for second.

USA Today columnist Susan Estrich acknowledged (4/6/95) the media's near-sycophantic demeanor toward sensationalized celebrities when she described how journalists performed at the Radio and Television Correspondents' dinner in Washington in early 1995. They paid more attention to what Kato Kaelin had to say than to President Clinton and they stood six deep in line to have their photographs taken with Kaelin. Also, when Newt Gingrich went on MTV in July, it was the reporters who wanted to discuss gossip while the young people in the audience wanted to talk about real issues.

The O.J. media orgy finally climaxed on Tuesday, October 3, with the announcement of the verdict. The televised verdict drew a combined 91

percent share of households watching TV on the networks and cable stations.

And when it all ended in October, media apologists rushed in to defend the unprecedented coverage by pointing out how much the public learned about the judicial system, spousal abuse, racism, and rogue cops. Nonetheless, it's probably best there will be no test on these subjects.

On the other hand, *San Francisco Examiner* columnist Robert Scheer pointed out (10/4/95) that a nation glued to O.J. TV missed out learning about a number of other subjects, including the White House signing of the Mideast peace accord which was blacked out on TV; or the questionable need for a post-Cold War military budget of $243 billion—$9 billion more than the Pentagon asked for; or that federal programs concerned with justice and race were being systematically destroyed in Washington.

In analyzing how the press covered O.J. this year, longtime media critic and *Censored* judge Ben Bagdikian found the news media "guilty in the first degree of compounding its pretrial sins." Bagdikian encouraged the media "to do what it insists is good journalism—to assign emphasis in the daily news on the basis of how important the subjects are to the community and country. Doing that is at least as valid as the way our news media assigned major daily importance to every detail, and some of the fantasies, of the O.J. trial."

In fear of becoming part of the problem, we'll close the book on O.J. by hoping that as the media recover from their O.J. hangover, they will realize how they failed to fulfill their responsibilities as a watchdog of society for much of 1994 and 1995. Many of the news stories, issues, and events preempted by O.J. during those years have been lost, or, at the least, are no longer as timely.

ANNIVERSARY JUNK FOOD NEWS

Nineteen-ninety-five also was distinguished as an anniversary news year. There were a number of significant, as well as insignificant, historic events which encouraged the media to devote considerable time and space to reminiscing about the past. "Anniversary news," like most junk food news, is an easy and profitable way to fill pages or newscasts when compared to hard news. It's also the kind of news that doesn't tend to rock the boat.

Following are just some of the many anniversary events that attracted the news media's spotlight in 1995:

> FIRST U.S. PIZZERIA OPENED (100TH ANNIVERSARY)
> THE WIRELESS TELEGRAPH (100)
> WOMEN'S SUFFRAGE (75)
> BIRTH OF *THE NEW YORKER* (70)
> SOCIAL SECURITY (60)
> END OF WORLD WAR II (50)
> UNITED NATIONS (50)
> MEDICARE/MEDICAID (30)
> "HOW TO STUFF A WILD BIKINI" (30)
> THE FIRST EARTH DAY (25)
> "DOONESBURY" DEBUT (25)
> MEETING OF RICHARD NIXON AND ELVIS PRESLEY (25)
> 1ST CONSUMER VCR (20)
> NANCY KERRIGAN/TONYA HARDING FRACAS (1)
> CONGRESSIONAL REPUBLICAN REVOLUTION (1)
> NORTHRIDGE CALIFORNIA EARTHQUAKE (1)

Junk food news stories normally focus on individuals or issues that are hyped out of proportion to their actual significance by the news media. However, occasionally a commercial product is so widely advertised and promoted that it generates widespread editorial coverage. Such was the case with Windows 95 in 1995.

The official launch of Windows 95, as reported by the *Wall Street Journal* (8/26/95), was a media circus rivaling a political convention as 500 reporters and dozens of TV crews descended on the Microsoft Corporation in Redmond, Washington. The *Journal* article also pointed out that marketing historians had "a hard time coming up with comparisons to this takeoff: the advent of the 1927 Model A or the 1960s Mustang in cars, perhaps; New Coke a decade ago; the first Super Bowl, or maybe the premiere of 'Gone With the Wind.'"

It is worth noting that the wizards of Madison Avenue were able to transform what was essentially a non-event—a software upgrade—into a major story that nearly challenged O.J.'s dominance of the news media in 1995.

The only two products able to achieve top junk food news status since this effort started were Clara Peller's "Where's the beef?" slogan in 1984 and Coca Cola's "new old classic Cherry Coke" in 1985.

THE TOP 10 JUNK FOOD NEWS STORIES OF 1995

To provide a record of Junk Food News stories, at the end of each year, I survey members of the national Organization of News Ombudsmen to solicit their selections for the most over-reported, least deserving news stories of the year.

Following are the top ten Junk Food News stories of 1995 as cited by the news ombudsmen. As you read them, compare how much you heard about them last year with how much you heard about the top ten *Censored* stories cited in Chapter 2.

1. O.J. SIMPSON
2. HUGH GRANT
3. KATO KAELIN
4. MIKE TYSON
5. WINDOWS 95
6. MICHAEL JACKSON
7. JERRY GARCIA
8. COLIN POWELL
9. MICKEY MANTLE
10. SHANNON FAULKNER

Rounding out the top 25 JFN nominations of 1995 were Neon Deion, "Showgirls," Miss America Swimsuit Contest, JFK Jr.'s *George*, "Waterworld," Bob Packwood, Baseball Strike, Susan Smith, Connie Chung, Christopher Reeve, Million Man March, Leno & Letterman, Cindy Crawford & Richard Gere, Jesse James, and the Unabomber .

TOP-RANKED JUNK FOOD NEWS STORIES OF THE PAST:

1984 Clara Peller's "Where's the beef?"
1985 Coca-Cola's new old classic Cherry Coke
1986 Clint Eastwood's campaign for mayor of Carmel
1987 The tribulations of Jim and Tammy Faye
1988 The trapped whales of Alaska
1989 Zsa Zsa Gabor's cop-slapping trial
1990 The marital woes of Donald and Ivana Trump
1991 The William Kennedy Smith rape trial
1992 Dan Quayle's misspelling of potato
1993 Amy Fisher & Joey Buttafuoco
1994 O.J. Simpson

COMMENTS BY NEWS OMBUDSMEN

Following are explanations suggested by some of the news ombudsmen who participated in the selection of the top 1995 Junk Food News subjects as to why the media tend to sensationalize such stories as those cited above:

"We're convinced this is what the public wants—that big TV ratings translate to high newspaper readership. And it is a break from the solemnity and murkiness of politics and other government shenanigans."—Lynn Feigenbaum, The *Virginian-Pilot*, Norfolk, Virginia.

"Because the editors think that their rivals will do those stories and due to the fact as well that all of them think that most people are interested in those stories."—Roger Jimenez, *La Vanguardia*, Barcelona, Spain.

"Because they have to do with much more money, power and sex than journalists are used to."—Marcelo Leite, *Folha De S. Paulo*, Sao Paulo, Brazil.

"Because the media have become peeping toms, reporting to the outside world all the misdeeds of the rich, the powerful, the tasteless, and the crooks. If public taste is to be raised to a higher level, the media have to draw lines about what is news and what is garbage."—Jean Otto, *Rocky Mountain News*, Denver, Colorado.

"The media think people are more interested in celebrities than news. It's pandering to the worst instincts in people."—Elissa Papirno, *Hartford Courant*, Hartford, Connecticut.

"I fear most of us are gluttons when it comes to 'Junk Food.' We also fear we may lose readers if we don't cater to this gluttony."—Phil Record, *Star-Telegram*, Ft. Worth, Texas.

"Surveys, ratings and polls show these are the kinds of stories a majority of people are reading, viewing or listening to—although many of these same viewers/readers are loathe to admit it. The overkill comes as a result of one national news source being afraid it will get 'scooped' or 'upstaged' by another."—Joe Sheibley, *The News-Sentinel*, Fort Wayne, Indiana.

"In many or most cases, a valid news story is seized upon and, often through 'pack' competition, turned into a looking-glass nightmare of sex, sensation, 'experts' who know no more than I do, and so on. *Most* days, for example, the Simpson trial was worth one paragraph on page 40 of your local paper. If that."—Emerson Stone, "News Practices" Columnist, *The Communicator Magazine*, Greenwich, Connecticut.

"'Junk food news' sells papers, airtime, and sadly, it's what many people want."—Gayle Williams, Gannett Suburban Newspapers, White Plains, New York.

AMERICA NEEDS MORE NEWS OMBUDSMEN

The ombudsmen, who annually name the top Junk Food News stories of the year for Project Censored, are members of one of the most select groups in America—the Organization of News Ombudsmen (ONO). It's their responsibility to make the news media more accountable to the public. And yet, while there are some 1,650 daily newspapers in America, there were only 35 official U.S. ombudsmen cited as ONO members in 1995, three less than the previous year.

Following is an explanation of why America needs far more ombudsmen than it has today. It was written by Bob Caldwell, the former public editor, or ombudsman, for *The Oregonian* in Portland, Oregon, and published November 12, 1995. It was Caldwell's last ombudsman column as he was named the *Oregonian*'s new editorial page editor. It is reprinted with his permission.

"MORE MEDIA OUTLETS NEED OMBUDSMEN"

"Nearly two years ago, *The Oregonian* started down a road that few news-papers travel and more should.

"*The Oregonian* created a news ombudsman's post, to explain how the paper works and to address reader complaints, comments and questions about news coverage.

"In general, news organizations are not prone to public self-criticism. That is illustrated by the fact that, according to the Organization of News

Ombudsmen, only 35 news organizations in the United States have ombudsmen.

"There are more than 1,500 daily newspapers in the country, at least three TV stations in most big cities and enough radio stations to reach, roughly, to Jupiter if you stacked them up.

"If you consider that most of them print or broadcast news in some form, then 35 ombudsmen is something less than peanuts.

"When asked about this embarrassment, many publishers, editors, station managers and news directors will offer excuses.

"A common one is that good editors and newsroom managers serve as their own ombudsmen. These people are in the news business, after all, and they're trained listeners, alert and empathetic. I admit that, in 25 years of journalism, I've used some version of that line myself once or twice.

"In reality, working newspeople take criticism the way cats take baths—unwillingly and with a lot of biting and scratching.

"This is no particular criticism of newspeople as human beings, although there is plenty of that around, too. Nobody likes having short-comings pointed out, and the pace of the newsroom does not lend itself to reflection.

"Those simply are facts. But they are facts that have a bearing on another subject—the distrust of the press that people have developed.

"There is a tendency in this business to pass off that distrust as part of a general malaise that afflicts all of the institutions of modern society. That may be true. But it also may be true that the distrust of other institutions in society is connected to distrust of the news media. It is difficult for people to trust a message when they do not trust the messenger.

"If I have concluded anything in the 22 months that I've been public editor of *The Oregonian*, it is that we—meaning this newspaper and the industry in general—are our own worst enemy in this regard.

"Not many people think the press is involved in some sort of conspiracy against the interests of the republic, but not many think it is the dispassionate, disinterested purveyor of reliable information that it should be.

"In March, for example, the Times Mirror Center for The People & The Press said four of five political and business leaders it surveyed agreed with the statement that 'the distinction between reporting and commentary has seriously eroded' in the news media. More surprisingly, 53 percent of the national reporters and editors surveyed and 44 percent of their local counterparts agreed.

"That perception, which I share, cuts more deeply into the credibility of the press than any other single thing.

"That may seem strange coming from someone whose next job will be to engage in commentary, but the key word in that survey question is 'distinction.' Good newspapers ought to offer good, in-depth coverage and good, provocative commentary but should keep the two things separate.

"If I could repeat the 22 months as ombudsman, I would try to approach that topic with greater clarity and in greater depth.

"This is a swan-song column, but it does not exactly sound a final note. If there is another key to building trust between readers and the newspaper, it is to establish a dialogue.

"During the past two years, readers have kept up their end of the dialogue, offering thousands of telephone calls—150 to 200 a week—and hundreds of letters, faxes and electronic-mail messages. They have offered complaints and criticism of everything from the paper's coverage of presidential politics to its inability to get the temperature numbers to match up on the weather page. Occasionally, they offered praise.

"(*Oregonian*) Editor Sandra M. Rowe plans to appoint a new public editor, probably after the first of the year, to keep the conversation going."

The limited number of ombudsmen in the United States, as pointed out by Bob Caldwell, is a sad commentary on the willingness of the news media to seek and address criticism. An ombudsman can be one of the most productive means of access to a newspaper available to readers. Yet there are only 35 of them in the United States! You could help bring about some change in media coverage by encouraging your local media to appoint an ombudsman. In writing your local editor, you might cite some of the reasons noted above or given in the "junk food news" chapter, "What Is An Ombudsman?," by Art Nauman, ombudsman for the *Sacramento Bee*, in the 1995 *Censored* Yearbook.

Nauman pointed out one primary reason for having an ombudsman: "To help make the paper more accountable to its readers. After all, newspapers enjoy protections and privileges given by the people—in the Constitution—to no other business enterprise. To say it another way, a newspaper is a major social and economic force in its community that potentially affects how people think and act. It should be willing to expose and critique its news-gathering process in the same way it continually demands that other community institutions account for themselves."

Roger Simms, chair of journalism at Murdoch University in Australia, spent several months in the U.S. in 1995 researching the role of ombudsmen, and offered six reasons a newspaper should have one: 1. Regular monitoring of community attitudes towards a newspaper; 2. Public relations function—lifting a paper's standing in the community; 3. Heading off potential legal trouble; 4. Impact on staff morale—a feeling among staff that the paper cares about its readers and that the ombudsman can help handle complaints; 5. Another column with the potential to draw new readers; 6. An answer to critics who say a paper is self-serving and insensitive to public criticism.

Given the social and political malaise of the nation and the failure of the press to report the symptoms, we need a free and aggressive press in American now more than ever before. More news ombudsmen could be an effective way to wake up some sleeping watchdogs.

CENSORED

"What experience and history teach is this—
that people and governments
never have learned anything from history,
or acted on principles deduced from it."
—Georg Wilhelm Friedrich Hegel

CHAPTER 6

An Eclectic Chronology of Censorship from 605 B.C. to 1995

The following eclectic chronology culls information and events from a variety of sources, both traditional and nontraditional.

A thorough reading of this chronology should make it clear that censorship is not merely an occasional social aberration, but rather a threat that has been with us from the earliest recorded times.

A thorough reading also should persuade you that censorship historically has been a tool of a powerful elite which attempts to control society through the manipulation of thought, speech, and all other forms of expression. There are, to my knowledge, very few examples, if any, where the poor or powerless are able to use censorship as a tool to influence decisions affecting themselves, let alone a wealthy and powerful elite.

In addition, this chronology should provide you with insights into how we as a society have supported rules, regulations, leaders and institutions that have fostered censorship.

Finally, I hope the following persuades you that freedom of expression is never permanently secured; it must be fought for and won each day. Project Censored is but one of many combatants who have fought against censorship. While the battle is never-ending, it is truly worthy.

A CENSORED CHRONOLOGY

605 B.C. Perhaps the earliest recorded case of censorship occurred when Jehoiakim, the king of Judah, burned Jeremiah's book of prophecies. This prescient event, found in the Bible (Jeremiah 36, 1-32), may also be the earliest example of self-censorship since Jeremiah had written the book at Jehoiakim's bidding.

500 B.C. While we revere the Greeks for their respect for freedom of speech, censorship was not unknown. In the fifth century B.C., poets, philosophers, musicians, authors, and others were subject to bans, persecution, and exile.

443 B.C. Most dictionaries trace censorship back to ancient Rome when two magistrates, called "censors," were appointed to conduct an annual census to register citizens and to assess their property for taxation and contract purposes. The censors also were authorized to censure and penalize moral offenders thought to be guilty of vice and immorality by removing their voting rights and tribe membership. This form of censorship was discontinued in 22 B.C. when emperors took over the censorial powers.

399 B.C. The ultimate form of censorship is death, and Socrates—one of the first Greek philosophers to express a rational defense of freedom of speech— became an early victim of it. After he was tried and convicted of impiety and of corrupting youth, Socrates was put to death. Ironically, his best-known pupil, Plato, outlined the first comprehensive system of censorship, particularly of the arts. In *The Republic*, Book II, Plato warned against allowing children to hear any "casual" tales by "casual" persons and called for the establishment of a censorship system for writers of fiction.

221 B.C. About two centuries after the appointment of censors in Rome, the Chinese launched their own office of censorship under the Ch'in dynasty (221-206 B.C.) Originally designed to critique the emperor's performance, the office of censor soon was used by the emperor to investigate and punish official corruption. The institution eventually became a huge bureaucracy that effectively ended with the overthrow of the Ch'ing dynasty in 1911.

213 B.C. One of China's most famous monarchs, Tsin Chi Hwangti, built the Great Wall of China (214-204 B.C.) He also exercised a most impressive act of censorship in 213 B.C. by ordering all books in China destroyed, except those concerning science, medicine, and agriculture. In addition, he executed 500 scholars and banished thousands of others.

48 B.C. The famous Alexandrian Library was burned on orders from Julius Caesar and some 700,000 rolls of manuscripts were lost forever. An effort was made to rebuild it, and this later library, known as the "Daughter Library," was destroyed in A.D. 389 by an edict of the Emperor Theodosius.

A.D. 58 In Acts 19:19 of the Bible, the Apostle Paul praised converts who burned books (worth 50,000 pieces of silver) in the purifying fires of orthodoxy, providing modern-day Christian censors with scriptural authorization for their book burning.

A.D. 95 Following-up on Paul's advice, the "Apostolic Constitutions," written by St. Clement of Rome, warned Christians that the Scriptures provided everything a true believer needed to read.

A.D. 499 Under Pope Gelasius, the concept of the Papal Index, a list of books unsuitable for Roman Catholics, first appeared. It was formalized in 1564 and still exists to this day.

1215 On June 15, King John of England, under pressure from English barons, sealed the Magna Carta at Runnymede, guaranteeing certain civil and political liberties to the English people.

1231 The Inquisition, an open season for censors, was launched by the Roman Catholic Church as a formal way of discovering heresy and punishing heretics. Thousands of scriptures were inspected, reviewed, and often destroyed by the Inquisitors—self-described defenders of the Truth of the Sacred Text—from 1231 to 1596. For almost four centuries, book burners also were empowered to burn authors at the stake.

1450 Johann Gutenberg invented the printing press, with its movable type, thereby providing the technological breakthrough for the intellectual revolution of the Renaissance and its challenge to the institution of censorship. It also threatened the tight control secular and religious leaders exercised over the production and distribution of information.

1484 The first legal guarantee of press freedom may be traced back to early 1484 during the brief reign of King Richard III of England. Found among a number of scrolls which recorded the acts and statutes approved during his reign was a statement asserting the media were, and should be, excluded from ordinary commercial regulation, according to Nicholas Russell, associate professor of the School of Journalism and Communications at the University of Regina, Saskatchewan.

1501 In an effort to protect the Church of Rome against heresy, Pope Alexander VI issued an edict banning the printing of books. Not unlike their colleagues in the Roman Catholic Church, leaders of the Protestant Reformation (including John Knox, Martin Luther, and John Calvin) persecuted heretics and papists. In England, Henry VIII burned copies of William Tyndale's

New Testament and had Thomas More beheaded for refusing to acknowledge the king's power over religion. In 1529, Henry VIII issued an official list of banned books, some 30 years before the widely known Roman Catholic Index was institutionalized. By 1586, prior restraint had run rampant in England where all books had to be read and approved by the Archbishop of Canterbury or the Bishop of London prior to publication.

1512 Nicolaus Copernicus published "Commentarious," his hypothesis on the revolutions of the heavenly bodies. It stated the earth was not the center of the universe but revolved around the sun. The theory, which contradicted the geocentric theory favored by the Catholic church, was condemned and placed on the Papal Index in 1616.

1517 Protesting papal censorship, the sale of indulgences, and other papal expedients, Martin Luther, an ordained priest, posted his 95 theses on the door of the Palast Church in Wittenberg, laying the foundations for the German Reformation and the Lutheran Church. Luther later was one of the prohibited authors cited in an abortive early version (1559) of the *Index of Prohibited Books*, formally authorized and published by the Roman Catholic Church in 1564.

1541 Concerned about nude figures in Michelangelo's fresco, "The Last Judgment," in the Sistine Chapel, Pope Paul IV ordered artists to paint over the more provocative parts to protect the innocent. During a major four-year restoration that was completed in 1993, Vatican authorities decided not to remove the draperies or "breeches" painted on to the Sistine nudes 452 years earlier. Gianluigi Colalucci, head of the Vatican museum's restoration project, explained, "The decision we took is of a historic nature, not an aesthetic one; we have chosen to respect the acts of the Council of Trent." It now appears the world will never again see the fresco exactly as Michelangelo painted it.

1564 After abortive attempts dating back more than a thousand years, the papacy successfully issued the formal *Index Librorum Prohibitorum* (Index of Prohibited Books) as authorized by the Council of Trent. Approximately 500 pages in length, it listed books and authors condemned by the Roman Catholic Church. While it survived until 1774 in France and 1834 in Spain, the Index (as it is known colloquially) remains in force for Roman Catholics up to present day. It is the longest-running, and possibly most effective, example of censorship in world history.

1633 Galileo Galilei was forced by the Inquisition to renounce and reject *Dialago*, published in 1632, which supported the theories of Copernicus concerning the revolutions of the planet. *Dialago* was added to the infamous Index where it remained until 1822.

1643 The British Parliament reintroduced the Licensing Act, ending a brief respite from censorship which occurred in 1640 with the abolishment of the Court of Star Chamber. It was this renewal of book licensing that instigated John Milton's eloquent plea for free speech a year later.

1644 *Areopagitica; a Speech of Mr. John Milton For the Liberty of Unlicenc'd Printing, To the Parlament of England*, published in 1644, is considered to be the English-speaking world's first and most powerful statement urging freedom of expression. Some of its better-known excerpts include:

> *Who kills a man kills a reasonable creature, God's image; but he who destroys a good book, kills reason itself. Give me the liberty to know, to utter, and to argue freely according to conscience, above all liberties. Though all the winds of doctrine were let loose to play upon the earth, so Truth be in the field, we do injuriously, by licensing and prohibiting to misdoubt her strength. Let her and Falsehood grapple; whoever knew Truth put to the worse in a free and open encounter?*

While Milton's eloquent statement is rightfully credited with being the genesis of press freedom in America, his treatise actually dealt with the right to license, or prior restraint, not with post-publication censorship. The latter finally was addressed by the First Amendment to the Constitution of the United States in 1791.

1690 A small, three-page newspaper, measuring just six by nine-and-one-half inches, titled "Numb. 1, PUBLICK OCCURRENCES Both FOREIGN and DOMESTICK, Boston, Thursday Sept. 25th, 1690," is generally agreed to be the first newspaper published in America. There was no "Numb. 2" because the governor and council issued a statement four days after its publication declaring their "High resentment and Disallowance of said Pamphlet, and order that the same be Suppressed and called in; strictly forbidding any person or persons for the future to Set forth any thing in Print without License first obtained." They found that the editor, Benjamin Harris, had printed "Reflections of a very high nature: As also sundry doubtful and uncertain Reports." While this was an inauspicious beginning for a free press in the New World, there remain many reflections of a very high nature that continue to be subject to censorship today.

1695 Because of increasing resistance, partially generated by Milton's *Areopagitica*, the Licensing Act in England was not renewed in 1695, a date which has come to signify the establishment of freedom of the press in England. However, this did not mark the end of censorship in that country. Prior censorship, through licensing, was replaced with punitive (or post-publication) censorship, a form that, though preferable to prior censorship, is still found in most societies to this day. This is not to say that prior censorship is no longer attempted: consider the case of *The Progressive* magazine, the target of the first case of press prior restraint in America (*U.S. v. Progressive*, 1979). Again, in 1988, the U.S. Supreme Court's Hazelwood decision gave school administrators prior restraint control over student newspapers.

1735 The John Peter Zenger case provided a classic example of an attempt at punitive, or post-publication, censorship in America; but it established truth as a defense against charges of libel. Zenger was arrested and charged with seditious libel for criticizing New York Governor William Cosby in his *New York Weekly Journal*. At the age of 80, Andrew Hamilton, one of the leading attorneys in the colonies, took on the case pro bono, considering the issue to be critical to the future of liberty. Putting Milton's *Areopagitica* at the core of the defense, Hamilton won the case with the presumption that truth could not be libelous. The case is often referred to as the birth of freedom of the press in America.

1764 *The Hartford* (Connecticut) *Courant*, the oldest continuously published newspaper in the United States, was founded on October 29. The oldest U.S. daily newspaper, the *New York Post*, was founded in 1801.

1765 The British Stamp Act of 1765 taxed all printed materials circulated in the colonies; the Taunted Acts of 1766 placed duties on American imports of glass, lead, paint, tea, and paper. Together these documents outraged colonial journalists and encouraged press protests until all duties, except those on tea, were removed in 1770. The famed Boston Tea Party (planned at the home of an editor of the *Boston Gazette*) followed in 1773. Then, in rapid succession, the British reacted with the Intolerable Acts of 1774, the First Continental Congress met that same year, and the first shot of the War of Independence was fired in 1775.

1776 In Philadelphia, on July 4, the Declaration of Independence was signed by representatives from the thirteen states of America. It opened with these words: "When in the Course of human events it becomes necessary for one people to dissolve the political bonds which have connected them with another...;" and it continued, "We hold these truths to be self-evident, that all men are created equal, that they are endowed by their Creator with certain unalienable Rights, that among these are Life, Liberty and the pursuit of Happiness..." These eloquent words, with their emphasis on liberty and equality, paved the way for a free society granting free speech and a free press.

1787 The Constitution of the United States was drafted in 1787, ratified in 1788, and went into effect on the first Wednesday of March 1789, thereby formally establishing the United States of America.

1789 The French Revolution specifically enshrined the freedoms of "speech, thought, and expression" in Clause 11 of its Declaration of the Rights of Man.

1791 On December 15, the first ten amendments, known collectively as the Bill of Rights, were added to the Constitution. These provisions established a formal contractual agreement between the government and its citizens, encompassing specific concerns not addressed in the Constitution. Foremost among these is Article I, dealing with the freedoms of religion, speech, the press, and the right of petition: "Congress shall make no law respecting an establishment of religion, or prohibiting the free exercise thereof; or abridging the freedom of speech, or of the press; or the right of the people peaceably to assemble, and to petition the Government for a redress of grievances." What might be most remarkable about this most extraordinary document is not what it says but what it does not say. There are no restrictions, contingencies, exclusions, or other provisos dealing with heresy, blasphemy, pornography, obscenity, defamation, national security, sedition, public morals, racism, sexism, libel, slander, political correctness, or a host of other social concerns that have threatened to dilute the strength of the First Amendment for more than 200 years.

1798 The ink was barely dry on the Bill of Rights when Congress enacted the Alien and Sedition Acts of 1798. The legislation would punish anyone who spoke, wrote, or published "Any false scandalous and malicious (speech) against the government of the United States" or used speech that would bring the President or Congress "into contempt or disrepute." Although the Acts expired in 1801, it wasn't until 1964 that the Supreme Court declared them "inconsistent with the First Amendment."

1802 The English Society for the Suppression of Vice was launched in England, paving the way for similar groups in the United States later in the 19th century.

1818 Dr. Thomas Bowdler, an early British version of Jerry Falwell, was an unsuccessful physician consumed with cleansing the language of any indelicate words or phrases. Specifically, he wanted to eliminate from Shakespeare "whatever is unfit to be read aloud by a gentleman in the company of ladies." In 1818, in London, he published his "Family Shakespeare" which was also widely distributed in the United States. The expurgated version of Shakespeare led to the term "bowdlerized," referring to this form of censorship.

1841 Ralph Waldo Emerson published his famed essay, "Self-Reliance." In this tribute to free expression, he wrote, "The virtue in most request is conformity. Self-reliance is its aversion. ... Whoso would be a man must be a non-conformist. ... A foolish consistency is the hobgoblin of little minds, adored by little statesmen and philosophers and divines."

1842 At the age of 24, Karl Marx began his career as a working journalist with an essay titled, "Remarks on the Latest Prussian Censorship Instruction." Censored by German authorities, it was published a year later by a German-exile press in Switzerland. Marx went on to decry censorship for protecting the interests of the elite and perpetuating the domination of the powerless by the powerful. Ironically, communist societies subsequently used censorship to protect the interests of the elite and to dominate the powerless. Marx himself went on to become one of the most censored authors of modern times, particularly, of course, in capitalist societies.

1842 While Marx was being censored in Germany, the U.S. Congress passed the Tariff Law of 1842, prohibiting "all indecent and obscene prints, paintings, lithographs, engravings, and transparencies" from being imported. In 1857, the law was expanded to include images, figures, and photographs, in order to prevent the importation of Greek statues of "questionable" taste into the U.S.

1856 French novelist Gustave Flaubert was charged with immorality and lasciviousness for publishing *Madame Bovary*. When Flaubert was acquitted, the book, which otherwise might have reached a small audience, became an instant bestseller. The first American edition was published in 1896.

1857 In England, the Obscene Publications Act of 1857 led to an early definition of obscenity. It was also known as the Campbell Act, named for its proponent, the Lord Chief Justice. To assure passage of his bill, Campbell defined an obscene work as one written for the single purpose of corrupting the morals of youth and designed to shock the sense of decency in any well-regulated mind.

1859 In his famous essay, "On Liberty," John Stuart Mill, who believed every man is competent to choose what he will read or hear, recorded his thesis on the expression of thought: "Who can compute what the world loses in the multitude of promising intellects combined with timid characters, who dare not follow out any bold, vigorous, independent train of thought, lest it should land them in something which would admit of being considered irreligious or immoral? ... No one can be a great thinker who does not recognize that as a thinker it is his first duty to follow his intellect to whatever conclusions it may lead. ... There is always hope when people are forced to listen to both sides. It is when they attend only one that errors harden into prejudices and truth itself ceases to have the effect of truth, by being exaggerated into falsehood."

1861 During the Civil War, the U.S. War Department warned journalists against providing any military information that would aid the enemy. The order was generally disregarded, though, leading to casualties. However, more responsible correspondents and editors proved able to report on the war while still concealing information of value to the enemy. In the North, the greatest censorship came from angry mobs who attempted to destroy newspapers with which they disagreed.

1861 William Makepeace Thackeray, founder and editor of *The Cornhill Magazine*, rejected Elizabeth Barrett Browning's poem, "Lord Walter's wife," as one of many poems and stories he thought to be indecent or indelicate.

1873 The New England Watch and Ward Society and the New York Society for the Suppression of Vice were founded for the purpose of pressuring publishers, editors, and news agents into rejecting controversial writers.

1873 Anthony Comstock was America's answer to England's Thomas Bowdler. Comstock, a religious fanatic whose motto was "Morals, Not Art or Literature," joined with the YMCA to found the New York Society for the Suppression of Vice. As head of this organization, he was given a monopoly by New York to eliminate vice in the state. He also succeeded in getting Congress to pass what was known as The Comstock Act of 1873, which consolidated various statutes and regulations dealing with "obscene, lewd, and lascivious" publications and specifically barred birth-control material from the mail.

Comstock was extraordinarily successful in "fighting vice." In 1874, he reported that in a two-year period, his society had seized 130,000 pounds of bound books along with 60,300 "articles made of rubber for immoral purposes." When he retired in 1915, he estimated that he had destroyed over 160 tons of "obscene" literature.

One of his great successes was the suppression of Paul Chabas' "September Morn," a romantic painting of a young nude girl bathing on the shore of a lake. The censored painting led to a controversy over the distinction between "nude" and "naked" that persisted for nearly 120 years. Finally, in 1992, Anne-Imelda Radice, acting head of the National Endowment for the Arts in the United States, announced her personal ability to differentiate between "nude" and "naked." She subsequently left the Foundation without revealing her exceptional insight.

1885 The board of trustees of the Concord Public Library in New Hampshire censored a book which "deals with a series of adventures of a very low grade of morality; it is couched in the language of a rough dialect, and all through its pages there is a systematic use of bad grammar. ... The book is flippant and irreverent. ... It is trash of the veriest sort." Mark Twain, the author of this dangerous book, *The Adventures of Huckleberry Finn*, responded by saying, "That will sell 25,000 copies for us, sure."

1896 A simple kiss in a play, "The Widow Jones," when seen magnified to a larger than life scale on a screen in the May Irwin-John C. Rice film "Kiss," resulted in the first known attempt at film censorship.

1900 The turn of the century marked the Golden Age of Muckraking—a brief, glowing uncensored moment in history when journalists exposed the ills of society, publishers provided the soapbox, people reacted with indignation, and politicians responded with corrective legislation. The first two decades of the 20th century were distinguished by the clamorous, sometimes sensationalized, efforts of investigative writers like Rheta Child Doss, Finley Peter Dunne, Frank Norris, Upton Sinclair, Lincoln Steffens, and Ida Tarbell. Their investigative style of journalism intrigued readers, exposed the widespread corporate and political corruption of the times, and paved the way for many of the social reforms that followed.

While President Theodore Roosevelt applied the term "muckrakers" to journalists in a pejorative manner, today it is considered a mark of distinction among some reporters and authors such as Jessica Mitford. Unfortunately, except for the contributions of a few notable journalists, like Drew Pearson, George Seldes, and I.F. Stone, contemporary America has not enjoyed a comparable period of socially aware, concerned, and effective journalism.

1909 Appearing before the Select Committee of both Houses of Parliament, which was considering censoring stage plays in 1909, George Bernard Shaw opened his testimony by citing his qualifications as a witness: "I am by profession a playwright...I am not an ordinary playwright in general practice. I am a specialist in immoral and heretical plays. My reputation has been gained by my persistent struggle to force the public to reconsider its morals. ... I object to censorship not merely because the existing form of it grievously injures and hinders me individually, but on public grounds." The statement, titled "The Necessity of Immoral Plays," was rejected by the Committee. Shaw subsequently published it as part of the preface to *The Shewing-Up of Blanco Posnet*. Shaw also pointed out, in *The Rejected Statement*, Part I, that "Assassination is the extreme form of censorship."

1911 From 1911 to 1926, the Hearst media empire used its various propaganda techniques to persuade the U.S. to declare war against Mexico. The public would have had a better understanding of Hearst's clamorous propaganda if it had known that his real motivation was to protect his family's land-holding of some 2500 square miles in Mexico against possible expropriation.

Apparently impressed by Hearst's endeavors, Colonel Robert Rutherford McCormick, owner of the *Chicago Tribune*, sent reporter George Seldes to Mexico in 1927 to cover the "coming war" with the United States. Seldes never did find a "war," but he did write a series of ten columns on the situation in Mexico. The first five echoed the official State Department line, supporting American business interests; the second five reported the other side of the issue which Seldes had observed or verified himself. Despite promises to publish all ten columns, the *Tribune* ran only the first five; disgusted with this obvious act of censorship, Seldes quit the *Tribune*.

1912 The first radio-licensing law was passed by Congress and signed by William Howard Taft. It authorized the Secretary of Commerce and Labor to assign wavelengths, time limits, and broadcast licenses. The only control at the time was a loose form of self-censorship by the stations whose taboos included lewd jokes and any discussion of birth control.

H.V. Kaltenborn, who lectured on current events over WEAF in New York became one of the first broadcasters to become embroiled in a controversy over the content of a radio talk. Kaltenborn had criticized Secretary of State Charles Evans Hughes regarding the way he had dealt with the Russians.

This led to a request from Washington, through the American Telephone and Telegraph Company, which leased the telephone lines to WEAF, that Kaltenborn be taken off the air. Recognizing the threat to its own best interests, WEAF acquiesced, and Kaltenborn left the station. AT&T saw nothing wrong with its actions; in fact, it acknowledged that it had "constant and complete" cooperation with governmental agencies and had indulged in censorship to maintain this cooperative relationship. The government's first attempt at electronic censorship was a resounding success.

Undaunted by the threat of censorship, radio expanded rapidly; by 1927 there were 733 stations and considerable interference on the broadcast bands. The near-chaotic situation ended with the passage of the Federal Radio Act of 1927, establishing the Federal Radio Commission (FRC). The Federal Communications Commission (FCC) was later established with passage of the Federal Communications Act of 1934.

1914 *The Woman Rebel*, a feminist newspaper edited by Margaret Sanger, advocated the practice of birth control. After five issues, it was stopped by the U.S. Post Office, which had the authority to censor the press at the time.

1917 The National Civil Liberties Bureau was founded and renamed the American Civil Liberties Union (ACLU) in 1920. The organization was created to deal with civil liberties problems arising out of World War I, including the Espionage and Sedition Acts, conscientious objectors, and political prisoners. It gained national recognition in the mid-1920s by defending the accused individuals in the Scopes trial, the Sweet case, and the Sacco-Vanzetti case. In 1988, the ACLU attracted widespread national attention when presidential candidate George Bush resorted to red-baiting by referring derisively to "card-carrying members" of the ACLU.

1917 World War I kept Congress busy churning out legislation designed to prevent any conceivable sign or sound of disloyalty from occurring. First, the Espionage Act of June 15 provided heavy fines and imprisonment for anyone encouraging disloyalty or obstructing recruitment; in practice, it made it easier to jail Wobblies, communist sympathizers, and radicals. Next, on October 6, came the Trading-with-the-Enemy Act, which called for the censorship of all messages sent abroad and required domestic media containing articles in a foreign language to file sworn translations with local postmasters. The travel ban aspect of the act was imposed against Cuba in 1962 by President John F. Kennedy; was eased by President Jimmy Carter in 1977; was re-imposed in 1982 by President Ronald Reagan; and was sustained by presidents George Bush and Bill Clinton.

1918 Following on the heels of the two paranoia-induced decrees cited above came the Sedition Act of May 16. This made it unlawful to "utter, print, write, or publish any disloyal, profane, scurrilous, or abusive language about the form of the government of the United States, of the Constitution of the United States, or the uniform of the Army or Navy of the United States." As if this were not sufficient, President Woodrow Wilson authorized the formation of the Committee on Public Information (CPI), a propaganda machine headed by George Creel, a journalist.

Now, for the first time, the brute forces of official censorship were buttressed by the slick techniques of propaganda, self-censorship, and disinformation, in what Creel called "a fight for the mind of mankind." And it worked. While the press eventually rejected CPI's manipulative efforts, most newspapers reportedly published all 6,000 press releases sent out by the CPI News Division.

In late November, *The Nation* magazine warned of the apparent control of the press not merely by the government and its legislation but also by the patriotic desire of the press itself to support the government in its efforts. This cheerleading function of the press was most recently observed during the Persian Gulf War in 1991.

1918 Lenin reintroduced censorship in the Soviet Union as a temporary emergency measure to protect the incipient Bolshevik regime against hostile propaganda, demonstrating how censorship is often rationalized as necessary for self-protection.

1918 The biggest censored story of World War I started on November 11, Armistice Day, when journalist George Seldes and three colleagues broke the Armistice regulations and drove into Germany to see what was happening.

Through luck and bravado, they managed to get an interview with Field Marshal Hindenburg. When Seldes asked him what ended the war, Hindenburg replied it was the American infantry attack in the Argonne that won the war. Without it, Germany would have held out much longer. As a form of punishment for breaking regulations, Seldes' story of Hindenburg's confession was suppressed by military censors, with the support of other U.S. journalists angry because they had been scooped.

The historic interview was never published, except by Seldes, who believed it could have altered the course of history. Hitler built Nazism on what Seldes called a total lie, i.e. that Germany did not lose the war on the battlefield but rather because of the Dolchstoss, or stab-in-the-back "by civilians," "by the Socialists," "by the Communists," and "by the Jews." Had the world known of Hindenburg's confession, Hitler might not have so easily manipulated German citizens into supporting his cause. We'll never know what might have been because of a military censor.

1918 While there were many victims of the repressive censorship laws of World War I, Eugene V. Debs was one of the most famous. Founder of the Social Democratic Party in the United States and five-time presidential candidate (between 1900 and 1920), Debs was tried for espionage for opposing the war effort. His citizenship was revoked and he was sentenced to ten years in prison. While in jail in 1920, he ran for president as the Socialist candidate and received nearly a million votes. President Harding commuted his sentence on Christmas Day 1921.

1919 In a Supreme Court ruling in the espionage case *Schenck v. United States,* Justice Oliver Wendell Holmes, delivering the unanimous opinion of the

Court, supported the ruling with the now-famed example of censorship warranted by a clear and present danger—"The most stringent protection of free speech would not protect a man in falsely shouting fire in a theatre and causing a panic."

1920 Walter Lippmann, an outstanding journalist, author, and ethicist of the time, issued an early warning about latter day journalists and media moguls in his essay, "Journalism and the Higher Law." He wrote, "Just as the most poisonous form of disorder is the mob incited from high places, the most immoral act the immorality of a government, so the most destructive form of untruth is sophistry and propaganda by those whose profession it is to report the news. The news columns are common carriers. When those who control them arrogate to themselves the right to determine by their own consciences what shall be reported and for what purpose, democracy is unworkable. Public opinion is blockaded."

1922 The Motion Picture Producers and Distributors of America (MPPDA) was formed as a self-censoring response to outside critics. The MPPDA, chaired by Will Hays, former Postmaster General and Chairman of the Republican National Committee, paved the way for the creation of a formal motion picture code in 1930.

1924 In *Literature and Revolution*, Leon Trotsky established the role of art in a revolutionary society as a service to the revolutionary state, with artists allowed to create in relative freedom but, of course, always under "watchful revolutionary censorship."

1925 John T. Scopes, a young high school teacher, was convicted of violating Tennessee's law that prohibited the teaching of biological evolution (Darwin's theory). In one of the most famous courtroom confrontations in American history, famed liberal attorney Clarence Darrow defended Scopes while William Jennings Bryan assisted the state with the prosecution. Scopes later was released on a technicality by the Tennessee State Supreme Court. But the evolution/creationism argument continues.

1927 The seeds for repressive censorship measures in Germany were sown when the Reichstag passed a morality law to protect young people from indecent prints and pictures. In the guise of maintaining morality among the youth, the law was used by the police to enter private homes, to supervise dancing in homes, and to protect children from parents. By the time the National Socialists came to power in 1933 with the appointment of Adolph Hitler as Chancellor, modern art was banned and leaders of the Expressionist movement were exiled.

1929 Boston earned its "Banned in Boston" epithet in late 1929 when a wave of censorship swept through the city resulting in what was called a "memorable wholesale book holocaust." Among the 68 books by prominent authors banned during that period were *What I Believe* by Bertrand Russell, *Oil* by Upton Sinclair, *An American Tragedy* by Theodore Dreiser, *Elmer Gantry* by Sinclair Lewis, *The Sun Also Rises* by Ernest Hemingway, and *Antic Hay* by Aldous Huxley.

1930 The Motion Picture Producers and Distributors of America (MPPDA) adopted its first Motion Picture Production Code (also known as the Hays Code after the head of the MPPDA). At first, adhering to it was strictly voluntary. Then, in 1933, in response to the National Legion of Decency—founded by the Catholic Church, which had started to review movies—the MPPDA established a stronger code and began to review all scripts. Acceptable films were given a Hays Office seal of approval.

In 1968, again in reaction to outside efforts at censorship, the Motion Picture Association of America (MPPDA became MPAA in 1948) developed a formal, but still voluntary, rating system of four categories: G for general audiences; PG for parental guidance suggested; R for restricted (children under 17 must be accompanied by a parent or guardian); and X (no one under 17 admitted). In 1984, the MPAA added a fifth category: PG-13 (parental guidance suggested for children under 13). In 1990, the X rating was revised to NC-17 (no children under 17 admitted). The X rating had become so popular among promoters of hard-core pornography, it was no longer suited for general use by the theaters. Released on September 23, 1995, "Showgirls," the first mainstream film to carry the NC-17 rating, was the second most popular film opening that weekend.

Finally, in mid-1992, the MPAA revamped its ratings once again, this time to include explanations as to why films are given ratings other than G. For example, the MPAA gave the film "Christopher Columbus—The Discovery" a PG-13 rating, noting that it included "some action violence" and "nudity."

Since its inception in 1930, the MPAA has claimed that the ratings code is not designed to censor a film but rather to warn parents about the content of a film.

1933 James Joyce's celebrated novel *Ulysses* broke the historic barrier of customs censorship when the New York Federal District Court and the Circuit Court of Appeals ruled it was not obscene within the meaning of federal statutes. Judge John Woolsey, of the District Court, said, "Although it contains...many words usually considered dirty, I have not found anything that I consider to be dirt for dirt's sake."

1934 The Federal Communications Act established the Federal Communications Commission (FCC) to succeed the earlier Federal Radio Commission, granting it the right to renew a license as long as the broadcaster operated in the "public interest, convenience, and necessity." It was explicitly stated that the FCC would not have the authority of censor; however, it did have the authority to withhold a license from a broadcaster not operating in the "public interest." Thus, while the FCC could not prohibit liquor advertising, it could emphasize that a station that did advertise liquor, which children could hear, would have to prove that it was acting in the public interest to do so when its license came up for renewal. Not surprisingly, stations have not accepted liquor advertising since.

Although the FCC was not allowed to practice censorship, it wasn't long before advertisers discovered they were not subject to the same restrictions. Cream of Wheat, which sponsored best-selling author Alexander Woollcott on CBS, received some complaints from listeners that Woollcott had made derogatory remarks about Adolph Hitler. When the author refused the advertiser's request to refrain from such remarks, his series was canceled.

1937 Automobile safety, essentially, has been a censored subject since the 1930s. Auto manufacturers haven't liked to acknowledge that driving can be hazardous to your health. Yet, in January 1937, Dr. Clair Straith, a plastic surgeon who specialized in treating facial injuries from auto accidents, published an article in the *American Medical Association Journal* warning of the dangers and suggesting ways the industry could make cars safer. Nonetheless, Detroit ignored the warnings and continued to stress power and speed.

Nearly three decades later, Ralph Nader, in *Unsafe At Any Speed*, wrote, "It is more than coincidental that radio, television, newspapers and magazines have so long ignored the role of vehicle design in producing...collisions." Not one out of 700 newspapers accepted the offer to run a serialization of his book. In September 1993, Health and Human Services Secretary Donna E. Shalala attributed a decrease in deaths from motor vehicle accidents to an increased use of safety belts and other safety devices and added, "We're now seeing how effective injury control programs and highway design can be."

1938 Information concerning the hazards of cigarette smoking was available as early as 1938 but was ignored, or censored, or played down by the media to such an extent that, even two decades later, only 44 percent of the public thought smoking was a cause of lung cancer. In 1994, 56 years after the hazards of smoking were first known, the national news media unleashed a torrent of information and exposés about the hazards of smoking. Ironically, even in the face of well-documented data, the tobacco manufacturers continued to deny such health hazards. Nonetheless, in 1994, cigarette consumption fell to its lowest level since World War II. In 1995, the tobacco industry responded with libel suits against its critics.

1938 The infamous House Un-American Activities Committee (HUAC) was founded under the chairmanship of Congressman Martin Dies, Jr. (D-TX) to "expose communist infiltration" in the Congress of Industrial Organizations (CIO) and in FDR's New Deal administration. This powerful congressional body was particularly successful in using the principle of guilt by association.

1938 *Fortune* magazine sent a copy of an editorial about hunger in America to six New York City daily newspapers; it warned of the dangers to a democracy when a third of its citizens were starving. The *New York Post* featured the editorial on its front page and noted that four of the six dailies, including *The New York Times*, completely ignored the story.

The issue continued to attract media attention even three years later when Senator Robert M. La Follette addressed the Senate, saying that 45 million people were below the safety line in nutrition. In addition, he said, "Twenty million families must live on not more than eight or nine cents per person per meal. About 14 percent of all American families must live on an average of five cents per person per meal." Again, *The New York Times*, which proudly claims it prints "All the news that's fit to print," failed to report a word of this the next day.

1938 On Halloween night, October 31, CBS's "Mercury Theater on the Air" broadcast a realistic dramatization of H.G. Wells' science fiction masterpiece, *War of the Worlds*. The response by terrified listeners across the country confirmed the potential power of radio.

1939 Communist dictator Joseph Stalin redefined the role of the artist in Russia to require active participation in the political guidance of the country. To accomplish this, Russian artists were expected to practice self-censorship in the interest of the state; those who didn't cooperate often vanished suddenly. It was not until late 1995 that one of the world's most remarkable modern art collections, consisting of Russian avant-garde art, was re-united in Greece for its first-ever public viewing. Avant-garde art had been banned by Stalin in the 1920s.

1940 On May 20, 1940, George Seldes—America's Emeritus Journalist and the most censored journalist in history—published Volume I, Number 1, of *In fact*, a biweekly newsletter for "the millions who want a free press." The premiere issue exposed a secret meeting of 18 prominent American leaders who decided to "do their utmost to abrogate existing neutrality legislation," reprimanded the press for its failure to reveal how a major soap manufacturer had been caught "fooling the American people through fake advertising," and warned readers about Father Coughlin and his anti-Semitic hate campaign. George Seldes, hailed as the grandfather of the alternative press and the creator of modern investigative journalism, died on July 2, 1995, at the age of 104. He also was a former Project Censored judge.

1940 Morris Ernst, one of the nation's leading crusaders against censorship, compiled and categorized a comprehensive list of works censored in the United States. The list included some of the world's greatest classics, including works by Homer, Shakespeare, Whitman, and Darwin.

1940 The American Library Association (ALA) established the Committee on Intellectual Freedom, now called the Office for Intellectual Freedom, one of the nation's leading advocates of the First Amendment and free speech. Part of the committee's responsibility is to guard, protect, defend, and extend intellectual freedom.

1940 "The Outlaw," a sexy western starring a sultry Jane Russell in a push-up bra designed by Howard Hughes, was denied the film industry's "seal of approval" because, as one judge put it, Jane Russell's breasts "hung over the picture like a thunderstorm spread out over a landscape." While the film is now available in the 95 and 103 minute versions, no one appears to have a copy of the original uncensored 117-minute version. And it wasn't until 1994 that the push-up bra, re-introduced as the Wonderbra, attained the "junk food news" stature it deserved.

1941 The Manhattan Project, the research effort that led to the atomic bomb, was launched in total secrecy. Within a few years, more than a half-million people across the U.S. were involved in one of the most secretive scientific projects in history. The successful information-control practices employed by the Manhattan Project paved the way for the news management, manipulation, and obfuscation, which has since characterized the nation's nuclear research, in peacetime as well as wartime. The longtime cover-up of human radiation experiments, which were not widely publicized until late 1993, is but one example of the "success" of those information-control techniques.

1941 An extraordinary two-year U.S. Senate investigation of the concentration of economic power in the U.S. concluded that the National Association of

Manufacturers (representing large corporations) and the United States Chamber of Commerce were receiving favored treatment from the press. Although similar charges often have been made since then, America's corporate elite and the press continue to deny that such favored treatment exists.

1941 World War II censorship was initiated when President Franklin Delano Roosevelt created the U.S. Office of Censorship with Byron Price, former executive news editor of The *Associated Press*, as director. Price had the authority to censor all international communications, including mail, cable, and radio. At its peak, the postal section of his office had more than 10,000 employees. Nonetheless, there was little public outrage over censorship during WWII, the result of Price's successful efforts to encourage editors and publishers to practice "voluntary cooperation" with the censorship program.

That effort, along with the Office of War Information (OWI), a propaganda organization headed by Elmer Davis, formerly with CBS News and *The New York Times*, co-opted the traditional negative reaction to information control. The fact that American citizens were more united behind the nation during WWII than WWI also aided the censorship effort. The Office of Censorship closed on August 15, 1945, a few hours after the surrender of Japan. Shortly after the end of the war, the OWI was succeeded by the United States Information Service, under the auspices of the State Department.

1947 "A Free and Responsible Press," a comprehensive and critical report on the status of the media, was issued by the Commission on Freedom of the Press, headed by Dr. Robert M. Hutchins, Chancellor of the University of Chicago. The study, funded by a $200,000 grant from Henry Luce, owner of *Time* and *Life*, found free speech to be in grave danger—not so much from the government as from those who controlled access to the media. The report warned, "One of the most effective ways of improving the press is blocked by the press itself. By a kind of unwritten law, the press ignores the errors and misrepresentation, the lies and scandals, of which its members are guilty." Not surprisingly, the landmark report was given a lukewarm reception by the press. Commenting on the press coverage of the Commission's report, Hutchins said, "Some treated it unfairly, some used untruthful headlines, and some just plain lied about it."

1947 The Dead Sea Scrolls, dating from approximately 22 B.C. to A.D. 100, were discovered in Wadi Qumran. They were almost immediately subjected to censorship by controlled access, which continued until 1991 when biblical scholars forced official researchers to share the information. Since then, access to the scrolls has increased, and by 1994 the Israel Antiquities Association was releasing microfiche and CD-ROM editions.

1947 Charlie Chaplin's "Monsieur Verdoux," a satirical film criticizing munitions makers and military leaders and espousing a more humanistic morality, drew protests and pickets by veterans and religious groups. The outcry resulted in the film's withdrawal from distribution. Chaplin, one of the world's greatest filmmakers and actors, whose impersonation of "the little tramp" created laughter everywhere it was shown, left the U.S. for a self-imposed exile in Switzerland.

1947 Prompted by allegations that the government was infiltrated by communist spies, President Harry S Truman issued an executive order establishing a loyalty-security program for government employees. The program paved the way for one of the nation's most repressive political periods, from 1949 to 1953, which came to be known as the McCarthy era, named after Senator Joseph McCarthy (R-Wisconsin). McCarthy, who incessantly charged that "card-carrying communists" had infiltrated our government from top to bottom, was one of the most feared and controversial men in U.S. Senate history. Following an historic television interview with consummate journalist Edward R. Murrow (see 1954), McCarthy was censured by the U.S. Senate on a vote of 67-22 and died a discredited disgrace in 1957.

1948 The Library Bill of Rights was adopted by the American Library Association to resist "all abridgment of the free access to ideas and full freedom of expression." With the First and Fourteenth Amendments to the Constitution as its foundation, the Bill took an unequivocal stand on the freedom to read and supported democracy in full measure, stating, "There should be the fullest practicable provision of material presenting all points of view concerning the problems and issues of our times, international, national, and local." America's librarians are the nation's first line of defense in the ongoing battle against censorship.

1948 Alfred Kinsey published *Sexual Behavior in the Human Male*, the first of the "Kinsey Reports," which influenced public attitudes toward sex, helped promote sexual freedom and expression, and, at the same time, provided a major target for censors. The second report, *Sexual Behavior in the Human Female*, was published in 1953.

1948 The Universal Declaration of Human Rights was adopted by the General Assembly of the United Nations as "Article XIX." It holds that freedom of expression is not the property of any political system or ideology but is, rather, a universal human right, now defined and guaranteed in international law. "Article 19" also became the name of an international human rights organization founded in England in 1986.

1949 Apparently seeing a threat of communism in certain murals on the walls of public buildings, Richard Nixon, then a Republican Congressman from California, wrote, "I believe a committee should make a thorough investigation of this type of art in government buildings with the view of obtaining removal of all that is found to be inconsistent with American ideals and principles." Nixon went on to even greater efforts at censorship as his career progressed.

1952 The Television Code, adopted by the National Association of Broadcasters, spoke eloquently about commercial television's responsibility to augment the "educational and cultural influence of schools, institutions of higher learning, the home, the church, museums, foundations, and other institutions devoted to education and culture." It also addressed the medium's specific responsibilities toward children and the community. The Code has since been subject to a number of interpretations and revisions. Potential dangers of censorship by the networks, affiliates, advertisers, and the government have yet to be addressed.

1953 On January 17, 1953, I.F. Stone published the first issue of *I.F. Stone's Weekly* in Washington, DC. Following in the footsteps of George Seldes, whom he cited as a mentor, Stone used his extraordinary investigative skills to criticize the U.S. government and its policies. The *Weekly* was an early and clamorous opponent to U.S. involvement in the Vietnam War. Stone's wit, wisdom, and outspoken criticism attracted more than 70,000 subscribers by the time the final issue was published in December 1971. They also attracted the attention of J. Edgar Hoover, the late FBI director, who ineffectually monitored Stone's activities for four decades.

1953 President Dwight D. Eisenhower, often maligned for his military background, warned of censorship during a talk at Dartmouth College: "Don't join the book burners. Don't think you are going to conceal faults by concealing evidence that they ever existed. Don't be afraid to go into your library and read every book as long as it does not offend your own ideas of decency. That should be the only censorship." In June 1953, in a letter to the American Library Association Convention, President Eisenhower wrote: "As it is an ancient truth that freedom cannot be legislated into existence, so it is no less obvious that freedom cannot be censored into existence."

1954 The evening of March 9, 1954, has been called television's finest hour. It was the night that Edward R. Murrow, on his weekly program "See It Now," permitted Senator Joseph R. McCarthy to destroy himself in front of millions of viewers. Murrow concluded his program saying, "The actions of the junior senator from Wisconsin have caused alarm and dismay amongst our allies abroad and given considerable comfort to our enemies. And whose fault is that? Not really his; for he didn't create this situation of fear, he merely exploited it and rather successfully. Cassius was right. 'The fault, dear Brutus, is not in our stars but in ourselves.'"

Referring to the years the press had permitted McCarthy to decimate Americans' civil rights, Murrow later said, "The timidity of television in dealing with this man when he was spreading fear throughout the land is not something to which this art of communication can ever point with pride. Nor should it be allowed to forget it." McCarthy was surely not the first demagogue to intimidate the press, nor will he be the last.

1957 The Supreme Court made its first significant effort to define obscenity. Until now it had worked with what was known as the Hicklin rule, a carry-over description of obscenity from British law, which ruled that obscenity had a tendency to deprave and corrupt those whose minds were open to such immoral influences (such as children) and into whose hands it might fall. In 1957, the Supreme Court replaced this extraordinarily strict inter-pretation of obscenity with what came to be known as the Roth-Memoirs Test. This ruling established three tests, or standards, for ruling a work obscene: 1) The dominant theme of the material, taken as a whole, appeals to an average person's prurient interest in sex; 2) the material is patently offensive because it affronts contemporary community standards, assuming a single national standard, relating to sexual matters; and 3) the material is utterly without redeeming social value. This test for obscenity, while less restrictive than Hicklin, permitted a wide range of legal maneu-vering and remained in effect until 1973.

1958 In defending the absolutist theory of the First Amendment, which holds that "no law" means no law, William O. Douglas, Supreme Court Justice, wrote: "The First Amendment does not say that there is freedom of expression provided the talk is not 'dangerous.' It does not say that there is freedom of expression provided the utterance has no tendency to subvert. It does not put free speech and freedom of the press in the category of housing, sanitation, hours of work, factory conditions, and the like, and make it subject to regulation for the public good. Nor does it permit leg-islative restraint of freedom of expression so long as the regulation does not offend due process. All notions of regulation or restraint by govern-ment are absent from the First Amendment. For it says in words that are unambiguous, 'Congress shall make no law...abridging the freedom of speech, or of the press.'"

1959 D.H. Lawrence's novel, *Lady Chatterly's Lover*, first published in Italy in 1928, was banned by the Federal Post Office Department when published in New York in 1959. The New York Postmaster withheld some 200,000 copies of a circular announcing the new Grove Press edition of the book. The Federal Courts subsequently ruled the book was not hard-core pornography and dismissed the banning restriction. *Lady Chatterly's Lover* and James Joyce's *Ulysses* are among the most important contemporary censorship cases. Both books, by noted literary artists, were subjected to obscenity charges; both were tried, appealed, and approved in federal courts; and both remain controversial to this day.

1959 Clarifying the distinction between freedom and pornography in a capitalist system versus a communist system, Soviet premier Nikita Khrushchev said, "This is a dance (the Can-Can) in which girls pull up their skirts. ... This is what you call freedom—freedom for the girls to show their backsides. To us it's pornography. The culture of people who want pornography. It's capitalism that makes the girls that way. ... There should be a law prohibiting the girls from showing their backsides, a moral law."

1960 A classic example of the potential dangers of news media self-censorship was provided by the events surrounding the Bay of Pigs disaster. In November 1960, editors of *The Nation* magazine tried to interest major news media in an article charging that the U.S. was preparing to invade Cuba, but no one took the story. While reports of the impending invasion were widely known throughout Central America, the American press followed the lead of *The New York Times* which dismissed the reports as "shrill...anti-American propaganda." Following the tragic, ill-fated invasion, President John F. Kennedy, who had persuaded the *Times* to withhold the story, acknowledged that had the press fulfilled its traditional watchdog role and reported the pending invasion, it would have saved the nation from a disastrous decision and the subsequent national disgrace; he told *The New York Times*: "If you had printed more about the operation, you could have saved us from a colossal mistake."

1960 *The New York Times v. Sullivan*—a landmark case in libel law, introduced the concept of malice in journalism. On March 29, 1960, *The New York Times* published a full-page ad signed by some 64 people who charged that thousands of black Southern students engaging in nonviolent protests had been deprived of their constitutional rights. The ad specifically cited an event that occurred in Montgomery, Alabama. L.B. Sullivan, the commissioner of public affairs in Montgomery at the time, filed a libel suit against The New York Times Company and others. In finding for *The Times*, Supreme Court Justice William J. Brennan Jr., said: "We are required in this case to determine for the first time the extent to which the constitutional protections for speech and press limit a State's power to award damages in a libel action brought by a public official against critics of his official conduct." In doing so in this case, the court ruled that it would be more difficult, under law, for a public official to win a libel suit than it is for a private citizen. The ruling now requires that the public official must prove that the statement was made with "actual malice"—that is, with knowledge that it was false, or with reckless disregard as to whether it was false. The 1981 movie, "Absence of Malice," starring Sally Field and Paul Newman, popularized this court decision regarding libel.

1963 Whatever the truth may be behind the assassination of President John F. Kennedy, the news media cannot justify their early and uncritical endorsement of the Warren Commission Report. Their initial attempts to silence the critics of the official version smacked of raw censorship. When a leading scholar offered to write an analysis of the commission's operations, *The New York Times* rejected the offer, saying, "The case is closed." Mark Lane's book on the same subject, *Rush To Judgment*, was not rushed to print. Lane could not find a publisher for 15 months and it was only published after the media decided the issue was acceptable for coverage as a "newsworthy controversy."

Lane's second book, *A Citizen's Dissent*, published in early 1968, records how his pleas for a national examination of the evidence were rejected by *Look, Life*, the *Saturday Evening Post* and others. When *UPI* was offered advance proof sheets, they replied they "would not touch it." This book provides what may be the most exhaustive and documented study ever undertaken of the mass media's use of hidden bias on one issue. Not surprisingly, three years after publication, Lane reported that he hadn't been able to discover "one newspaper story in the mass media noting that the book had been published." Lane said that several media representatives told him: "We will bury that book with silence." And they did.

Incredibly, the media's conspiracy-like efforts to attack anything critical of the original Warren Commission Report's interpretation of the assassination was still in evidence in 1991. The press left no stone unturned in its criticism of film producer and director Oliver Stone and his movie, "JFK," which did not support the commission's findings. The effort was so exceptional, Stone had to hire one of the nation's leading public relations firms, Hill & Knowlton, to counteract the attacks and defend himself.

Indicative of the extent of censorship surrounding the Kennedy assassination was the way Abraham Zapruder's eight-millimeter film of the assassination was handled. This extraordinary bit of footage, which recorded the actual assassination, raised serious questions about the Warren Commission's version of the event. The film, originally purchased by Time Inc. and later sold back to Zapruder, was not shown on national television until 1975, when it was aired on Tom Snyder's late-night "Tomorrow" show. Finally, in November 1994, the Zapruder film was placed in the Library of Congress' registry of American film. It was the first amateur film to be so honored.

1963 "The CBS Evening News" with Walter Cronkite was expanded to 30 minutes, becoming network TV's first half-hour nightly newscast. The evening TV news originally started in the mid-fifties as a 15 minute dose of headlines. In 1980, Ted Turner would create the first 24-hour-a-day news programming with Cable News Network (CNN).

1966 In passing the Freedom of Information Act (FOIA), Congress established the American public's "right to know." It was signed into law by President Lyndon Johnson and went into effect on July 4, 1967. Unfortunately, years of information control and manipulation, as well as disdain for the FOIA by the Reagan/Bush administrations, encouraged federal agencies to find ways to circumvent it. Today, it can be extremely time-consuming and expensive for the public—as well as the press—to use it.

1966 At 10 a.m., on February 10, the U.S. Senate Foreign Relations Committee began hearings on the Vietnam war with the testimony of Ambassador George F. Kennan. Over the objections of Fred W. Friendly, president of CBS News, the network aired a fifth CBS rerun of "I Love Lucy" instead of the hearings. Because of that decision, Friendly quit CBS and subsequently wrote *Due to Circumstances Beyond Our Control...* to tell what happened. The book begins with a quotation: "What the American people don't know can kill them." And it did. More than 58,000 Americans died in Vietnam, and many tens of thousands of returned Vietnam veterans have died from war-related problems since.

1968 Dr. Paul Ehrlich's book *The Population Bomb* created a stir with its prediction that mass famines would plague the world within 20 years. Ehrlich warned that to avoid the tragedy of overpopulation, birth rates must be curbed. In 1971, media critic Robert Cirino, referring to Ehrlich's book, was equally prescient with his observation, "Experts have been making urgent pleas for controlling population and pollution for the last twenty-five years. But did the news media alert us in time?" Ehrlich's prediction has been tragically fulfilled with the African famines of the 1980s and 1990s, yet his warning continues to go unheeded. The earth's population is now growing at a rate of more than 100 million a year, and few people or institutions, including the press, seem to be aware that this is indeed a problem.

1968 The Columbia University Center for Mass Communications in New York offered all three networks a documentary using U.S. Army footage which depicted the horrifying effects of the atomic bomb on individual Japanese victims. The Army had suppressed the film since 1945 and only released it at the insistence of the Japanese government. The film was described by Columbia University Professor Sumner J. Glimcher as "perhaps the best argument for people to live in peace." All three networks rejected the offer to run the documentary, telling the University they just weren't interested; nor did they use the Army's film, which also was available to them, to produce a documentary of their own.

1968 On March 16, some 570 South Vietnamese civilians were slaughtered in Mylai by the U.S. military. Although the massacre was reported over the radio in South Vietnam and in French publications, neither the U.S. press nor that of any other country challenged the official Pentagon version that 128 "Reds" had been killed. Ronald Ridenhour, a former soldier, spent six months investigating the tragedy and talking to witnesses before trying to interest federal officials and the media in the story. He contacted the President, Secretary of State, Secretary of Defense, numerous congressmen, *Life, Look, Newsweek, Harper's*, major newspapers, two wire services, and at least one of the networks. Neither the politicians nor the media were interested.

By September 1969, nearly 18 months after the tragedy, David Leonard, a reporter for the *Columbus Enquirer*, followed up on a lead about Lt. William Calley Jr., and published a front-page story about him. Again the media ignored it, and the story died. In October, Seymour Hersh, then a freelance writer in Washington, DC, investigated the report and tried to sell his version to several publications, including *Life* and *Look*. Again they were not interested. He finally sold the story to the *Dispatch News Service*, which released it on November 13; at last, the media put the tragic massacre on the national agenda.

1968 On September 24, "60 Minutes" was launched on the CBS television network. The weekly hour-long program became known for its hard-hitting investigative reports and went on to become the most popular show in the history of television. The "father" of television news magazines celebrated its 27th anniversary in 1995.

1968 The critical need for mass media coverage of social problems, and the potential impact such coverage can have, was made clear when CBS-TV

News broadcast a documentary, titled "Hunger in America." The documentary stirred a public debate, made hunger a national issue overnight, and has had a lasting impact. The U.S. Department of Agriculture expanded its food program to more counties, increased its monthly surplus of food going to the poor, and called for an expansion of the food stamp program.

1968 "The Final Report: President's Task Force on Communications Policy," published December 7, was highly critical of the nation's commercial television system. It strongly recommended creating a television communications system that would ensure a diversity of ideas and tastes, so that all minorities and majorities could be represented on television. President Johnson refused to make the report public before he left office, and the new president, Richard Nixon, delayed its release for another four months, until May 1969. Neither Johnson nor Nixon should have been worried; when the media finally did get the report, they essentially suppressed the potentially explosive information. The *Los Angeles Times* "covered" the report in a two-inch article on Page 2 under the daily news roundup; *The New York Times* reported it under a small headline in the middle of Page 95.

1969 "The Smothers Brothers Comedy Hour," a weekly entertainment program, was canceled by CBS for failing to cooperate with the network's program-previewing policies. According to the brothers, the program was often censored by CBS, with up to 75 percent of a program being edited out before being aired. In one classic case of broadcasting censorship, as cited by Robert Cirino in his book *Power to Persuade*, CBS asked Pete Seeger, the famed folk singer who was blacklisted by broadcasters for 17 years, to drop the following verse from one of his songs on the Smothers Brothers program. It referred to the position in which the U.S. found itself in Vietnam in 1967:

> *But every time I read the papers*
> *That old feeling comes on;*
> *We're waist deep in the Big Muddy*
> *And the big fool says to push on.*

When Seeger refused to drop the verse, CBS censored the entire song, prompting Seeger to say, "It is wrong for anyone to censor what I consider my most important statement to date. ... I think the public should know that the airwaves are censored for ideas as well as for sex."

1969 In a letter to *The New York Times*, Charles Tower, chairman of the National Association of Broadcasters Television Board, proposed an interesting new definition of censorship. Tower criticized *The Times* for attacking CBS-TV for "censoring" social commentary on the Smothers Brothers show (see above). He suggested, "There is a world of difference between the deletion of program material by Government command and the deletion by a private party (such as a broadcaster). ... Deletion by Government command is censorship. ... Deletion of material by private parties ... is not censorship." While Tower's definition was spurious as well as self-serving, there are probably some who would support his thesis, even now.

1969 The U.S. Supreme Court granted specific protection for student expression rights. The Court's decision in *Tinker v. Des Moines Independent Community School District*, often called the "black armbands case," allowed students to wear black armbands as a symbolic expression of protest against the Vietnam war. The Court declared that neither students nor teachers "shed their constitutional rights to freedom of speech or expression at the schoolhouse gate."

1969 In August, the outrageous but historic three-day Woodstock Music and Art Fair in New York State paved the way for future rock festivals by showing it was possible to overcome censorship rules and regulations set-up by local authorities to prevent such festivals. In August 1994, a commercialized, plastic, 25th anniversary version of Woodstock failed to generate any reported efforts at censorship but it did become a nomination for "junk food news story" of 1994.

1969 On November 13, during a speech in Des Moines, Iowa, Vice President Spiro Agnew launched a series of scurrilous and unsubstantiated attacks on the nation's media, accusing them of favoring liberals. His stand was applauded by the vast majority of media owners who shared Agnew's opinion. These accusations are still used today to support the pervasive myth of "the liberal American media."

1970 Agnew continued his verbal assault, attacking the underground press, rock music, books, and movies for luring American youth into a drug culture. He told his audience, "You need a Congress that will see to it that the wave of permissiveness, the wave of pornography, and the wave of moral pollution never become the wave of the future in our country." In a speech in Las Vegas, he specifically criticized radio stations for playing songs that contain "drug culture propaganda." On March 5, 1971, the FCC issued a notice to broadcasters, holding them responsible for airing songs that would "promote or glorify the use of illegal drugs" and made it abundantly clear that any station ignoring this notice could lose its license.

1970 On May 4, four students protesting the Cambodian incursion during the Vietnam War were killed by the National Guard on the Kent State

University campus in Ohio, a tragic example of the ultimate form of censorship—assassination.

1970 *How To Talk Back To Your Television Set*, a strident criticism of television by Nicholas Johnson, a former member of the FCC, cites a series of CBS-TV documentaries that were "shelved, turned down, or killed," including "a 'hard-hitting' documentary on homosexuals gutted before showing by the management. ... an 'in-depth investigation' of Saigon corruption, also tabled. ... film footage of North Vietnam rejected for broadcast. ... an hour production on [the] black middle class, dumped ... a project on 'Police Brutality,' turned into 'an industrial promo film for sponsor IBM' ... a probe of the military industrial complex, ultimately devoted to 'the nomenclature of military rockets.'" Johnson also noted that CBS had pending for several years a project on "Congressional ethics"; he wondered whether we'd ever see it. The relevancy of the subjects of those censored documentaries to today's social problems is self-evident.

1970 The President's Commission on Obscenity and Pornography failed to find evidence linking obscene materials to criminal behavior, a conclusion that led both President Richard M. Nixon and the U.S. Senate to reject the report. The lesson was not lost on President Ronald Reagan, who later appointed Attorney General Edwin Meese to direct his own Commission on Pornography in 1985.

1971 Robert Cirino, a secondary school teacher in San Fernando, California, published an extraordinary book, *Don't Blame the People: How the news media use bias, distortion and censorship to manipulate public opinion.* After being rejected by mainstream publishers, Cirino published the book himself. Following its success as a college textbook, it was picked up and published by Random House in 1972. Cirino's closing paragraph sums up the role of the press in America and suggests a solution:

"The effort to improve the quality of life in America has to be first the fight to save America from the distorted view of reality presented by the communication industry. It is a fight to restore the average man's participation in government by really letting him decide important questions. It is the average man, the man who doesn't have large corporate interests to protect, that is the strength of a democracy. His reasoning ability and sense of justice enacted into decisions and policies constitute the type of government envisioned by those who wrote America's Declaration of Independence. There has never been a better idea of governing a nation. Our major mistakes have not been the result of democracy, but of the erosion of democracy made possible by mass media's manipulation of public opinion. This erosion could only be stopped in the unlikely event that the

Courts, the Congress and the American people were to demand that all political viewpoints have equal control over access to a mass communication system that is not for sale to anyone."

1971 On June 13, *The New York Times* started to print the Pentagon Papers, part of a top-secret 47-volume government study of decision-making on Vietnam. Two days later, *The Times* was barred from continuing the series. In pleading its right to publish the papers before the Supreme Court, *The Times*, in effect, appeared to abandon the First Amendment in proposing the establishment of guidelines for prior restraint. Supreme Court Justice William O. Douglas warned *The Times*: "The First Amendment provides that Congress shall make no laws abridging the freedom of the press. Do you read that to mean that Congress can make some laws abridging freedom of the press?" It was, added Justice Douglas, "a very strange argument for *The Times* to be making." On June 30, the Supreme Court, by a 6-3 vote, told *The Times* it could go ahead and print the rest of the material.

1971 In December, I.F. Stone, marking the end of a special era in journalism, published the last issue of *I.F. Stone's Weekly*. In his essay, "Notes On Closing, But Not In Farewell," Stone wrote: "To give a little comfort to the oppressed, to write the truth exactly as I saw it, to make no compromises other than those of quality imposed by my own inadequacies, to be free to follow no master other than my own compulsions, to live up to my idealized image of what a true newspaper man should be and still be able to make a living for my family—what more could a man ask?"

1971 "The Selling of the Pentagon," a hard-hitting CBS documentary, told the American people how much money the Pentagon was spending to buy a favorable public image for itself. Congress, particularly Rep. F. Edward Hebert, chair of the House Armed Services Committee, and members of the Nixon administration were outraged. When CBS-TV rebroadcast the show about a month later, it had to add 15 minutes of rebuttal from Hebert (who called it "un-American"), Vice President Spiro Agnew (who called it a "vicious broadside against the nation's defense establishment"), and Secretary of Defense Melvin Laird (often caricatured with a missile head). The House Committee on Interstate and Foreign Commerce unsuccessfully attempted to subpoena the film, and a committee vote to request a contempt citation against CBS had to be voted down.

1972 The June break-in of the Democratic National Committee offices in the Watergate complex by the Republican CREEP (Committee to Re-elect the President) sparked one of the biggest political cover-ups in modern history. And the press, to its lasting shame, was an unwitting, if not willing, partner in the cover-up. The break-in, by CREEP employees known as the "plumbers," was described as a "two-bit burglary" not worthy of press attention. It didn't manage to get on the national news agenda until after November, when Richard Nixon was re-elected with a landslide vote. Carl Bernstein and Bob Woodward, both with the *Washington Post*, eventually made it a national story. Bernstein noted that out of some 2,000 full-time reporters for major news organizations, just 14 were assigned to the story on a full-time basis, even six months after the break-in. When Walter Cronkite tried to do an extraordinary two-part series on Watergate on the "CBS-TV Evening News," before the election, a phone call from the Nixon White House to Bill Paley, chair of CBS, resulted in Cronkite's scheduled program being reduced. The power of a President to directly intervene and censor the nation's leading broadcast news organization was revealed. Ironically, 21 years after the Watergate break-in, when the government released three additional hours of the tapes to the public, Nixon was heard plotting to deflect the blame for the break-in and calculating that Watergate was "a Washington son-of-a-bitching story" most Americans would shrug off.

1972 The Supreme Court ruled that dancing, even topless dancing, was a type of expression entitled to protection under the First Amendment. This judicial ruling encouraged the growth of topless, and eventually bottomless, dancing in bars throughout America.

1972 The Supreme Court ruled that the Central Intelligence Agency could preview its employees' speeches and publications to protect against any disclosure of classified information. In 1980, this ruling was expanded to include pre-publication review of all materials, including unclassified information. This decision was based on a case involving a former CIA agent who published a book criticizing U.S. actions during the Vietnam War. The book contained no classified information.

1972 The first issue of the *Index On Censorship* was published, acknowledging that "the need for such a magazine would become clear in the next few years"—and it has. The *Index*, an international advocate of free expression, focuses on the censorship, banning, and exile of writers and journalists throughout the world. In 1994, it was relaunched with a new format but without a change in its focus on international censorship.

1973 Beginning with the case of *Miller v. California*, the Supreme Court refined the Roth-Memoirs 1957 definition of obscenity, replacing national standards with local community standards. What is known as the Miller Test for obscenity is used today by American courts to determine whether a work is, by law, obscene. Written material is legally obscene under the following three conditions: 1) An average person, applying contemporary local community standards, finds that the work, taken as a whole, appeals to prurient interest; 2) The work depicts, in a patently offensive way, sexual conduct specifically defined by applicable state law; and 3) The material lacks serious literary, artistic, political, or scientific value.

1973 "Sticks and Bones"—a dramatic, filmed version of an award-winning stage drama about the homecoming of a blind Vietnam veteran and his callous reception—was scheduled to be shown on CBS on March 9. Just four days before air date, CBS executives postponed the program, saying it would be "unnecessarily abrasive to the feelings of millions of Americans whose lives or attention were dominated at the time by the returning POWs and other veterans." Joseph Papp, producer of the film, called the postponement "a cowardly cop-out, a rotten affront to freedom of speech." When the drama was finally shown five months later, only 91 affiliate stations carried it (less than half of the 184 that normally would carry the network's programs). Many advertisers canceled their commercials.

1975 Ruling on the constitutionality of a Tennessee ban on the rock musical "Hair," the U.S. Supreme Court decided that live theater had legal protection against prior restraint, as was the case with books, movies, and other forms of expression.

1976 Project Censored, the national media research project focusing on news media censorship, was founded by Carl Jensen, Ph.D., at Sonoma State University, Rohnert Park, California. The top ten *Censored* stories of 1976 were:

1. Jimmy Carter and the Trilateral Commission
2. Corporate Control of DNA
3. Selling Banned Pesticides and Drugs to Third World Countries
4. The Oil Price Conspiracy
5. The Mobil Oil/Rhodesian Connection
6. Missing Plutonium and Inadequate Nuclear Reactor Safeguards
7. Workers Die for American Industry
8. Kissinger, the CIA, and SALT
9. Worthless or Harmful Non-prescription Drugs
10. The Natural Gas "Shortage"

1976 On June 2, Don Bolles, investigative reporter for the *Arizona Republic* was permanently "censored" when his car exploded in the parking lot of the Hotel Chardon in Phoenix. Bolles was investigating a lead dealing with massive land frauds, political payoffs, the underworld, and corporate crime. Following the assassination, nearly 100 journalists, organized as the Investigative Reporters and Editors Inc. (IRE), produced a 23-installment series on crime and corruption in Arizona. John Harvey Adamson, who admitted to planting the dynamite under Bolles' car, testified that Bolles was killed as a favor to Kemper Marley, one of Arizona's richest and most powerful figures and a target of Bolles' exposés. Ironically, in 1993, the University of Arizona named one of its buildings after Kemper Marley following a $6 million contribution to the university. Marley died in 1990 at 83.

1977 The FCC outlawed a monologue, "Seven Words You Can't Say On Radio" by comedian George Carlin, from being broadcast on radio or television. While the words still have shock value in print, they're surely not strangers on television, particularly on cable. The seven words that assured Carlin of lasting First Amendment fame were "shit," "piss," "fuck," "cunt," "cocksucker," "motherfucker," and "tits."

1977 When the ACLU defended the rights of the Nazi party to demonstrate in Skokie, near Chicago, 15 to 20 percent of ACLU members dropped their membership in protest. While the Illinois Appellate Court gave the Nazis permission to demonstrate but not to wear the swastika, the Illinois Supreme Court subsequently ruled that the Nazis had a right to display the swastika.

1977 The problem of decommissioning nuclear power plants—one of Project Censored's top ten censored stories of 1977—wasn't discovered until some of the original plants and reactors had to be shut down. In two cases, the costs for dismantling the plant ran almost as high as the original construction costs. Decommissioning nuclear power plants remains an unresolved and under-covered issue in 1996.

1978 The specter of sterility was raised when researchers discovered that the average sperm count among American men had dropped substantially since a landmark study done less than 30 years earlier. The research revealed that the probable causes were industrial and agricultural chemicals similar to the DBCP pesticide (which, earlier, had led to male sterility at a chemical plant), and that the trend may represent a potential sterility threat to the entire male population. The threat, one of the top ten *Censored* stories of the year, wasn't dramatic enough to attract the attention of the mass media at the time.

1979 The longest-lasting case of government censorship by prior restraint of a publication began March 9. A Federal District Court in Wisconsin imposed a temporary restraining order on *The Progressive*, a Wisconsin-based monthly magazine, censoring publication of the article, "The H-Bomb Secret: How We Got It, Why We're Telling It." The government claimed that the description of how a hydrogen bomb was designed would help foreign countries produce H-bombs more swiftly. But the

Supreme Court finally acknowledged the true intent of the First Amendment on September 17, when it ruled the magazine could publish the article.

1979 To find cheap labor and to escape U.S. health and safety regulations, increasing numbers of major American corporations set up branches or contracted jobs under "sweatshop" conditions in Third World countries. This story—one of the top ten *Censored* stories of 1979—attracted national attention during the 1992 presidential election year, as unemployment plagued workers in the U.S., and health problems and environmental pollution threatened workers in Third World countries.

1980 The top *Censored* story of 1980, "Distorted Reports of the El Salvador Crisis," launched more than a decade of top ten *Censored* stories dealing with underreported or biased reports of U.S. intervention in Central America.

1981 The American people were told that the over-regulation of business and the "declining moral fiber of the American worker" had caused the worst economic crisis since the depression. But Maurice Zeitlin, a UCLA economic sociologist, testifying before the California Senate Committee on Industrial Relations, charged that we no longer had a competitive economy, and that monopoly, militarism, and multinationalization were at the root of our economic crisis. His testimony, cited as the top *Censored* story of 1981, also suggested that we could expect more of the same until the root causes are examined and changed.

1982 President Reagan established an oppressive system of security classification with his Executive Order 12356. It reversed a trend toward openness on the part of previous administrations by eliminating what was known as the balancing test. Now it was no longer necessary to weigh the public's need to know against the need for classification. In addition, the Executive Order reduced the threshold standard for classification. That same year, Project Censored cited Reagan as "America's Chief Censor" for his efforts to reduce the amount of information available to the public about the operation of the government, the economy, the environment, and public health, and for his attempts to weaken the Freedom of Information Act.

1982 *The Media Monopoly*, by Ben Bagdikian, was published, revealing that just 50 corporations control half or more of the media in America.

1983 National Security Decision Directive 84 (NSDD 84), issued by the Reagan Administration in March, required all government personnel with access to classified materials to sign a lifetime secrecy pledge.

1984 Fulfilling the Orwellian expectations of the year, President Reagan implemented NSDD 84—the largest censoring apparatus ever known in the United States. For the first time in history, millions of federal employees were required to submit their speeches, articles, and books for prepublication review by their superiors for the rest of their lives. Under pressure from Congress, the administration suspended the pre-publication review provision in September 1984, but a 1986 General Accounting Office report on its impact concluded that the suspension had little effect, and that pre-publication review was alive and well in America.

1984 On September 14, CBS reporter Mike Wallace appeared on the "Phil Donahue Show" and predicted that one of the segments he was working on for "60 Minutes" could possibly change the course of the presidential election. The story focused on one of Ronald Reagan's closest friends, Nevada Senator Paul Laxalt, who was high on Reagan's list of potential Supreme Court nominees. Journalists investigating Laxalt found he had accepted political contributions from supporters linked to organized crime, received highly questionable loans, tried to limit FBI investigations into Nevada gaming operations and owned a Carson City casino that engaged in illegal skimming operations. After being contacted by Laxalt and his attorney, CBS decided not to run the story. And although the story didn't have a chance to change the course of the 1984 election, as predicted by Wallace, Ronald Reagan never nominated Laxalt to the Supreme Court.

1985 President Ronald Reagan appointed Attorney General Edwin Meese to head his Commission on Pornography. The members, reportedly hand-picked for their support of censorship, spent considerable time investigating erotic films, books, and magazines protected by the First Amendment. Based on the testimony of the Rev. Donald Wildmon, executive director of the National Federation of Decency, the Commission sent a letter to 26 major corporations, including K-mart, Southland (7-Eleven stores), and Stop N Go Stores, that accused them of selling and distributing pornography by selling publications such as *Playboy* and *Penthouse*. A U.S. District Court subsequently ruled the commission had threatened the First Amendment rights of magazine publishers and distributors and ordered the letter withdrawn. In 1994, a U.S. District Court in Los Angeles struck a blow for readers' rights when it overturned a ban on sexually explicit magazines at Los Angeles fire stations, saying the First Amendment gives firefighters the right to read publications such as *Playboy*.

1985 The drive for profits, coupled with the apparent collapse of the FCC, led to a frenzy of media mergers and paved the way for an international information monopoly. Consumer advocate Ralph Nader warned of the increased threat of censorship resulting from conglomerate self-interest: "Self-censorship is alive and well in the U.S. media."

1986 The American Library Association (ALA) charged the Reagan administration with efforts to eliminate, restrict, and privatize government documents; with launching an official new "disinformation" program that permitted the government to release deliberately false, incomplete and misleading information; and with developing a new category of "sensitive information," restricting public access to a wide range of previously unclassified data. While the ALA charges were well-documented, they were ignored by the major news media.

1986 FAIR, Fairness & Accuracy In Reporting, an anti-censorship organization based in New York, was formed to shake up the establishment-dominated media. It draws attention to important news stories that have been neglected or distorted by the media, and defends working journalists when they are muzzled.

1986 Article 19, an international human rights organization named after Article XIX of the Universal Declaration of Human Rights (see 1948), was founded in London to document and fight censorship on an international basis. The UN declaration holds, "Everyone has a right to freedom of opinion and expression; this right includes freedom to hold opinions without interference and to seek, receive and impart information and ideas through any media regardless of frontiers."

1986 The final report of Attorney General Edwin Meese's Commission on Pornography was released. As expected, it simply ignored the First Amendment. But what can you expect from Edwin Meese, the subject of a 1984 *Censored* story that charged him with directing a secret operation involving a variety of illegal and unconstitutional activities while a California state official in the late '60s and early '70s. That operation was aimed at subverting the anti-war movement in California.

1987 The continuing consolidation of media ownership raised critical questions about the public's access to a diversity of viewpoints as Ben Bagdikian updated his 1982 book, *The Media Monopoly*. He found that just 26 corporations now controlled the majority of America's media enterprises. Bagdikian also predicted that by the 1990s, a half dozen giant firms would control most of the world's media.

1988 The British government imposed a ban on broadcasters, preventing them from transmitting the speech of representatives of specified organizations in Northern Ireland—including not only outlawed republican and loyalist paramilitary groups but also Sinn Fein, a legal political party. The ban, meant to deny publicity to terrorists, would be lifted on September 16, 1994.

1988 In what many consider to be an unconstitutional ruling, the U.S. Supreme Court's *Hazelwood* decision provided renewed support for censorship through the use of prior restraint. In essence, the court gave high school administrators the power to censor student publications in advance. The ruling reversed a long-time trend of First Amendment support for freedom of expression issues on high school campuses. Oddly enough, this violation of the First Amendment has been ignored by the major news media. Despite widespread ongoing student protest, it is still unchallenged in 1996.

1988 Top *Censored* story of this election year revealed how the major mass media ignored, overlooked, or undercovered at least ten critical stories reported in America's alternative press that raised serious questions about the Republican presidential candidate, George Bush. The stories dated from his reported role as a CIA "asset" in 1963 to his Presidential campaign's connection with a network of anti-Semites with Nazi and fascist affiliations in 1988.

1988 Author Salman Rushdie's novel, *The Satanic Verses*, was attacked by Muslims for sacrilege and blasphemy. On February 14, 1989, the Ayatollah Khomeini issued a "fatwa," or death sentence, on Rushdie who went into hiding. Khomeini died four months later of cancer. On February 14, 1994, the fifth anniversary of Khomeini's death sentence, Iranian leaders publicly renewed their pledge to find and kill Rushdie, saying the late Khomeini's death decree would never be rescinded. In a similar case, feminist author Taslima Nasrin went into hiding in her native Bangladesh in June 1994 after Muslim extremists offered a $5,000 reward for her death. Extremist groups were infuriated by a report that Nasrin had called for a revision of the Koran, the Islamic holy book. Nasrin said she was misquoted but had called for changes in strict rules that limit Bangladeshi women to housework and child-rearing. On August 10, Nasrin fled to Sweden where she vowed to continue her fight against Muslim extremism.

1989 Fulfilling his 1987 predictions about world media conglomerates, Ben Bagdikian revealed in a well-documented article in *The Nation* that five global media lords already dominated the fight for hundreds of millions of minds throughout the world. Further, these media monopolies conceded that they may control most of the world's important newspapers, magazines, books, broadcast stations, movies, recordings, and video cassettes by the turn of the century. The Big Five of 1989:

Time Warner Inc., the world's largest media corporation
German-based Bertelsmann AG, owned by Reinhard Mohn
Rupert Murdoch's News Corporation Ltd., of Australia
Hatchette SA, of France, world's largest producer of magazines
U.S.-based Capital Cities/ABC Inc.

1989 On December 20, the United States invaded Panama to overthrow the regime of Manuel Noriega, who would surrender on January 3, 1990. Subsequent news reports concerning the actual death toll, the legal implications of the invasion, and the Bush-Noriega relationship, revealed that the press pool concept of censorship, developed for the 1983 Grenada War, succeeded in preventing the public from knowing what transpired in Panama.

1990 In April, for the first time in history, an American museum and its director faced criminal charges for pandering obscenity. Their crime was a display of erotic art photographs by Robert Mapplethorpe. The director, Dennis Barrie, and the Contemporary Arts Center in Cincinnati were both acquitted of pandering in October. As a result, Cincinnati earned the nickname "Censornati."

1990 The flawed coverage of events leading up to the Persian Gulf crisis was the top *Censored* story of the year. Traditional press skepticism of government/military activities was the first casualty in the days immediately following Iraq's invasion of Kuwait as the U.S. media became cheerleaders for the Bush Administration's military policy.

1991 For the second year in a row, the top *Censored* story of the year focused on the Gulf War. It revealed how the networks rejected uncensored videotape footage of the heavy Iraqi civilian damage, the result of American-led bombing campaigns. Instead, the networks continued to publicize the Pentagon-approved, high-tech, smart-bomb, antiseptic, non-threatening version of the war. The second overlooked story of the year revealed a number of specific Gulf War issues that didn't receive the coverage they deserved, while the #6 story provided photographic evidence that challenged President Bush's original explanation for our rapid deployment in the Gulf.

1991 On May 24, the Supreme Court, in a ruling as unconstitutional as its earlier *Hazelwood* decision, upheld a Reagan administration interpretation of Title X, the Public Health Services Act, that prohibited abortion counseling at federally funded family planning clinics. The 1987 interpretation suggested that Title X "required physicians and counselors to withhold information about abortion even from patients who were at medical risk from continuation of the pregnancy." The Court ruled that the word "abortion" cannot be uttered in any of America's 4,500 federally supported clinics that provide aid and counseling to millions of poor women. In essence, the United States Supreme Court ruled that First Amendment free speech rights are a function of federal funding. The abortion "gag rule" was repealed by President Clinton in January 1993.

1991 In the introduction to Volume IV of *The Right To Know*, published in 1992 by the DataCenter, in Oakland, California, Zoia Horn, a long-time champion of intellectual freedom and the public's right to know, made the following comments about how we "celebrated" the 200th anniversary of the Bill of Rights: "The 200th anniversary of the Bill of Rights should have been the occasion for a reaffirmation of democratic principles. Unfortunately, it fizzled into just another public relations campaign— profiting Philip Morris, Inc., the sponsor of a widely viewed exhibit. Many people polled during the Persian Gulf War saw no contradiction between the censorship and manipulation of the media by the Pentagon, and the Bill of Rights. Indeed, previous polls revealed that a disturbing number of citizens, asked to read the Bill of Rights, thought it was a communist document, and thus rejected parts of it. Ignorance of our basic democratic tenets requires a serious, massive, educational campaign at all age levels, through all mediums of communication."

1992 The Department of Defense and a group of self-selected media executives agreed on nine out of ten ground rules for press coverage of America's next military engagement. The contested and unresolved issue concerned prior restraint on the part of the military. The policy, which apparently "supplements" the First Amendment, evolved from the pool concept of censorship developed by the Reagan administration for the Grenada War, subsequently refined by the Bush administration for the Panama invasion, and finally given a full-scale test during the Gulf War—where it failed.

1992 The Center for the Study of Commercialism (CSC) invited 200 media outlets to a press conference to be held on March 11 in Washington, DC. The purpose was to reveal how advertisers, one of the nation's most powerful media voices, influence, corrupt, and censor a free press. Not a single radio or television station or network sent a reporter and only two newspapers, the *Washington Post* and the *Washington Times*, bothered to attend. The *Post* didn't run a story on the press conference while the *Times* (also known as the Capital's Moonie Paper since it is owned by Sun Yung Moon) ran one but didn't name the advertisers cited in the CSC study. The well-documented study, which has been seen by few Americans, was titled "Dictating Content: How Advertising Pressure Can Corrupt A Free Press."

1992 In the June introduction to "Less Access To Less Information By and About the U.S. Government: XVIII," the American Library Association, Washington Office, reflected on how the Reagan/Bush administrations significantly limited access to public documents and statistics and warned that it might get worse, given the increasing commercialization of what was once public information. By contrast, in the June 1993 introduction, the ALA reported that in its first year in office, "the Clinton Administration has improved public access to government information." However, it also added, there are still barriers to access.

1993 In his latest update on the increasing monopolization of the media, the Fourth Edition of *The Media Monopoly*, Ben Bagdikian reported that fewer than 20 corporations now own and control the majority of the media in America.

1993 Franklyn S. Haiman, John Evans Professor Emeritus of Communication Studies at Northwestern University and leading First Amendment scholar, systematically challenges the criminalization of purely expressive behavior, sometimes referred to as speech act theory, because it is felt to be offensive, provocative, or even dangerous. In his book *"Speech Acts" and the First Amendment*, Haiman persuasively argues that controlling speech is neither constitutional nor effective as a means of preventing antisocial conduct.

1993 Reminiscent of an attempt to censor a film titled "Kiss," nearly a century ago (see 1896), the director of a children's theater in Dallas ordered a kiss eliminated from a wedding scene after a businessman complained because the actor was black and the actress was white. The actor went ahead and kissed his "bride" in the production of "Ramona Quimby" anyway, and, after a flood of complaints, the director officially reinstated the kiss in the performance. The specious grounds for kiss-censorship moved from race to gender in 1994 when a kissing scene between two men on the May 18 episode of television's "Melrose Place" was cut from the final production.

1993 An ABC-TV movie about a Marine held hostage during the Vietnam war was itself held hostage for more than two years. "The Last P.O.W.: The Bobby Garwood Story" was finally broadcast on June 28, about two and a half years after its originally scheduled air date. ABC reportedly felt "it was inappropriate to air it" in early 1991 during the Gulf War since it raised questions about patriotism. The rationale sounds much the same as that given for the CBS censorship of "Sticks and Bones" in 1973.

1993 Robert Maynard, 56, a high school dropout who rose to become the first African-American owner-publisher of a major metropolitan daily newspaper, died of cancer. Before buying the *Oakland Tribune*, Maynard was a pioneering black journalist and founder of the Institute for Journalism Education in Oakland, which has trained more than 600 minority journalists to be reporters, editors and managers. Maynard also had served as a judge for Project Censored.

1993 The Uniform Defamation Act, a complex and widely criticized approach to reforming libel law across the country, was replaced with a version more acceptable to the media. The Uniform Correction or Clarification of Defamation Act of 1993 allows for the publication of a correction or clarification to mitigate damages, or even to settle a claim completely, and it sets up a framework and timetable for the process.

1993 IRE (Investigative Reporters & Editors) announced one of its most ambitious projects ever with the development of a computerized bulletin board service that would provide a comprehensive news and information library available to journalists throughout the world.

1993 The top *Censored* story of the year focused on the failure of the mass media to widely report that the United States had become one of the most dangerous places in the world for young people. A study by the United Nations Children's Fund revealed that nine out of ten young people murdered in industrialized countries are slain in the U.S.

1994 In late March, 70 leading editors, publishers, politicians, lawyers, and scholars at the First Hemispheric Conference on Free Expression, meeting in Mexico City, declared, "A society of free individuals cannot remain free without free speech and freedom of the press." Asserting there must be no law abridging freedom of speech or press, and supporting it with ten basic principles, the historic document reinforces the Universal Declaration of Human Rights adopted on December 10, 1948, by the General Assembly of the United Nations as "Article XIX" (see 1948). The Inter American Press Association, meeting in Guatemala City a week after the Hemispheric conference, declared its support for the declaration.

1994 On May 3, the right of reviewers and other journalists to express their opinions was upheld in a remarkable ruling by the U.S. Court of Appeals for the District of Columbia. Admitting to a "mistake of judgment," the Court reversed its ruling of February 18 which found *The New York Times* guilty of libeling author Dan E. Moldea in a review of his book on the National Football League and organized crime. In doing so, the Court reinforced the First Amendment rights of journalists, as well as reviewers, to publish their opinions.

1994 In an historic, unanimous First Amendment decision, issued on June 13, the Supreme Court advanced the free speech rights of all Americans. The court unanimously ruled that cities may not bar residents from posting signs on their own property. The case began when the community of Ladue, Missouri, refused to permit a resident to display an 8 x 11 inch sign in an upstairs window of her house. The simple little sign read: "For Peace in the Gulf."

1994 The U.S. Supreme Court ruled that television cable operators have the same rights and protections under the Constitution as other media. In ruling on the *Turner Broadcasting System Inc. v. Federal Communications Commission* case, the Court concluded that cable programmers and cable operators engage in and transmit speech and thus are entitled to the protection of the First Amendment.

1994 On July 29, the Interactive Digital Software Association announced a video game rating system for games on cartridges, compact discs, and diskettes, based on samples of content. The categories include Early Childhood, ages 3+; Kids to Adults, ages 6+; Teens, ages 13+; Mature, ages 17+; and Adults only.

1994 On August 15, the "Voice of America," the official U.S. Information Agency (USIA) propaganda arm of the U.S. Department of State, started to offer digital audio newscasts in 15 foreign languages over the Internet, the reputedly uncontrollable international system of computer networks. Since the USIA is officially prohibited from distributing program materials in the U.S., the Internet carries a disclaimer warning that the material is "provided exclusively for recipients outside the United States."

1994 *Amerika*, the monthly magazine published by the U.S. Information Agency, was another casualty of the end of the Cold War when it folded in September 1994 after 38 years of publication. William Harwood, deputy public affairs officer at USIA, said the publication, originally designed to counter Soviet propaganda, "was about the only thing you could read that wasn't filled with propaganda."

1994 One of the most important libel trials in modern media history continued through 1995. Psychoanalyst Jeffrey Masson had sued journalist Janet Malcolm for libel by misquoting him in a 1983 *New Yorker* magazine article. The first round ended in June 1993, when a jury found that five quotes attributed to Masson had been fabricated or distorted and that Malcolm was aware that two of them were libelous. The second round ended in September 1993, when a U.S. District Judge dismissed Masson's suit against the *New Yorker* but granted a new libel trial to Malcolm. The third round ended November 2, 1994, when a federal jury cleared Malcolm of libeling Masson. However, this might not be the end of the decade-long libel suit since Masson announced a week later that he would appeal. In

August 1995, Malcolm said she had accidentally found the missing notes containing three quotes at the center of the case. The case was still on appeal when the year ended.

1994 President Bill Clinton signed an executive order on November 10 approving the declassification of 44 million documents stored at the National Archives. There are still some 281 million pages of classified material from before 1964 and hundreds of millions more held by the Pentagon, Central Intelligence Agency, and other executive branch agencies.

1994 The Supreme Court limited the range of free speech on November 14 when it reversed a Circuit Court of Appeals ruling that said City College of New York violated Professor Leonard Jeffries' free-speech rights when it removed him as chairman of CCNY's Black Studies department. Jeffries was accused of making an anti-Semitic speech.

1994 In late December, Random House announced it would publish A *Long Fatal Love Chase*, a novel by Louisa May Alcott that had been censored more than a century earlier for being too sensational.

1994 The top *Censored* story of the year revealed that the National Institute for Occupational Safety and Health (NIOSH) had still not notified some 169,000 American workers that they had been exposed to hazardous materials at their worksites as discovered during NIOSH studies in the early 1980s.

1995 On February 18, Boris Yeltsin, president of Russia, banned the Russian media from advertising alcohol, tobacco, and the services of unregistered healers. The decree, which took effect immediately, called such Western-style advertisements a threat to public health.

1995 The U.S. District Court for the District of Columbia expanded protection for commercial speech by rejecting a ten million dollar libel suit by author Mark Lane against Random House. Random House ran an ad for *Case Closed*, a book by Gerald Posner supporting the Warren Commission report, which featured Lane and other conspiracy theorists.

1995 In early March, on the 50th anniversary of the death of Anne Frank in a concentration camp, Doubleday published an unabridged edition of her diary, titled *Diary of a Young Girl: The Definitive Edition*. It turns out that her father, Otto Frank, had edited out about 30 percent of the original publication.

1995 In late March, in an act reminiscent of its earlier index of books forbidden to Catholics, the Vatican press office publicly condemned a book on clerical crime, including murder, witchcraft, and sex. The book, *Saints and*

Sinners, by Monsignor Filippo Tamburini, was declared an "abuse" that should be "strongly deplored." And, on March 24, under pressure from the Catholic League, Walt Disney's Miramax changed the national release date of its controversial movie, "Priest," so it wouldn't coincide with Good Friday.

1995 On April 19, the U.S. Supreme Court approved anonymous pamphleteering by ruling that states cannot require people to sign leaflets and other political literature. The court said anonymous pamphleteering adheres to "an honorable tradition of advocacy and of dissent."

1995 On April 30, the National Science Foundation turned supervision of the Internet over to a group of commercial services. The Internet originated 26 years earlier when the Department of Defense launched its predecessor, ARPANET, to ensure the government's ability to communicate in case of a nuclear attack.

1995 Gustave Courbet's explicit painting of a reclining nude, "The Origin of the World," was displayed in June at the Orsay Museum in Paris after more than a century of scandal, secrecy, and censorship.

1995 On June 14, three leading software companies formed the Information Highway Parental Empowerment Group to create industry standards for rating content and for the software that would filter out offensive material based on the ratings. The three companies, Microsoft Corp., Netscape Communications Inc., and Progressive Networks Inc., said it would be a voluntary rating system administered by an independent organization.

1995 On June 29, the U.S. Supreme Court issued two rulings perceived by conservative Christians as major victories for religious freedom. In one 5-4 vote, the court ruled the University of Virginia violated the free speech rights of a student group by refusing to provide funds for its Christian magazine while subsidizing other student publications. In another ruling, by a 7-2 vote, the court ruled against Ohio for preventing the Ku Klux Klan from displaying a large wooden cross in front of the state capitol.

1995 In July, Secretary of Education Richard Riley distributed to all public schools a new directive concerning religious activities which allows students to express personal religious views or beliefs—but does not permit schools to endorse religious activity or doctrine.

1995 The era of the typewriter came to an inauspicious end on July 5 when the Smith Corona Corporation, the last U.S. typewriter manufacturer, filed for bankruptcy. The first mass produced typewriter was manufactured by E. Remington and Sons in 1874.

1995 The Federal Communications Commission eliminated the "prime time access rule" on July 28. It required network-affiliated stations to reserve one hour of prime time for shows not produced by ABC, CBS, or NBC. The rule originated in 1970 to provide programming diversity when the three networks had little competition.

1995 In September, Charles L. Klotzer, founder and editor of the *St. Louis Journalism Review* (SJR), announced the transfer of ownership of the monthly review to Webster University, in St. Louis, Missouri. *SJR*, which critiqued the St. Louis media scene for 25 years, was the only journalism review that focused on media coverage in a single city. The transfer was to take effect January 1, 1996.

1995 In keeping with its penchant for censorship dating back to at least 499 A.D., the Roman Catholic Church inaugurated in September a national toll-free movie review line giving "moral ratings" to current movies and videos. The review, sponsored by the Catholic Communications Campaign, provides both the U.S. Catholic Conference Classification rating and the traditional Motion Picture Association of America rating along with a brief description of the film. The toll-free number is 800/311-4222.

1995 In an ironic move, the United Nations censored its own 50th anniversary commemorative book, A *Vision of Hope*. United Nations officials deleted the names of countries the U.N. itself had cited for human rights violations, excised an account of corruption in the election of the World Health Organization director, and banned any reference to the Dalai Lama, the exiled leader of Tibet.

1995 The Supreme Court of Canada, in a 5-4 decision, ruled on September 21 that the Tobacco Products Control Act of 1988, which banned almost all advertising of tobacco products, was unconstitutional.

1995 Former Soviet President Mikhail Gorbachev warned that the information revolution could raise much of the world from poverty or it could divide global society between the info-rich and the info-poor. He made the statement September 29 at the first State of the World Forum, sponsored by the San Francisco-based Gorbachev Foundation.

1995 On October 27, the R.J. Reynolds company announced it was pulling Joe Camel, one of the most controversial characters in advertising history, from its billboards after nearly eight years. Joe Camel, long under criticism for his appeal to kids, will continue to be used in print advertising and in-store promotions.

1995 The 70-year-old evolution/creationism argument continues. On June 29, the U.S. Supreme Court let stand a ruling barring an Orange County public school teacher from suing his employer for compelling him to teach evolution as fact. See 1925 for the Scopes Trial.

1995 The aptly titled Telecommunications Deregulation Bill, which would virtually eliminate all regulation of the U.S. communications industry, was named the top *Censored* story of the year. The major media failed to highlight the threat to the nation's "marketplace of ideas" from mega-media monopolies, a *Censored* story several times in the past.

THE WRITER AND THE ASTERISK

A writer owned an Asterisk,
And kept it in his den,
Where he wrote tales (which had large sales)
Of frail and erring men;
And always, when he reached the point
Where carping censors lurk,
He called upon the Asterisk
To do his dirty work.

Stoddard King (1889-1933)

BIBLIOGRAPHY TO CHRONOLOGY

American Library Association, Washington Office. "Less Access To Less Information By and About the U.S. Government: XVIII and XXI." Washington, DC.: American Library Association, June 1992 and June 1993.

Attorney General. "Commission on Pornography Final Report, July 1980, Vol. I & II." Washington, DC: U.S. Department of Justice, 1980.

Bagdikian, Ben H. *The Information Machines: Their Impact on Men and the Media.* New York: Harper & Row, 1971.

Bagdikian, Ben H. *The Effete Conspiracy and Other Crimes By the Press.* New York: Harper & Row, 1972.

Bagdikian, Ben H. *The Media Monopoly.* Boston: Beacon Press, 1983,1992.

Bartow, Edith Merwin. *News and These United States.* New York: Funk & Wagnalls Company, 1955.

Black, Jay, and Jennings Bryant. *Introduction to Mass Communication.* Third Edition. Dubuque, Iowa: Wm. C. Brown Publishers, 1992.

Boyle, Kevin, ed. *Article 19: Information, Freedom and Censorship.* New York: Times Books, 1988.

Busha, Charles H., ed. *An Intellectual Freedom Primer.* Littleton, Colorado: Libraries Unlimited, Inc., 1977.

Cirino, Robert. *Don't Blame the People.* Los Angeles: Diversity Press, 1971. (Later published by Random House, 1972.)

Cirino, Robert. *Power To Persuade: Mass Media and the News.* New York: Bantam Books, 1974.

Curry, Richard O., ed. *Freedom at Risk: Secrecy, Censorship, and Repression in the 1980s.* Philadelphia: Temple University Press, 1988.

D'Souza, Frances, Editorial Team Director. *Article 19: Information Freedom and Censorship.* Chicago: American Library Association, 1991.

DeGrazia, Edward. *Censorship Landmarks.* New York: R.R. Bowker Co., 1969.

Downs, Robert B., ed. *The First Freedom.* Chicago: American Library Association, 1960.

Emery, Edwin. *The Press and America: An Interpretative History of the Mass Media,* Third Edition. Englewood Cliffs, New Jersey: Prentice-Hall, Inc., 1972.

Ernst, Morris L. and Alexander Lindey. *The Censor Marches On.* New York: Da Capo Press, 1971.

Friendly, Fred. *Due To Circumstances Beyond Our Control...* New York: Vintage Books, 1967.

Goetz, Philip W. *The New Encyclopædia Britannica.* Chicago: Encyclopædia Britannica, Inc., 1991.

Haiman, Franklyn S. *"Speech Acts" and the First Amendment.* Carbondale: Southern Illinois University Press, 1993.

Hentoff, Nat. *The First Freedom: The Tumultuous History of Free Speech in America.* New York: Delacorte Press, 1980.

Hoffman, Frank. *Intellectual Freedom and Censorship: An Annotated Bibliography.* Metuchen, New Jersey: Scarecrow Press, 1989.

Horn, Zoia, Nancy Gruber, and Bill Berkowitz, eds. *The Right To Know,* Volume 4. Oakland, California: Data Center, 1992.

Hoyt, Olga G. and Edwin P. *Freedom of the News Media.* New York: The Seabury Press, 1973.

Jansen, Sue Curry. *Censorship: The Knot That Binds Power and Knowledge.* New York: Oxford University Press, 1988.

Jenkinson, Clay. "From Milton to Media: Information Flow in a Free Society." *Media&Values.* Spring 1992.

Johnson, Nicholas. *How To Talk Back To Your Television Set.* New York: Bantam Books, 1970.

Kendrick, Alexander. *Prime Time: The Life of Edward R. Murrow.* Boston: Little, Brown and Company, 1969.

Kent, Allen and Harold Lancour, eds. *Encyclopedia of Library and Information Science,* Volume 4. New York: Marcel Dekker, 1970.

Knight, Arthur. *The Liveliest Art: A Panoramic History of the Movies.* New York: New American Library, 1957.

Lee, Martin A. and Norman Solomon. *Unreliable Sources: A Guide to Detecting Bias in News Media.* New York: Lyle Stuart, 1990.

Lippmann, Walter. *Liberty and the News.* New York: Harcourt, Brace and Howe, 1920.

Liston, Robert A. *The Right To Know: Censorship in America.* New York: Franklin Watts, Inc., 1973.

McCormick, John and Mairi MacInnes, eds. *Versions of Censorship.* Garden City, New York: Anchor Books, 1962.

McKeon, Richard, Robert K. Merton, and Walter Gellhorn. *The Freedom to Read: Perspective and Program.* New York: R. R. Bowker Company, 1957.

Minor, Dale. *The Information War.* New York: Hawthorn Books, Inc., 1970.

Mott, Frank Luther. *American Journalism: A History of Newspapers in the*

United States through 260 Years: 1690 to 1950. New York: The Macmillan Company, 1950.

The New York Public Library. *Censorship: 500 Years of Conflict*. New York: Oxford University Press, 1984.

Parenti, Michael. *Inventing Reality: The Politics of the Mass Media*. New York: St. Martin's Press, 1986.

Pember, Don R. *Mass Media Law*. Fifth Edition. Dubuque, Iowa: Wm. C. Brown Publishers, 1990.

Powledge, Fred. *The Engineering of Restraint: The Nixon Administration and the Press*. Washington, DC: Public Affairs Press, 1971.

Project Censored. "The 10 Best Censored Stories: 1976-1995." Rohnert Park, CA: Censored Publications, 1976-1995.

Rivers, William L., and Wilbur Schramm. *Responsibility in Mass Communication: Revised Edition*. New York: Harper & Row, 1969.

Seldes, George. *Lords of the Press*. New York: Julian Messner, Inc., 1938.

Seldes, George. *Witness to a Century: Encounters With the Noted, the Notorious, and the Three SOBs*. New York: Ballantine Books, 1987.

Sills, David L. ed. *International Encyclopedia of the Social Sciences*, Volume 2. New York: The Macmillan Company & The Free Press, 1968.

Stephens, Mitchell. *A History of News From the Drum to the Satellite*. New York: Viking, 1988.

Stone, I.F. "Notes On Closing, But Not In Farewell." *I.F. Stone's Bi-Weekly*, December 1971.

Tebbel, John. *The Media in America*. New York: Thomas Y. Crowell Company, 1974.

Theiner, George. *They Shoot Writers, Don't They?* London: Faber and Faber, 1984.

Wallraff, Günter. *Wallraff: The Undesirable Journalist*. London: Pluto Press Limited, 1978.

Widmer, Kingsley, and Eleanor. *Literary Censorship: Principles, Cases, Problems*. Belmont, California: Wadsworth Publishing Company, 1961.

THIS MODERN WORLD

by TOM TOMORROW

IT'S **WIRED**--THE MAGAZINE ABOUT NEW FORMS OF COMMUNICATION WHOSE WACKY USE OF TYPE AND BACKGROUNDS OFTEN RENDERS IT **COMPLETELY UNREADABLE...**

OH, DON'T BE SUCH A **LUDDITE!**

YES--**CONTENT** IS SO **OLD-FASHIONED!** WHAT MATTERS IN THE **INFORMATION AGE** ...IS **LAYOUT!**

WIRED

WIRED CELEBRATES ITS SUBJECT WITH **GUSTO!** AS ONE EDITOR RECENTLY COMMENTED, "TECHNOLOGY IS NOT NEUTRAL--TECHNOLOGY IS ABSOLUTELY 100% POSITIVE!"

HMM--SO THE DISTRESS I AM CURRENTLY EXPERIENCING--

--IS SIMPLY THE RESULT OF YOUR OUT-MODED "SECOND WAVE" THINKING!

WIRED IS TO THE NINETIES WHAT **PLAYBOY** WAS TO THE SIXTIES--A MAGAZINE LARGELY DEVOTED TO CONVINCING IMPRESSIONABLE YOUNG MEN THAT **NOTHING** IS HIPPER THAN BEING A **GOOD CONSUMER...**

IF I ONLY HAD A QUADROPHONIC HI-FI SYSTEM-- **THEN** I'D GET THE BABES!

IF I ONLY HAD A POWERFUL MULTI-MEDIA SYSTEM-- **THEN** I'D GET THE BABES!

OF COURSE, **WIRED** IS ULTIMATELY MORE THAN A MERE **MAGAZINE**--IT'S A **WAY OF LIFE**... NOT UNLIKE, SAY, THE **UNIFICATION CHURCH...**

YOU SIMPLY DON'T UNDERSTAND OUR ADVANCED PARADIGM.

WE SCORN AND PITY YOU.

WOULD YOU LIKE TO BUY A COPY OF OUR **NEW ISSUE?**

TOM TOMORROW © 11-22-95

CENSORED Resource Guide

One of Project Censored's long-standing goals is to improve the lines of communication between the public and the media that serve the public. Just knowing where to direct concerns, compliments, ideas or even offers to help is a question many people have when trying to reach either the alternative or establishment media.

With this in mind, Project Censored assembled a simple, easy-to-use and dependable resource guide for anyone who wants to contact the media to follow up on these stories or to get actively involved in doing something about an issue or the media.

Following is a collection of names, addresses, phone and fax numbers, and e-mail addresses, when available, for a variety of organizations, individuals, and electronic and print media outlets that might prove useful.

Although this information was current as of late 1995, you may want to double-check to ensure the names, addresses, etc., are still accurate. If you are aware of any changes and/or corrections to the list, please send them to Censored Resource Guide, Sonoma State University, Rohnert Park, CA 94928.

We plan to update the list in the 1997 edition of CENSORED! If you have any additions that should be included, please send them to the same address.

ALTERNATIVE BROADCAST/FILM/VIDEO PRODUCERS & ORGANIZATIONS

8MM NEWS COLLECTIVE
c/o Squeaky Wheel
372 Connecticut Street
Buffalo, NY 14213
Tel: 716/884-7172

THE 90'S CHANNEL
2010 14th Street, #209
Boulder, CO 80302
Tel: 303/442-8445
Fax: 303/442-6472

ALTERNATIVE RADIO
2129 Mapleton
Boulder, CO 80304
Tel: 303/444-8788
Fax: 303/546-0592

ALTERNATIVE VIEWS
Box 7297
Austin, TX 78713
Tel: 512/477-5148
Fax: 512/471-4806

AMERICA'S DEFENSE MONITOR
1500 Massachusetts Ave., NW
Washington, DC 20005
Tel: 202/862-0700
Fax: 202/862-0708
E-mail: cdi @ igc.apc.org

BLACK PLANET PRODUCTIONS/
NOT CHANNEL ZERO
P.O. Box 435, Cooper Station
New York, NY 10003-0435
Tel: 212/886-3701
Fax: 212/420-8223

CALIFORNIA NEWSREEL
149 9th Street, Suite 420
San Francisco, CA 94103
Tel: 415/621-6196

COMMON GROUND
Stanley Foundation
216 Sycamore Street, Suite 500
Muscatine, IA 52761
Tel: 319/264-1500

CUBA VA FILM PROJECT
12 Liberty Street
San Francisco, CA 94110
Tel: 415/282-1812
Fax: 415/282-1798

DIVA-TV
c/o ACT-UP
135 W. 29th Street, #10
New York, NY 10001
Tel: 212/564-2437

EARTH COMMUNICATIONS
(Radio For Peace International)
SJO 577, P.O. Box 025216
Miami, FL 33102-5216
Tel: 506/249-1821 (Costa Rica)
Fax: 506/249-1095 (Costa Rica)
E-mail: rfpicr@sol.racsa.co.cr

EDUCATIONAL VIDEO CENTER
60 E. 13th Street, 4th Fl.
New York, NY 10003
Tel: 212/254-2848

EL SALVADOR MEDIA PROJECT
335 W. 38th Street, 5th Fl.
New York, NY 10018
Tel: 212/714-9118
Fax: 212/594-6417

EMPOWERMENT PROJECT
3403 Highway 54 West
Chapel Hill, NC 27516
Tel: 919/967-1963
Fax: 919/967-1863

ENVIROVIDEOS
P.O. Box 629000
El Dorado Hills, CA 95762
Tel: 1/800/227-8955

FILMFORUM
6522 Hollywood Blvd.
Los Angeles, CA 90028
Tel: 213/466-4143
Fax: 213/466-4144

FREE RADIO BERKELEY/
FREE COMMUNICATIONS
COALITION
1442 A Walnut Street, #406
Berkeley, CA 94709
Tel: 510/644-3779
or 510/464-3041
E-Mail: frbspd @ crl.com

GLOBALVISION
1600 Broadway, Suite 700
New York, NY 10019
Tel: 212/246-0202
Fax: 212/246-2677
E-mail: globalv@well.com
http://www.igc.apc.org/globalvision

INDEPENDENT TELEVISION
SERVICE
190 Fifth Street East, Suite 200
St. Paul, MN 55101
Tel: 612/225-9035
Fax: 612/225-9102

LABOR BEAT
37 S. Ashland Avenue
Chicago, IL 60607
Tel: 312/226-3330

MEDIA NETWORK/
ALTERNATIVE MEDIA
INFORMATION CENTER
39 W. 14th Street, #403
New York, NY 10011
Tel: 212/929-2663
Fax: 212/929-2732

NATIONAL ASIAN AMERICAN
TELECOMMUNICATIONS
ASSOCIATION
346 9th Street, 2nd Fl.
San Francisco, CA 94103
Tel: 415/863-0814
Fax: 415/863-7428

NATIONAL FEDERATION
OF COMMUNITY BROADCASTERS
666 11th Street, NW, Suite 805
Washington, DC 20001
Tel: 202/393-2355

PACIFICA NETWORK NEWS
702 H Street, NW, Suite 3
Washington, DC 20001
Tel: 202/783-1620
Fax: 202/393-1841

PACIFICA RADIO ARCHIVE
3729 Cahuenga Blvd., West
North Hollywood, CA 91604
Tel: 818/506-1077
Fax: 818/506-1084
E-mail: ppspacific@igc.apc.org

PAPER TIGER TV/DEEP DISH
339 Lafayette Street
New York, NY 10012
Tel: 212/420-9045
Fax: 212/420-8223

PEOPLE'S VIDEO NETWORK
2489 Mission Street, #28
San Francisco, CA 94110
Tel: 415/821-6545
or 415/ 821-7575
Fax: 415/821-5782

P.O.V. (Point Of View)
330 W. 19th Street, 11th Fl.
New York, NY 10011-4035
Tel: 212/989-8121
Fax: 212/989-8230

RISE AND SHINE PRODUCTIONS
300 West 43rd Street, 4th Fl.
New York, NY 10036
Tel: 212/265-2509

TELEMUNDO NETWORK
2470 West 8th Avenue
Hialea, FL 33010
Fax: 305/888-7610

THIRD WORLD NEWSREEL
Camera News, Inc.
335 West 38th Street, 5th Fl.
New York, NY 10018
Tel: 212/947-9277
Fax: 212/594-6417

UNPLUG
360 Grand Avenue
P.O. Box 385
Oakland, CA 94610
Tel: 510/268-1100

VIDEO DATABANK
112 S. Michigan Avenue, 3rd Fl.
Chicago, IL 60603
Tel: 312/345-3550
Fax: 312/541-8072

THE VIDEO PROJECT:
FILMS AND VIDEOS FOR A SAFE
AND SUSTAINABLE WORLD
5332 College Avenue, Suite 101
Oakland, CA 94618
Tel: 510/655-9050
or: 1/800-4-PLANET
Fax: 510/655-9115

"VIEWPOINTS" SERIES
c/o PBS
1320 Braddock Place
Alexandria, VA 22314-1698
Tel: 703/739-5000
PBS Comment Line: 1/800/272-2190

ZEITGEIST FILMS, LTD.
247 Centre Street, 2nd Fl.
New York, NY 10013
Tel: 212/274-1989
Fax: 212/274-1644

ALTERNATIVE & ELECTRONIC NEWS SERVICES

ACTIVIST NEWS NETWORK
P.O. Box 51170
Palo Alto, CA 94303
Tel: 415/493-4502
Fax: 415/493-4564

ALTERNET-Alternative News Network
77 Federal Street
San Francisco, CA 94107
Tel: 415/284-1420
Fax: 415/284-1414
CompuServe ID: 71362,27

CALIFORNIA ALTERNATIVE
NEWS BUREAU
1015 20th Street
Sacramento, CA 95616
Tel: 916/498-1234
Fax: 916/498-7920
E-mail: newsreview@aol.com

INSIGHT FEATURES
Networking for Democracy
3411 Diversey, Suite 1
Chicago, IL 60647
Tel: 312/384-8827
Fax: 312/384-3904

INTERNET
(SEE LIBRARY AND
REFERENCE SOURCES)

INTERPRESS SERVICE
Global Information Network
777 United Nations Plaza
New York, NY 10017
Tel: 212/286-0123
Fax: 212/818-9249

LATIN AMERICA DATA BASE
Latin American Institute
University of New Mexico
801 Yale Blvd., NE
Albuquerque, NM 87131-1016
Tel: 800/472-0888
or 505/277-6839
Fax: 505/277-5989

NEWS INTERNATIONAL
PRESS SERVICE
6161 El Cajon Blvd., #4
San Diego, CA 92115
Tel: 619/563-9218
Fax: 619/563-1514

PACIFIC NEWS SERVICE
450 Mission Street, Room 506
San Francisco, CA 94105
Tel: 415/243-4364

PEACENET; ECONET; CON-
FLICTNET; LABORNET
INSTITUTE FOR GLOBAL
COMMUNICATIONS
18 DeBoom Street
San Francisco, CA 94107
Tel: 415/442-0220
Fax: 415/546-1794

PEOPLE'S NEWS AGENCY
7627 16th Street, NW
P.O. Box 56466
Washington, DC 20040
Tel: 202/829-2278
Fax: 202/829-0462
E-mail: proutwdc@prout.org

ALTERNATIVE PERIODICALS
& PUBLICATIONS

14850 MAGAZINE
Public Communications, Inc.
104 N. Aurora Street, Suite 3
Ithaca, NY 14850
Tel: 607/277-1021
Fax: 607/277-0801

ACROSS THE LINE
Seeds of Peace
P.O. Box 12154
Oakland, CA 94604
Tel: 510/420-1799

THE ADVOCATE
6922 Hollywood Blvd., Suite 1000
Los Angeles, CA 90028
Tel: 213/871-1225
Fax: 213/467-6805
E-mail: info@advocate.com

AFRICA NEWS
P.O. Box 3851
Durham, NC 27702
Tel: 919/286-0747
Fax: 919/286-2614

AGAINST THE CURRENT
Center for Changes
7012 Michigan Avenue
Detroit, MI 48210
Tel: 313/841-0161
Fax: 313/841-8884

AKWESASNE NOTES
Mohawk Nation
P.O. Box 196
Rooseveltown, NY 13683-0196
Tel: 518/358-9531
Fax: 613/575-2935

ALTERNATIVE PRESS REVIEW
C.A.L. Press
P.O. Box 1446
Columbia, MO 65205-1446
Tel: 314/442-4352

ALTERNATIVES
Lynne Rienner Publishers
1800 30th Street, Suite 314
Boulder, CO 80301-1032
Tel: 303/444-6684
Fax: 303/444-0824

AMICUS JOURNAL
40 W. 20th Street
New York, NY 10011
Tel: 212/727-2700
Fax: 212/727-1773

ANIMAL'S AGENDA
P.O. Box 25881
Baltimore, MD 21224
Tel: 410/675-4566

ARMS SALES MONITOR
Federation of American Scientists
307 Massachusetts Avenue, NE
Washington, DC 20002
Tel: 202/675-1018
Fax: 202/675-1010
E-mail: llumpe@fas.org

THE BAFFLER
Box 378293
Chicago, IL 60637

THE BALTIMORE SUN
501 N. Charles Street
Baltimore, MD 21201
Tel: 410/332-0920

BLACK SCHOLAR
P.O. Box 2869
Oakland, CA 94609
Tel: 510/547-6633
Fax: 510/547-6679

THE BODY POLITIC
P.O. Box 2363
Binghamton, NY 13902
Tel: 607/648-2760
Fax: 607/648-2511
E-mail: annebower@delphi.com

BORDER/LINES
P.O. Box 459
Toronto, Ontario M5S 2S9
Canada
Tel: 416/921-6446
Fax: 416/921-3984

THE BOSTON PHOENIX
126 Brookline Avenue
Boston, MA 02215
Tel: 617/536-5390
Fax: 617/859-8201

THE BOYCOTT QUARTERLY
Center for Economic Democracy
P.O. Box 30727
Seattle, WA 98103-0727
E-mail: boycottguy@aol.com

BREAD AND JUSTICE
Southern California Interfaith Hunger
Coalition
2449 Hyperion, Suite 100
Los Angeles, CA 90027
Tel: 213/913-7333
Fax: 213/664-1725

BROADCASTING & CABLE
1705 DeSales Street, NW, Ste. 600
Washington, DC 20036
Tel: 202/659-2340

BULLETIN OF THE ATOMIC
SCIENTISTS
Education Foundation for Nuclear
Science
6042 South Kimbark Avenue
Chicago, IL 60637
Tel: 312/702-2555
Fax: 312/702-0725
E-mail: bullatomsci@igc.apc.org

CANADIAN DIMENSION
707-228 Notre Dame Ave., Rm.401
Winnipeg, MB R3B 1N7
Canada
Tel: 204/957-1519
Fax: 204/943-4617

CAPITAL EYE
Center for Responsive Politics
1320 19th Street, NW, #700
Washington, DC 20036
Tel: 202/857-0044
Fax: 202/857-7809
E-mail: info@crp.org

CASCADIA TIMES
25-6 NW 23rd Pl., #406
Portland, OR 97210
Tel: 503/223-9036
E-mail: cascadia@desktop.org

THE CHRONICLE OF HIGHER
EDUCATION
1255 23rd Street, NW
Washington, DC 20037
Tel: 202/466-1000
Fax: 202/296-2691

THE CHRONICLE OF
PHILANTHROPY
1255 23rd St., NW, 7th Floor
Washington, DC 20037
Tel: 202/466-1200
Fax: 202/466-2078

THE CIRCLE
1530 East Franklin Avenue
Minneapolis, MN 55404
Tel: 612/879-1760
Fax: 612/879-1712

CITIZENS CLEARINGHOUSE
FOR HAZARDOUS WASTES
P.O. Box 6806
Falls Church, VA 22040

CITY PAPER
Baltimore's Free Weekly
812 Park Avenue
Baltimore, MD 21201
Tel: 410/523-2300
Fax: 410/523-2222

COMMON CAUSE MAGAZINE
2030 M Street, NW
Washington, DC 20036
Tel: 202/833-1200
Fax: 202/659-3716

CONGRESSIONAL QUARTERLY
WEEKLY REPORT
1414 22nd Street, NW
Washington, DC 20037
Tel: 202/887-8500
Fax: 202/728-1863

CONNECT
The Center for Media Literacy
1962 South Shenandoah Street
Los Angeles, CA 90034
Tel: 310/559-2944
Fax: 310/559-9396

CONSUMER REPORTS
101 Truman Avenue
Yonkers, NY 10703
Tel: 914/378-2000

COUNTERPOISE
1716 SW Williston Avenue
Gainesville, FL 32608
Tel: 904/335-2200
Fax: call first
E-mail: willett@freenet.ufl.edu

COUNTER PUNCH
Institute for Policy Studies (IPS)
Newsletter Project
1601 Connecticut Ave., NW
Washington, DC 20009

COVERTACTION QUARTERLY
1500 Massachusetts Ave., NW, #732
Washington, DC 20005
Tel: 202/331-9763
Fax: 202/331-9751

CRESTED BUTTE CHRONICLE
& PILOT
P.O. Box 369
Crested Butte, CO 81224
Tel: 303/349-6114

CROSSROADS
Institute for Social and Economic
Studies
P.O. Box 2809
Oakland, CA 94609
Tel: 510/843-7495
E-mail: crossroads@igc.apc.org

CUBA ADVOCATE
1750 30th Street, #152
Boulder, CO 80301
Tel: 303/447-2286

CULTURAL DEMOCRACY
P.O. Box 545
Tucson, AZ 85702
Tel: 602/791-9359
E-mail: cdemocracy@aol.com

CULTURAL SURVIVAL QUARTERLY
Cultural Survival, Inc.
46 Brattle Street
Cambridge, MA 02138
Tel: 617/441-5400
Fax: 617/441-5417

THE DAILY CITIZEN
P.O. Box 57365
Washington, DC 20037
Tel: 202/429-6929
Fax: 202/659-1145

THE DAYTON VOICE
1927 N. Main Street, Suites 7&8
Dayton, OH 45405
Tel: 513/275-8855
Fax: 513/275-6056

DEADLINE
Center for War, Peace
and the News Media
New York University
10 Washington Place, 4th Fl.
New York, NY 10003
Tel: 212/998-7960
Fax: 212/995-4143

DE TODO UN POCO
2830 5th Street
Boulder, CO 80304
Tel: 303/444-8565
Fax: 303/545-2074

DEFENSE MONITOR
1500 Massachusetts Ave., NW
Washington, DC 20005
Tel: 202/862-0700
Fax: 202/862-0708
E-Mail: cdi@igc.apc.org

DENVER WESTWORD
P.O. Box 5970
Denver, CO 80217
Tel: 303/296-7744

(DIS)CONNECTION
c/o Autonomous Zone
1573 N. Milwaukee Ave., #420
Chicago, IL 60622
Tel: 312/278-0775
E-mail: ugwiller@bgu.edu

DISSENT
521 Fifth Avenue
New York, NY 10017
Tel: 212/595-3084

DOLLARS AND SENSE
1 Summer Street
Somerville, MA 02143
Tel: 617/628-8411
Fax: 617/628-2025

E: THE ENVIRONMENTAL
MAGAZINE
P.O. Box 5098
Westport, CT 06881
Tel: 203/854-5559
Fax: 203/866-0602

EARTH ISLAND JOURNAL
300 Broadway, Suite 28
San Francisco, CA 94133-3312
Tel: 415/788-3666
Fax: 415/788-7324

THE ECOLOGIST
Agriculture House, Bath Road
Sturminster Newton
Dorset DT10 IDU, U.K.
Tel: 011-44-1258-473476
E-mail: ecologist@gn.apc.org

ECONEWS
879 Ninth Street
Arcata, CA 95521
Tel: 707/822-6918
Fax: 707/822-0827
E-mail: nec@igc.apc.org

THE EL SALVADOR WATCH
c/o CISPES
19 W. 21st Street, Room 502
New York, NY 10010
Tel: 212/229-1290

EMERGE:
BLACK AMERICA'S
NEWS MAGAZINE
One B.E.T. Plaza
1900 W Place, NE
Washington, DC 20018-1211
Tel: 202/608-2093
Fax: 202/608-2598

ENVIRONMENTAL ACTION
6930 Carroll Avenue, Suite 600
Takoma Park, MD 20912
Tel: 301/891-1100
Fax: 301/891-2218

ENVIRONMENTAL IMPACT
REPORTER
P.O. Box 1834
Sebastopol, CA 95473
Tel: 707/823-8744

ESSENCE MAGAZINE
1500 Broadway
New York, NY 10036
Tel: 212/642-0600

EXTRA!
Fairness and Accuracy in Reporting
130 W. 25th Street
New York, NY 10001
Tel: 212/633-6700
Fax: 212/727-7668
E-mail: info@fair.org
http://www.fair.org./fair/

FACTSHEET 5
c/o Seth Friedman
P.O. Box 170099
San Francisco, CA 94117-0099
Tel: 415/668-1781

FAT!SO?
P.O. Box 423464
San Francisco, CA 94142-3464
http://www.fatso.com

FIFTH ESTATE
4632 Second Avenue
Detroit, MI 48201
Tel: 313/831-6800

FEMINIST LIBRARY NEWSLETTER
5 Westminster Bridge Road
London, SE1 7XW, England
Tel: 011-44-1-928-7789

FOOD & WATER JOURNAL
Food and Water, Inc.
RR1, Box 68D
Walden, VT 05873
Tel: 802/563-3300
Fax: 802/563-3310

FOOD FIRST NEWS
Institute for Food & Development Policy
398 60th Street
Oakland, CA 94618
Tel: 510/654-4400

FOREIGN AFFAIRS
58 E. 68th Street
New York, NY 10021
Tel: 212/734-0400

FREE THINKER FORUM
Project Freedom
P.O. Box 14447
St. Louis, MO 63178
Tel: 618/637-2202
E-mail: profreedom@aol.com

FRONT LINES RESEARCH
Public Policy Institute
Planned Parenthood Federation of
America
810 Seventh Avenue
New York, NY 10019
Tel: 212/261-4721
Fax: 212/261-4352

GAO REPORTS & TESTIMONY
U.S. General Accounting Office
Washington, DC 10548-0001
Tel: 202/512-6000

GENDER & MASS MEDIA
Stockholm University-JMK
P.O. Box 27861
S-115 93
Stockholm, Sweden

GLOBAL EXCHANGES
2017 Mission Street, Suite 303
San Francisco, CA 94110
Tel: 415/255-7296

GLOBAL PESTICIDE CAMPAIGNER
Pesticide Action Network
116 New Montgomery, #810
San Francisco, CA 94105
Tel: 415/541-9140
Fax: 415/541-9253

GRASSROOTS ECONOMIC
ORGANIZING NEWSLETTER
P.O. Box 5065
New Haven, CT 06526
Tel: 203/389-6194

GREEN MAGAZINE
P.O. Box 381
Mill Harbour
London E14 9TW
England

HARD TIMES
c/o L.A. Village View
2342 Sawtelle Blvd.
Los Angeles, CA 90064
Tel: 310/477-0403

HEALTH LETTER
1600 20th St.,NW
Washington, DC 20009
Tel: 202/588-1000

HIGH COUNTRY NEWS
P.O. Box 1090
Paonia, CO 81428
Tel: 303/527-4898

THE HUMAN QUEST
Churchman Co., Inc.
1074 23rd Avenue N.
St. Petersburg, FL 33704-3228
Tel: 813/894-0097

HUNGRY MIND REVIEW
1648 Grand Avenue
St. Paul, MN 55105
Tel: 612/699-2610

HURACAN
P.O. Box 7591
Minneapolis, MN 55407

THE IDLER
15 St. Stephens Gardens
London, W2 5NA, England
Tel: 011-44-171-792-3501

IN CONTEXT
P.O. Box 11470
Bainbridge Island, WA 98110
Tel: 206/842-0216
Fax: 206/842-5208

THE INDEPENDENT
540 Mendocino Avenue
Santa Rosa, CA 95401
Tel: 707/527-1200
Fax: 707/527-1288

INDEX ON CENSORSHIP
Writers & Scholars Educational Trust
33 Islington High Street
London N1 9LH
United Kingdom
Tel: 011-44-171-278-2313
Fax: 011-44-171-278-1878
E-mail: index@indexcen.democ.co.uk

INDUSTRIAL WORKER
103 W. Michigan Avenue
Ypsilanti, MI 48197-5438
Tel: 313/483-3548
Fax: 313/483-4050
E-mail: iww@igc.apc.org

INSIGHT
3600 New York Avenue, NE
Washington, DC 20002
Tel: 202/636-8810

IN THESE TIMES
2040 N. Milwaukee Avenue, 2nd Fl.
Chicago, IL 60647-4002
Tel: 312/772-0100
Fax: 312/772-4180

IRE JOURNAL: INVESTIGATIVE
REPORTERS & EDITORS
P.O. Box 838
University of Missouri
School of Journalism
Columbia, MO 65205
Tel: 314/882-2042
Fax: 314/882-5431

ISSUES IN SCIENCE &
TECHNOLOGY
1636 Hobart Street, NW
Washington, DC 20009
Tel: 202/986-7217
Fax: 202/986-7221

KLANWATCH
P.O.Box 548
Montgomery, AL 36104
Tel: 205/264-0286
Fax: 205/264-0629

LA GACETA
P.O. Box 5536
Tampa, FL 33675
Tel: 813/248-3921
Fax: 813/247-5357

LABOR NEWS FOR WORKING
FAMILIES
I.I.R., 2521 Channing Way
Berkeley, CA 94720
Tel: 510/643-6814
Fax: 510/642-6432

LATIN AMERICAN PERSPECTIVES
2455 Teller Road
Newbury Park, CA 91320
Tel: 805/499-0721
Fax: 805/499-0871

LEFT BUSINESS OBSERVER
250 W. 85th Street
New York, NY 10024-3217
Tel: 212/874-4020

LEGAL TIMES
1730 M Street, NW, Suite 802
Washington, DC 20036
Tel: 202/457-0686

LONDON INDEPENDENT
40 City Road
London EC1Y 2DB
England

MEDIA AND VALUES
Media Action Research Center
475 Riverside Drive, Suite 1901
New York, NY 10115
Tel: 212/865-6690
Fax: 212/663-2746

MEDIA BYPASS
P.O. Box 5326
Evansville, IL 47716
Tel: 812/477-8670
Fax: 812/477-8677

MEDIA, CULTURE AND SOCIETY
Sage Publications
6 Bonhill Street
London, EC24 4PU, England

MEDIACULTURE REVIEW
77 Federal Street
San Francisco, CA 94107
Tel: 415/284-1420
Fax: 415/284-1414

THE METRO TIMES
743 Beaubien, Suite 301
Detroit, MI 48226
Tel: 313/961-4060
Fax: 313/961-6598

MIGHT MAGAZINE
150 Fourth Street, Suite 650
San Francisco, CA 94103
Tel: 415/896-1528
E-mail: mightmag@aol.com

MOTHER JONES
731 Market Street, Suite 600
San Francisco, CA 94103
Tel: 415/665-6637
Fax: 415/665-6696

MS. MAGAZINE
230 Park Avenue
New York, NY 10169
Tel: 212/551-9595

MUCKRAKER
Center for Investigative Reporting
568 Howard Street, 5th Fl.
San Francisco, CA 94105-3008
Tel: 415/543-1200
Fax: 415/543-8311

MULTINATIONAL MONITOR
P.O. Box 19405
Washington, DC 20036
Tel: 202/387-8034
Fax: 202/234-5176
E-mail: monitor@essential.org

THE NATION
72 Fifth Avenue
New York, NY 10011
Tel: 212/242-8400
Fax: 212/463-9712

NATIONAL CATHOLIC REPORTER
P.O. Box 419281
Kansas City, MO 64141
Tel: 816/531-0538
Fax: 816/968-2280

NATIONAL REVIEW
150 E. 35th Street
New York, NY 10016
Tel: 212/679-7330
Fax: 212/696-0309

THE NEIGHBORHOOD WORKS
Center for Neighborhood Technology
2125 West North Avenue
Chicago, IL 60647
Tel: 312/278-4800

THE NEW INTERNATIONALIST
55 Rectory Road
Oxford OX4 1BW, U.K.
Tel: 011-44-186-572-8181
Fax: 011-44-186-579-3152
E-mail: newint@gn.apc.org

NEW PERSPECTIVES QUARTERLY
10951 W. Pico Blvd., 3rd Fl.
Los Angeles, CA 90064
Tel: 310/474-0011
and 800/336-1007

THE NEW REPUBLIC
1220 19th Street, NW
Washington, DC 20036
Tel: 202/331-7494
Fax: 202/331-0275

NEW STATESMAN & SOCIETY
Foundation House
Perseverance Works
38 Kingsland Road
London, E2 8DQ, England

NEW TIMES, INC.
P.O. Box 5970
Denver, CO 80217

NEW YORK NATIVE
That New Magazine, Inc.
P.O. Box 1475
Church Street Station
New York, NY 10008

NEWS FROM INDIAN COUNTRY
Rt. 2, Box 2900A
Hayward, WI 54843

NEWSLETTER ON
INTELLECTUAL FREEDOM
American Library Association
50 E. Huron Street
Chicago, IL 60611
Tel: 312/280-4223
Fax: 312/440-9374

NEWT WATCH!
Public Citizen
2000 P Street, NW
Washington, DC 20036

NORTH COAST XPRESS
P.O. Box 1226
Occidental, CA 95465
Tel: 707/874-1453
  or 707/874-3104

NUTRITION ACTION
HEALTHLETTER
Center for Science in the Public Interest
1875 Connecticut Ave., NW, Suite 300
Washington, DC 20009-5728

OPEN EYE
BM Open Eye
London, WC1N 3XX
Tel: 011-44-195-625-0654

OUT
The Soho Building
110 Greene Street, Suite 800
New York, NY 10017
Tel: 212/334-9119
Fax: 212/334-9227

PACIFIC SUN
P.O. Box 5553
Mill Valley, CA 94942
Tel: 415/383-4500
Fax: 415/383-4159

PBI/USA REPORT
Peace Brigades Int'l/USA
2642 College Avenue
Berkeley, CA 94704
Tel: 510/540-0749
Fax: same; call first
E-mail: pbiusa@igc.apc.org

PEACE REVIEW:
A Transnational Quarterly
Peace & Justice Studies
University of San Francisco
2130 Fulton Street
San Francisco, CA 94117
Tel: 415/666-6349/6496
Fax: 415/666-2346
E-mail: eliasr@usfca.edu

PEACEWORK
American Friends Service Committee
2161 Massachusetts Ave.
Cambridge, MA 02140
Tel: 617/661-6130
Fax: 617/354-2832

THE PEOPLE'S WARRIOR
P.O. Box 488
Rockwall, TX 75087
Tel: 1-800/771-1992
or 214/771-1991

PERCEPTIONS MAGAZINE
c/o 10734 Jefferson Blvd., Suite 502
Culver City, CA 90230
Tel: 310/313-5185
 or 800/276-4448
Fax: 310/313-5198

PITTSBURGH POST-GAZETTE
Box 957
Pittsburgh, PA 15222
Tel: 412/263-1100

POZ MAGAZINE
1279 Old Chelsea Station
New York, NY 10113-1279
Tel: 212/242-2163
E-mail: pozmag@aol.com

PREVAILING WINDS MAGAZINE
Center for the Preservation of Modern
History
P.O. Box 23511
Santa Barbara, CA 93121
Tel: 805/899-3433
Fax: 805/899-4773

PRISON LEGAL NEWS
P.O. Box 1684
Lake Worth, FL 33460
Tel: 407/547-9716

THE PROGRESSIVE
409 E. Main Street
Madison, WI 53703
Tel: 608/257-4626
Fax: 608/257-3373

PROPAGANDA REVIEW
Media Alliance
814 Mission Street, Suite 205
San Francisco, CA 94103
Tel: 415/546-6334

PUBLIC CITIZEN
1600 20th Street, NW
Washington, DC 20009
Tel: 202/588-1000
Fax: 202/588-7799
E-mail: pnye@citizen.org

THE PUBLIC EYE
Political Research Associates
120 Beacon Street, 3rd Fl.
Somerville, MA 02143-4304
Tel: 617/661-9313

RACHEL'S ENVIRONMENT &
HEALTH WEEKLY
c/o Environmental Research Foundation
Box 5036
Annapolis, MD 21403-7036
Tel: 410/263-1584
Fax: 410/263-8944
E-mail: rachel@rachel.clark.net

RANDOM LENGTHS
P.O. Box 731
San Pedro, CA 90733

REAPPRAISING AIDS
c/o Charles A. Thomas, Jr.
7514 Girard Ave., #1-331
La Jolla, CA 92037

REASON
3415 S. Sepulveda Blvd., Suite 400
Los Angeles, CA 90034
Tel: 310/391-2245

RECONSTRUCTION
1563 Massachusetts Avenue
Cambridge, MA 02138
Tel: 617/495-0907
Fax: 617/496-5515

THE RECORDER
625 Polk Street
San Francisco, CA 94102

RED PEPPER
Socialist Newspaper Publications, Ltd.
3 Gunthorpe Street
London, E1 7RP, England
Tel: 011-44-171-247-1702
E-mail: redpepper@online.rednet.co.uk

RETHINKING SCHOOLS
1001 E. Keefe Avenue
Milwaukee, WI 53212
Tel: 414/964-9646
Fax: 414/964-7220

REVOLUTIONARY WORKER
P.O. Box 3486
Chicago, IL 60654

ROC-ROCK OUT CENSORSHIP
P.O. Box 147
Jewett, OH 43986

ROLLING STONE
1290 Ave. of the Americas, 2nd Fl.
New York, NY 10104
Tel: 212/484-1616
Fax: 212/767-8203

THE SAN FRANCISCO BAY
GUARDIAN
520 Hampshire
San Francisco, CA 94110
Tel: 415/255-3100
Fax: 415/255-8762

SANTA BARBARA NEWS PRESS
715 Anacapa Street
Santa Barbara, CA 93101
Tel: 805/564-5200

SANTA CRUZ SENTINEL
P.O. Box 638
Santa Cruz, CA 95061
Tel: 408/423-4242
Fax: 408/429-9620

SANTA ROSA SUN
1275 Fourth Street, #608
Santa Rosa, CA 95404
Tel: 707/544-3448
Fax: 707/544-4756

SECRECY & GOVERNMENT
BULLETIN
Federation of American Scientists
307 Massachusetts Avenue, NE
Washington, DC 20002
Tel: 202/675-1012

SF WEEKLY
425 Brannan Street
San Francisco, CA 94107
Tel: 415/541-0700
Fax: 415/777-1839

S.O.A. WATCH
P.O. Box 3330
Columbus, GA 31903

SOCIAL POLICY
25 W. 43rd Street, Room 620
New York, NY 10036
Tel: 212/354-8525
Fax: 212/642-1956

SOJOURNERS
2401 15th Street, NW
Washington, DC 20009
Tel: 202/328-8842
Fax: 202/328-8757

SOUTHERN EXPOSURE
P.O. Box 531
Durham, NC 27702
Tel: 919/419-8311
Fax: 919/419-8315

SPIN
6 West 18th Street
New York, NY 10011
Tel: 212/633-8200
Fax: 212/633-9041

SPIRIT OF CRAZY HORSE
Leonard Peltier Defense Committee
International Office
P.O. Box 583
Lawrence, KS 66044
Tel: 913/842-5774
Fax: 913/842-5796

THE SPOTLIGHT
300 Independence Avenue, SE
Washington, DC 20003
Tel: 202/544-1794

THE STRANGER
1202 E. Pike Street, Suite 1225
Seattle, WA 98122-3934
Tel: 203/323-7002

STRATEGIES
Strategies for Media Literacy
1095 Market Street, Suite 617
San Francisco, CA 94103
Tel: 415/621-2911

THE SUN
107 N. Roberson Street
Chapel Hill, NC 27516
Tel: 919/942-5282

TASK FORCE CONNECTIONS
National Task Force on AIDS Prevention
973 Market St., Suite 600
San Francisco, CA 94103
Tel: 415/356-8110
Fax: 415/356-8138

TEXAS OBSERVER
307 West 7th Street
Austin, TX 78701-2917
Tel: 512/477-0746
Fax: 512/474-1175

THIRD FORCE
Center for Third World Organizing
1218 East 21st Street
Oakland, CA 94606-9950
Tel: 510/533-7583

THRESHOLD
Student Environmental Action Coalition
(SEAC)
P.O. Box 1168
Chapel Hill, NC 27514-1168
Tel: 919/967-4600
Fax: 919/967-4648
E-mail: seac@igc.apc.org

TIBET PRESS WATCH
International Campaign for Tibet
1518 K Street, NW, Suite 410
Washington, DC 20005

TIKKUN
251 W. 100th Street, 5th Fl.
New York, NY 10025
Tel: 212/864-4110
Fax: 212/864-4137

TOWARD FREEDOM
209 College Street
Burlington, VT 05401
Tel: 802/658-2523
Fax: 802/658-3738
E-mail: mavmedia@aol.com

TRANSITION
1430 Massachusetts Ave., 4th Fl.
Cambridge, MA 02138
Tel: 617/496-2847

TRANSPORTATION ALTERNATIVES
92 St. Mark's Place
New York, NY 10009
Tel: 212/475-4600

TURNING THE TIDE
People Against Racist Terror
P.O. Box 1990
Burbank, CA 91507

U. THE NATIONAL COLLEGE
MAGAZINE
1800 Century Park East #820
Los Angeles, CA 90067-1503
Tel: 310/551-1381
Fax: 310/551-1659
E-mail: editor@umagazine.com

UNCLASSIFIED
Association of National Security Alumni
2001 S Street, NW, Suite 740
Washington, DC 20009
Tel: 202/483-9325

THE URBAN ECOLOGIST
Urban Ecology
405 14th Street, Suite 701
Oakland, CA 94612
Tel: 510/251-6330
E-mail: urbanecology@igc.apc.org

URGENT ACTION BULLETIN
Survival International
11-15 Emerald Street
London WC1N 3QL
United Kingdom
Tel: 011-44-171-242-1441
Fax: 011-44-171-242-1771

URGENT ACTION NEWSLETTER
Urgent Action Program Office
Amnesty International USA
P.O. Box 1270
Nederland, CO 80466-1270
Tel: 303/440-0913
Fax: 303/258-7881
E-mail: sharris@igc.apc.org

UTNE READER
1624 Harmon Place, Suite 330
Minneapolis, MN 55403
Tel: 612/338-5040
Fax: 612/338-6043
E-mail: editor@utne.com
http://www.utne.com

VIBE
205 Lexington Avenue, 3rd Fl.
New York, NY 10016
Tel: 212/522-7092
Fax: 212/522-4578

VILLAGE VOICE
36 Cooper Square
New York, NY 10003
Tel: 212/475-3300
Fax: 212/475-8944

WAR AND PEACE DIGEST
War and Peace Foundation
32 Union Square East
New York, NY 10003-3295
Tel: 212/777-6626
Fax: 212/995-9652

WASHINGTON FREE PRESS
1463 E. Republican Street, #178
Seattle, WA 98112
Tel: 206/233-1780
E-Mail: freepres @ scn.org

THE WASHINGTON SPECTATOR
London Terrace Station
P.O. Box 20065
New York, NY 10011

WELFARE MOTHER'S VOICE
Welfare Warriors
4504 North 47 Street
Milwaukee, WI 53218

WHO CARES: A JOURNAL OF
SERVICE AND ACTION
511 K Street, NW, Suite 1042
Washington, DC 20005
Tel: 202/628-1691
Fax: 202/628-2063
E-mail: info@whocares.mag

WHOLE EARTH REVIEW
27 Gate Five Road
Sausalito, CA 94965
Tel: 415/332-1716
Fax: 415/332-3110

WILD FOREST REVIEW
P.O. Box 86373
Portland, OR 97286
Tel: 503/788-1998

WILLAMETTE WEEK
Portland's Newsweekly
822 SW 10th Avenue
Portland, OR 97205
Tel: 503/243-2122
Fax: 503/243-1115

WIRED MAGAZINE
520 Third Street, 4th Fl.
San Francisco, CA 94107
Tel: 415/222-6205
Fax: 415/222-6209

WOMEN'S HEALTH LETTER
2245 E. Colorado Blvd., Suite 104
Pasadena, CA 91107-3651
Tel: 818/798-0638
Fax: 818/798-0639

WOMENSTRUGGLE!
P.O. Box 54115
Minneapolis, MN 55454
Tel: 612/729-8543

THE WORKBOOK
Southwest Research and
Information Center
P.O. Box 4524
105 Stanford, S.E.
Albuquerque, NM 87106
Tel: 505/262-1862
Fax: 505/262-1864

WORKING MOTHER MAGAZINE
230 Park Avenue
New York, NY 10069
Tel: 212/551-9500
Fax: 212/551-9757

WORLD POLICY JOURNAL
65 Fifth Avenue, Suite 413
New York, NY 10003
Tel: 212/229-5808
Fax: 212/229-5579

WORLD PRESS REVIEW
200 Madison Avenue, Suite 2104
New York NY 10016
Tel: 212/889-5155
Fax: 212/889-5634

WORLD WATCH
Worldwatch Institute
1776 Massachusetts Avenue, NW
Washington, DC 20036
Tel: 202/452-1999
Fax: 202/296-7365

YO!-YOUTH OUTLOOK
Pacific News Service
450 Mission Street, Room 506
San Francisco, CA 94105
Tel: 415/243-4364

YOUTH ACTION FORUM
Youth Action Network
100 Adelaide Street W., Suite 906
Toronto, Ontario, Canada
Tel: 1/800/718-LINK
  or 416/368-2277
Fax: 416/368-8354

Z MAGAZINE
116 Botolph Street
Boston, MA 02115
Tel: 617/787-4531
Fax: 508/457-0626

FREE PRESS/RIGHT-TO-KNOW PUBLICATIONS & ORGANIZATIONS

THE ADVOCACY INSTITUTE
1730 Rhode Island Ave., NW
Suite 600
Washington, DC 20036-3118
Tel: 202/659-8475

ALLIANCE FOR COMMUNITY
MEDIA
666 11th Street, NW, Suite 806
Washington, DC 20001-4542
Tel: 202/393-2650
Fax: 202/393-2653
E-mail: alliancecm@aol.com

ALLIANCE FOR CULTURAL
DEMOCRACY
P.O. Box 545
Tucson, AZ 85702
Tel: 602/791-9359

ALTERNATIVE PRESS CENTER
P.O. Box 33109
Baltimore, MD 21218-0401
Tel: 410/243-2471
Fax: 410/235-5325
E-mail: altpress@igc.apc.org

AMERICAN LIBRARY ASSOCIATION
OFFICE FOR INTELLECTUAL
FREEDOM
50 E. Huron Street
Chicago, IL 60611
Tel: 312/280-4223
or 800/545-2433
Fax: 312/280-4227

ARTICLE 19: INTERNATIONAL
CENTRE AGAINST CENSORSHIP
33 Islington High Street
London N1 9LH
England
Tel: 011-44-171-278-9292
Fax: 011-44-171-713-1356

ASSOCIATION OF
ALTERNATIVE NEWSWEEKLIES
(AAN)
1001 Connecticut Ave., NW, Ste. 822
Washington, DC 20036-4104
Tel: 202/822-1955
Fax: 202/822-0929

BILL OF RIGHTS JOURNAL
175 Fifth Avenue, Room 814
New York, NY 10010
Tel: 212/673-2040
Fax: 212/460-8359

CALIFORNIA FIRST AMENDMENT
COALITION
926 J Street, Suite 1406
Sacramento, CA 95814-2708
Tel: 916/447-2322
Fax: 916/447-2328

CALIFORNIANS AGAINST
CENSORSHIP TOGETHER (ACT)
1800 Market Street, Suite 1000
San Francisco, CA 94103
Tel: 510/548-3695

THE CENTER FOR DEMOCRACY
AND TECHNOLOGY (CDT)
1001 G Street, NW, 500 East
Washington, DC 20001
Tel: 202/637-9800
Fax: 202/637-0968
E-mail: info@cdt.org
http://www.cdt.org

CENTER FOR MEDIA EDUCATION
1511 K Street, NW, Suite 518
Washington, DC 20005
Tel: 202/628-2620
Fax: 202/628-2554

CENTER FOR THIRD WORLD
ORGANIZING
1218 East 21st Street
Oakland, CA 94606-9950
Tel: 510/533-7583

CIVIC MEDIA CENTER
1636 West University Avenue
Gainesville, FL 32603
Tel: 904/373-0010

CIVIL LIBERTIES
American Civil Liberties Union
132 W. 43rd Street
New York, NY 10036
Tel: 212/944-9800
Fax: 212/869-9065

COALITION vs PBS CENSORSHIP
P.O. Box 485
Santa Monica, CA 90406-0485
Tel: 310/315-4779
Fax: 310/315-4773
E-mail: 72607,2610@compuserve.com

COMMITTEE TO PROTECT
JOURNALISTS
330 Seventh Ave., 12th Fl.
New York, NY 10001
Tel: 212/465-1004
Fax: 212/465-9568

CONSUMER PROJECT ON
TECHNOLOGY
P.O. Box 19367
Washington, DC 20036

CULTURE WATCH
Data Center
464 19th Street
Oakland, CA 94612
Tel: 510/835-4692
Fax: 510/835-3017
E-mail: datactr@tmn.com

DATA CENTER
Right-to-Know Project
464 19th Street
Oakland, CA 94612
Tel: 510/835-4692
Fax: 510/835-3017
E-mail: datactr@tmn.com

ELECTRONIC FRONTIER
FOUNDATION
P.O. Box 170190
San Francisco, CA 94117
Tel: 415/668-7007
Fax: 415/668-7007
E-mail: info@eff.org
http://www.eff.org

ENVIRONMENTAL RESEARCH
FOUNDATION
Box 5036
Annapolis, MD 21403-7036
Tel: 410/263-1584
Fax: 410/263-8944
E-mail: rachel@rachel.clark.net

FEMINISTS FOR FREE EXPRESSION
2525 Times Square Station
New York, NY 10108
Tel: 212/713-5446

FIRST AMENDMENT CENTER
Society of Professional Journalists
1050 Connecticut Avenue, NW
Suite 1206
Washington, DC 20036
Tel: 202/628-1411

FIRST AMENDMENT CONGRESS
1445 Market Street, Suite 320
Denver, CO 80202
Tel: 303/820-5688
Fax: 303/534-8774

FREEDOM FORUM
1101 Wilson Blvd.
Arlington, VA 22209
Tel: 703/528-0800
Fax: 703/284-3570

FREEDOM FORUM
First Amendment Center
1207 18th Avenue South
Nashville, TN 37212
Tel: 615/321-9588

FREEDOM FORUM
Media Studies Center
Columbia University
2950 Broadway
New York, NY 10027-7004
Tel: 212/678-6600
Fax: 212/678-6663

FREEDOM OF EXPRESSION
FOUNDATION
5220 S. Marina Pacifica
Long Beach, CA 90803
Tel: 310/985-4301
Fax: 310/985-2369

FREEDOM OF INFORMATION
CENTER
20 Walter Williams Hall
University of Missouri at Columbia
Columbia, MO 65211
Tel: 573/882-4856
Fax: 573/882-9002
E-mail: jourke@muccmail.missouri.edu

FREEDOM OF INFORMATION
CLEARINGHOUSE
P.O. Box 19367
Washington, DC 20036
Tel: 202/588-7790

FREEDOM WRITER
Institute for First Amendment Studies
P.O. Box 589
Great Barrington, MA 01230
Tel: 413/274-3786

FREE PRESS ASSOCIATION
P.O. Box 15548
Columbus, OH 43215
Tel: 614/291-1441

FREE RADIO BERKELEY/
FREE COMMUNICATIONS
COALITION
1442-A Walnut Street, #406
Berkeley, CA 94709
Tel: 510/464-3041
E-Mail: frbspd @ crl.com.

THE GAP MEDIA PROJECT
142 W.S. College Street
Yellow Springs, OH 45387
Tel: 513/767-2224
Fax: 513/767-1888

THE GIRAFFE PROJECT
P.O. Box 759
Langley, WA 98260
Tel: 206/221-7989

GLOBAL INFORMATION NETWORK
777 U.N. Plaza
New York, NY 10017
Tel: 212/286-0123
Fax: 212/818-9249
E-mail: ipsgin@igc.apc.org

GOVERNMENT ACCOUNTABILITY
PROJECT
810 First Street, NE, Suite 630
Washington, DC 20002-3633
Tel: 202/408-0034
Fax: 202/408-9855

THE GUSTAVUS MYERS CENTER
FOR THE STUDY OF HUMAN
RIGHTS IN NORTH AMERICA
2582 Jimmie
Fayetteville, AR 72703-3420
Tel: 501/442-4600
 and 501/575-4301
E-mail: jbennet@comp.uark.edu

HEAL
Hanford Education Action League
1720 North Ash Street
Spokane, WA 99205
Tel: 509/326-3370

HISPANIC EDUCATION AND MEDIA
GROUP
P.O. Box 221
Sausalito, CA 94966
Tel: 415/331-8560

THE HUCK BOYD NATIONAL
CENTER FOR COMMUNITY MEDIA
School Of Journalism
105 Kedzie Hall
Kansas State University
Manhattan, Kansas 66506-1501
Tel: 913/532-6890
Fax: 913/532-7309

HUMAN RIGHTS WATCH
FREE EXPRESSION PROJECT
485 Fifth Avenue
New York, NY 10017
Tel: 212/972-8400
Fax: 212/972-0905
E-mail: hrwnyc@hrw.org

INFACT
256 Hanover Street
Boston, MA 02113
Tel: 617/742-4583
Fax: 617/367-0191

INSTITUTE FOR FIRST
AMENDMENT STUDIES
P.O. Box 589
Great Barrington, MA 01230
Tel: 413/528-3800
E-mail: ifas@crocker.com

INTER AMERICAN PRESS
ASSOCIATION
2911 NW 39th Street
Miami, FL 33142
Tel: 305/634-2465
Fax: 305/635-2272

THE INVESTIGATIVE
REPORTING FUND
P.O. Box 7554
Asheville, NC 28802
Tel: 704/259-9179
Fax: 704/251-1311

LEONARD PELTIER DEFENSE
COMMITTEE
P.O. Box 583
Lawrence, KS 66044
Tel: 913/842-5774

LEONARD PELTIER FREEDOM
CAMPAIGN
c/o International Action Center
39 West 14th Street, Room 206
New York, NY 10011
Tel: 212/633-6646
Fax: 212/633-2889

LIBRARIANS AT LIBERTY
CRISES Press, Inc.
1716 SW Williston Rd.
Gainesville, FL 32608
Tel: 904/335-2200

MEDIA ACTION RESEARCH
CENTER
P.O. Box 320
Nashville, TN 37202
Tel: 615/742-5451
Fax: 615/742-5419

MEDIA COALITION/AMERICANS
FOR CONSTITUTIONAL FREEDOM
1221 Avenue of the Americas, 24th Fl.
New York, NY 10020
Tel: 212/768-6770
Fax: 212/391-1247

MEDIA/ED
The Media Education Foundation
26 Center Street
Northhampton, MA 01060
Tel: 413/586-4170
Fax: 413/586-8398

MEDIA REPORT TO WOMEN
10606 Mantz Road
Silver Spring, MD 20903
Tel: 301/445-3230

MEIKLEJOHN CIVIL LIBERTIES
INSTITUTE
P.O. Box 673
Berkeley, CA 94701
Tel: 510/848-0599
Fax: 510/848-6008

MSRRT NEWSLETTER
Chris Dodge/Jan DeSirey
4645 Columbus Ave., S.
Minneapolis, MN 55407
E-mail: cdodge@hennepin.lib.mn.us

NATIONAL COALITION
AGAINST CENSORSHIP
275 7th Avenue, 20th Fl.
New York, NY 10001
Tel: 212/807-6222
Fax: 212/807-6245
E-mail: ncacnetcom.com

NATIONAL COMMITTEE AGAINST
REPRESSIVE LEGISLATION
3321 12th Street, NE
Washington, DC 20017
Tel: 202/529-4225
Fax: 202/526-4611
E-mail: kgage@igc.apc.org

OMB WATCH
1742 Connecticut Avenue, NW
Washington, DC 20009-1171
Tel: 202/234-8494
Fax: 202/234-8584

PEOPLE FOR THE AMERICAN WAY
2000 M Street, NW, Suite 400
Washington, DC 20036
Tel: 202/467-4999
Fax: 202/293-2672

POLITICAL RESEARCH ASSOCIATES
120 Beacon Street, 3rd Fl.
Somerville, MA 02143-4304
Tel: 617/661-9313
Fax: 617/661-0059

PROGRESSIVE MEDIA PROJECT
409 East Main Street
Madison, WI 53703
Tel: 608/257-4626
Fax: 608/257-3373
E-mail: pmp@peacenet.org

PROJECT ON GOVERNMENT
OVERSIGHT
2025 Eye Street, NW, Suite 1117
Washington, DC 20006-1903
Tel: 202/466-5539
Fax: 202/466-5596

REPORTERS' COMMITTEE
FOR FREEDOM OF THE PRESS
1735 Eye Street, NW, Suite 504
Washington, DC 20006
Tel: 202/466-6312

STUDENT PRESS LAW CENTER
1101 Wilson Blvd., Suite 1910
Arlington, VA 22911
Tel: 703/807-1904
Fax: 703/807-2109
E-mail: splc@capaccess.org

THE THOMAS JEFFERSON CENTER
FOR THE PROTECTION OF FREE
EXPRESSION
400 Peter Jefferson Place
Charlottesville, VA 22901-8691
Tel: 804/295-4784
Fax: 804/296-3621

TREATMENT REVIEW
AIDS Treatment Data Network
611 Broadway, Ste. 613
New York, NY 10012-2809
Tel: 800/734-7104
Fax: 212/260-8869
E-mail: AIDSTreatD@aol.com

UNDERGROUND PRESS
CONFERENCE
Mary Kuntz Press
P.O. Box 476617
Chicago, IL 60647
Tel: 312/486-0685
Fax: 312/226-1168

WORLD PRESS FREEDOM
COMMITTEE
c/o The Newspaper Center
11600 Sunrise Valley Drive
Reston, VA 22091
Tel: 703/648-1000
Fax: 703/620-4557

WOMEN'S INSTITUTE
FOR FREEDOM OF THE PRESS
3306 Ross Place, NW
Washington, DC 20008-3332
Tel: 202/966-7783

JOURNALISM/MEDIA ANALYSIS PUBLICATIONS & ORGANIZATIONS

ACCURACY IN MEDIA
(AIM)
4455 Connecticut Avenue, NW
Suite 330
Washington, DC 20005
Tel: 202/364-4401
Fax: 202/364-4098

ADBUSTERS: A Magazine of
Media and Environmental Strategies
The Media Foundation
1243 W. Seventh Avenue
Vancouver, British Columbia
Canada V6H 1B7
Tel: 604/736-9401
Fax: 604/737-6021

THE AMERICAN EDITOR
ASNE
P.O. Box 4090
Reston, VA 22090-1700
Tel: 703/648-1144
Fax: 703/476-6125
E-mail: asne@aol.com

AMERICAN JOURNALISM REVIEW
8701 Adelphi Road
Adelphi, MD 20783
Tel: 301/431-4771
Fax: 301/431-0097

AMERICAN SOCIETY OF
JOURNALISTS AND AUTHORS
1501 Broadway, Suite 302
New York, NY 10036
Tel: 212/997-0947
Fax: 212/768-7414

ASIAN AMERICAN
JOURNALISTS ASSOCIATION
1765 Sutter Street, Suite 1000
San Francisco, CA 94115
Tel: 415/346-2051
Fax: 415/931-4671
E-mail: aaja1@aol.com

THE ASPEN INSTITUTE
Communications and Society Program
1333 New Hampshire Avenue, NW
Suite 1070
Washington, DC 20036
Tel: 202/736-5818
Fax: 202/467-0790

ASSOCIATION FOR EDUCATION
IN JOURNALISM AND MASS
COMMUNICATION
1621 College Street
University of South Carolina
Columbia, SC 29208
Tel: 803/777-2005

ASSOCIATION OF AMERICAN
PUBLISHERS
220 E. 23rd Street
New York, NY 10010
Tel: 212/689-8920
Fax: 212/696-0131

ASSOCIATION OF HOUSE
DEMOCRATIC PRESS ASSISTANTS
House of Representatives
Box 70035
Washington, DC 20024
Tel: 202/224-9154
Fax: 202/225-4951

BAY AREA CENSORED
Media Alliance
814 Mission Street, Suite 205
San Francisco, CA 94103
Tel: 415/546-6334

BLACK PRESS INSTITUTE
2711 E. 75th Place
Chicago, IL 60649
Tel: 312/375-8200
Fax: 312/375-8262

BLACK WOMEN IN PUBLISHING
P.O Box 6275
FDR Station
New York, NY 10150
Tel: 212/772-5951

CENTER FOR INVESTIGATIVE
REPORTING
568 Howard Street, 5th Fl.
San Francisco, CA 94105-3008
Tel: 415/543-1200
Fax: 415/543-8311

CENTER FOR MEDIA AND PUBLIC
AFFAIRS
2100 L Street, NW, Suite 300
Washington, DC 20037-1526
Tel: 202/223-2942
Fax: 202/872-4014

CENTER FOR MEDIA EDUCATION
1511 K Street, NW, Suite 518
Washington, DC 20005
Tel: 202/628-2620
Fax: 202/628-2554

CENTER FOR MEDIA LITERACY
1962 South Shenandoah Street
Los Angeles, CA 90034
Tel: 310/559-2944
Fax: 310/559-9396

CENTER FOR THE STUDY
OF COMMERCIALISM
1875 Connecticut Avenue, NW
Suite 300
Washington, DC 20009-5728
Tel: 202/332-9110
Fax: 202/265-4954

CENTER FOR WAR, PEACE AND
THE NEWS MEDIA
New York University
10 Washington Place, 4th Fl.
New York, NY 10003
Tel: 212/998-7960
Fax: 212/995-4143

CHRISTIC INSTITUTE
5276 Hollister Avenue
Santa Barbara, CA 93111
Tel: 805/967-8232
Fax: 805/967-5060

CITIZENS FOR MEDIA LITERACY
34 Wall Street, Suite 407
Asheville, NC 28801
Tel: 704/255-0182
Fax: 704/254-2286
E-mail: cml@unca.edu

COLUMBIA JOURNALISM REVIEW
700 Journalism Building
Columbia University
New York, NY 10027
Tel: 212/854-1881
Fax: 212/854-8580

COMMUNICATIONS CONSORTIUM
AND MEDIA CENTER
1333 H Street, NW, Suite 700
Washington, DC 20005
Tel: 202/682-1270
Fax: 202/682-2154

COMMUNITY MEDIA WORKSHOP
c/o Columbia College
600 S. Michigan Avenue
Chicago, Il 60605-1996
Tel: 312/663-1600, ext.5498
Fax: 312/663-3227

CULTURAL ENVIRONMENT
MOVEMENT/CULTURAL
 INDICATORS
University City Science Center
3624 Market Street, One East
Philadelphia, PA 19104
Tel: 215/387-5303
Fax: same as above

DOWNS MEDIA EDUCATION
CENTER
P.O. Box 1170
Stockbridge, MA 01262
Tel: 413/298-0262
Fax: 413/298-4434

EDITOR AND PUBLISHER
11 W. 19th Street
New York, NY 10011
Tel: 212/675-4380
Fax: 212/929-1259

ESSENTIAL INFORMATION
P.O. Box 19405
Washington, DC 20036
Tel: 202/387-8030
Fax: 202/234-5176

FAIRNESS AND ACCURACY
IN REPORTING (FAIR)
130 W. 25th Street
New York, NY 10001
Tel: 212/633-6700
Fax: 212/727-7668
E-mail: info@fair.org
http://www.fair.org/fair/

FUND FOR INVESTIGATIVE
JOURNALISM
1755 Massachusetts Avenue, NW
Washington, DC 20036
Tel: 202/462-1844

GLAAD
Gay and Lesbian Alliance
Against Defamation
150 W. 26th Street, Suite 503
New York, NY 10001
Tel: 212/807-1700
Fax: 212/807-1806

GLAAD MEDIA WATCH/SFBA
1360 Mission Street, Suite 200
San Francisco, CA 94103
Tel: 415/861-2244
Fax: 415/861-4893
E-Mail: glaad sfba @ aol.com

THE INDEPENDENT
Association of Independent
Video and Film (AIVF)
625 Broadway, 9th Fl.
New York, NY 10012
Tel: 212/473-3400
Fax: 212/677-8732

INSTITUTE FOR
ALTERNATIVE JOURNALISM
77 Federal Street
San Francisco, CA 94107
Tel: 415/284-1420
Fax: 415/284-1414
CompuServe: 71362, 27

INSTITUTE FOR MEDIA ANALYSIS
145 W. 4th Street
New York, NY 10012
Tel: 212/254-1061
Fax: 212/254-9598

INVESTIGATIVE JOURNALISM
PROJECT
Fund for Constitutional Government
122 Maryland Avenue, NE, Suite 300
Washington, DC 20002
Tel: 202/546-3732
Fax: 202/543-3156

INVESTIGATIVE REPORTERS
& EDITORS
P.O. Box 838
University of Missouri
School of Journalism
Columbia, MO 65205
Tel: 314/882-2042
Fax: 314/882-5431
E-mail: jourire@mucc.mail.missouri.edu

JOURNALISM QUARTERLY
George Washington University
Journalism Program
Washington, DC 20052
Tel: 202/994-6226

JUST THINK FOUNDATION
221 Caledonia Street
Sausalito, CA 94965
Tel: 415/289-0122
Fax: 415/289-0123
E-mail: think@justthink.org

MEDIA ACCESS PROJECT
2000 M Street, NW, Suite 400
Washington, DC 20036
Tel: 202/232-4300
Fax: 202/223-5302

MEDIA ALLIANCE
814 Mission Street, Suite 205
San Francisco, CA 94103
Tel: 415/546-MEDIA
Fax: 415/546-6218

MEDIAFILE
814 Mission Street, Suite 205
San Francisco, CA 94103
Tel: 415/546-6523
Fax: 415/546-6218

THE MEDIA INSTITUTE
1000 Potomac Street, NW, Suite 301
Washington, DC 20007
Tel: 202/298-7512
Fax: 202/337-7092
E-mail: tmi@clark.net

MEDIA WATCH
P.O. Box 618
Santa Cruz, CA 95061-0618
Tel: 408/423-6355
Fax: 408/423-6355
E-mail: mediawok@aol.com

NATIONAL ALLIANCE FOR MEDIA
EDUCATION
655 13th Street, Suite 210
Oakland, CA 94612
Tel: 510/451-2717

NATIONAL ASSOCIATION OF
BLACK JOURNALISTS
11600 Sunrise Valley Drive
Reston, VA 22091
Tel: 703/648-1270
Fax: 703/476-6245

NATIONAL ASSOCIATION OF
HISPANIC JOURNALISTS
National Press Bldg., Suite 1193
Washington, DC 20045
Tel: 202/662-7145
Fax: 202/662-7144

NATIONAL CONFERENCE OF
EDITORIAL WRITERS
6223 Executive Boulevard
Rockville, MD 20852
Tel: 301/984-3015

NATIONAL INSTITUTE FOR
COMPUTER ASSISTED REPORTING,
IRE
P.O. Box 838
University of Missouri
School of Journalism
Columbia, MO 65205
Tel: 314/882-2042
Fax: 314/882-5431
E-mail: jourire@mucc.mail.missouri.edu

NATIONAL LESBIAN & GAY
JOURNALISTS ASSOCIATION
874 Gravenstein Hwy., S., Suite 4
Sebastopol, CA 95472
Tel: 707/823-2193
Fax: 707/823-4176
E-mail: exeoffice@aol.com

NATIONAL NEWSPAPER
ASSOCIATION
1627 K Street, NW, Suite 400
Washington, DC 20006
Tel: 202/466-7200
Fax: 202/331-1403

NATIONAL TELEMEDIA COUNCIL
120 East Wilson Street
Madison, WI 53703
Tel: 608/257-7712

NATIONAL WRITERS UNION
873 Broadway, Room 203
New York, NY 10003
Tel: 212/254-0279

THE NEW CITIZEN
Citizens for Media Literacy
34 Wall Street, #407
Asheville, NC 28801
Tel: 704/255-0182
Fax: 704/254-2286
E-mail: cml@unca.edu

NEWSPAPER ASSOCIATION
OF AMERICA
11600 Sunrise Valley Drive
Reston, VA 22091
Tel: 703/648-1000
Fax: 703/620-4557

THE NEWSPAPER GUILD
8611 Second Avenue
Silver Spring, MD 20910
Tel: 301/585-2990

NEWSPAPER RESEARCH JOURNAL
Scripps Hall School of Journalism
Ohio University
Athens, OH 45701
Tel: 614/593-2590
Fax: 614/593-2592

NEWSPRINTS
Essential Information
P.O. Box 19405
Washington, DC 20036
Tel: 202/387-8030

NEWSWORTHY
Minnesota News Council
822 Marquette Ave., Suite 200
Minneapolis, MN 55402
Tel: 612/341-9357

ORGANIZATION OF
NEWS OMBUDSMEN
c/o Art Nauman
Sacramento Bee
P.O. Box 15779
Sacramento, CA 95852
Tel: 916/442-8050
http://www.infi.net/ono/

PR WATCH
Center for Media and Democracy, Inc.
3318 Gregory Street
Madison, WI 53711
Tel: 608/233-3346
Fax: 608/238-2236

PROJECT CENSORED
Sociology Department
Sonoma State University
1801 E. Cotati Avenue
Rohnert Park, CA 94928-3609
Tel: 707/664-2500
Fax: 707/664-2108
E-mail: project.censored@sonoma.edu

PROJECT CENSORED CANADA
School of Communication
Simon Fraser University
Burnaby, BC V5A 1S6, Canada
Tel: 604/291-4905
Fax: 604/291-4024
E-mail: censored@sfu.ca

PUBLIC MEDIA CENTER
446 Green Street
San Francisco, CA 94133
Tel: 415/434-1403
Fax: 415/986-6779

PUBLIC MEDIA MONITOR
Council for Public Media
P.O. Box 4703
Austin, TX 78765

QUILL
Society of Professional Journalists
16 S. Jackson Street
P.O. Box 77
Greencastle, IN 46135-0077
Tel: 317/653-3333
Fax: 317/653-4631
E-mail: spj@internetmci.com

ROCKY MOUNTAIN MEDIA WATCH
Box 18858
Denver, CO 80218
Tel: 303/832-7558
Fax: same

ST. LOUIS JOURNALISM REVIEW
8380 Olive Boulevard
St. Louis, MO 63132
Tel: 314/991-1699
Fax: 314/997-1898

SOCIETY OF ENVIRONMENTAL
JOURNALISTS
P.O. Box 27280
Philadelphia, PA 19118
Tel: 215/247-9710
E-mail: SEJoffice@aol.com

SOUTHWEST ALTERNATE MEDIA
PROJECT
1519 West Main
Houston, TX 77006
Tel: 713/522-8592
Fax: 713/522-0953

STRATEGIES FOR MEDIA LITERACY
1095 Market Street, Suite 617
San Francisco, CA 94103
Tel: 415/621-2911
Fax: 415/255-9392

TIMES MIRROR CENTER FOR THE
PEOPLE & THE PRESS
1875 Eye Street, NW, Suite 1110
Washington, DC 20006
Tel: 202/293-3126

TYNDALL REPORT
135 Rivington Street
New York, NY 10002
Tel: 212/674-8913
Fax: 212/979-7304

WOMEN IN COMMUNICATIONS
3717 Columbia Pike, Suite 310
Arlington, VA 22204
Tel: 703/920-5555
Fax: 703/920-5556

LIBRARY & REFERENCE SOURCES

THE ACTIVIST'S ALMANAC:
The Concerned Citizen's Guide
to the Leading Advocacy Organizations
in America
By David Walls, 1993
Simon & Schuster Fireside Books
New York

ALTERNATIVE PRESS INDEX
Alternative Press Center, Inc.
P.O. Box 33109
Baltimore, MD 21218
Tel: 410/243-2471
Fax: 410/235-5325

CENTER FOR DEFENSE
INFORMATION
Library for Press and Public
1500 Massachusetts Avenue, NW
Washington, DC 20005
Tel: 202/862-0700
Fax: 202/862-0708
E-Mail: cdi @ igc.apc.org

CONNECTING TO THE INTERNET
O'Reilly & Associates, 1993
101 Morris Street
Sebastopol, CA 95472
Tel: 707/829-0515
http://www.ora.com/

DIRECTORY OF ELECTRONIC
JOURNALS, NEWSLETTERS AND
ACADEMIC DISCUSSION LISTS
by Kovacs and Strangelove
Association of Scientific
and Academic Publishing
1527 New Hampshire Avenue, NW
Washington, DC 20036

ECOLINKING: EVERYONE'S GUIDE
TO ONLINE INFORMATION
by Don Rittner, 1992
Peachpit Press
2414 6th Street
Berkeley, CA 94710

ENCYCLOPEDIA OF ASSOCIATIONS
1993 ed., 4 vols.
Gale Research Inc., Detroit and London

ERIC
Clearinghouse on Information &
Technology
Syracuse University
Schools of Information
Studies/Education
4-194 CST
Syracuse, NY 13244-4100
Tel: 315/443-3640

THE FEDERAL INTERNET SOURCE
Published by National Journal Inc.
And The Internet Letter
1501 M Street, NW, Suite 300
Washington, DC 20005
Tel: 800/424-2921
E-mail: njcirc@clark.net

FORBES MEDIA GUIDE
1400 Route 206 N.
P.O. Box 89
Bedminster, NJ 07921
Tel: 908/781-2078
Fax: 908/781-6635

FROM RADICAL
TO EXTREME RIGHT
A bibliography of current periodicals
of protests, controversy, advocacy and
dissent
by Gail Skidmore and Theodore Jurgen
Spahn, 1987, 3rd ed.
Scarecrow Press, Inc.
Metuchen, NJ, and London

GALE DIRECTORY OF
PUBLICATIONS AND
BROADCAST MEDIA
1992 ed., 3 vols, plus supplement
Gale Research Inc., Detroit and London

THE INTERNATIONAL DIRECTORY
OF LITTLE MAGAZINES AND
SMALL PRESSES
Len Fulton, ed., 30th ed., 1994/95
Dustbooks
P.O. Box 100
Paradise, CA 95967

THE LEFT INDEX:
A QUARTERLY INDEX TO
 PERIODICALS OF THE LEFT
Reference and Research Services
Santa Cruz, CA

LIBRARY JOURNAL
249 N. 17th Street
New York, NY 10011
Tel: 212/463-6700

MACROCOSM USA: POSSIBILITIES
FOR A NEW PROGRESSIVE ERA
Sandi Brockway, ed., 1992
Macrocosm USA, Inc.
P.O. Box 185
Cambria, CA 93428-8030
Tel: 805/927-8030
Fax: 805/927-1713
BBS (MacroNet): 805/927-1987

NATIONAL FORUM ON
INFORMATION LITERACY
c/o American Library Association
50 East Huron Street
Chicago, IL 60611

THE PEOPLE'S RIGHT TO KNOW:
MEDIA, DEMOCRACY AND THE
INFORMATION HIGHWAY
by Frederick Williams and John V.
Paulik, eds.
Lawrence Erlbaum Associates, 1994.

PROGRESSIVE PERIODICALS
DIRECTORY
by Craig T. Canan
2nd ed., 1989
Progressive Education
P.O. Box 120574
Nashville, TN 37212

RIGHT-TO-KNOW NETWORK
(RTK NET)
OMB Watch
1742 Connecticut Ave., NW
Washington, DC 20009-1171
Tel: 202/234-8494
Fax: 202/234-8584

ULRICH'S INTERNATIONAL
PERIODICALS DIRECTORY
34th ed., 1996, 5 vols.
R.R. Bowker, Reed Refeerence Publishing
121 Chanlon Road
New Providence, NJ 07974
Tel: 800/521-8110
Fax: 908/665-2867

THE WHOLE INTERNET:
USER'S GUIDE AND CATALOG
2nd ed.
by Ed Krol
O'Reilly & Associates, 1994
101 Morris Street
Sebastopol, CA 95472
Tel: 707/829-0515
http://www.ora.com

THE WORKING PRESS
OF THE NATION, 1996 ed.
Reed Reference Publishing
121 Chanlon Road
New Providence, NJ 07974
Tel: 800/521-8110
Fax: 908/665-2867

NATIONAL BROADCAST AND CABLE MEDIA

48 HOURS
CBS News
524 W. 57th Street
New York, NY 10019
Tel: 212/975-4848

60 MINUTES
CBS News
524 W. 57th Street
New York, NY 10019
Tel: 212/975-2006

20/20
ABC News
147 Columbus Avenue
New York, NY 10023
Tel: 212/456-2020
Fax: 212/456-2969

ABC WORLD NEWS TONIGHT
47 W. 66th Street
New York, NY 10023
Tel: 212/456-4040

AMERICAN JOURNAL
CBS
402 E. 76th Street
New York, NY 10021
Tel: 1-800/EDI-TION

ASSOCIATED PRESS RADIO
NETWORK
1825 K Street, NW, Suite 710
Washington, DC 20006
Tel: 202/736-9500
Fax: 202/736-1199

CBS EVENING NEWS
524 W. 57th Street
New York, NY 10019
Tel: 212/975-3693

CBS THIS MORNING
524 W. 57th Street
New York, NY 10019
Tel: 212/975-2824

CHRISTIAN BROADCASTING
NETWORK
700 CBN Center
Virginia Beach, VA 23463-0001
Tel: 804/523-7111

CONUS COMMUNICATIONS
3415 University Avenue
Minneapolis, MN 55414
Tel: 612/642-4646

CNN
One CNN Center
Box 105366
Atlanta, GA 30348
Tel: 404/827-1500

CNN
Washington Bureau
820 First Street, NE
Washington, DC 20002
Tel: 202/898-7900

C-SPAN
400 N. Capitol Street, NW, Suite 650
Washington, DC 20001
Tel: 202/737-3220
Fax: 202/737-3323

CROSSFIRE
CNN
820 First Street, NE
Washington, DC 20002
Tel: 202/8989-7951

THE CRUSADERS
1011-F West Alameda Avenue
Burbank, CA 91506
Tel: 818/556-2155
Fax: 818/556-2111

DATELINE
NBC News
30 Rockefeller Plaza, Room 510
New York, NY 10112
Tel: 212/664-6170

DAY & DATE
CBS-TV
514 West 57th Street, 6th Fl.
New York, NY 10019
or 1-800/884-1136

DAY ONE
ABC News
147 Columbus Avenue, 8th Fl.
New York NY 10023
Tel: 212/456-6100

PHIL DONAHUE SHOW
30 Rockefeller Plaza
New York, NY 10019
Tel: 212/975-2006

ESPN
ESPN Plaza
Bristol, CT 06010
Tel: 203/585-2000

EYE TO EYE
CBS News
555 W. 57th Street
New York, NY 10019
Tel: 212/975-2000

FACE THE NATION
CBS News
2020 M Street, NW
Washington, DC 20036
Tel: 202/457-4481

FOOD NOT BOMBS RADIO
NETWORK
3145 Geary Blvd., #12
San Francisco, CA 94118
Tel: 415/386-9209

FRONTLINE
125 Western Avenue
Boston, MA 02134
Tel: 617/783-3500
Fax: 617/254-0243

FRONT PAGE
FOX
5746 W. Sunset Blvd., #F-158
Los Angeles, CA 90028-8588

THE GERALDO RIVERA SHOW
555 West 57th Street
New York, NY 10019
Tel: 212/265-8520

GOOD MORNING AMERICA
ABC News
147 Columbus Avenue
New York, NY 10023
Tel: 212/456-5900
Fax: 212/456-7290

HIGHTOWER RADIO
1800 W. 6th Street
Austin, TX 78711
Tel: 512/477-5588
or 800/AGITATE
Fax: 512/478-8536

HOME BOX OFFICE
1100 Avenue of the Americas
New York, NY 10036
Tel: 212/512-1329

INSIGHT (Radio program)
The Progressive
409 E. Main Street
Madison, WI
Tel: 608/257-4626
Fax: 608/257-3373

INVESTIGATIVE REPORTS
Arts & Entertainment Network
235 E. 45th Street
New York, NY 10017
Tel: 212/661-4500

LARRY KING LIVE TV
CNN
820 First Street, NE
Washington, DC 20002
Tel: 212/898-7900

MACNEIL/LEHRER NEWSHOUR
New York Office:
WNET-TV
356 W. 58th Street
New York, NY 10019
Tel: 212/560-3113

MACNEIL/LEHRER NEWSHOUR
Washington Office:
Arlington, VA 22206
Tel: 703/998-2870

JULIANNE MALVEAUX SHOW
Pacifica Radio
702 H Street, NW
Washington, DC 20001
Tel: 202/783-3100
Fax: 202/462-6612
E-mail: jmnia@aol.com

MEET THE PRESS
NBC News
4001 Nebraska Avenue, NW
Washington, DC 20016
Tel: 202/885-4200
Fax: 202/362-2009

MORNING EDITION:
ALL THINGS CONSIDERED
National Public Radio
635 Massachusetts Ave., NW
Washington, DC 20001-3753
Tel: 202/414-2000
Fax: 202/414-3329

BILL MOYERS
Public Affairs Television
356 W. 58th Street
New York, NY 10019
Tel: 212/560-6960

MTV NEWS
1515 Broadway, 24th Fl.
New York, NY 10036
Tel: 212/258-8000

NATIONAL PUBLIC RADIO
635 Massachusetts Ave., NW
Washington, DC 20001-3753
Tel: 202/414-2000
Fax: 202/414-3329

NBC NIGHTLY NEWS
30 Rockefeller Plaza
New York, NY 10112
Tel: 212/664-4971

NIGHTLINE (New York)
ABC News
47 W. 66th Street
New York, NY 10023
Tel: 212/456-7777

NIGHTLINE (Washington DC)
ABC News
1717 DeSales Street, NW
Washington, DC 20036
Tel: 202/887-7360

NOW
NBC News
30 Rockefeller Plaza
New York, NY 10112
Tel: 212/664-7501

OUT ACROSS AMERICA
Network Q
884 Monroe Avenue
Atlanta, GA 30308
Tel: 800/368-0638
E-mail: networkQ@aol.com

PBS
1320 Braddock Place
Alexandria, VA 22314-1698
Tel: 703/739-5000
Fax: 703/739-5295
PBS Comment Line: 1/800/272-2190

PERSPECTIVES-ABC RADIO
125 West End Avenue
New York, NY 10023
Tel: 212/456-5554

PRI-PUBLIC RADIO
INTERNATIONAL
100 North Sixth Street, Suite 900 A
Minneapolis, MN 55403
Tel: 612/338-5000
Fax: 612/330-9222

PRIMETIME LIVE
ABC News
147 Columbus Avenue
New York, NY 10023
Tel: 212/456-1600

RADIO FREE EUROPE/
RADIO LIBERTY
1201 Connecticut Avenue, NW
Suite 1100
Washington, DC 20036
Tel: 202/457-6900
Fax: 202/457-6997

RELIABLE SOURCES
CNN
820 First Street, NE
Washington, DC 20002
Tel: 202/898-7900

RUSH LIMBAUGH
WABC Radio
2 Penn Plaza, 17th Fl.
New York, NY 10121
Tel: 212/613-3800
 or 800/282-2882
Fax: 212/563-9166

STREET STORIES
CBS News
555 W. 57th Street
New York, NY 10019
Tel: 212/975-8282

THIS WEEK WITH DAVID BRINKLEY
ABC News
1717 DeSales Street, NW
Washington, DC 20036
Tel: 202/887-7777

TODAY SHOW
NBC News
30 Rockefeller Plaza
New York, NY 10112
Tel: 212/664-4249

TURNER BROADCASTING SYSTEM
1 CNN Center
Atlanta, GA 30348-5366
Tel: 404/827-1792

TV NATION
P.O. Box 5297
New York, NY 10085
Tel: 212/474-5800
E-mail: tvnatfans@aol.com

OPRAH WINFREY
Harpo Productions
P.O. Box 9909715
Chicago, IL 60690
Tel: 312/633-1000

WE THE PEOPLE
Jerry Brown-Radio
200 Harrison Street
Oakland, CA 94607
Tel: 510/836-DARE
 and 800/426-1112

NATIONAL COLUMNISTS

RUSSELL BAKER
The New York Times
229 W. 43rd Street
New York, NY 10036

DAVID BRODER
The Washington Post
1150 15th Street, NW
Washington, DC 20071

ALEXANDER COCKBURN
The Nation
72 Fifth Avenue
New York, NY 10011
Tel: 212/242-8400
Fax: 212/463-9712

JEFF COHEN/NORMAN SOLOMON
c/o Creators Syndicate
5777 W. Century Blvd., Suite 700
Los Angeles, CA 90045
Tel: 310/337-7003

ROBERT NOVAK
Chicago Sun Times
401 N. Wabash Avenue
Chicago, IL 60611
Tel: 312/321-3000
Fax: 312/321-3084

ELLEN GOODMAN
The Boston Globe
P.O. Box 2378
Boston, MA 02107
Tel: 617/929-2000

NAT HENTOFF
The Village Voice
36 Cooper Square
New York, NY 10003
Tel: 212/475-3300
Fax: 212/475-8944

JIM HIGHTOWER
1800 W. 6th Street
Austin, TX 78711
Tel: 512/477-5588
Fax: 512/478-8536

MOLLY IVINS
Fort Worth Star-Telegram
P.O. Box 1870
Fort Worth, TX 76101
Tel: 817/390-7400
Fax: 817/390-7520

JAMES KILPATRICK
Universal Press Syndicate
4900 Main Street, 9th Fl.
Kansas, MO 64112
Tel: 800/255-6734
or 816/932-6600

MORTON KONDRACKE
ROLL CALL
900 Second Street, NE
Washington, DC 20002
Tel: 202/289-4900
Fax: 202/289-5337

JULIANNE MALVEAUX
c/o King Features Syndicate
216 E. 45th Street
New York, NY 10017

MARY MCGRORY
The Washington Post
1150 15th Street, NW
Washington, DC 20071
Tel: 202/334-6000

CLARENCE PAGE
Chicago Tribune
435 N. Michigan Avenue
Chicago, IL 60611
Tel: 312/222-3232

TOM PETERS
555 Hamilton Avenue
Palo Alto, CA 94301

ANNA QUINDLEN
New York Times
229 W. 43rd Street
New York, NY 10036
Tel: 212/556-1234

A.M. ROSENTHAL
New York Times
229 W. 43rd Street
New York, NY 10036
Tel: 212/556-1234

MIKE ROYKO
Chicago Tribune
435 N. Michigan Avenue
Chicago, IL 60611
Tel: 312/222-3232

WILLIAM SAFIRE
New York Times
1627 Eye Street, NW
Washington, DC 20006
Tel: 202/862-0330
Fax: 202/862-0340

GEORGE WILL
Newsweek
444 Madison Avenue
New York, NY 10022
Tel: 212/350-4000

NATIONAL PUBLICATIONS & NEWS SERVICES

ASSOCIATED PRESS
National Desk
50 Rockefeller Plaza
New York, NY 10020
Tel: 212/621-1600

BRITISH MEDICAL JOURNAL
B.M.A. House
Tavistock Square
London WC1H 9JR
England
Tel: 011-44-171-383-6123
Fax: 011-44-171-383-6403

CHICAGO TRIBUNE
435 N. Michigan Avenue
Chicago, IL 60611
Tel: 312/222-3232

CHRISTIAN SCIENCE MONITOR
One Norway Street
Boston, MA 02115
Tel: 617/450-2000

COPLEY NEWS SERVICE
1100 National Press Building
Washington, DC 20045
Tel: 202/737-6960

COX ENTERPRISES, INC.
P.O. Box 105357
Atlanta, GA 30348
Tel: 404/843-5123

DOW JONES NEWS SERVICE
P.O. Box 300
Princeton, NJ 08543
Tel: 609/520-4638

FORTUNE
Time Warner, Inc.
Time & Life Building
Rockefeller Center
New York, NY 10020
Tel: 212/586-1212

HARPER'S MAGAZINE
666 Broadway
New York, NY 10012-2317
Tel: 212/614-6500
Fax: 212/228-5889

KNIGHT-RIDDER NEWS SERVICE
790 National Press Building
Washington, DC 20045
Tel: 202/383-6080

LOS ANGELES TIMES
Times-Mirror Square
Los Angeles, CA 90053
Tel: 800/528-4637

MCCLATCHY NEWS SERVICE
P.O. Box 15779
Sacramento, CA 95852
Tel: 916/321-1895

NATIONAL JOURNAL
1501 M Street, NW, Suite 300
Washington, DC 20005
Tel: 202/739-8400

NATIONAL NEWSPAPER ASSOCIA-
TION
1525 Wilson Boulevard, Suite 550
Arlington, VA 22209-2434
Tel: 703/907-7900
Fax: 703/907-7901

NEWSNET
945 Haverford Road
Bryn Mawr, PA 19010
Tel: 610/527-8030

NEWSWEEK
444 Madison Avenue
New York, NY 10022
Tel: 212/350-4000

NEWSDAY
235 Pinelawn Road
Melville, NY 11747-4250
Tel: 516/843-2020

NEW YORK TIMES
229 W. 43rd Street
New York, NY 10036
Tel: 212/556-1234

NEW YORK TIMES
Washington Bureau
1627 Eye Street, NW, 7th Fl.
Washington, DC 20006
Tel: 202/862-0300
Fax: 202/862-0340

PR NEWSWIRE
810 7th Avenue
New York, NY 10019
Tel: 800/832-5522

REUTERS INFORMATION SERVICES
1700 Broadway
New York, NY 10019
Tel: 212/603-3300
Fax: 212/603-3446

SAN FRANCISCO CHRONICLE
901 Mission Street
San Francisco, CA 94103
Tel: 415/777-1111
Fax: 415/512-8196

SAN FRANCISCO EXAMINER
110 Fifth Street
San Francisco, CA 94103
Tel: 415/777-2424
Fax: 415/512-1264

SCRIPPS/HOWARD NEWS SERVICE
1090 Vermont Avenue, NW, Suite 1000
Washington, DC 20005
Tel: 202/408-1484

STATES NEWS SERVICE
1333 F Street, NW
Washington, DC 20004
Tel: 202/628-3100

SUBURBAN NEWSPAPERS OF
AMERICA
401 North Michigan Avenue
Chicago, IL 60611
Tel: 312/644-6610

TIME MAGAZINE
Time Warner, Inc.
Time & Life Building
Rockefeller Center
New York, NY 10020-1393
Tel: 212/522-1212

TRIBUNE MEDIA SERVICES
64 E. Concord Street
Orlando, FL 32801
Tel: 800/332-3068
 or 407/420-6200

UNITED PRESS INTERNATIONAL
1400 Eye Street, NW
Washington, DC 20005
Tel: 202/898-8000

U.S. NEWS & WORLD REPORT
2400 N Street, NW
Washington, DC 20037
Tel: 202/955-2000
Fax: 202/955-2049

USA TODAY
1000 Wilson Boulevard
Arlington, VA 22229
Tel: 703/276-3400

WALL STREET JOURNAL
200 Liberty Street
New York, NY 10281
Tel: 212/416-2000

WASHINGTON POST
1150 15th Street, NW
Washington, DC 20071
Tel: 202/334-6000

THE WASHINGTON TIMES
National Weekly Edition
3600 New York Avenue, NE
Washington, DC 20002
Tel: 202/636-3008

APPENDIX B

Alternative Writer's Market

In the past, I've suggested that if you are a freelance journalist writing an exposé of the cozy relationship between *The New York Times* and the nuclear power industry, your best market probably would be *Lies Of Our Times* (LOOT), a publication devoted to ongoing analysis of the nation's esteemed daily. And I pointed out that you wouldn't find LOOT in the traditional resource book, *Writer's Market: Where & How To Sell What You Write*, published annually by Writer's Digest Books, but you would find it in the "Alternative Writer's Market" published in the *Censored* Yearbook.

Unfortunately, now you won't find LOOT in the *Censored* Yearbook either. As has happened with a number of our productive sources over the years, LOOT ceased publication in 1995 due to a lack of financial resources. Ed Herman, former senior editor of LOOT, said it definitely was not due to a lack of subjects to expose.

However, as also happens frequently with the alternative media, there are aspiring new publishers willing to take up the gauntlet. Investigative authors will find 35 additional markets cited in this year's "Alternative Writer's Market," bringing the total number of listings to 77.

Included among them is a new publication—*Counterpoise*—that will specifically feature reviews of new books that have been ignored or censored by the traditional review media. *Counterpoise* is sponsored by the Social Responsibilities Roundtable of the American Library Association.

Another encouraging sign for investigative freelance journalists is that *The Nation*, one of our most prolific sources for censored stories, is increasing the amount of freelance investigative reporting in its pages.

Bruce Shapiro, associate editor of *The Nation*, said, "The magazine is expanding its commitment to investigative reporting because radical change in American politics and the economy demands it and because too many publications have retreated from quality investigative journalism. We seek stories that illuminate crucial issues. We're especially interested in corporate crime, the politics of health care, national security and intelligence, immigration, political corruption, prisons, technology and the changing workplace, education, civil rights and civil liberties, plus the news media."

Throughout its 20-year history, Project Censored has received numerous queries from journalists and authors seeking publishers for exposés that challenge the conventional wisdom of the establishment press. It is this ongoing succession of queries that led to the development of the following guide.

All names and addresses have been updated where necessary in the third edition of the "Alternative Writer's Market" (AWM). This edition includes a number of new publications and features some of the most promising markets open to investigative journalists.

If you know of any additional listings that should be included in the 1997 AWM, please write the "Alternative Writer's Market," Project Censored, Sonoma State University, Rohnert Park, CA 94928, for a listing application.

Also, if you are aware of any changes and/or corrections for the current list, please send them to the same address.

14850 MAGAZINE
104 N. Aurora Street
Ithaca, NY 14850
Tel: 607/277-1021 Fax: 607/277-0801
Editor-in-Chief: Corey Shane

14850 Magazine, named after its zip code, is published monthly. About 95 percent of its articles are provided by freelance writers. It is interested in interviews, reviews, opinion, and think pieces, ranging from 800 to 1,600 words.
 Rates: $30 in credit
 Queries not required; send SASE for Writer's Guidelines; response time is two weeks.
 Tips: "We like local stuff, but we're wide open; we've done pieces on JFK, Leonard Peltier, health care, censorship, and other political issues. We really publish a pretty broad array of material."—Editor-in-Chief Corey Shane

THE ADVOCATE
6922 Hollywood Boulevard, Suite 1000
Los Angeles, CA 90028
Tel: 213/871-1225 Fax: 213/467-6805
E-mail: info@advocate.com

The Advocate is a biweekly with about 80 percent of its articles provided by freelance writers. It is interested in articles, profiles, and interviews with an average length of 1,500 words.

Rates: Negotiable

Queries with published clips required; send SASE for Writer's Guidelines; response time is two weeks.

AKWESASNE NOTES
P.O. Box 196
Mohawk Nation
Rooseveltown, NY 13683-0196
Tel: 518/358-9531 Fax: 613/575-2935
Editor: Salli Benedict

Akwesasne Notes is a quarterly publication with about 75 percent of its articles provided by freelance writers. It is interested in articles, profiles, book reviews, music reviews, interviews, letters-to-the-editor, poetry.

Rates: Yes, though very minimal

Queries with published clips required; response time is two to four weeks.

Tips: "Environmental, Native issues across the U.S. and Canada, Native/natural issues of aboriginal people."—Jann Day/Mark Neursisian

ALTERNATIVE PRESS REVIEW
P.O. Box 1446
Columbia, MO 65205-1446
Tel: 314/442-4352
Editor: Jason McQuinn

Alternative Press Review is a quarterly publication that monitors and reports on the activities and performance of America's alternative media. About 10 percent of its articles are provided by freelance writers. It is interested in articles, profiles, and book reviews covering alternative media and their relationship to society, radical movements, and mainstream media.

Rates: 2 cents per word for reprints or reviews; 5 cents per word for original articles

Queries with published clips required; send SASE for Writer's Guidelines; response time is one to two months.

Tips: "We're looking for critical, perceptive assessments about alternative media organizations, conferences, publications, genre, movements; no puff pieces."—Editor Jason McQuinn

AMERICAN JOURNALISM REVIEW
8701 Adelphi Road
Adelphi, MD 20783
Tel: 301/431-4771 Fax: 301/431-0097
Editor: Rem Rieder

The American Journalism Review, formerly the Washington Journalism Review, is published ten times a year. About 80 percent of its articles are provided by freelance writers. It is interested in articles, analysis, book reviews, interviews, exposés, upwards of 2,000 words; short pieces of 500-700 words.

Rates: Features—20 cents a word; short features—$100

Queries with published clips required; response time three to four weeks.

Tips: "Read the magazine before submitting **queries**; know what we've done, what we do, what we're looking for. We're always looking for good ideas, especially investigations of media coverage."—Associate Editor Chip Rowe

BACKGROUNDERS
(See FOOD FIRST NEWS & VIEWS)

THE BAFFLER
P.O. Box 378293
Chicago, IL 60637
Editor: Thomas Frank

The Baffler is a quarterly publication with about 80 percent of its articles provided by freelance writers. It is interested in articles, profiles, book reviews, interviews, opinion pieces, essays, and exposés ranging from 500 to 10,000 words.

    Rates: Offered

    Queries not required; response time is six months.

    Tips: "Read the magazine first."

BORDER/LINES MAGAZINE
P.O. Box 459, Stn. P.
Toronto, Ontario
Canada M58 2S9
Fax: 416/921-3984
Managing Editor: Julie Jenkinson

Border/Lines is published February, June, September/October with 100 percent of its articles provided by freelance writers. It is interested in articles, profiles, book reviews, interviews, opinion pieces, essays and exposés, with a maximum length of 4,000 words.

    Rates: $75 to $250

    Queries with published clips required; send SASE for Writer's Guidelines; response time is three months.

    Tips: "Please write in for formal guidelines. Be sure to include an SASE with all requests and your articles."— Managing Editor Julie Jenkinson

BOYCOTT QUARTERLY
P.O. Box 30727
Seattle, WA 98103-0727
E-mail: BoycottGuy@aol.com
Editor: Zachary D. Lyons

Boycott Quarterly, is, as it name suggests, published quarterly; please contact publisher for dates. Currently a low percentage of its articles are provided by freelance writers. It is interested in articles, opinion pieces, and exposés, ranging from 1,500 to 2,000 words.

    Rates: Free subscription only

    Queries with published clips required; response time varies.

    Tips: "Boycotts, corporate injustice and irresponsibility, related topics, reports on economic democracy topics (co-ops, barter, farmers markets, etc.). We solicit or produce in-house almost all articles but like to reprint well-written articles on related topics published elsewhere."—Editor Zachary D. Lyons

THE BULLETIN OF THE ATOMIC SCIENTISTS
6042 S. Kimbark Avenue
Chicago, IL 60637
Fax: 312/702-0725

The Bulletin of the Atomic Scientists publishes both solicited and unsolicited manuscripts dealing with nuclear issues. While the Bulletin is a serious magazine, it is not a scholarly journal. Articles should be written in a lively style and should be suitable for the non-technical reader. In most cases, articles should be no longer than 3,000 words.

Queries with published clips are suggested; send SASE for Writer's Guidelines.

CALIFORNIA ALTERNATIVE NEWS BUREAU
1015 20th Street
Sacramento, CA 95616
Tel: 916/498-1234 Fax: 916/498-7920
Editor: Tom Johnson

The California Alternative News Bureau is a monthly news service which includes 15 California alternative papers among its subscribers. About 50 percent of its articles are provided by freelance writers. It is interested in hard news, features, and profiles of statewide California interest. Articles range from 500 to 2,000 words.

Rates: $100 to $400 depending on quality and work involved

Queries with published clips required; response time normally within a week.

Tips: "Take a story the mainstream papers have missed or downplayed, and, with lively writing tell Californians about it. No polemics, editorials. If you want your audience outraged, reflect it in your writing, not your lead."—Editor Tom Johnson

CANADIAN DIMENSION (CD)
228 Notre Dame Ave., Room 401
Winnipeg, Manitoba, R3B1N7
Canada
Tel: 204/957-1519 Fax: 204/943-4617
Office Manager: Michelle Torres

Canadian Dimension (CD) relies on freelance writers for about 25 percent of its material. It is primarily interested in articles (2,000 words maximum) and book reviews (750 words maximum).

Rates: 10 cents per published word; maximum of $300 per article

Queries preferred; send SASE for Writer's Guidelines; response time is two months.

Tips: "We're looking for articles on issues affecting women, gays/lesbians, aboriginals, the environment, and labour."

CASCADIA TIMES
25-6 Northwest 23rd Place, #406
Portland, OR 97201
Tel: 503/223-9036
E-mail: cascadia@desktop.org
Editor: Paul Koberstein

Cascadia Times, a regional publication with a focus ranging from San Francisco to Alaska, is published monthly. About 75 percent of its articles are provided by freelance writers. It is interested in investigative journalism on the environment and health, and book reviews on the same subjects. It publishes six to eight articles monthly, ranging from 500 to 3,000 words.

Rates: 20 cents per word

Queries not required; send SASE for Writer's Guidelines; response time is up to two weeks.

Tips: "No opinion pieces, please."— Editor Paul Koberstein

CITY PAPER
Baltimore's Free Weekly
812 Park Avenue
Baltimore, MD 21201
Tel: 410/523-2300 Fax: 410/523-8437
Managing Editor: Heather Joslyn

The City Paper is a weekly newspaper distributed free in the Baltimore area. About 50 percent of its articles are provided by freelance writers. It is interested in articles, profiles, book reviews, interviews, essays, exposés, all of which should have a strong Baltimore connection.

Rates: $25 to $400 depending on length

Queries with published clips required; response time normally two weeks; send SASE for Writer's Guidelines.

Tips: "We are particularly interested in the issues, people, and character of Baltimore City."

COMMON CAUSE MAGAZINE
2030 M Street, NW
Washington, DC 20036
Tel: 202/833-1200 Fax: 202/659-3716
Editor: Vicki Kemper

Common Cause Magazine, longtime scourge of Washington's political high-rollers, is published quarterly. About 30 percent of its articles are provided by freelance writers. It is primarily interested in investigative political pieces.

Rates: Vary

Queries not required

Tips: "We're interested in articles about money in politics, political corruption, real-life impacts of government policy, and social issues."—Editor Vicki Kemper

COUNTERPOISE
1716 SW Williston Road
Gainesville, FL 32608
Tel: 904/335-2200 Fax: (Phone first)
E-mail: willett@freenet.ufl.edu
Editor: Charles Willett

Counterpoise is a new alternative review journal which will be published quarterly starting January 1997. It will be sponsored by the Social Responsibilities Round Table of the American Library Association. It expects that about 50 percent of its articles will be provided by freelance writers. It is interested in articles, profiles, book reviews, opinion pieces, essays, and exposés. Write for details.

Rates, Query requirements, Writer's Guidelines, response time, etc., not yet determined

Tips: "Interested in reviews by librarians and other qualified persons of noteworthy new titles ignored or dismissed by the mainstream review media. Volunteers should write the editor, enclosing samples of their work."—Editor Charles Willett

COUNTER PUNCH
P.O. Box 18675
Washington, DC 20036
Tel: 202/986-3665 Fax: 202/986-3665
Editors: Ken Silverstein and Alexander Cockburn

Counter Punch is published twice monthly. About five percent of its articles are provided by freelance writers. It is specifically interested in politics with a Washington, DC angle.

Rates: Very low, negotiable

Queries not required; response time is a week.

COVERTACTION QUARTERLY
1500 Massachusetts Ave., NW
Room 732
Washington, DC 20005
Tel: 202/331-9763 Fax: 202/331-9751
Editors: Terry Allen and Phil Smith

CovertAction Quarterly, a publication that lives up to its name, is naturally published quarterly. From 50 to 80 percent of its articles are provided by freelance writers. It is interested in substantive articles, well-researched (with footnotes), exposés, interviews, etc. Average article length is 4,000-5,000 words, sometimes longer.

Rates: Negotiable

Queries with published clips required; send SASE for Writer's Guidelines; response time is 10 days.

Tips: "We're interested in stories about U.S. and allied intelligence operations (foreign and domestic), non-intelligence related topics demonstrating U.S. intervention or involvement, right-wing and/or racist activities, environmental issues, private (non-governmental) activities of a secret and/or detrimental nature."— Director of Research Louis Wolf

CULTURAL DEMOCRACY
P.O. Box 545
Tucson, AZ 85702
Tel: 602/791-9359

Cultural Democracy is a quarterly publication of the Alliance for Cultural Democracy, an 18-year-old national network of community and neighborhood-based cultural workers.

Rates: None

Queries not required; response time is two weeks to two months; send SASE for Writer's Guidelines.

Tips: "We are looking for writings that express the interconnection between cultural rights, community, arts, and ecology and ongoing, or historical, examples of projects or programs reflecting these concerns."

THE DAYTON VOICE
1927 N. Main Street, Suites 7&8
Dayton, OH 45405
Tel: 513/275-8855 Fax: 513/275-6056
Editor: Marrianne McMullen

The Dayton Voice is an alternative weekly that focuses primarily on local, state, or regional news and entertainment features surrounding the Dayton, Ohio area. About 80 percent of its articles are provided by freelance writers. It is interested in investigative reporting, profiles, and popular culture features. Article length ranges from 500 to 2,500 words.

Rates: $30 to $50

Queries not required but preferred; send SASE for Writer's Guidelines; response time is two weeks.

DE TODO UN POCO
2830-5th Street
Boulder, CO 80304
Tel: 303/444-8565 Fax: 303/545-2074
E-mail: tmoore@igc.apc.org
Editors: Nancy Sullo and Tom Moore

De Todo Un Poco is specifically interested in "first-hand" news and analysis about Central America and the Caribbean. About 10 percent of its articles are provided by freelance writers. It is interested in articles, profiles, and opinion pieces ranging up to 500 words.

Rates: None

Queries required; response time is two weeks.

Tips: "Particularly interested in 'first-hand experience' pieces. News and analysis pertaining to Central America and the Caribbean. In general, should be 500 words or less. We have a different 'focus' (nation or theme) each month and only have space for material pertaining to this focus. Inquire first; we're happy to hear your ideas."— Editor Nancy Sullo

DETROIT METRO TIMES
743 Beaubien, Suite 301
Detroit, MI 48226
Tel: 313/961-4060

The Detroit Metro Times is a weekly newspaper; about 70 percent of its material is provided by freelance writers. It is interested in articles, profiles, reviews, opinion pieces of 600 to 3,500 words on cutting edge culture and progressive political and social change. It is not interested in consumer news or mainstream religion, medicine, or sports.

Rates: None cited

Queries with published clips required; response time two weeks.

Tips: "We are interested in feminism, progressive politics, analysis of U.S. government and corporate abuse, environmentalism, race relations, danger of the right-wing, media monopoly and manipulation, etc."— Jim Dulzo

DOLLARS AND SENSE
1 Summer Street
Somerville, MA 02143
Tel: 617/628-8411 Fax: 617/628-2025
Editors: Betsy Reed and Marc Breslow

Dollars and Sense is a bimonthly magazine that focuses on economic issues and perspectives not normally found in *Forbes Magazine* or the *Wall Street Journal*. About 20 percent of its articles are provided by freelance writers. It will consider full-length features, interviews, and book reviews (200-600 words each) for publication.

Rates: Regrets that it cannot compensate authors at this time

Queries required; response time is a month; send SASE for Writer's Guidelines.

Tips: "Articles on progressive economics and political economy will be of interest."—Editor Betsy Reed

E: THE ENVIRONMENTAL MAGAZINE
P.O. Box 5098
Westport, CT 06881
Tel: 203/854-5559 Fax: 203/866-0602
Managing Editor: Jim Motavalli

E: The Environmental Magazine is a bimonthly magazine that focuses on the environment as its name suggests. About 75 percent of its articles are provided by freelance writers. It is interested in environment-oriented articles, interviews, exposés, news briefs, feature stories, as well as health-related articles, eco-home, and eco-tourism.

Rates: Twenty cents a word

Queries with published clips required; send SASE for Writer's Guidelines; response time is 4 to 6 months with an acknowledgment in one week.

Tips: "Investigative exposé pieces are good; anything that takes the corporate superstructure to task."

EARTH ISLAND JOURNAL
300 Broadway, Suite 28
San Francisco, CA 94133-3312
Tel: 415/788-3666 Fax: 415/788-7324
Editor: Gar Smith

Earth Island Journal is an environmental-oriented quarterly magazine. Only about 5 percent of its articles are provided by freelance writers. However, half-page (500 words) and full page (1,000 words) stories are most likely to win consideration; feature-length reports (1,500-3,000 words) occasionally come from outside writers.

Rates: Year's free subscription in exchange

Queries required; response time normally ten days to three months; send SASE for Writer's Guidelines.

Tips: "Our beat: 'Local News From Around the World.' First-person reports on under-reported environmental stories from abroad—particularly with a U.S. hook. Is some U.S. corporation causing harm overseas? Are there solutions from abroad that we can apply in the U.S.?"—Editor Gar Smith

ENVIRONMENTAL ACTION MAGAZINE
6930 Carroll Avenue, Suite 600
Takoma Park, MD 20912
Tel: 301/891-1100 Fax: 301/891-2218

Environmental Action Magazine (EA) is a quarterly magazine that primarily explores the human environment. About 10 percent of its articles are provided by freelance writers. While it is mainly interested in book reviews and essays by established experts/leaders in particular fields, it does publish a few investigative pieces.

Rates: Up to $300 but most authors are unpaid

Queries with published clips and résumé required; response time four to eight weeks.

Tips: "We stopped taking most freelance work in 1992 due to budget cuts and reduced frequency of the magazine. EA focuses primarily on the human environment (as opposed to wilderness issues) and on issues relating to the environmental movement itself. Issues in 1996 will focus on big money in politics and its effects on the environment; transportation; and strategies to target corporate power."—Magazine Associate Francis Wilkins

EXTRA!
130 W. 25th Street
New York, NY 10001
Tel: 212/633-6700 Fax: 212/727-7668
Editor: Jim Naureckas

EXTRA! is a bimonthly news media review journal published by Fairness and Accuracy In Reporting, a national media watchdog organization. It is interested in well-documented articles related to issues of media bias.

Rates: Ten cents a word

Queries not required; send SASE for Writer's Guidelines.

Tips: "Stories should focus more on the media than on the information not reported by the media. We look at media coverage of specific issues relating to government control of the media, corporate interference, racial and gender bias, etc."—Editor Jim Naureckas

FACTSHEET FIVE
P.O. Box 170099
San Francisco, CA 94117
Tel: 415/668-1781 Fax: 415/668-1781
Editor: R. Seth Friedman

Factsheet Five, a publication that focuses exclusively on Zines, is published four times a year. About 30 percent of its articles are provided by freelance writers. It primarily prints reviews but also publishes a number of freelance articles covering Zines, publishing, and the alternative/underground culture.

Rates: Range from $50 to $100

Queries not required but published clips are welcome; send SASE for Writer's Guidelines; response time is one month.

Tips: "Factsheet Five is exclusively devoted to the world of Zines. While we do print an occasional political piece, we only accept them from writers who have written for us before. We only accept articles about Zine culture from new writers."—Editor R. Seth Friedman

FOOD FIRST NEWS & VIEWS BACKGROUNDERS
398 60th Street
Oakland, CA 94618
Tel: 510/654-4400 Fax: 510/654-4551
Managing Editor: Kathleen McClung

Food First News & Views, and its companion publication, Backgrounders, are quarterly publications of the Food First Institute. Both publications explore the causes of hunger, poverty, and environmental deterioration. Less than 10 percent of their articles are provided by freelance writers. They are interested in short articles or interviews with a 2,000-word maximum.

Rates: Negotiable; small stipend only

Queries with published clips required; response time is one to two months.

Tips: "Food First is a non-profit research and education center focusing on the root causes of hunger, poverty, and environmental deterioration. Most of our writers are on staff or closely associated with the institute."—Managing Editor Kathleen McClung

FREETHINKER FORUM
8945 Renken Road
Staunton, IL 62088
or P.O. Box 14447
St. Louis, MO 63178
Tel: 618/637-2202 Fax: 618/637-2666
E-mail: profreedom@aol.com
Editor/Publisher: Susan Duncan

Freethinker Forum is a monthly publication focusing on liberal issues and individuals. About 50 percent of its articles are provided by freelance writers. It is interested in political (liberal) articles, interviews with liberal activists, politicians, etc., opinion pieces, and essays, with a liberal bent only. Length usually ranges from a minimum of 500 words to a maximum of 3,000 words.

Rates: $50 for 500 words; $100 for 1,000 to 2,000 words; longer articles negotiable; all paid on publication

Queries not required; send SASE for Writer's Guidelines; response time is 21 days.

Tips: "Commentary on the state of

the country under conservative rule, liberal activism, feminist issues, animal rights, anti-religion or exposés involving religious zealots, etc., environmental issues, single mothers, welfare, the penal system."—Editor Susan Duncan

FRONT LINES RESEARCH

Public Policy Institute
Planned Parenthood Federation of America
810 7th Avenue
New York, NY 10019
Tel: 212/261-4721 Fax: 212/261-4352
Editor: Frederick Clarkson

Front Lines Research features "journalism with footnotes" in defense of reproductive health, education, and democracy. It is published bimonthly. About 20 percent of its articles are provided by freelance writers. It is interested in investigative, analytical, rigorous, footnoted, documentary features on the radical right. Maximum length is 2,000 words plus footnotes.
   Rates: 10 cents per word plus expenses
   Queries with published clips required; send SASE for Writer's Guidelines; response time is two weeks.
   Tips: "Considerable expertise on the far-right is a pre-requisite. We are generally publishing definitive work in this field. The style is a mix of investigative journalism and academic journalism. I call it journalism with footnotes. Stories in this journal should be compelling reading and have a long shelf life."—Editor Frederick Clarkson

GLOBAL EXCHANGES

2017 Mission Street
Suite 303
San Francisco, CA 94110
Tel: 415/255-7296
Editor: Kevin Danaher

Global Exchanges is a quarterly publication which focuses on international affairs and citizen diplomacy. Only about two percent of its articles are provided by freelance writers. It publishes in February, May, August, and October.
   Rates: None
   Queries with published clips required; send SASE for Writer's Guidelines; response time is one to two weeks.

HARD TIMES

c/o L.A. View
2342 Sawtelle Boulevard
Los Angeles, CA 90064
Tel: 310/477-0403
Founder/Editor/Publisher:
Len Doucette

Hard Times, an aptly named publication about homelessness, is published bi-monthly. One hundred percent of its articles are provided by freelance writers. One hundred percent of its funds are from street sales of the paper.
   Rates: Can't afford to pay writers
   Queries not required.
   Tips: "We are dedicated to educating the general public about all issues regarding homelessness. We welcome all submissions but are unable to guarantee publication."—Editor Len Doucette

HIGH COUNTRY NEWS
P.O. Box 1090
Paonia, CO 81428
Tel: 303/527-4898

High Country News is a regional Colorado publication with a national impact. It is published biweekly. Ninety percent of its articles are provided by freelance writers. It is interested in magazine-style leads, essays on environmental issues, planning, shorter roundups on local issues with regional resonance.

Rates: Twenty cents a word and up

Queries with published clips required; send SASE for Writer's Guidelines; response time varies.

Tips: "Read the paper first, know what we cover, and where we are in that coverage."

THE HUMAN QUEST
1074 23rd Avenue N.
St. Petersburg, FL 33704-3228
Tel: 813/894-0097
Editor: Edna Ruth Johnson

The Human Quest is a bimonthly national magazine that is "in the mail on the 25th of the month." One hundred percent of its material is provided by freelance writers. Emphasis of The Human Quest is world peace; its religious conviction is spiritual humanism. It welcomes thoughtful articles ranging from 150 to 500 to 1,000 words in length.

Rates: None

Queries not required; response time normally within a week; in lieu of formal guidelines, editor will "happily furnish a copy of the publication" on request.

Tips: "The Human Quest is an independent journal of religious humanism, under the sponsorship of The Churchman Associates, Inc. It is edited in the conviction that religious journalism must provide a platform for the free exchange of ideas and opinions; that religion is consonant with the most advanced revelations in every department of knowledge; that we are in a fraternal world community; and that the moral and spiritual evolution of man is only at the beginning."—Editor Edna Ruth Johnson

THE INDEPENDENT FILM & VIDEO MONTHLY
625 Broadway, 9th Floor
New York, NY 10012
Tel: 212/473-3400 Fax: 212/677-8732
Editor: Patricia Thomson

The Independent Film & Video Monthly is a national magazine with about 90 percent of its articles provided by freelance writers. It is interested in news articles, 500-800 words; profiles of film/video makers, distributors, festival directors, 700-1,000 words; business, legal, technical articles, 700-1,200 words; features 1,500-3,000 words.

Rates: News articles, $50; profiles, $100; features, 10 cents a word

Queries with published clips required; response time from two weeks to two months.

Tips: "Interested in film/video-related articles that are not too theoretical or too mainstream. Recent features include 'The Money Game: Foundation Insiders Explain the Rules,' and 'Made in Japan: Current

Trends in Japanese Independent Filmmaking.'"—Michele Shapiro.

INDEX ON CENSORSHIP
33 Islington High Street
London, England N1 9LH
Tel: 171-278-2313 Fax: 171-278-1878
E-mail:
index@indexcen.demon.co.uk
indexoncenso@gn.apc.org
Editor: Ursula Owen

Index on Censorship is an international bimonthly review and analysis of censorship issues. It is interested in articles, profiles, book reviews, interviews, opinion pieces, essays, exposés, etc. Also interested in factual news and analytic articles on censorship and freedom of expression issues. Articles range from 800 to 4,000 words.

Rates: £60 per 1,000 words for original pieces

Queries not required.

Tips: Special interests include "All areas concerned with freedom of expression and censorship, world-wide (including Britain)."—Editor Ursula Owen.

INDUSTRIAL WORKER
103 W. Michigan Avenue
Ypsilanti, MI 48197-5438
Tel: 313/483-3548 Fax: 313/483-4050
E-mail: iww@igc.apc.org
Editor: Jon Bekken

Industrial Worker, a labor-oriented publication, is published monthly. About 10 percent of its articles are provided by freelance writers. It is interested in labor-related articles, profiles, book reviews, interviews, opinion pieces, essays, and exposés, up to about 500 words maximum.

Rates: Free subscriptions

Queries not required; response time is one month.

Tips: "Labor and social issues from a progressive perspective."—General Secretary/Treasurer Fred Chase

IN THESE TIMES
2040 N. Milwaukee
Chicago, IL 60647
Tel: 312/772-0100 Fax: 312/772-4180
Editor: James Weinstein; Managing Editor: Jim McNeill

In These Times (ITT) is a biweekly news and views magazine. About 50 percent of its articles are provided by freelance writers. It is interested in articles, profiles, book reviews, interviews, opinion pieces, essays, and exposés.

Rates: None cited

Queries with published clips required; response time normally two to three weeks; send SASE for Writer's Guidelines.

Tips: "Writers should be familiar with the magazine before sending submissions. A huge percentage of our rejections are pieces that are submitted by writers who obviously haven't read ITT."—Managing Editor Jim McNeill

LEFT BUSINESS OBSERVER
250 W. 85th Street
New York, NY 10024
Tel: 212/874-4020 Fax: 212/874-3137
E-mail: dhenwood@panix.com
Editor: Doug Henwood

Left Business Observer is published monthly and features all the business news you won't find in the *Wall Street Journal*. From 10 to 20 percent of its articles are provided by freelance writers. It is interested in articles and reviews on economics and politics—all genres okay.

Rates: Twelve cents a word

Queries with published clips required; response time is one week.

Tips: "Know the publication—be smart, witty, interesting, and radical."—Editor Doug Henwood

LIBRARIANS AT LIBERTY
1716 SW Williston Road
Gainesville, FL 32608
Tel: 904/335-2200 Fax: (Phone first)
E-mail: willett@freenet.ufl.edu
Editor: Charles Willett

Librarians at Liberty (L@L) provides an unrestrained opportunity for critics to sound off about censorship regarding libraries and the book trade. It is published semi-annually. About 50 percent of its articles are provided by freelance writers. It is interested in non-fiction articles, profiles, book reviews, interviews, opinion pieces, essays, and exposés, ranging from 250 to 2,000 words. L@L is anti-copyright. The editor reserves the right to edit all material submitted.

Rates: $30 to $50

Queries not required; there is no response unless published.

Tips: "Non-fiction only. Censorship, self-censorship of/by libraries and the book trade. All aspects of the alternative press related to libraries. Material which deals frankly and honestly with issues of independent, non-corporate writing and libraries. Gives library workers, publishers, booksellers, and users an unconstrained opportunity to express their concerns."
—Editor Charles Willett

MEDIAFILE
814 Mission Street, Suite 205
San Francisco, CA 94103
Tel: 415/546-6523 Fax: 415/546-6218
Editor: Larry Smith

Media/File is a bimonthly newspaper published by the Media Alliance, an organization of more than 3,000 San Francisco Bay Area media professionals. About 80 percent of its articles are provided by freelance writers. It is interested in articles and analyses relating to the media, with a specific interest in the San Francisco Bay Area; book reviews on books about media; profiles of interesting media workers; and investigative media exposés encouraged.

Rates: Depends on experience; frequently trade

Queries not required but helpful along with published clips; response time normally in two weeks; send SASE for Writer's Guidelines.

Tips: "Media, First Amendment, censorship issues are our bag."—Editor Larry Smith

MOTHER JONES
731 Market Street, Suite 600
San Francisco, CA 94103
Tel: 415/665-6637 Fax: 415/665-6696
Editor: Jeffrey Klein; Managing Editor: Katharine Fong

Mother Jones is a bimonthly magazine known for its investigative journalism and exposés, and its coverage of social issues, public affairs, and popular culture. Most of its articles are written by freelancers. It is interested in hard-hitting investigative reports exposing government, corporate, scientific, institutional cover-ups, etc.; thoughtful articles that challenge conventional wisdom on national issues; and people-oriented stories on issues such as the environment, labor, the media, health care, consumer protection, and cultural trends. "Outfront" stories run 250-500 words; short features run 1,200-3,000 words, and longer features run 3,000-5,000 words.

Rates: 80 cents per word for commissioned stories

Queries with published clips required; send SASE for Writer's Guidelines; please do not query by phone or fax.

Tips: "Keep in mind that our lead time is three months and submissions should not be so time-bound that they will appear dated. We are not a news magazine."

MIGHT
150 4th Street, #650
San Francisco, CA 94103-3048
Tel: 415/896-1528 Fax: 415/974-1216
E-mail: mightmag@aol.com
Editors: David Eggers, David Moodie, Paul Tullis

Might, published bi-monthly, does not want to see anything about Generation X! Its freelance articles range from 10 to 80 percent depending on the issue. It is interested in well-researched hard journalism up to 5,000 words; profiles and interviews up to 2,500 words; pranks up to 2,000 words; satire up to 2,000 words, book reviews up to 1,000 words. No personal essays.

Rates: "Nobody here gets paid, including the editors. We hope that to change in '96."

Queries with published clips required ("unless you're somebody we've heard of;" for writer's guidelines, read the magazine; response time ranges from one day to four months.

Tips: "No first person, nothing about Generation X."—Editor Paul Tullis

Ms.
230 Park Avenue
New York, NY 10169
Tel: 212/551-9595

Ms. is a bimonthly magazine that focuses primarily on women's issues and news. About 80 percent of its articles are provided by freelance writers. It is interested in articles, profiles, book reviews, opinion pieces, essays, and exposés. Article lengths: most departments, 1,200 words; features, 3,000-4,000 words; U.S. news, 1,000-2,000 words.

Rates: Between 70 cents and $1 per word, approximately

Queries with published clips required; address **queries** to Manuscripts Editor; response time about 12 weeks; send SASE for Writer's Guidelines.

MULTINATIONAL MONITOR

P.O. Box 19405
Washington, DC 20036
Tel: 202/387-8030 Fax: 202/234-5176
E-mail: monitor@essential.org
Editor: Robert Weissman

The Multinational Monitor is a monthly news magazine that focuses on the activities and escapades of multinational corporations. About 50 percent of its articles are provided by freelance writers. It is interested in articles, profiles, book reviews, interviews, essays, exposés, features and news items relating to multinational corporate issues. No fiction.

Rates: Ten cents a word

Queries required; send SASE for Writer's Guidelines.

Tips: "Issues include all topics related to the activities of multinational corporations and their impact on labor, health, consumer issues and environment, especially in the Third World." —A. Freeman

THE NATION

72 Fifth Avenue
New York, NY 10011
Tel: 212/242-8400 Fax: 212/463-9712
Editor-in-Chief: Katrina Vanden Heuvel

The Nation is a weekly magazine (biweekly through the summer) dedicated to reporting on issues dealing with labor, national politics, business, consumer affairs, environmental politics, civil liberties, and foreign affairs. About 75 percent of its articles are provided by freelance writers. It is interested in articles, book reviews, opinion pieces, essays, and exposés.

Rates: $75 per Nation page

Queries with published clips required; normal response time is four weeks; send SASE for Writer's Guidelines.

Tips: "Leftist politics."—Dennis Selby

NATIONAL CATHOLIC REPORTER

P.O. Box 419281
Kansas City, MO 64141
Tel: 816/531-0538 Fax: 816/968-2280
Editor: Tom Fox

The National Catholic Reporter is published weekly from September through May with the exception of Thanksgiving week and the first week in January. It publishes articles, profiles, book reviews, interviews, opinion pieces, essays, exposés, features and news items. About 50 percent of its articles are provided by freelance writers. Average length is from 750 to 1,500 words.

Rates: Fifteen cents a word

Queries required.

NEWSLETTER ON INTELLECTUAL FREEDOM

50 E. Huron Street
Chicago, IL 60611
Tel: 312/280-4223 Fax: 312/280-4227
Editor: Judith F. Krug

The Newsletter On Intellectual Freedom is a bimonthly magazine published by the American Library Association (ALA). Book reviews are published in every issue of the NEWSLETTER. Interested reviewers should contact the ALA Office for Intellectual Freedom for guidelines.

Articles focusing on intellectual freedom, freedom of the press, censorship, and the First Amendment will be considered for publication.

Rates: Pro bono

Queries required; send SASE for Writer's Guidelines.

Tips: "Authors should contact the Office for Intellectual Freedom for information and guidelines."—Editor Judith Krug

OPEN EYE
BM Open Eye
London, WC1N 3XX, U.K.
Tel: 0441-956-250654
E-mail: an74570@anon.penet.fi

Open Eye is a new British publication which is dedicated to "challenging media censorship." It cites its publication schedule as Yearly/Bi-yearly. About 50 percent of its articles are provided by freelance writers. It is particularly interested in exposés which it says is its specialty, particularly investigation of military and security services. Other subject areas include Green and Transpersonal issues, radical politics, and books reviews on these topics. Maximum length is 4-5,000 words.

Rates: Costs only

Queries required; response time is one month.

Tips: "Open Eye uncovers the issues the media conceals."

PACIFIC SUN
P.O. Box 5553
Mill Valley, CA 94942
Tel: 415/383-4500 Fax: 415/383-4159
E-mail: PSun@aol.com
Publisher/Editor: Steve McNamara;
Managing Editor: Linda Xiques

Pacific Sun is a weekly newspaper published on Wednesdays, circulated primarily in Marin and Sonoma counties in northern California. About 75 percent of its articles are provided by freelance writers. It is interested in articles, profiles, book reviews, interviews, and exposés. In-depth articles are 2,500-3,000 words; short newsy articles are 800 words; short features range from 1,200 to 1,500 words; and reviews are 500-800 words.

Rates: $75 to $150 to $400

Queries with published clips required; send SASE for Writer's Guidelines; response time is one month.

Tips: "We are a local interest paper. No national or international news unless there is a strong Marin/Sonoma hook."—Managing Editor Linda Xiques

PEACE REVIEW: A TRANSNATIONAL QUARTERLY
Peace & Justice Studies
University of San Francisco
2130 Fulton Street
San Francisco, CA 94117
Tel: 415/666-6349/6496 Fax: 415/666-2346/388-2631
E-mail: eliasr@usfca.edu
Editor: Robert Elias

Peace Review is a quarterly, multidisciplinary journal of essays addressing broad issues of peace, human rights, and development. It publishes relatively short essays, ranging from 2,500 to 3,500 words, short reviews of not more than 800 words, and brief biographies of distinguished peace activists. A transnational journal with distribution to more than 40 countries, it is edited for a wide readership.

Rates: Fifty offprints of each essay accepted for publication and a copy of the relevant journal issue

Queries not required; send SASE for Writer's Guidelines (each issue is organized around a particular theme).

Tips: "We are most interested in the cultural and political issues surrounding conflicts occurring between nations and peoples. Relevant topics include war, violence, human rights, political economy, development, culture and consciousness, the environment, and related issues."

THE PEOPLE'S WARRIOR

P.O. Box 488
Rockwall, TX 75087
Tel: 214/771-1991
Publisher: David Parker

The People's Warrior is a monthly publication which seeks to explore and profile legal or political corruption. About 90 percent of its articles are provided by freelance writers. All articles, profiles, book reviews, interviews, opinion pieces, essays, and exposés that deal with legal or political corruption will be given serious consideration. Manuscript length varies from two through ten typewritten, single-spaced pages.

Rates: $45 credit for 12-month subscription

Queries not required; response time is two weeks.

Tips: "We're particularly interested in well-documented articles which profile legal or political corruption."—Publisher David Parker

PERCEPTIONS MAGAZINE

c/o 10734 Jefferson Boulevar, Suite 502
Culver City, California
Postal Zone 90230
Tel: 310/313-5185 or 800/276-4448
Fax: 310/313-5198
E-mail: Perceptions@Primenet.Com
Editor: Judi V. Brewer

Perceptions Magazine is a bimonthly with 100 percent of its articles written by freelance writers. It is interested in articles, profiles, book reviews, interviews, essays, and exposés up to 2,500 words.

Rates: Gratitude, $5, and three magazines

Queries required; send SASE for Writer's Guidelines; response time is less than six weeks.

Tips: "Must read magazine first before enquiry."

PRISON LEGAL NEWS

P.O. Box 1684
Lake Worth, FL 33460
Tel: 407/547-9716
Editors: Paul Wright and Dan Pens

Prison Legal News, a monthly publication, focuses on prison related issues. About 30 percent of its articles are provided by freelance writers. It is interested in articles, book and video reviews, commentary, and exposés, ranging from 500 to 3,000 words.

Rates: Complimentary subscriptions

Queries not required; send SASE for Writer's Guidelines; response time is two weeks.

Tips: "Prison struggle, prison-related issues, legal analysis relating to prison civil rights."—Editor Paul Wright

THE PROGRESSIVE
409 E. Main Street
Madison, WI 53703
Tel: 608/257-4626 Fax: 608/257-3373
Editor: Matt Rothschild

The Progressive is a politically-oriented monthly magazine. About 80 percent of its articles are provided by freelance writers. It is interested in features, 2,500 words; activist profiles, 750 words; Q&A, 2,500 words; book reviews, 300-1,500 words; and exposés, 2,500-3,500 words.

Rates: Features, $300; book reviews, $150; interviews, $300; exposés, $300; and activist profiles, $100

Queries preferred with published clips; normal response time is ten days; send SASE for Writer's Guidelines.

PUBLIC CITIZEN MAGAZINE
1600 20th Street, NW
Washington, DC 20009
Tel: 202/588-1000 Fax: 202/588-7799
E-mail: pnye@citizen.org
Editor: Peter Nye

Public Citizen Magazine is published six times a year and focuses on national policy issues and their impact on the public. About 15 percent of its articles are provided by freelance writers. It is interested in book reviews, 400 words (two reviews per magazine page); features up to 4,500 words; profiles of extraordinary individuals who work for improving their local community up to three pages.

Rates: Negotiable, $400 tops; buys one-time rights only

Queries required; normal response time is two weeks.

Tips: "Our articles deal with national policy involving accountability of corporations and the government. It's best to read our magazine and be familiar with how our stories are published, their slant. We also rely heavily on facts, quotes, specific information."—Editor Peter Nye

RETHINKING SCHOOLS
1001 E. Keefe Avenue
Milwaukee, WI 53212-1710
Tel: 414/964-9646 Fax: 414/964-7220
Managing Editor: Barbara Miner

Rethinking Schools is a publication that focuses on analysis or critique of current educational policy, theory, or practice. From 5 to 10 percent of its articles are provided by unsolicited freelance writers. Its essays range from 600 to 2,000 words; how-to-articles (first-person reflections, tips on classroom materials, curriculum, and practices) are 200 to 1,500 words; poetry, student work, bibliography, and photos/graphics also considered.

Rates: From none to small

Queries not required; published clips preferred; send SASE for Writer's Guidelines; response time is six to eight weeks.

SOJOURNERS
2401 15th Street, NW
Washington, DC 20009
Tel: 202/328-8842 Fax: 202/328-8757
Editor: Jim Wallis

Sojourners is published monthly (10 times a year) and about 25 percent of its articles are provided by freelance writers. It is interested in features on issues of faith, politics, and culture (1,800-3,200 words); book, film, and music reviews (600-1,000 words).

Rates: Features, $100-$200; reviews, $40

Queries not required; submit published clips; normal response time is six to eight weeks; send SASE for Writer's Guidelines.

SONOMA COUNTY INDEPENDENT

540 Mendocino Avenue
Santa Rosa, CA 95401
Tel: 707/527-1200 Fax: 707/527-1288
E-mail: Indy@livewire.com
Editor: Greg Cahill

Sonoma County Independent is an alternative weekly newspaper in Sonoma County in northern California. From 60 to 75 percent of its articles are provided by freelance writers. It is interested in 2,000 to 3,000 word news features, usually in-depth local stories, but always looking for well-written people-oriented features identifying social or cultural trends. Also interested in 600-750 words on books, music, film, and theater columns, as well as opinion pieces.

Rates: Ten cents a word for news and features (more when appropriate); $35-$60 for columns

Queries with published clips required; send SASE for Writer's Guidelines; response time is two weeks.

Tips: "We are less interested in 'topics' than interesting people who can tell the 'story' within the topic. Writing style is always important, and our publication is always on the lookout for good writers who are good story-tellers."—Editor Greg Cahill

SOUTHERN EXPOSURE

P.O. Box 531
Durham, NC 27702
Tel: 919/419-8311
Editor: Pat Arnow

Southern Exposure is a quarterly magazine that focuses on Southern politics and culture. About 50 percent of its articles are provided by freelance writers. It is interested in investigative journalism, essays, profiles, book reviews, oral histories, and features on Southern politics and culture.

Rates: $50-$250

Queries not required; submit published clips; normal response time is four to six weeks; send SASE for Writer's Guidelines. Send $5.00 for a sample copy.

THE SPOTLIGHT

300 Independence Avenue, S.E.
Washington, DC 20003
Tel: 202/544-1794
Managing Editor: Fred Blahut

The Spotlight is a Washington, DC-based weekly newspaper which focuses on political/economic issues. About 20 percent of its articles are provided by freelance writers. It is interested in articles, opinion, and profiles ranging from 700 to 1,000 words.

Rates: Negotiable

Queries required; response time is three weeks.

Tips: "Economic-Nationalism, American-First Politics, Constitutional Rights."

ST. LOUIS JOURNALISM REVIEW
8380 Olive Boulevard
St. Louis, MO 63132
Tel: 314/991-1699 Fax: 314/997-1898

The **St. Louis Journalism Review** is a regionally based but nationally oriented journalism review magazine published monthly except for combined issues in July/August and December/January. About 80 percent of its articles are provided by freelance writers. It is interested in articles, profiles, interviews, opinion pieces, essays, and exposés dealing with the news media.

Rates: $20 to $100

Queries not required; normal response time is three to four weeks.

Tips: "While the St. Louis region is of primary interest, national and international pieces dealing with media criticism are considered."

STREET NEWS
445 West 49 Street
New York, NY 10019
Tel: 212/247-3548 Fax: 212/247-1412
Editors: Lee Stringer,
Indio Washington

Street News, an aptly titled monthly newspaper, provides "a forum for the soul and spirit of the street." Most of its pieces are written by freelancers. It is interested in articles, first person pieces, fiction, humor, and occasional exposés that express a street perspective and address political questions pertinent to people on the streets. The paper also accepts some general interest stories.

Rates: $45 to $50 for assigned pieces only.

Queries: send a story proposal and clips, if available; send SASE for manuscript returns; response time is about two weeks.

Tips: "Many of our writers are homeless, or have been so in the past. But we like to feature some general interest stories and articles."—Editor Lee Stringer

THE SUN
107 N. Roberson Street
Chapel Hill, NC 27516
Tel: 919/942-5282
Editor: Sy Safransky

The Sun is published monthly. About 90 percent of its articles are provided by freelance writers. It is interested in interviews and essays.

Rates: $100 to $500

Queries not required; send SASE for Writer's Guidelines; response time is three months.

Tips: "Send $3.50 for a sample copy before submitting."

TEXAS OBSERVER
307 W. 7th Street
Austin, TX 78701
Tel: 512/477-0746 Fax: 512/474-1175
Editor: Lou Dubose

Texas Observer, a publication that focuses on Texas but creates national waves, is published every two weeks. About 50 percent of its articles are provided by freelance writers. It is interested in articles, profiles, book reviews, interviews, essays, and exposés.

Rates: Meager

Tips: "Texas-oriented politics and culture."—Associate Editor Michael King

THIRD FORCE MAGAZINE

1218 E. 21st Street
Oakland, CA 94606
Tel: 510/533-7583 Fax: 510/533-0923
Managing Editor: John Anner; Senior
Editor: Andrea Lewis

Third Force Magazine, a bimonthly, is interested in "Issues and actions in communities of color." It will consider virtually any article that offers a fresh and interesting look at issues that relate to communities of color—especially political analysis, grassroots organizing, low-income communities, etc. It is not interested in pop-psychology, self-help, fashion and beauty, business success stories, etc. About 70 percent of its articles are provided by freelance writers.

Rates: Negotiable

Queries with published clips, or writing sample, preferred; send SASE for Writer's Guidelines; response time is from four to six weeks.

Tips: "We're interested in grassroots organizing, gender and sexuality issues, low-income communities and class issues, political and cultural analysis relating to communities of color, multi-racial coalition efforts, police and community safety issues, etc. All issues must relate to, or be of interest to, communities of color."—Senior Editor Andrea Lewis

TIKKUN MAGAZINE

251 W. 100th Street, 5th Floor
New York, NY 10025
Tel: 212/864-4110 Fax: 212/864-4137
Editor & Publisher: Michael Lerner

Tikkun is a bimonthly magazine that focuses on political and cultural issues. It is interested in articles, profiles, book reviews, interviews, opinion pieces, essays, exposés, features and news items; all types of material of varying lengths.

Rates: Varies

Queries not required; normal response time is four months.

Tips: "Political/cultural critiques—magazine has a liberal/progressive slant but does publish all sorts of viewpoints. A non-profit magazine."

TOWARD FREEDOM

209 College Street
Burlington, VT 05401
Tel: 802/658-2523 Fax: 802/658-3738
E-mail: mavmedia@aol.com
Editor: Greg Guma

Toward Freedom, an international journal of news, analysis, and advocacy, is published eight times a year. About 75 percent of its articles are provided by freelance writers. It is interested in international perspectives: features from 2,000 to 3,000 words; international news reports from 800 to 1,200 words; reviews, essays. Focus on human rights, politics and culture, environment, women, global media, post-nationalist movements, and creative solutions to world problems.

Rates: 10 cents per printed word

Queries required; send SASE for Writer's Guidelines; response time is 30 days.

Tips: "Query with one to three ideas; we look for writers who combine research with direct experience and a passionate approach. Special issues each year, e.g. environment and native peoples, global media and women. We cover the world with special emphasis on revealing relationships between cultures and political trends. Profiles also welcome."—Editor Greg Guma

TURNING THE TIDE: JOURNAL OF ANTI-RACIST ACTIVISM, RESEARCH & EDUCATION

P.O. Box 1990
Burbank, CA 91507
Tel: 310/288-5003
E-mail: mnovickttt@igc.apc.org
Editor: Michael Novick

Turning the Tide: Journal of Anti-Racist Activism, Research & Education is published quarterly in March, June, September, and December. From 30 to 40 percent of its articles are provided by freelance writers. It is interested in articles, profiles, book reviews, interviews, opinion pieces, essays, exposés, and poetry.

Rates: In contributor's copies

Queries preferred but not required; send 9x12 envelope and 78-cents postage for sample copy; response time is one to two months.

Tips: "We would like to see material that looks at far-reaching solutions, as well as thorough analyses of the problems related to issues of racism, sexism, and colonialism. We prefer material at no higher than a low high school reading level, light on rhetoric."—Editor Michael Novick

U. THE NATIONAL COLLEGE MAGAZINE

1800 Century Park East, #820
Los Angeles, CA 90067
Tel: 310/551-1381 Fax: 310/551-1659
E-mail: umagazine@aol.com
    editor@umagazine.com
Editor: Frances Huffman

U. The National College Magazine focuses on collegiate subjects and publishes 9 issues a year. About 90 percent of its articles are provided by freelance writers. It is looking for college news briefs: 300 words; feature articles: 1,000 words; profiles and interviews of celebrities, authors, athletes, politicians, etc.: 1,000 words; opinion pieces: 500 words; mini-features: 400 words; movie previews and music reviews: 100 words.

Rates: Range from $25 to $100

Queries with published clips required (by phone, fax, or mail); send SASE for Writer's Guidelines; response time is one to two months.

Tips: "Our articles are written by college students and must have a college focus."—Editor Frances Huffman

UTNE READER

1624 Harmon Place
Minneapolis, MN 55403
Tel: 612/338-5040
Managing Editor: Lynette Lamb

The **Utne Reader** is an eclectic bimonthly magazine that has earned the reputation of being the *Reader's Digest* of the alternative media. About 20 percent of its articles are provided by freelance writers. It is interested in short essays, articles, and opinion pieces.

Rates: $100-$500

Queries not required; submit published clips; normal response time is two to three months; send SASE for Writer's Guidelines.

Tips: "We use unsolicited material most often in our 'Gleanings' section. Most of our other freelance articles are assigned. The majority of *Utne Reader* articles are reprinted from other publications."—Managing Editor Lynette Lamb

THE WASHINGTON FREE PRESS
1463 E. Republican, #178
Seattle, WA 98112
Tel: 206/233-1780
E-mail: freepres@scn.org

The Washington Free Press emphasizes investigative reporting with a focus on Seattle or the Northwest. It is published six times a year. About 35 percent of its articles are provided by freelance writers. It is interested in feature stories, from 700 to 4,000 words, on labor, environmental, political, cultural, or media-critical topics; book reviews (chiefly of Northwest authors) 700 words or less; interviews at 1,200 words.

Rates: "All of our writing is volunteer"

Queries required with published clips; send SASE for Writer's Guidelines; response time is two weeks.

Tips: "Please contact us first with story idea before you write the whole shebang! Address queries to Submissions Editor."

WASHINGTON SPECTATOR
541 E. 12th Street
New York, NY 10009
Tel: 212/995-8527 Fax: 212/979-2055
Editor: Ben Franklin; Publisher: Phillip Frazer

The Washington Spectator is a small, but influential, political watchdog newsletter published 22 times a year. About 10 percent of its articles are provided by freelance writers. It is primarily interested in articles and exposés.

Rates: Varies: 50 cents a word and up

Queries with published clips required; normal response time is one week.

Tips: "Write a very brief (one page maximum) note as a first proposal."—Publisher Phillip Frazer

WHO CARES: A JOURNAL OF SERVICE AND ACTION
1511 K Street, NW, Suite 1042
Washington, DC 20005
Tel: 202/628-1691 Fax: 202/628-2063
E-mail: info@whocares.org
Editors: Heather McLeod, Cheryl Cole-Dodwell, Leslie Crutchfield

Who Cares Magazine, the only national publication covering the cutting edge of community service and activism, is published quarterly. It is interested in "Partners in Change" articles on service programs throughout the country (1,000 to 1,300 words); features (1,500 to 2,500 words); entrepreneurial programs (1,500 to 2,500 words); and department items ranging from 100 to 1,500 words.

Rates: Small stipends or minimal fees-per-word for commissioned articles; solicited features negotiable

Queries required with published clips; send SASE for Writer's Guidelines.

Tips: "Who Cares informs its readers through incisive, nonpartisan coverage of new service initiatives; inspires them with profiles of volunteers making a difference; and challenges them to consider new solutions to old problems."

WILLAMETTE WEEK

822 SW 10th Avenue
Portland, OR 97205
Tel: 503/243-2122 Fax: 503/243-1115
Editor: Mark Zusman

Willamette Week is an alternative weekly newspaper published and distributed in the Portland, Oregon, area. About 50 percent of its articles are provided by freelance writers. It is interested in articles (if regional in perspective), interviews, book reviews, music reviews, profiles—again with a regional focus.

Rates: Ten cents a word

Queries with published clips required; normal response time is about three weeks; send SASE for Writer's Guidelines.

WRITER'S GUIDELINES

P.O. Box 608
Pittsburg, MO 65724
Fax: 417/993-5544
Publisher & Editor: Susan Salaki

Writer's Guidelines is a bimonthly magazine designed to help writers get published. About 99 percent of its articles are provided by freelance writers. It is interested in articles, book reviews, interviews, opinion pieces, and essays that will help writers.

Rates: Depends on quality of material

Queries not required; normal response time is two weeks; send SASE for Writer's Guidelines.

Tips: "Use a friendly relaxed style in your material but not chummy. Our objective is to help writers get published. If your article or essay contains information that will make that happen, we want to see it. We look for material the other writer publications usually overlook."—Editor Susan Salaki

Top 10 Censored Reprints

1 CENSORED

Tele-communications Deregulation: Closing Up America's "Marketplace Of Ideas"

The following is a letter by Ralph Nader, James Love and Andrew Saindon, of Public Citizen's Consumer Project on Technology, to the editor of TAP-INFO, an Internet newsletter by the Taxpayer Assets Project, available from listproc–@tap.org.TAP-INFO, July 15, 1995.

Dear Editor:

We are writing to offer the enclosed materials as an aid to understanding the current telecommunications legislation in Congress, and to urge your newspaper's editorial board to oppose key provisions of these bills.

On June 15, 1995 the U.S. Senate passed S.652. This bill would:

■ allow one entity to own more television stations, by eliminating all nationwide numeric restrictions on the number of stations owned by a single entity, and raising the national "audience cap" for a single entity from 25 percent to 35 percent;

■ eliminate all FCC rules on the number of AM and FM radio stations in the same geographic market or nationally which can be owned by a single entity, allowing one entity to own every AM and FM radio station in the United States;

■ allow telephone companies to enter electronic publishing; and

■ relax the current ban on cross-ownership of telephone and cable systems. Telephone companies will be allowed to purchase outright cable systems that have fewer than 20,000 subscribers, or in places with fewer than 50,000 inhabitants. Because about 36 percent of all cable subscribers are served by systems with fewer than 20,000 subscribers, and 37 percent of the U.S. population lives in "places" with fewer than 50,000 inhabitants, the total effect of the relaxation of the current cross-ownership ban will be significant.**

The House of Representatives is considering similar legislation, H.R. 1555, which will go even further than the Senate legislation. Under the version of H.R. 1555 that was reported from the House Committee on Commerce on May 25, 1995, the Congress would:

■ eliminate all nationwide numeric restrictions on the number of broadcast television stations owned by a single entity, and raise the national "audience cap" for a single entity from 25 percent to 50 percent (within one year and one day);

■ eliminate the current ban on cross-ownership of VHF and UHF stations in the same market, and give the FCC authority to allow joint ownership of two VHF stations in the same market;

■ eliminate all FCC rules on the number of AM and FM radio stations in the same geographic market or nationally which can be owned by a single entity, allowing one entity to own every AM and FM radio station in the United States;*

■ lift the current FCC ban on joint ownership of a broadcast radio or TV license and a newspaper in the same market;

■ overturn the current statutory provisions which have the effect of prohibiting telephone companies from purchasing and operating TV stations;***

■ explicitly prohibit the FCC from adopting any rules which prohibit any non-broadcasting entity from obtaining a broadcast license or network of broadcast licenses;***

■ allow telephone companies to enter electronic publishing; and relax the current ban on telephone and cable mergers, through a series of exemptions for "rural" areas, systems in franchise areas with fewer than 50,000 inhabitants, or systems owned by small operators in smaller markets. As noted above, these exemptions, taken together, are likely to cover a large portion of the population, leading to many "one wire" communities.

As significant as these changes are, it is conceivable that even more sweeping changes will be made once H.R. 1555 reaches the full House for a vote.

It should also be noted that the FCC's rules for the new Personal Communications Services (PCS) licenses allow the current telecommunications incumbents (local exchange telephone, cable and cellular) to obtain licenses for most of the new wireless spectrum. For example, in much of California, the incumbent providers of telephone, cable and cellular services will be allowed to acquire up to 100 Mhz of the 120 Mhz of the new spectrum (up to 110 Mhz after the year 2000). And the FCC has not adopted any rules limiting cross-ownership of Direct Broadcast Satellite (DBS) licenses, allowing cable companies, for example, to occupy scarce DBS spectrum which should be used by competitors to the wired cable systems.

Moreover, in the Senate, S. 652 would overturn the FCC's common carrier Video Dial Tone (VDT) rules, by allowing telephone companies entering into the video market to operate as cable companies, with unregulated rates and closed systems and no common carrier access rights to unaffiliated entities.

We believe that Congress is moving the law in the wrong direction, toward greater concentration and fewer choices for consumers, under the guise of "greater competition." Laws and rules that limit cross-ownership and concentration not only enhance competition, a putative goal of the new legislation, but they also serve important non-economic goals, by promoting a greater diversity of programming, and enhancing opportunities for local ownership.

In a sense, this is a move toward a Brazilian Globo-lization of the media, placing ever greater power in the hands of fewer giant media moguls. The predictable result will be less diversity, more pre-packaged programming, and fewer checks on political power. That these provisions are being included in legislation that is being sold as pro-competition is particularly galling. If the goal of the legislation is simply to encourage more competition for local and long distance telephone service, or to allow the telephone companies to compete against cable companies, it is hardly necessary to eliminate nationwide concentration rules for broadcast radio, greatly relax concentration rules for broadcast television, allow same-market telephone company/cable mergers, allow same-market joint ownership of newspapers and broadcast television and radio, or pave the way for telephone company purchases of local television stations. These are gra-tuitous assaults on competition, diversity, and political pluralism.

The far reaching changes that would occur under S. 652 or H.R. 1555 have been widely criticized by virtually all of the active public interest groups engaged in the current debate. The Consumer Federation of America, Consumers Union, the Media Access Project and the Center for Media Education have all issued strong criticisms of the provisions of the bills which would allow for greater concentrations of power, as have well known press critics such as Tom Shales, whose biting critique of the legislation in the June 13, 1995 issue of *the Washington Post* led to the June 14, 1995 Nightline show, titled "New Communications Law a Power Giveaway?" The House is now preparing to debate H.R. 1555, perhaps as soon as the last week in July. It is important to have a broader public examination of these issues before then.

Congress, at the least, should retain existing limits on concentration of ownership of broadcast radio and television licenses, and rules prohibiting same-market joint ownership of newspapers and broadcast radio and television licenses. Local exchange telephone companies should not be allowed to buy cable operators in their own service areas.

Moreover, Congress should bolster existing restrictions on concentration and cross-ownership with provisions that address the new technologies and new regulatory enviroment. In particular, we should do more to ensure that wireless spectrum is licensed to new market entrants, rather than the well-entrenched incumbent players, revisiting the question of cross-ownership restrictions on PCS spectrum and taking steps to reserve DBS licenses to entities not controlled by cable or local exchange telephone companies. And, given the very new and different role of the local exchange telephone companies in providing information services and video programming, we believe that it is important to establish limits on the range of media outlets that these large companies can control. In particular, we believe it is important to prevent local exchange telephone companies from acquiring newspapers and broadcast radio or television licenses in their own service areas.

For more information, please contact James Love at 202/387-8030 (love @tap.org). Thank you for your attention to this important issue.

Notes:
* Concentration would only be limited by anti-trust laws. ** The definition and conditions for cable systems that are eligible for buy-out or merger are poorly drafted and sometimes contradictory in the Senate bill, leading to some confusion about which systems will qualify. The House language described below is clearer and also broader than the Senate version, authorizing more mergers. *** However, on a case-by-case basis, the FCC may deny a license to an entity if it finds that the combination of a license and a non-broadcast entity will lead to "undue concentration of media voices."

2 ☐CENSORED☐

The Budget Does Not Have To Be Balanced on The Backs Of The Poor

"CUT CORPORATE WELFARE: NOT MEDICARE,"
By John Canham-Clyne; *Public Citizen*, July/August 1995

In late June the House and Senate passed a joint resolution calling for nearly $1 trillion in cuts to Medicare, Medicaid, education, and social welfare to achieve a balanced budget by 2002. House Budget Committee Chairman John Kasich (R-Ohio) called the GOP budget blueprint "a fair and meaningful plan to bring our deficit to zero over the next seven years." But Public Citizen's analysis shows that Congress could go a long way toward balancing the budget without slashing programs for seniors, working families, and the poor just by cutting subsidy payments to major corporations.

Although no single line item in the budget is entitled "corporate welfare," the federal budget and tax codes are rife with huge subsidies to business—the sums involved make traditional "pork barrel" spending look like chicken feed. Over the past few months, Washington-based policy organizations across the political spectrum have produced lists of corporate subsidies and tax breaks costing taxpayers from $53 billion to $167.2 billion annually.

Public Citizen's line-by-line analysis of the two congressional budget plans found the Senate would cut corporate welfare by less than $10 billion over seven years, or 1 percent of total spending cuts, while the House budget outline calls for a larger, but still token $35 billion, or less than 3 percent of the $1.4 trillion in spending reductions.

Public Citizen President Joan Claybrook said that subsidies for the wealthiest and most powerful U.S. corporations would miss the budget axe. "The proposed $250 billion, or 15 percent cut in Medicare, demands serious sacrifice from the more than 80 percent of seniors with incomes below $25,000—yet big corporations on the public dole are not asked to sacrifice at all," Claybrook said. "This enormous disparity amounts to a virtual declaration of class warfare by the new conservative majority in Congress."

The phrase "corporate welfare" describes a wide range of direct and indirect subsidies, tax breaks, credit and insurance programs, public property giveaways, production and import quotas, research contracts, procurement abuse, and other policies benefiting selected firms or industries at taxpayers expense. An exact figure on the total corporate welfare budget is difficult to assess, but the figures run into the tens and hundreds of billions of dollars per year.

Janice Shields, coordinator of the Corporate Welfare Project at Ralph Nader's Essential Information, identified $167.2 billion in annual corporate welfare in a March report (see "Corporate Welfare Costs Taxpayers $167.2 Billion, New Study Shows," May/June, Public Citizen). The conservative Cato Institute has targeted 125 spending programs costing taxpayers $86 billion, and the centrist Progressive Policy Institute proposed repealing spending and tax subsidies that would save $265 billion over five years.

Federal corporate welfare in the budget falls into nine categories:

Direct Subsidies. The federal government pays these directly to corporate business operations. For example, under the Market Promotion Program, the U.S. Department of Agriculture in 1993 gave $75 million for overseas product advertising, including $500,000 to advertise Campbell's soup and $10 million to promote beer, wine, and liquor.

Indirect Subsidies. The Forest Service, for example, spends $100 million annually building access roads through national forests to assist timber companies' logging operations—over 340,000 miles in total.

Bailouts. From Lockheed and Chrysler to the S&L industry, the bigger the failure, the more likely Uncle Sam will save it. The most recent example is this year's so-called "Mexican peso bailout." It is more of a bailout for American banks, Wall Street, and wealthy individuals who made bad investments in Mexican bonds than assistance to the Mexican economy as a whole.

The Los Angeles Times reports that within three weeks of receiving $20 billion in U.S. loans to shore up its ailing economy the Mexican government spent more than $4 billion to pay off high-risk bonds held by "American insurance companies, mutual fund investors, Wall Street brokerage houses, Mexican banks, and the richest of Mexico's rich,...who were well aware of the risks when they bought the bonds before Mexico's economy began to unravel."

Below Market and *Guaranteed Loans.* The federal government sometimes loans businesses money at below-market interest rates, or offers the full faith and credit of the U.S. government as a guarantee to a lender if a business opportunity should go sour.

Loan guarantees represent a relatively small amount of direct spending, but expose the Treasury to enormous risk. The Overseas Private Investment Corporation guarantees loans to American businesses seeking to invest in politically unstable countries. Banks would not otherwise lend to these operations, but with the U.S. Treasury as a backstop, nobody is at risk—except U.S.taxpayers—if a war or revoltion overseas shuts down a project covered by an OPIC-guaranteed loan.

Meanwhile, the student loan program allows banks to profit from risk-free loans that are guaranteed by the government and could be made directly to students at a lower cost.

Insurance. If loan guarantees are a ticking time bomb in the federal budget, then the practice of limiting the liability of certain businesses is a nuclear time bomb. The Price-Anderson Act, for example, makes it likely that almost the entire cost of a Chernobyl-style nuclear catastrophe would be shifted to taxpayers or the victims.

"For those who decry a 'cycle of dependency' among recipients of social welfare, here is the real thing," Bill Magavern, director of Public Citizen's Critical Mass Energy Project, said of taxpayer insurance and the web of other subsidies for the nuclear industry. "Without government subsidies like Price-Anderson propping it up, the nuclear industry might not exist at all."

Tax Expenditures. The largest of all corporate welfare programs are specially targeted tax loopholes and provisions in the tax code. Estimates of the total cost of tax expenditures vary widely. Citizens for Tax Justice recently identified $412 billion in savings over five years by closing 10 loopholes. Several of the largest tax expenditure programs are particularly harmful to average Americans because they encourage companies to move plants, jobs, and investment outside the United States. (see sidebar, "Fire an American Worker...").

As the House prepares deep cuts in social programs, its budget resolution proposes a huge increase in tax expenditures through repeal of the Alternative Minimum Tax. The AMT was established to ensure that profitable corporations, many of which became so adept at taking deductions and exclusions that they paid no taxes at all, would pay at least a minimum federal income tax each year. The congressional Joint Committee on Taxations estimates that AMT repeal will be a $16.9 billion boon to business over the next five years.

Desperate to find savings for $350 billion in total tax cuts, House Budget

Committee Chairman John Kasich proposed cutting special interest tax expenditures by $25 billion over five years, but his Republican colleagues rejected the idea. Ways and Means Committee Chairman Bill Archer (R-Texas) told *The Wall Street Journal* that closing loopholes amounts to a "tax increase" that would "never happen on Chairman Archer's watch."

Public Property Giveaways. The United States, unlike most nations, does not collect full royalties on use of public property for private gain. The classic example is the 1872 Mining Act, still in effect, that permits mining on federal land for the nominal charge of $5 an acre. If the federal government charged a modest 8 percent royalty on the value of minerals extracted, it would bring in $200 million a year—compared to nothing today.

A much larger—virtually incalculable—source of corporate welfare occurs when the government gives away the clean air, water, and other environmental resources through lack of enforcement, deregulation, or neglect. For example, a pending GOP-sponsored bill would immunize private companies from billions of dollars in toxic waste clean-up costs under Superfund.

Trade Barriers. Certain industries enjoy trade protection, despite the fact that they have no hope of competing economically. U.S. government trade quotas on imported sugar cost the taxpayer virtually nothing—but they cost consumers over $1.4 billion a year in higher sugar prices.

Traditionally, corporate subsidies have been extremely difficult to root out of the budget and tax code because a shield of campaign contributions protects them from congressional action. Federal government subsidies for ethanol fuels will cost $3.6 billion over the next five years. Sixty percent of all ethanol is produced by agribusiness giant Archer Daniels Midland, which in December donated $2.5 million in "soft money" to the Republican Party—the largest single political contribution in American history. Archer Daniels Midland also donated money to the Democratic Party prior to the 1994 election, but afterward directed more of its money to the Republican party.

Giveaways of Government Intellectual Property for Private Use. This includes tens of millions of taxpayer dollars a year for federally funded research contracts to develop new drugs, aircraft for the National Air and Space Administration, and weapons systems for the Department of Defense. These government-financed projects develop products that private companies sell at profits without paying royalties back to the government or taxpayers.

The Kindest Cuts. With so much corporate welfare flowing, politicians can easily posture as opposing it without attacking their favored supporters. Among the few business subsidies congressional Republicans have cut are some that may serve defensible policy purposes. The House, for example, would eliminate a $7 million minority business development program in the Department of Transportation, but maintain 40 times that much in annual grants and loans to subsidize weapons exports.

"Congressional Republicans justify huge cuts in health care and education by claiming there's a fiscal emergency," notes Congress Watch Director Michael Calabrese, "But as they lower the budgetary lifeboats, they are tossing women, children, the elderly, and the poor over the side to keep the wealthiest and most powerful in our society afloat."

FIRE AMERICAN WORKERS...GET A CORPORATE WELFARE CHECK

Corporate welfare is by no means a domestic affair. Several corporate welfare programs encourage American businesses to invest in foreign countries, help drive down wages, and send jobs overseas.

According to Lori Wallach, director of Public Citizen's Global Trade Watch, exporting jobs through corporate welfare is part of a broader pattern of U.S. international economic policy. "U.S. trade policy is tailored to benefit the largest corporations at the expense of most Americans," she said. "Proof of this—in addition to trade agreements like NAFTA and GATT—is in taxpayer funds used to subsidize corporations to move operations from the United States to countries like Haiti, Costa Rica and China. Such arrangements are lose-lose: Americans lose jobs and tax dollars, while other nations receive slave wage jobs, pollution and, in many cases, inhuman working conditions."

■ *OPIC Loan Guarantees.* Overseas Private Investment Corporation programs encourage corporations to invest precious capital overseas rather than in the United States.

■ *Corporate Foreign Tax Credit.* Corporations are allowed to reduce their U.S. tax bills one dollar for every dollar paid in foreign taxes. By treating royalties paid to oil exporting countries as "taxes," oil companies have escaped literally hundreds of billions of dollars in taxes over the past four decades. Forcing corporations to deduct foreign taxes as a business expense—as they do with U.S. state taxes—could save $35 to $40 billion. According to a recent Citizen Action study, the oil industry alone will avoid paying $5 billion this year through the foreign tax credit.

■ *USAID Business Promotion Programs.* Between 1980 and 1991, the U.S. Agency for International Development poured more than $1 billion worth of U.S. development and humanitarian aid into Haiti, facilitating the development of assembly factories for U.S. textile and electronic companies. At the same time, a series of dictatorships suppressed Haiti's labor and pro-democracy movements. When President Jean Bertrand Aristide took office in 1991, his government sought to double the minimum wage from $2 to $4 per day. USAID gave the Haitian business community $7 million to lobby against the increase and other "anti-business" measures like social security and health care taxes.

WHAT YOU CAN DO

A new Essential Information study released by Ralph Nader's Corporate Welfare Project shows that corporations receive more than three times the amount of federal spending paid in social welfare to poor recipients. The Study, Aid for Dependent Corporations, identified 153 federal programs totalling $167.2 billion that benefits corporations this year—a cost of $1,388 to each taxpayer. By contrast, Aid to Families with Dependent

Children and other forms of social welfare, including food stamps, housing assistance, and child nutrition, cost $50 billion a year, or $415 for individual taxpayers, the study shows. Copies of Aid to Dependent Corporations are available for $10 from Essential Information, P.O. Box 19367, Washington DC 20036. Tel. 202/387-8034.

John Canham-Clyne is research director at Public Citizen's Congress Watch.

3 CENSORED

Child Labor In The U.S. Is Worse Today Than During The 1930s

"WORKING IN HARM'S WAY"

By Ron Nixon; *Southern Exposure,*
Fall / Winter 1995

On June 11, 1993, 14-year-old Wyonnie Simons of Eastover, South Carolina, went to work on a local cattle farm in the nearby town of Hopkins. Originally hired to pick up paper and cut grass, Simons, a dedicated worker, was soon assigned other responsibilities. "He loved to work," said Betty Simons, Wyonnie's mother. "He was willing to help anyone." Just 10 days after beginning the job, Simons was killed while driving a forklift.

Four days after Simons' death, 17-year-old Jamie Hoffman of Rock Hill,

South Carolina, was killed while moving explosives in a warehouse. Provisions of the Fair Labor Standards Act could have shut the operation down after the accident, but Southern International, a fireworks company that owned the warehouse, was allowed to stay open because it was one of the busiest times of the year—the week of the Fourth of July.

Both incidents were clear violations of state labor laws and the Fair Labor Standards Act (FLSA), the federal law which prohibits youths under 18 from working in hazardous occupations. Both companies could have faced penalties as high as $10,000 under the FLSA, but neither company was fined. According to reports filed by investigators with the South Carolina Department of Labor, Licensing and Regulation, the agency that oversees child labor, both companies were issued warnings and "educated on child labor" laws. One of the youths' families has resorted to litigation: Betty Simons is suing the farm for her son's death. "It's not the money," Simons said. "It's the tragic loss of life."

The U.S. Bureau of Labor Statistics estimates that there are five million youth in the work force. The federal agency does not collect data on workers below the age of 15. Most young workers have jobs in restaurants, retail, and farm work with most *reported* injuries in the first two. Farm work is notably unregulated when it comes to young workers, and there are no real estimates of how many young farm workers there are. Such a lack of oversight means that many of the nation's children may be working in situations detrimental to their social and educational development, health, and in some cases, their lives. But as long as there is so little information available and so little regulation, many of the uses and abuses of children in the work force will remain hidden.

The information that is available from numerous studies and news reports documents violations of child labor laws throughout the South:

In North Carolina, researchers using data from medical examiners found that 71 children and teenagers died during the 1980s as a result of injuries sustained on the job. Eighty-six percent of the deaths resulted from working conditions that violated the Fair Labor Standards Act.

In Florida and Texas, investigations found rampant abuse of children in the garment industry. In one case, Jones of Dallas Manufacturing, Inc., a company that makes clothes for J.C. Penney and Sears, was fined for using a contractor who employed children. One child was 5 years old.

According to data from the Bureau of Labor Statistics, Louisiana had the highest percentage of 16 to 19-year-olds killed on the job in the South from 1980 to 1989. The national average of all work-place deaths of 16 to 19-year-olds killed was just over 4 percent. The state ranked third nationally, behind Utah and Oklahoma.

Nationally, a 1990 report by the General Accounting Office, the investigative wing of Congress, found that child labor violations had risen 150 percent between 1983 and 1989. The number of children caught working illegally during this time by the Department of Labor jumped from 9,200 to 25,000 nationwide.

In 1992, a National Institute of Occupational Safety and Health (NIOSH) report found that 670 youths age 16 to 17 were killed on the job from 1980 to 1989. Seventy percent of the deaths involved violations of the FLSA. A second NIOSH report found that more than 64,100 children went to the emergency room for work-related injuries in 1992.

Why do children continue to be injured, even killed on the job, despite state and federal laws regulating child labor and two highly publicized crackdowns on violators in 1991? Answers to this question are not easy to find but can be unearthed in data from federal and state departments of labor, reviews of numerous studies, and interviews with state and federal labor department officials, child labor advocates, and medical researchers.

At various times minor reforms have been made at both the federal and state levels, but several barriers continue to prevent children from being adequately protected in the workplace. A patchwork of inefficient data collection systems fails to monitor the total number—much less the well-being—of youth in the workplace. Enforcement of the FLSA is lax. Cultural beliefs about the worth of work for children are strong. Perhaps most importantly, various business trade groups lobby successfully to keep child labor laws from being strengthened and, in many cases, to weaken existing laws.

"Child labor today is at a point where violations are greater than at any point during the 1930s," said Jeffrey

Newman of the National Child Labor Committee, an advocacy group founded in 1904. "It's very sad, and it doesn't speak well to our understanding and commitment to our children."

THE LAW, THE COURT, THE LAW. . .

Efforts to protect children from exploitation in the workplace began in the early 1900s. Unable to get individual states to pass strong laws to protect the health and safety of young workers, reformers like Jane Addams, Lewis Hine, Mary "Mother Jones" Harris, the National Consumers League, and others turned their attention to the federal government. In 1916 they persuaded the government to pass the Keatings-Owen Act, the first piece of federal legislation regulating child labor. Signed into law by President Woodrow Wilson, the bill prohibited the interstate commerce of goods produced by children under the age of 14 and established an eight-hour workday for youth under the age of 16.

The bill had tremendous support from the labor unions, churches, and the two major political parties. But two states that depended heavily on child labor, North and South Carolina, objected to the bill's provisions. After the bill became law, a judge in North Carolina declared it unconstitutional, arguing that it interfered with interstate commerce. The federal Supreme Court agreed, and the law was struck down.

In 1919 reformers tried again. A bill similar to the Keatings-Owen Act passed, imposing a 10 percent tax on the net profits of manufacturers who employed children below the age of 14.

Again the North Carolina judge declared the law unconstitutional, this time stating that the act infringed on the rights of states to impose taxation measures. Again the U.S. Supreme Court sided with North Carolina.

Reformers then tried to pass a constitutional amendment. Opponents launched an all-out assault. Farmers were told that under the proposed amendment, children would not be allowed to work on the farms. Mothers were told that they could be fined just for sending their children to the store or to run errands. Though Congress approved the amendment, the states refused to ratify it.

Resistance to laws restricting child labor was most apparent in the South where booming textile industry depended heavily on children for a supply of cheap labor. In 1890 children numbered 25,000 in the textile industry. By 1900 the number was 60,000. Until the 1920s, one quarter of the region's textile workers were boys under the age of 16 and girls under the age of 15. "The children of the South, many of them, must work," said one mill owner. "It is a question of necessity."

Hubert D. Stephens, U.S. Senator from Mississippi from 1923 to 1935, went even further, calling child labor reform a "socialist movement" designed to "destroy our government." The Senator warned Southern parents that under the proposed child labor laws, "the child becomes the absolute property of the federal government."

Despite such scare tactics, the National Recovery Administration, a federal agency created during the New

Deal, banned employment of children below the age of 16 in most industries in the early 1930s. The U.S. Supreme Court invalidated the restriction in 1935.

Finally, in 1938, during a period of increased automation in American industries and declining child labor, the Fair Labor Standards Act (FLSA) passed. The act, which was drafted under the direction of labor leader Sidney Hillman, limited the maximum number of work hours for 14 and 15-year-olds, prohibited certain occupations, and raised the minimum age for full-time employment to 16. The FLSA remains the major piece of federal regulation governing child labor.

UNTOLD THOUSANDS

Today, 57 years after the passage of the FLSA, millions of children in the United States are in the work force, and a large number are exposed to hazardous working conditions. How many? "No one really knows," said Jeffery Newman of the National Child Labor Committee.

There is no comprehensive national data collection system that accurately tracks the number of working youth, their occupation, where they work, or how many are injured or killed on the job. "The numbers that you do get are relatively meaningless," Newman said. He believes that even the best figures underestimate the number of working children by 25 to 30 percent.

Charles Jeszeck of the General Accounting Office (GAO) won't go as far as calling the numbers meaningless, but says, "The data that we have on children's work are very conservative,

because they are derived from woefully inadequate data systems." To illustrate the extent of under-reporting by employers (to regulators), Jeszeck pointed out that the GAO's review of independent census data identified at least 166,000 youth age 15 and 16 working in prohibited occupations like construction.

"The number of minority children working may be the most under-counted," Jeszeck said. "We found that although white youth are more likely to work, minority children are more likely to work in unreportable jobs like agriculture or other 'hazardous' industries like manufacturing or construction. They also work more hours a week but fewer weeks a year than whites." Data on youth below the age of 14 are not routinely collected, he said, "So right off the top you have a distorted picture of working youth."

On the state level, things aren't much better. In response to the Freedom of Information Act requests, most state officials admitted that information on children in the work force is rarely collected in a comprehensive or even consistent format.

Kathleen Dunn of East Carolina University and Carolyn Runyan of the Injury Prevention Center at the University of North Carolina at Chapel Hill had the same difficulty in 1992 when they began researching young workers. "There is no standardized method for keeping track of work-related injuries [for youth]," Runyan said. "North Carolina has a good system for keeping track of injuries and deaths in general, but for youth we don't expect to need the information, so the data are not routinely collected."

Part of the problem, Runyan explained, is the perception of doctors or medical examiners who record the cause of injury or death. "Many medical examiners have in their minds some kind of age cut-off when it comes to work-place deaths or injuries," Dunn said. "So if a child is below a certain age they won't even consider an injury to the child as a work-related injury. This is a problem across the country," she said. "What we need is education for medical examiners and standardization of [criteria for] work-related injuries for youth."

FIELD OF TEENS

Counting or tracking the number of young farm workers is even more difficult. Most states exempt agriculture from requiring work permits or age certificates, and the Bureau of Labor Statistics' annual survey overlooks millions of children who work on the farm, since the minimum age reported is 15. "But under exemptions in the FLSA, it's legal for children as young as 10 and 11 to work. The problem is most people simply don't think that children under 12 work," said Diana Mull of the Association of Farmworkers Opportunities Programs.

The United Farm Workers Union and studies on migrant children estimate that 800,000 children work in agriculture. According to the *Wall Street Journal*, 23,500 are injured and another 300 die on the farm each year. All of these numbers are conservative, farm worker advocates say. "There is huge under-reporting in the number of

children working in agriculture," said Mull.

The Consumer Product Safety Commission used to monitor the number of children's injuries caused by farm equipment and pesticides. But in 1994, the federal agency stopped collecting such data due to budget constraints, said Art Donovan of the commission staff.

Although the Environmental Protection Agency estimates that there are about 300,000 acute illnesses and injuries from exposure to farm pesticides for all workers, little data are available on the actual number of children exposed. According to studies, children are more susceptible than adults to the effects of pesticides. Children absorb more than adults per pound of body weight, but the EPA standards for protecting workers from exposure to pesticides are based on adults only. According to a GAO study, the EPA "believes that studies monitoring field exposure to pesticides and laboratory animal studies on age-related toxic effects indicated no reason to specifically regulate children differently."

The GAO also found that all pesticide illness reports, except for California's, were limited in scope, detail, and quality of information. The study concluded that there was no way to determine accurately the national incidence or prevalence of pesticide illness in the farm sector.

Inspectors are unlikely to get even a chance to look for children working illegally on a farm. According to a provision in the annual appropriations bill, the U.S. Department of Labor prevents

OSHA from inspecting farms which claim less than 11 workers. The provision is supposed to protect small family farms from regulations that apply to corporate agribusiness. But giant farms circumvent inspection by hiring contractors to provide labor instead of hiring workers directly. "The farm labor contractor is the only one that shows up on the books as an employee," said farm worker activist Mull, "giving the farm only one worker on its books. Therefore these big farms that can have as many as 50 or 60 workers are exempt from inspection, and the farm escapes responsibility for complying with the labor laws."

A farm owner can also record only one person on the books when in reality an entire family, including the children, could be working under that one person's social security number.

"If we had better data and could flesh out the number of kids actually working legally and illegally, as well as those injured and killed, we might be able to raise the awareness of the public and Congress and get something done," said the GAO's Jeszeck. He advocates a centralized national data collection system.

Catherine A. Belter of the National Parent Teacher Association is more emphatic. Testifying before a congressional hearing in February, Belter warned legislators of the immediate need for a comprehensive data collection system for working children in order to form a strategy of prevention. "Until the U.S. has an accurate number of child[work]-related injuries and fatalities, finding the appropriate statutory or regulatory policy that will protect youth is impossible," Belter said. "America must do a better job than continuing to take a patchwork approach to developing and amending child labor laws and regulations."

ENFORCEMENT BLUES

Getting a national data collection system in place is just part of the solution to protecting young people in the workplace, advocates say. "Enforcement is a major problem," said Linda Golodner, executive director of the National Consumers League and co-chair of the Child Labor Coalition.

Few states have full-time child labor inspectors, and in Georgia and Alabama, laws prohibit agencies from assessing fines even when they do find children working in violation of the law. Mississippi has no labor department and Maryland has no child labor enforcement division. But even when agencies have the ability to assess fines, the penalties are rarely significant enough to deter repeat violations. In South Carolina, the fine for violating the state child labor law is $50. In Florida, the state agency can only issue a warning for the first violation regardless of the severity of the injury that may result—including death.

Further problems arise as local departments cut back on enforcement due to budget constraints. They turn over enforcement to the federal government, but a shrinking budget is causing cuts in enforcement by the U.S. Department of Labor as well.

The number of Department of Labor inspectors has dropped from 989 in 1991 to 791 in 1994, and the department has no full-time investigators assigned exclusively to child labor. Investigators in the Wage and Hour Division enforce 96 laws and regulations, including child labor, said Bob Cuccia of the Department of Labor. "Child labor is one of our major focuses," he added. But a GAO study in 1990 found that investigators spend only about 5 percent of their time on child labor.

Nationally, recorded child labor violations dropped from a high of nearly 40,000 in 1990 to just over 8,000 in 1994. Cuccia attributes the decline to the 1991 crackdown called "Operation Childwatch" and to "education and outreach to businesses from the Department of Labor." While child labor violations did decrease tremendously, inspections also decreased by two thirds. In 1990 the department conducted 5,889 inspections, fining businesses a total of $8,451,268. In 1994 the number of inspections dropped to just over 2,000.

"Businesses don't worry about being inspected unless there's some horrible incident," said Darlene Adkins, coordinator of the Child Labor Coalition. "I'm not saying that anyone wants to harm children. It's just that child labor laws aren't a priority for most businesses."

A 1992 report from the National Safe Workplace Institute bears out Adkins' observations. The report found that the average business could expect to be inspected once every 50 years or so by the wage and hour division. According to the United Food and Commercial Workers Union, it would take the Occupational Safety and Health Administration 23 years just to inspect all high-risk workplaces, including those where youth work.

Even when companies are inspected and violations are found, the maximum penalty of $10,000 per violation is rarely enforced. A prime example is Food Lion, the supermarket chain based in Salisbury, North Carolina. In 1992, the company agreed to settle charges of 1,436 child labor violations with the Department of Labor. Most of the violations, according to the company's 10K form filed with the Securities and Exchange Commission, were for allowing employees under the age of 18 to operate balers—machines that compress cardboard boxes that are rated as too hazardous for minors to use. Food Lion paid an estimated $1,000,000 for the violations. The fines amounted to $714 per violation—far below the federal maximum.

"If Food Lion had paid the maximum amount, the fines would have totaled over $14 million," said Darlene Adkins of the Child Labor Coalition.

KIDS SEWING AND SOWING

While restaurants and supermarket chains, two industries that employ large numbers of youth, have been scrutinized by state and federal regulators over the past several years, little attention has been given to the garment and the agricultural industry. "These industries are where you find the most vulnerable kids," said Linda Golodner of the National Consumers League. In Florida and Texas, many kids still work in "sweatshop" conditions reminiscent of the 1920s.

An investigation by the *Fort Lauderdale Sun-Sentinel* found that the

$1.2 billion garment industry in Dade County, Florida, the nation's third largest garment center, is riddled with flagrant violations that go virtually unpunished by the government.

Jorge Rivero, Miami district director of the U.S. Department of Labor, concedes that children are working in the garment industry. But unless inspectors catch a child at work or someone admits that children are working in the industry, there is little that can be done, he said. Many garment workers are contracted by manufacturers and work at home where their kids help.

"We've never had any success in fining the garment industry," Rivero said. "I don't know why it's so hard, but it is. We go out every year and do directed investigations, basically at random, without [waiting for] complaints. We've done this for the last 30 years. It's unusual to get a complaint."

State officials, Rivero said, have limited resources and in most cases turn over enforcement to the federal Department of Labor, which lacks the manpower to make a dent in the illegal employment of children.

"Many employers in Dade County have no fear of the Labor Department enforcement efforts," an International Ladies Garment Workers Union representative testified at a 1989 hearing. "They're not hiding."

Labor officials in the state of Texas experience similar problems. In the Dallas/Fort Worth area, officials estimate that 8,000 to 40,000 Asian immigrants are employed by the garment industry. Most work at home where children sometimes work alongside their parents late into the night. As in

Florida, the state labor department has little success in curbing such violations because of lack of personnel. Recent Asian immigrants may have little choice in letting their children work and, would be unlikely to report violations. One Asian-American garment worker believes it is simply tradition in Asian families. "The family works together like always. Just like on the farm, the whole family, including the children, work."

Jeffrey Newman of the National Child Labor Committee disagrees. "Whenever you see a child working in the garment industry under sweatshop conditions, it is exploitation," he said.

Though legislation and enforcement in the garment industry are weak, children working in agriculture receive even less protection. Most states exempt agriculture from child labor laws altogether. And on the federal level, various exemptions in the labor laws allow farm children to work at much younger ages than in other industries.

For example, 16 and 17-year-olds can do hazardous work in agriculture, while the age for similar work in other industries is 18. Ten and 11-year-olds can be employed if the farmer gets a waiver from the Department of Labor, simply by proving that *not* employing 10 and 11-year-olds would cause severe economic hardship to the farm.

How can farming be so loosely regulated when the National Safety Council has defined agriculture as the most dangerous occupation, behind construction? The answer lies in the history of the FLSA. "The FLSA was a piece of New Deal legislation that had to appeal to Southern Dixiecrats," said Elaine Broward, a labor historian at Harvard University. At that time, farming was the lifeblood of the Southern economy. More than half the population lived on farms, and youth regularly worked. But recent changes in agricultural production have radically altered the industry. It is no longer a small-time activity.

"In 1938 the dangers of agriculture were not as well-known as they are now," said Cynthia Schneider, staff attorney with the Migrant Legal Program in Washington, D.C. "The use of pesticides and the type of farm equipment used today make agriculture more dangerous than it ever was."

In North Carolina, state labor department officials made similar observations after reviewing a 1993 study by Kathleen Dunn and Carolyn Runyan. They found that 71 people age 11 to 19 were fatally injured while working on the job between 1980 and 1990. Twenty-seven percent of those who died were involved in farm activities. After a review of state policies, Tom Harris, director of the state wage and hour division, asked federal officials to add provisions to current child labor laws barring work in hazardous activities. Harris also recommended the exemptions for children in agriculture be repealed.

"From a safety standpoint, there is no reason today for a farm/non-farm dichotomy in our child labor laws and regulations," Harris said.

FAMILY VALUES: GET TO WORK!

The traditional American belief in the value of children working presents another obstacle to reforms suggested by Harris and others. Medical historian David Rosner of Baruch College in New York said that child labor has a long history that complicates attempts to restrict or regulate it. "We have deep-seated social and cultural values that play against serious attempts at protecting kids," Rosner said. "Americans are deeply ambivalent about child labor," he said. "We see work as redemptive and as a morally legitimate method of self-improvement."

Indeed, beliefs about the value of work permeate the American psyche. In 1925 the National Industrial Conference Board of the U.S. National Association of Manufacturers claimed that working as a child was "desirable and necessary for complete education and maturity, . . . as well as for the promotion of good citizenship and the social and economic welfare."

More recently, according to professor Dario Menateau of the University of Minnesota, groups such as the President's Science Advisory Committee in 1973, the National Panel on High School and Adolescent Education in 1976, and the Carnegie Council in 1979 have all asserted that work can contribute to adolescent learning of socially accepted norms, values, and behaviors. "Working during the teen years is usually seen by these groups as a helpful medium available in modern society that facilitates the transition to adult life," Menateau said.

The myth is that these kids have to work to help support their families, said Linda Golodner of the National Consumers League. "Very, very few work to help their families," she said. "They're getting money to buy concert tickets, designer sneakers, cars, and things like that. We feel that it's OK [for them] to have a job, just so that their hours are limited and they're not sacrificing these educational years or their childhood." While it may be true that most children work for their own spending money, in agriculture it is a different story.

Diana Mull of the Association of Farmworkers Opportunities Programs said, "The myth is that in agriculture, children are simply doing chores and that they are helping out the family. For most of the work being done in agriculture, the wages are so low that everyone [in a family] has to work just to make ends meet. One should wonder how this in any way teaches kids the value of a dollar or work when they see their parents eking out a meager living moving from place to place. How to be exploited, how to be abused, that's something we want to teach kids, right?"

So what skills and responsibilities do kids learn at work? It depends on the job, experts say. In a 1992 study of learning in the workplace, researchers Ellen Greenberger and Laurence Steinberg observed that, "The typical jobs available to youth do little to inspire a high degree of commitment and concern."

The authors said that jobs for most youth do not require use of even the most basic academic skills. Food service workers, manual laborers, and cleaners spend an average of 2 percent or less of their time at work reading, writing, or doing arithmetic. Cleaning, carrying and moving objects from one place to another take up between 14 and 55 percent of the time of the average food service or retail sales job. "Adolescents . . . had few illusions about the degree of expertise their work called for," Greenberger and Steinberg concluded. "Nearly half felt that a grade-school education or less would suffice to enable them to perform their jobs."

Quality of work may be low, but quantity of work can be too high. Another study found that students who work more than 20 hours a week were less likely to do homework, earn A's, or take college preparatory courses. "While the drop in grades may be unimportant to a 4.0 student, for the marginal student it could be significant," said Maribeth Oaks of the National Parent Teacher Association.

Professor Menateau, who has studied working children for more than 20 years, said schools have changed their curricula to accommodate work. "I'd hate to say that education is being watered down," he said, "but the schools are adjusting. They simply aren't demanding the amounts of homework and the academics that they used to because students are doing so many other things."

FOLLOW THE MONEY

If lack of data, lax enforcement, and deep-seated beliefs hamper efforts to reform child labor laws, lobbying efforts by various business trade organizations make reform nearly impossible. In 1992, when former Senator Howard Metzenbaum introduced legislation to establish a national work permit system and national standards for reporting injuries suffered by minors, pressure from the restaurant industry successfully killed the measure in committee.

Likewise, when the House Judiciary Committee considered child labor laws that would have subjected employers to a $250,000 fine and imprisonment for violations that resulted in serious injury to minors, a lobbying campaign from the restaurant industry again killed the bill in committee.

The restaurant industry has good reason to fear changes in the child labor laws. According to *Restaurant Business,* an industry trade publication, the nation's 400,000 restaurants employed over 1 million teenagers age 16 to 19 in 1993. The National Restaurant Association—Washington's other NRA—a trade organization of 200,000 restaurants and proprietors, has quietly managed to prevent any changes in the nation's child labor laws. And with a Republican Congressional majority receptive to its agenda, the NRA seems poised to weaken existing laws.

The NRA is not alone. The Food Marketing Institute (FMI) has lobbied against strengthening child labor provisions in the FLSA. Representing the nation's supermarket chains and other food stores, FMI earlier this year lobbied to repeal a section of the FLSA that prohibits children under the age of 18 from operating cardboard compactors and balers. Bills to repeal the ban were introduced in both the House and the Senate.

The FMI may prevail despite testimony from child labor advocates, a NIOSH report that found 50 accidents as a result of operating balers, and support for the ban from Department of Labor officials. Supporters of the repeal on balers call it "a chance to create summer jobs in your district without spending a dime of taxpayer's money," as they wrote in a joint letter to potential sponsors. Repealing the baler ban would entice more supermarkets to hire young people without fear of being charged a penalty for letting kids throw boxes into the machines.

Supporters of the ban are stunned by the relative ease the FMI has had in pushing its baler repeal. "We have simply been reduced to commenting on the proposed changes," said Debbie Berkowitz of the United Food and Commercial Workers Union, who is urging Congress to maintain the ban.

In the nation's capital, money talks, and both the NRA and FMI have talked generously to potential supporters of their agenda. According to the Center For Responsive Politics, the NRA gave a total of $658,844 to 279 candidates in the 1994 election, making it one of the 50 largest PACs in the country. The NRA gave 73 percent of its contributions to Republican candidates, mostly to the U.S. House. Senators received larger amounts on average—$5,089 compared to $2,057 for House members.

In 1994 the FMI gave $452,465, with more than 68 percent going to Republican candidates. More than 70 percent of the FMI contributions went to House members, with Senators receiving an average of larger amounts $3,061, compared to $1,186 for House members. Rep. Thomas Ewing (R-IL) and Sen. Larry Craig (R-ID), both sponsors of the bills to repeal the ban on balers, received contributions from the FMI.

A representative of the trade organizations denies that the contributions influence voting. "Political giving helps," Herman Cain, chair and executive officer of Godfathers Pizza and a former president of the NRA, told the *Wall Street Journal*, "But it does not buy a decision ... The only thing it has done in many instances is give us access."

This access has successfully stalled or killed any attempts to improve workplace protection for children. According to Federal Election Commission data gathered by the National Library on Money and Politics, members of both the House and Senate committees that oversee work-place laws have received $109,350 and $70,815 from the NRA and FMI, respectively, for 1991-1994.

House Speaker Newt Gingrich has been a favorite of both the NRA and the FMI. Since 1991 Gingrich has received over $27,000 from both PACs. He picked up another $230,000 from other PACs in the restaurant industry for his extra-curricular fundraising operations including his nationally televised college class called "Renewing America." According to Federal Election Commission data, House Majority Leader Dick Armey (R-TX) received $6,500 and Rep. Tom DeLay (R-IL) $8,500 from the FMI and NRA combined. In total, said *Common Cause*, the restaurant industry has given $1.3 million to Republican candidates in recent years.

Republicans "cherish the restaurant folks for all the help that they have given the party," Rep. Armey told the *Wall Street Journal*. "That puts them clearly within the favored category. You know the old adage—dance with the ones that brung you."

Rep. Tom DeLay has taken this advice to heart. The NRA helped to plug DeLay's run for majority whip of the House by shoring up support and campaign contributions in the Republican freshman class. Earlier this year, when DeLay pulled together a coalition of anti-regulation groups called Project Relief, the NRA was awarded one of the seats on the task force. Chaired by Bruce Gates, a lobbyist with the grocery industry which includes the FMI, Project Relief, according to its mission statement, is "committed to changing fundamentally the process by which the federal government regulates."

If Project Relief gets its way, "past and proposed regulations governing such food industry areas as food safety, transportation, and occupational safety [including child labor laws] would be subject to much greater scrutiny," Gates told the *Progressive Grocer*, a trade publication.

According to FEC data analyzed by the Environmental Working Group in Washington, D.C., the 115 PACs that make up Project Relief gave House Republicans $10.3 million in 1994. Most of Project Relief's contributions have been bestowed upon members of the House and Senate Regulatory Task Forces, committees set up under the new Republican majority to oversee changes in regulations. On the House side, Rep. DeLay, who chairs the House Regulatory Task Force, received

$38,423. In the Senate, Kay Bailey Hutchison (R-TX) received $331,733.

DeLay has fingered nearly 60 rules and regulations for weakening or outright abolition, including child labor restrictions, which the restaurant and grocery industries say are being imposed on them by the federal government. "We would like to give them as much flexibility as possible," Rep. Bill Goodling (R-PA), chairman of the committee in charge of overhauling child labor laws, told the *Wall Street Journal*.

Other plans of Project Relief are to do away with OSHA and NIOSH entirely or to reduce their functions, a move that would have a devastating effect on work-place safety as a whole and on child labor particularly.

"I'm not encouraged about activity that is being generated in the House and Senate this year," said Linda Golodner, of the National Consumers League. "We'd love to see some action. But with the anti-regulatory attitude in the Congress, I don't feel optimistic."

WHAT TO DO

Action on the state level may hold more promise, Golodner said. The Child Labor Coalition is using model state legislation to push for reforms on the state level. The Coalition is urging legislators to:

Provide equal protection under the child labor laws for young migrant and seasonal farm workers. This provision would set a minimum age of 14 for employment of agricultural workers, the same as for non-agricultural workers. It would also set a maximum number of work hours while school is in session and prohibit minors from working in hazardous occupations and around hazardous substances.

Require work permits for all working minors that will give information on the number of youth employed and the industries employing them.
u Require labor education about workplace rights and responsibilities under the FLSA prior to a youth's initial employment.

Provide enhanced enforcement provisions and specific enforcement financing. Under this proposal, the state department of labor would publish and disseminate the addresses and names of each employer who had repeated and intentionally violated child labor laws and specify the type of violations. The information would be disseminated to students, parents, employers, and educators.

Establish stiffer penalties for employers who are child labor violators. This provision would make anyone found repeatedly violating child labor laws ineligible for any grant, contract, or loan provided by a state agency for five years. Repeat offenders would be ineligible to employ a minor during this period. The Department of Labor would be required to disseminate a list of offenders to parents and authorities.
Several states are considering adopting all or portions of the legislation. "Just looking at the law and making a couple of regulatory changes can be helpful," Golodner said. "Regulatory changes on the state level put the focus back on education for youth and save lives."

Intern Terri Boykin provided research assistance and additional reporting.

4 CENSORED

The Privatization of the Internet

"KEEPING ON-LINE SPEECH FREE: STREET CORNERS IN CYBERSPACE"

By Andrew L. Shapiro;
The Nation, July 3, 1995

You probably didn't notice, but the Internet was sold a few months ago. Well, sort of: The federal government has been gradually transferring the backbone of the U.S. portion of the global computer network to companies such as I.B.M. and M.C.I. as part of a larger plan to privatize cyberspace. But the crucial step was taken on April 30, when the National Science Foundation shut down its part of the Internet, which began in the 1970s as a Defense Department communications tool. That left the corporate giants in charge.

Remarkably, this buyout of cyberspace has garnered almost no protest or media attention, in contrast to every other development in cyberspace—particularly Senator James Exon's proposed Communications Decency Act, which would criminalize "obscene, lewd, lascivious, filthy, or indecent" speech on computer networks. Yet issues of ownership and free speech are inextricably linked. Both raise the vexing question of what role—if any—government should play in cyberspace and, consequently, of what this new frontier will become.

The chorus of opposition to Exon's misguided proposal is right on; the bill deserves to be scrapped. But as cyberspace becomes privatized and commercialized, we should also be skeptical of the laissez-faire utopianism of many of Exon's critics. They say that cyberspace is a bastion of free expression and that users can regulate themselves. "No government interference!" is their rallying cry. In the context of censorship, this sounds right. But in the context of ownership, it is wrong. Speech in cyberspace will not be free if we allow big business to control every square inch of the Net. The public needs a place of its own.

This seems simple enough. And yet the issue of who owns cyberspace has been overlooked because it's difficult in the abstract to see what's at stake here. So let's get concrete: Consider two models of cyberspace that represent what total privatization deprives us of and what it leaves us with.

In the first model—this is what we're being deprived of—you use a computer and modem to go on-line and enter a virtual world called Cyberkeley. As you meander down the sidewalk, you find a post office, libraries and museums, shopping malls full of stores, and private clubs that service a limitless variety of clientele, from those who want spiritual guidance, **tips** on gardening or legal advice to those with a penchant for live sex or racist hatemongering. You also encounter vibrant public spaces—some large like a park or public square, others smaller like a town hall or street corner. In these public forums, some people are talking idly, others are heatedly debating social issues. A few folks are picketing outside a store where hard-core pornography is sold, others are protesting the post office's recently increased mail rates and one lone activist outside the Aryan Militia's hangout hands out leaflets urging racial unity. Most people are just passing through, though you and they can't help but take notice of the debaters, the demonstrators, even the leafleter.

In the second cyberspace model—which is what we're getting—you enter an on-line world called Cyberbia. It's identical to Cyberkeley, with one exception: There are no spaces dedicated to public discourse. No virtual sidewalks or parks, no heated debate or demonstrators catching your attention, no street-corner activist trying to get you to read one of her leaflets. In fact, you can shape your route so that you interact only with people of your choosing and with information tailored to your desires. Don't like antiabortion activists, homeless people, news reports about murders? No problem—you need never encounter them.

Cyberbia is tempting. People can organize themselves in exclusive virtual communities and be free of any obligation to a larger public. It is, perhaps, the natural result of a desire for absolute free choice, customization and control. But, at least for now, cyberspace must be treated as an extension of, rather than an alternative to, the space we live in. Consequently, it should be clear that Cyberbia—like suburbia—simply allows inhabitants to ignore the problems that surround them off-line. In Cyberkeley, by contrast, people may be inconvenienced by views they don't want to hear. But at least there are places where bothersome, in-your-face expression flourishes and is heard. These public forums are essential to an informed citizenry and to pluralistic, deliberative democracy itself.

Unfortunately, cyberspace is shaping up to be more like Cyberbia than Cyberkeley. That's because the consensus among on-line boosters—from the terminally wired hackers to the cyberwonks at the Electronic Frontier Foundation to Newt Gingrich, Al Gore and other Third Wave lawmakers—is that all cyberspace should be privately owned and operated. While their fears of government abuse or inefficient centralization may be legitimate, presenting the choice as one between totalitarian control and a total absence of publicly owned space is misleading. These extreme alternatives prevent us from moving toward something like Cyberkeley—a model of cyberspace that is mostly private, but which preserves part of this new domain as a public trust, a common space dedicated to citizens' speech. Without this hybrid vision, it is unlikely that we will realize the democratic possibilities of this new technology.

All this becomes readily apparent if one steps back from the cyberspace framework and contemplates how our anemic public discourse came to be. By the 1960s, crucial victories for freedom of expression had been won in the courts against government attempts to suppress labor activists, Communists, civil rights activists and war protesters. At the heart of these victories was the public forum doctrine, which minimizes government control of speech in areas such as sidewalks and parks, disallowing restrictions based on content or viewpoint. As the Supreme Court said in 1939, these special locations were "held in trust for the use of the public...for purposes of assembly, communicating thoughts between citizens, and discussing public questions."

From the 1960s to the present, as Owen Fiss of Yale Law School has argued, speech on the street corner has become increasingly silent as a result of two concurrent trends: the rise of electronic media and the privatization of spaces that had previously been public—a prime example being the center of commerce, now the shopping mall. For a brief time, with the F.C.C.'s fairness doctrine for broadcasters and a 1968 Supreme Court decision that granted labor picketers access to a privately owned mall, there was reason to believe that speech might remain diverse and unfettered in the new locales. But the Supreme Court slowly and surely chipped away at what Justice William Brennan called "robust public debate." It limited citizen access to radio and television, and it allowed speech to be restricted not only in private shopping malls but also in certain publicly owned spaces, such as airports and post offices. Property owners and even municipalities acting in "private" capacities were able to use the First Amendment to exclude dissenting voices by arguing that they should not have to associate with speech with which they disagreed.

Given this history, it should be clear how important public forums in cyberspace could be—as a way of keeping debate on-line robust and as a direct remedy for the dwindling number of such spaces in our physical environment. A remarkable incident shows further why this is so.

In 1990 the on-line service Prodigy started something of a revolt among some of its members when it decided to raise rates for those sending large volumes of e-mail. Protesters posted messages claiming they were being penalized for speaking frequently; they sent e-mail to Prodigy's on-line advertisers threatening a boycott. In response, Prodigy not only read and censored their messages, it summarily dismissed the dissenting members from the service. A spokesman for the company, which is a joint venture of Sears and I.B.M., wrote unapologetically in a New York Times opinion piece that the company would continue to restrict speech as it saw fit, including speech criticizing the company.

This example, extreme as it is, demonstrates the difference between Cyberkeley, which has public forums, and Cyberbia, which does not. In the latter, there is no way for the aggrieved Prodigy members to picket the on-line service in an area that its patrons will see (nor is there any higher authority to which they can appeal); thus the company has no incentive to refrain from suppressing dissent. Sure, the dissenters can open their own shop, but they'll probably be lost in some distant corner of cyberspace. By contrast, in Cyberkeley, the protesters would have access to the virtual sidewalk outside Prodigy; they would be able to protest the company's rate hike—and the fact that they were kicked out simply for airing a contrarian view—in a way that Prodigy members and nonmembers alike would hear.

Undoubtedly, some will argue that the Prodigy incident was an anomaly and that cyberspeech is already as free as it needs to be. But like the protests of the Prodigy dissidents, all speech in cyberspace is, in three fundamental ways, less free than speech in a traditional public forum.

First, cyberspeech is expensive, both in terms of initial outlay for hardware and recurring on-line charges. For millions of Americans, this is no small obstacle, especially when one considers the additional cost of minimal computer literacy. While it is true that speech becomes cheaper once you've gained access to cyberspace—sending a message to 1,000 people costs little more than sending it to one—the initial threshold cost of this entry remains prohibitively high; the specter of information haves and have-nots is already upon us. This problem might be alleviated somewhat through subsidized access to cyberspace via public computer terminals (which have been established with success in Santa Monica and other cities), lower connection costs for low-income users (as with telephone service) and even something as idiosyncratic as Speaker Gingrich's tax breaks for laptops.

Second, speech on the Net is subject to the whim of private censors who are not accountable to the First Amendment. More and more, travelers in cyberspace are using commercial on-line services such as America Online and Compuserve, which, like Prodigy, have their own codes of decency and monitors who enforce them. Even those who prefer the more anarchic Usenet discussion groups are subject to regulation by self-appointed system operators and moderators. Since these censors are private agents, not state actors, disgruntled users have no First Amendment claim. Fortunately, most monitors, even at commercial on-line services, are not heavy-handed. But this is not always the case and, more important, there is no legal way to insure that it will be.

Third, speech in cyberspace can be shut out by unwilling listeners too easily. With high-tech filters, Net users can exclude all material from a specific person or about a certain topic. This feature may protect children from inappropriate speech, but adults should not be able to steer clear of "objectionable" views, particularly marginal political views, so easily.

Together, these three points demonstrate why on-line speech is less free than it seems and, again, why Cyberkeley is preferable to Cyberbia. They also show why the cyberwonks' solution to Net regulation—a laissez-faire print model that treats all users as writers rather than, say, speakers—is inadequate: We're either paying to publish in mass-circulation periodicals where editors are free to censor us or we're writing pamphlets no one knows about because there's no public space in which to distribute them.
linespace[

So how do we reverse the onslaught of commercialization and move from Cyberbia to Cyberkeley? Congress could recognize the important public function of private on-line services and thus require them to save a place for dissenting speech, just as the Supreme Court required a privately owned "company town" to do in 1946. Eli Noam of Columbia University suggests as much when he says that computer networks "become political entities" because of their quasi-governmental role—taxing members, establishing rules, resolving conflicts. However, this remedy would probably be as unpopular today among courts and legislators as newspaper right-of-reply statutes and the F.C.C. fairness doctrine.

A more appropriate solution might be for Congress and state and local governments to establish forums in cyberspace dedicated explicitly to public discourse. This entails more than just setting up a White House address on the Internet or even starting the virtual equivalent of PBS or NPR. These public forums must be visible, accessible and at least occasionally unavoidable—they must be street corners in cyberspace.

Through regulation or financial incentives, Congress might be able to get users of commercial and academic on-line services to pass through a public gateway before descending into their private virtual worlds. This gateway could provide either a comprehensive list or a representative sample (depending on technological capacities) of issues that are being discussed in public cyberforums, which the user can—if she chooses—enter and exit with a simple click of the mouse. The entry point might also register how many citizens are speaking in each forum and how long the discussion there has been going on.

Though Net users might initially see the public gateway as an imposition, it really isn't different from the burden of exposure that they accept in their everyday lives. To get to a store or private club one must, at least momentarily, traverse the square or travel the street. As on a real public sidewalk, a virtual pedestrian can try to ignore what's there and pass right by. Most probably will. But some will be enticed to listen and even to argue. More important, all will have at least the opportunity to hear truly free speech outside the control of private interests—and, like expression in any public forum, free from government censorship.

Even if Cyberkeley is technically feasible, skeptics of regulation from the left and right will question whether it is legal or even good policy. And this is precisely where the false choice between libertarianism and authoritarianism should be abandoned. In a liberal democracy, the people have a right to demand that government promote speech in a content-neutral way, particularly speech that is drowned out by the voices of the moneyed and powerful.

Admittedly, this state obligation to make speech available that otherwise would be unheard may seem unfamiliar to First Amendment absolutists who take it as an article of faith that, in all matters pertaining to freedom of expression, government should simply stay out of the way. But in fact, just as the state protects citizens from unfair market conditions, it also has a role to play when the marketplace of ideas fails and there is outright domination of some views. This is the same reason our government gives—and should give more, as European nations do—grants to marginal artists, postal subsidies to small magazines of opinion and free use of cable channels to community organizations. As the Supreme Court said last year in Turner Broadcasting v. FCC, "Assuring that the public has access to a multiplicity of information sources is a governmental purpose of the highest order, for it promotes values central to the First Amendment."

Cyberkeley might also help solve other Net snafus. For example, controversial political discussions on-line are sometimes destroyed by a phenomenon called "spamming," in which an individual endlessly replicates a message in order to silence his opponents. Open discourse is effectively shut down. In a public forum, government cannot censor speech, but it can impose minimal "time, place and manner" restrictions, particularly in order to maintain the fairness of public debate. Thus, just as the state might prohibit use of a 100-decibel loudspeaker at 2 A.M. in Times Square, it might also turn down the volume on those who drown out other speech by spamming.

More mundane problems might also be ameliorated. For example, as political campaigns buy time on commercial on-line services, public cyberforums could take on an important role for candidates with little money. While Bob Dole is chatting with America On-line subscribers, his grass-roots opponents should be able to set up a soapbox on the virtual sidewalk outside.

If cyberspace is deprived of public forums, we'll get a lot of what we're already used to: endless home shopping, mindless entertainment and dissent-free chat. If people can avoid the unpalatable issues that might arise in these forums, going on-line will become just another way for elites to escape the very nonvirtual realities of injustice in our world. As the wired life grows exponentially in the coming years, we'll all be better off if we can find a street corner in cyberspace.

Shapiro, Andrew, "Keeping On-Line Speech Free: Street Corners in Cyberspace," *The Nation* magazine. © 1995 The Nation Company Inc.

5 CENSORED

U.S. Pushes Nuclear Pact But Spends Billions To Add Bang To Nukes

"U.S. SEEKS ARMS INGREDIENT AS IT PUSHES NUCLEAR PACT"

By Thomas W. Lippmann; *The Washington Post*, May 1, 1995

WASHINGTON—Even as the United States urges the rest of the world to extend indefinitely a treaty requiring signatories to work toward elimination of nuclear weapons, the Energy

Department is planning a multibillion-dollar project to resume production of a radioactive gas used to enhance the bang of American nuclear warheads.

The department is planning to announce this summer what kind of facility it plans to build to produce the gas tritium, the crucial element in thermonuclear weapons, and where it plans to build it.

The choice is between a huge particle accelerator, using theoretically workable but untested technology, and a nuclear reactor, which would be the first reactor ordered in the United States since the 1979 Three Mile Island nuclear accident.

Either choice involves immense political, financial, environmental and national security risks, and the issue is emotionally wrenching as well.

The U.S. delegation to the 178-nation conference meeting in New York to discuss extension of the Nuclear Nonproliferation Treaty is already under pressure from some countries to do more to eliminate nuclear weapons, as that treaty requires. But U.S. national security strategy presumes a continued, if diminished, reliance on a nuclear arsenal.

Many officials of the Clinton administration are averse to nuclear power and do not want the federal government to sponsor construction of a reactor. But many career staff members in the Energy Department and the Pentagon have long supported the nuclear industry and favor the reactor method of producing the tritium needed for the weapons program.

Energy Secretary Hazel O'Leary is under intense congressional pressure to choose the reactor option and to build it at the Energy Department's Savannah River, S.C., weapons plant where all of the tritium for the nation's nuclear arsenal has been produced.

The choice facing O'Leary appears to come down to this: invest billions of federal dollars in a particle accelerator or accept a proposal from a nuclear industry consortium to use mostly private funds to construct a reactor.

Proponents of the accelerator option argue that scientists have proved its viability and that building an accelerator avoids the questions of safety and of radioactive waste disposal associated with nuclear reactors.

Proponents of the reactor say that the proposed multipurpose reactor's design has been judged safe by the Nuclear Regulatory Commission and that the privately owned reactor would cost the government as much as $15 billion less than the accelerator over its planned 40-year life.

© 1995, *The Washington Post*. Reprinted with permission.

6 CENSORED

Radical Plan From Newt Gingrich's Think Tank To Gut FDA

"AGENCY UNDER ATTACK"

By Leslie Weiss; *Mother Jones*, September/October 1995

The Food and Drug Administration, sometimes criticized in past years for being too cozy with corporations, has lately come under attack for exactly the opposite failing. A powerful bloc of critics in industry and the Republican Congress is pushing to overhaul the FDA, claiming the agency is too tough on drug companies, unnecessarily inhibiting innovation and delaying the approval of new drugs and medical devices.

Leading the charge is Speaker of the House Newt Gingrich, who has labeled the FDA number one "job-killer" in the country, and called its head, David Kessler, "a bully and a thug." Gingrich's Progress & Freedom Foundation has announced a radical plan to privatize much of the FDA's oversight of drugs and medical devices. Not surprisingly, the foundation has financial backing from some of the biggest names in the pharmaceutical industry, including Bristol-Myers Squibb Co., Eli Lilly & Co., and Marion Merrell Dow. Glaxo, manufacturer of Imitrex (see main story), has also given an undisclosed amount to the foundation, in addition to contributions of approximately $325,000 to the Republican Party and Republican candidates (including $4,000 to Gingrich) in the last election alone. As a whole, the drug industry contributed more than $1.6 million to the Republican Party in the 1993-94 election cycle.

If enacted, the Progress & Freedom Foundation's plan will place responsibility for drug development, testing, and review in the hands of private firms hired by the drug companies themselves, while retaining a weakened FDA to rubber-stamp their recommendations. Additionally, the plan limits the liability of drug companies that place dangerous drugs on the market. An interim report on the foundation's study was released in June; the final version is due out later this fall.

Under the plan, government-licensed firms called DCBs—drug (or device) certifying bodies—would be retained by drug companies to develop, test, and review new products. According to the proposal, "competition between firms would inevitably produce a lower-cost, faster, and higher-quality development and approval process."

FDA spokesperson Jim O'Hara offers an alternative view: "What this report proposes is dismantling many of the safeguards that protect the public from drugs and devices that are unsafe or just don't work. This is basically a proposal that says public health and safety are commodities for the marketplace."

Though drug testing and review would be privatized under the plan, the FDA would still exist and would theoretically have final say on new products. However, the report states there would be "a strong presumption that private certification decisions would not be overturned without substantial cause." Further, the FDA would not be authorized to request additional testing or data, and it would "have to exercise its veto within a fixed time period (e.g., 90 days) after which the drug would automatically receive FDA approval."

The Progress & Freedom Foundation's plan also limits the liability of drug companies should a patient be injured or killed by a dangerous drug or medical device. According to the proposal, a victim could not sue for punitive damages if the manufacturer of the product could show that it had met regulatory standards—however weakened—during development and testing.

Dr. Sidney Wolfe, director of Public Citizen's Health Research Group, says the plan to limit corporate liability is "hypocrisy at the very least."

Even some in the drug industry believe the Progress & Freedom Foundation's proposal goes too far. Steve Berchem of the Pharmaceutical Research and Manufacturers of America says that while some drug reviews can be handled by the private sector, it would be a mistake to weaken the FDA's authority over product approvals. "We need an FDA that maintains public confidence," Berchem says.

Nonetheless, the political writing on the wall is clear. Earlier this year, the FDA announced steps to reform itself, including the creation of a pilot program to allow private companies to review some medical devices. But this compromise isn't going to satisfy the hard-liners. Progress & Freedom Foundation spokesperson Rick O'Donnell says the FDA proposals "don't actually hit at the heart of the systemic problems that our plan is addressing."

As the battle to reshape the FDA heats up in the coming months, the Progress & Freedom Foundation will coordinate its efforts with those of other heavily funded right-wing attacks. But look for Newt and Company to draw their proposals directly from the foundation's plan.

© 1995 The Foundation for National Progress

7 CENSORED

Russia Injects Earth With Nuke Waste

"POISON IN THE EARTH: A SPECIAL REPORT; NUCLEAR ROULETTE FOR RUSSIA: BURYING UNCONTAINED WASTE"

By William J. Broad; *The New York Times*, November 21, 1994 (Reprinted in the *Santa Cruz Sentinel*, "Russia Injects Earth With Nuke Waste," November 21, 1994)

For more than three decades, Russian scientists have disclosed, the Soviet Union and now Russia secretly pumped billions of gallons of atomic waste directly into the earth. They say the practice continues today.

Though the Russians defend the practice as safe, it is at odds with accepted global standards for nuclear waste disposal and is contrary to what they have previously said they were doing.

The disclosure has set off a debate among experts over the likely consequences of the radioactive injections, which some experts say represent a new kind of nuclear danger that might haunt the planet for centuries.

The Russians told a small group of Western experts that Moscow had injected about half of all the nuclear waste it ever produced into the ground at three widely dispersed sites, all thoroughly wet and all near major rivers.

The injections violate the accepted rules of nuclear waste disposal, which require it to be isolated in impermeable containers for thousands of years. The Russian scientists claim the practice is safe because the wastes have been injected under layers of shale and clay, which in theory cut them off from the Earth's surface.

But already the wastes at one site have leaked beyond the expected range and "spread a great distance," the Russians told the small group of international scientists, who were handpicked to receive the news. The Russians did not say whether the distance was meters or kilometers or whether the poisons had reached the surface.

Decades or centuries might pass before scientists know whether the injections are calamitous or benign.

Some American experts say that in all likelihood things will work out favorably but that close study is prudent. "Does it have the potential for impacting the environment in Russia and the world?" said Dr. Clyde W. Frank, a top official of the Energy Department. "We're a long way from understanding that. We're dealing with a long-term situation."

But others say the injections could be one of the deadliest assaults ever on the Earth's environment. "Far and away, this is the largest and most careless nuclear practice that the human race has ever suffered," said Dr. Henry W. Kendall, a Nobel laureate in physics at the Massachusetts Institute of Technology, who learned of the injections while advising the federal government. "It's just an enormous scale of irresponsibility."

Repeated efforts to reach Nikolai N. Yegorov, a high official of the Russian Ministry of Atomic Energy and leader of the delegation that made the disclosure, were unsuccessful.

The Russian experts say they began injecting the waste as a way to avoid the kind of surface-storage disasters that began to plague them in the 1950s. But by any measure, the injections were one of the Cold War's darkest secrets.

Moscow said nothing of large injections and dissembled publicly by claiming to stand by accepted standards for radioactive waste disposal. Moreover, the injections are yet another environmental black mark against Moscow, which before the disclosures was already being criticized for environmental recklessness.

The three sites are at Dimitrovgrad near the Volga River, Tomsk near the Ob River, and Krasnoyarsk on the Yenisei River. The Volga flows into the Caspian Sea and the Ob and Yenisei into the Arctic Ocean.

The amount of radioactivity injected by the Russians is up to three billion curies. By comparison, the accident at the Chernobyl nuclear power plant released about 50 million curies of radiation, mostly in short-lived isotopes that decayed in a few months. The accident at Three Mile Island discharged about 50 curies.

A curie is the amount of radiation given off by one gram of radium and, in any nuclear material, is equal to the disintegration of 37 billion atoms per second. An old-style luminous watch dial with 12 radium dots emitted about three one-thousandths of a curie of radiation.

The injected wastes include cesium-137, with a half life of 30 years, and strontium-90, with a half life of 28 years and a bad reputation because it binds readily with human bones. A half life is the time it takes for half of a radioactive substance to decay into atoms that are less complex and often less harmful to humans.

The Russians are working with the Department of Energy, which runs America's nuclear complex, to try to better predict how far and fast the radioactive waste is likely to spread through aquifers.

At best, the Russian waste may stay underground long enough to be rendered largely harmless by the process of radioactive decay.

At worst, it might leak to the surface and produce calamities in Russia and areas downstream along the rivers. If the radioactivity spread through the world's oceans, experts say, it might prompt a global rise in birth defects and cancer deaths.

The benign scenario is more likely than the calamitous one, many experts say. But uncertainties persist, partly because there are no comparative data on the large-scale injection of radioactive waste, diminishing the accuracy of forecasts.

8 CENSORED

Medical Fraud Costs The Nation $100 Billion Annually— Or More
"MEDSCAM"
By L.J. Davis; *Mother Jones*, March/April 1995

Consider the following cautionary tale: In 1981, the Senate Special Committee on Aging undertook a pioneering study of the extent and nature of medical insurance fraud. To assist the committee in its thinking, the legislators called upon Dr. Richard Joseph Kones, a Philadelphia cardiologist who had been convicted of submitting fraudulent bills in excess of $500,000 to the public and private insurance systems of three states. To the doctor's disingenuous surprise, he had actually been paid.

"The problem is that nobody is watching," he told the senators. "The system is extremely easy to evade. The forms I sent in were absolutely outrageous. I was astounded when some of those payments were made."

In the seven years since he'd first stumbled upon a felon's pot of gold in 1974, Kones had been convicted of fraud no fewer than five times. Dr. Kones, in effect, begged Congress to stop him before he billed more.

But Congress didn't stop him. In 1990, not long after he was released from a Texas jail, Kones was able, despite his record, to get his Pennsylvania medical license reinstated. According to the FBI, he was soon up to his old tricks, submitting outrageous bills that charged insurers anywhere from $2,500 to $5,000 for a single visit by a single patient. "I can't get into specifics," says John Narvaez, the FBI agent in charge of the latest investigation, "but if you saw his claim submissions to the insurance companies, you wouldn't believe them."

When Kones was finally hauled in again last year, he was charged with 200 counts of mail fraud for billing in excess of $1 million over four years. The trial is pending.

For two decades, Dr. Kones had remarkable success milking the fee-for-service system that has been the standard form of reimbursement since modern medical insurance was introduced in the 1930s: A doctor performs (or pretends to perform) a professional service, and the insurance companies or the government pay the doctor for it. Under managed care—the wave of the future, no matter what happens in Washington, since many employers and insurance companies want it—the perverse, fraud-porous incentives of fee-for-service will presumably vanish, because health care providers will be placed on salary. Unfortunately, the medical investigators contacted during the course of this investigation agree that health care theft will simply mutate like a virus, adapting itself to changed circumstances.

The United States' $1 trillion annual health bill is 14 percent of the gross domestic product, making the medical industry the largest business in the land. Of this sum, a staggering amount is stolen. According to the National Health Care Anti-Fraud Association (an alliance of insurance companies, concerned individuals, and federal and state agencies), the yearly swag totals between $31-$53 billion. According to a widely quoted 1992 report by the General Accounting Office, the annual bill has probably hit $100 billion. Other investigators estimate the amount is as high as $250 billion. In fact, as an extensive Mother Jones investigation has discovered, no one really has the foggiest notion of how much money is stolen from the medical system every year—and no one has any way of finding out.

We are no longer dealing with the usual handful of physicians who make an extra buck by fudging on the bill, or the bogus patients who fake an injury for the insurance money, although both are with us always. Fraud is perpetrated at every level, even down to the taxicab companies who receive insurance money for driving elderly patients to their appointments. For a couple of decades, Congress has dutifully held hearings, listened to hair-raising testimony, wrinkled its brow, and occasionally passed corrective legislation. But while some of the perpetrators are caught, an unknown but substantial number continue to laugh all the way to the bank, with money obtained from the citizenry through inflated insurance premiums and lost tax monies.

Part of the problem stems from the always-vexing nature of white-collar crime. When a grocery store is robbed, the court is presented with a simple question: Is the guy standing before the bar of justice the guy who robbed the store? In white-collar cases, the question is whether a crime has been committed at all—and the more complex the crime, the harder it is to prove. Gathering evidence can take two to four years. Presenting it to the judge and jury takes even more time, and the outcome is far from certain: A court, faced with a pile of hard-to-understand documents and a defendant who is a pillar of the community, may be disinclined to convict. Small wonder, then, that the government and insurance companies often seem to lack enthusiasm when it comes to recovering stolen insurance money in court.

More than 4 billion private and government health insurance claims are processed annually. For seemingly sound, humanitarian reasons, a number of states require that private insurance claims be processed and paid swiftly, in as little as 15 days, giving investigators a vanishingly small amount of time to prevent fraud before it occurs.

When a claim seems suspicious, an investigator must decide whether a health care provider is a possible crook or merely incompetent or overzealous. (A RAND study of 4.4 million Medicare beneficiaries revealed that in permissive jurisdictions, patients were 11 times more likely to have a hip operation, 6 times more likely to have a knee replaced, and 3 times more likely to have a coronary bypass than in jurisdictions where the rules were less generous.) Moreover, according to Dr. Marc J. Roberts, professor of political economy and health policy at Harvard, 90 percent of all hospital bills are wrong—not necessarily fraudulent, but wrong.

Until recently, many of the nation's 1,200 claims payers showed little interest in medical insurance fraud—it was far easier to tack an invisible surcharge onto premiums. Even when they do investigate fraud, insurers face formidable obstacles. Often, a successful practitioner of medical insurance fraud will file claims with a number of companies, concealing the extent of the crime by charging a hundred bucks here and a hundred bucks there until it adds up to real money. Anti-trust and civil liability laws make it difficult for insurers to share information, and though some states have passed laws granting them limited immunity, companies are still reluctant to cooperate with one another, according to the GAO. Meanwhile, the government's efforts are undermanned, underfunded, and woefully inadequate.

Although Medicare and Medicaid were created in 1965, no specialized police force was established until 1978, giving the bad guys, according to Bill Whatley Jr., president of the National Association of Medicaid Fraud Control Units, "a 13-year head start, and we never caught up. The people who put this program together didn't believe that the [health care providers] in the program would commit fraud, because medicine was such a high calling."

There are currently 42 state Medicaid anti-fraud units, run by the states but largely funded with federal money; since 1978, they have successfully prosecuted more than 7,000 cases, which looks good until examined closely.

"We have no idea how much fraud falls through the cracks," says Whatley, an Alabama deputy attorney general. "I just doubled the number of my investigators, and my caseload doubled. If I tripled the investigators, the caseload would triple."

Because the Medicaid units are state-controlled, the quality of prosecution varies—and according to Ed Kuriansky, New York's chief anti-fraud investigator, no state uses all its share of the federal money available. Furthermore, the state units only patrol the Medicaid system; at the federal level, at least nine agencies have some responsibility for investigating medical fraud, with the task falling mostly on the FBI and the Office of the Inspector General (OIG) of the Department of Health and Human Services, where the story is different but no more encouraging.

"There were always a limited amount of resources," says Richard Kusserow, a former FBI agent who was inspector general from 1981 to 1992 (at which point he was hired as part of the damage-control effort of a hospital chain convicted of fraud). "When you think about the gigantic programs and the very limited number of investigators available, it's shocking. On the federal side, there are only about 125 [full-time] investigators. Now it's going to be cut again. You'll have 100 investigators left for some 250 programs, among them Medicare and Medicaid." With 4 billion annual claims, each investigator at the OIG or FBI faces a load of millions of possible cases—this, just to determine whether or not a crime might have occurred.

The irony is that prosecuting medical insurance fraud is one of the government's few profit centers, returning about $72 for every taxpayer dollar spent; even allowing for the usual bureaucratic exaggeration, the monies recovered are substantial—to say nothing of the money that is saved when a fraudulent practitioner is removed from circulation.

The government and private insurance companies are finally awakening to the problem, and they promise wonders when computers are turned loose on the paperwork, instantly detecting suspicious billing patterns. But while computers may help to identify possible problem areas, human beings will still have to investigate them. The government agencies remain understaffed, and legal problems still constrain private insurers from sharing information in all but a dozen or so states.

Proponents of managed care claim it will eliminate powerful incentives for fraud by replacing the fee-for-service system with flat-rate payments, but not one investigator contacted by Mother Jones expects managed care to eradicate medical fraud. "It'll just wear a new jacket," says San Martin, chief investigator for Medi-Cal. Large-scale managed care has already come to several states, and investigators have already begun to detect certain patterns. Under managed care, fraudulent profits can be maintained by providing less care, pretending to provide more, and bribing public officials to look the other way. "You get paid a certain amount of money at the beginning of the year to treat a certain number of people," says Dr. Alan A. Stone, professor of law and medicine at Harvard. "The more you have left at the end of the year, the richer you are. A patient comes in with a stomachache, and you say, 'Here's an antacid. Don't bother me.' When you introduced the profit motive into health care, the whole industry became permeated with greed."

It seems safe to say that the Republican obsession with deregulation and market economics will make an unknowably bad situation unknowably worse. Under the market theories so popular in the conservative quarters now ascendant, mad, bad, and dangerous medical practitioners are supposed to be driven out of business as consumers make informed health care choices. Unfortunately, when it comes to health care, an informed consumer is a near-mythical beast, rarely encountered.

"Ordinary market principles cannot apply to the health care industry," says Dr. Stone. "The basic problem is the problem of information. The patient knows he's sick, but he relies on the physician to identify the illness. Take the doctor in Rhode Island who implanted a pacemaker into every elderly patient who came in. He was putting pacemakers into every patient with mild congestive failure, just to make money. But how were the patients to know that?"

With the free marketeers now riding high and the Oval Office occupied by a man who seems to want nothing more than Newt Gingrich's approval, the future looks very bleak indeed. After all, fraudulent medical providers have had 30 years to perfect their act.

"The only ones who aren't confused," says New York anti-fraud investigator Ed Kuriansky, "are the crooks."

A GLOSSARY OF MEDICAL FRAUD

UPCODING

A doctor performs one medical procedure and charges the insurer for another, more profitable (or permissible) one. A variant of this popular fraud was described in a Senate report: A Texas medica equipment supplier billed Medicare nearly $1 million by charging $1,300 for orthotic body jackets designed to keep patients upright, but instead supplied wheelchair pads that cost between $50 and $100.

UNBUNDLING

The whole is sometimes worth less than the sum of its parts. A wheelchair broken down into its components—a wheel here, a seat there—with a separate bill for each, can mean a significant profit. According to a Senate report, a glucose monitoring kit may cost $12 in a drugstore; unbundled, the kit costs Medicare up to $250.

PHARMACY FRAUD

A corrupt pharmacist, often abetted by a physician and a patient, dispenses a generic drug rather than a brand-name drug and pockets the difference. Or, a pharmacist fills an insured prescription, buys it back at a discount from the patient, then sells it again. Or, a patient receives a drug with street value and peddles it, so everybody gets paid: the pharmacist, the prescribing physician, the patient-entrepreneur who sells the drug on the street, and the person who buys it, often for another resale. New York investigators have raided apartments piled high with thousands of prescription drugs.

PSYCHIATRIC SCHEMES

In the 1980s, the nation experienced an epidemic of clinical depression, as hospital chains filled their beds with teenagers, the overweight, and substance abusers. For insurance purposes, these people weren't young or heavy or addicted—they were depressed, whether they liked it or not. Private insurance companies estimate that psychiatric schemes cost them millions.

HOME HEALTH CARE

This rich field for the plow of fraud includes overbilling, billing for services not rendered, kickbacks, the use of untrained (i.e., inexpensive) personnel, and the delivery of unnecessary equipment, such as the ever-popular wheelchair, to people who don't need it.

GHOST PATIENTS, ETC.

There are doctors who work more than 24 hours a day and doctors who continue to treat patients after they're dead. In New York, investigators found corrupt podiatrists who issued prescriptions for orthopedic shoes to corrupt patients who took the prescriptions to corrupt shoestores, where they exchanged them for sneakers, high heels, and loafers. Nearly $30 million in insurance money vanished.

© 1995 The Foundation for National Progress

L.J. Davis is a contributing editor to *Harper's and Buzz magazines, and a frequent contributor to Mother Jones.*

9 | CENSORED |

U.S. Chemical Industry Fights For Toxic Ozone-Killing Pesticide

"CAMPAIGN AGAINST METHYL BROMIDE: OZONE-KILLING PESTICIDE OPPOSED"
By Anne Schonfield; *Earth Island Journal,* Winter 1995

Methyl bromide is a pesticide that is at least 50 times more destructive to the ozone layer, molecule for molecule, than chlorofluorocarbons (CFCs). Most methyl bromide is applied to tomatoes, strawberries, peppers, tobacco and nursery crops. In 1992, the United Nations estimated that methyl bromide is responsible for five to ten percent of current worldwide ozone depletion, a share that is expected to increase to 15 percent by the year 2000.

Methyl bromide is extremely toxic and is known to cause acute and chronic health effects. Farmworkers, pesticide applicators and people living or working where methyl bromide is used can suffer poisoning, neurological damage and reproductive harm. The chemical is so toxic to humans and animals that the Environmental Protection Agency (EPA) classifies it as a Category I acute toxin, the most deadly category of substances.

For 60 years, methyl bromide has been used to kill pests in soils and buildings, and on agricultural products. In 1991, the US accounted for nearly 40 percent of the pesticide's worldwide use. Soil fumigation to sterilize soil before crops are planted is by far the largest use of methyl bromide in the US.

In a 1994 assessment, the United Nations listed elimination of methyl bromide as the most significant remaining approach (after phaseout of CFCs and halons) to reducing ozone depletion. Eliminating all emissions of methyl bromide from agricultural, structural and industrial activities by the year 2001 would achieve a 13 percent reduction in the level of ozone-depleting chemicals reaching the stratosphere over the next 50 years.

HEALTH EFFECTS OF EXPOSURE

Methyl bromide is toxic to the central nervous system and damages lungs kidneys, eyes and skin. Recovery from the more severe symptoms of methyl bromide toxicity, such as pneumonia, severe weakness, paralysis and heart problems, can take days to several months. Studies show that harmful concentrations of methyl bromide can drift several miles from the site of fumigation, posing a threat to nearby residents and workers who may be exposed to the gas. Unlike other commonly used pesticides, however, methyl bromide is believed to leave little or no residues on most foods.

Under the Clean Air Act the EPA has mandated a halt to methyl bromide production and import in the US in 2001, but manufacturers and agricul-tural users have mounted a formidable campaign to delay the ban. Because no gradual phaseout is required, methyl bromide can be used without major restriction until 2001. Since the act does not prohibit the use of existing stocks after 2001, application of the pesticide can continue as long as stockpiled supplies last.

A tax on methyl bromide—like that currently imposed on other ozone-depleting chemicals— should be required to pressure users and producers to reduce their dependence on methyl bromide and to stimulate the shift to available alternatives before the phaseout date. The Congressional Budget Office estimates that a methyl bromide tax could generate nearly $1 billion over five years.

The Montreal Protocol, the principal international treaty on ozone-depleting substances, officially recognized methyl bromide as an ozone-depleting chemical in 1992, but will not decide on an international phaseout until November, 1995. Resistance stems primarily from industries in countries with large methyl bromide producers and users, including the US, Israel, Japan and France.

METHYL BROMIDE ALTERNATIVES

Numerous alternatives to methyl bromide exist, including using organic soil additives, soil solarization, crop rotation and biological pest control in farming. Controlled atmosphere and heat/cold treatments are proven alternatives on harvested crops and in structures.

Several of the key pesticides proposed as methyl bromide replacements by the chemical industry are already known to threaten human health and the environment. For example, the soil fumigant 1,3-D (Telone) is considered a probable human carcinogen by the EPA. Metam-sodium, another popular chemical replacement, causes birth defects in laboratory animals.

The Methyl Bromide Global Coalition (MBGC)—a group of seven international methyl bromide users and producers—has launched a multimillion dollar lobbying campaign to keep methyl bromide on the market. In early 1994, members of the MBGC, along with the agribusiness and chemical industries, sued EPA to stop the phaseout of methyl bromide.

While some nations are actively fighting a methyl bromide phaseout, other countries have already banned or vigorously regulated the chemical. In 1992, the Netherlands eliminated all soil fumigation with methyl bromide and other countries, including, Denmark, Germany and Switzerland, have taken similar actions.

The Methyl Bromide Alternatives Network (MBAN), formed in 1993, is a coalition of environmental, agricultural and labor organizations working to phase out methyl bromide and replace it with affordable, environmentally sound alternatives. In 1995, MBAN will approach food manufacturers that use methyl bromide, like Gerber, Hershey and Nabisco, to switch to alternatives that do not deplete the ozone layer. MBAN will also pressure the EPA to accelerate the US phaseout of methyl bromide and the Department of Agriculture to focus on developing and promoting alternatives. Throughout the year,

MBAN will urge delegates to the Montreal Protocol to sign a global methyl bromide phaseout agreement in 1995.

WHAT YOU CAN DO: *Write the EPA demanding a label on all products using methyl bromide, ask your groceries to stock organic produce and demand non-chemical termite services from pest-control companies. For more information, contact MBAN at 116 New Montgomery St., #810, San Francisco CA 94105; (415) 541-9140; fax (415) 541-9253; email: panna@panna.org.*

10 CENSORED

The Broken Promises of NAFTA

"NAFTA'S CORPORATE CON ARTISTS"
By Sarah Anderson and Kristyne Peter; *Covert Action Quarterly*, Fall 1995

"A GIANT SPRAYING SOUND"
By Esther Schrader; *Mother Jones*, January/February 1995

NAFTA'S CORPORATE CON ARTISTS
It was not hard to figure out who was who in the halls of the congressional office buildings on November 15, 1993, two days before the vote on the North American Free Trade Agreement (NAFTA). There were clusters of people wearing labor union caps and jackets; they were lobbying against the

trade pact. Then there were the crowds of dark-suited men in matching red, white, and blue neckties; they were with the pro-NAFTA business coalition, USA*NAFTA.

The patriotic neckties were just a minor tactic in one of the most expansive lobbying efforts in the history of corporate America. Calling itself a grassroots organization, USA*NAFTA gave new meaning to the term by enlisting *Fortune* 500 companies as captains to whip up support for the agreement in each of the 50 states. An army of more than 2,000 member corporations provided backup.

The USA*NAFTA coalition promised that the free trade pact would be all things to all people. It would improve the environment, reduce illegal immigration by raising Mexican wages, deter international drug trafficking, and most importantly, create a net increase in high-paying U.S. jobs. In the final days of the battle for passage, USA*NAFTA worked closely with the White House NAFTA war room to sway undecided members of Congress. According to the *Wall Street Journal*, coalition members studied the fence-sitters' campaign contribution lists and urged the top corporate donors to turn up the heat. Many firms complied by promising new jobs in the member's district or threatening to withhold future contributions.

Today, less than two years after the agreement became law, USA*NAFTA's own members are blatantly breaking the coalition's grand promises. Many of the firms that only a short time ago were extolling the benefits of NAFTA for U.S. workers and communities have cut jobs, moved plants to Mexico, or continued to violate labor rights and environmental regulations in Mexico.

The best available information on NAFTA layoffs comes from the U.S. Department of Labor's (DoL) NAFTA Transitional Adjustment Assistance (TAA). This program provides retraining and other benefits to U.S. workers after the DoL certifies that they were laid off because of a shift in production to Mexico or Canada or an increase in imports from those countries. Between January 1, 1994, and July 10, 1995, 62,000 workers filed claims for this assistance; 35,000 of them were certified. It should be noted that recipients of NAFTA-TAA benefits are only a fraction of the total number of NAFTA-related layoffs, since many workers are not aware of the program or apply for a general retraining program with more generous benefits. A University of Maryland study estimates that in 1994, more than 150,000 U.S. jobs were cut as a result of increased consumer imports from Mexico.

Even these limited data reveal that USA*NAFTA members have carried out NAFTA-related layoffs at a rate surprising even to cynics. If only for public relations purposes, they might have held off on the job cuts until the ink on the agreement was a little drier. However, by July 10 (only 18 months into the agreement), USA*NAFTA firms were already responsible for 40 NAFTA-related layoffs affecting 7,785 U.S. workers. Another 4,626 workers from 24 plants operated by coalition companies applied for NAFTA-TAA benefits during this time and were rejected, in some cases simply because the Department of Labor was unable to verify a shift in production.

Dozens of USA*NAFTA companies carried out NAFTA-related layoffs, but a few member firms deserve special attention for their ability to quickly harness the agreement's benefits for themselves at the expense of workers and communities.

ALLIED SIGNAL

At the helm of USA*NAFTA was Lawrence Bossidy, CEO of AlliedSignal, a diversified manufacturing firm which produces auto parts and defense equipment. As chief spokesperson, Bossidy made countless public and media appearances to persuade Americans that NAFTA would be good for them.

While lauding the benefits of the agreement for society at large, Bossidy was quick to deny any suggestion that it would provide incentives for his own company to move jobs to Mexico. In August 1993, CNN anchor Lou Dobbs asked him, "Do you think jobs will move to Mexico [under NAFTA]? For example, would your company, would you put jobs in Mexico?" Bossidy replied, "I think quite the contrary, Lou. I think the jobs that were to move to Mexico have already moved there. I mean, there's more than 700,000 employees in the Mexican maquiladoras now!"

Less than two years later, Bossidy's firm could boast the most NAFTA-related layoffs. As of July, AlliedSignal workers in five cities have petitioned for NAFTA-TAA benefits. The DoL approved the claims in three communities (Greenville, Ohio; El Paso, Texas;

and Orangeburg, South Carolina). Claims from workers in Danville, Illinois, and Eatontown, New Jersey, were rejected, even though the New Jersey workers say that AlliedSignal left little doubt that the company was moving jobs south. In the months leading up to the layoffs, New Jersey workers were sent to provide training in one of the company's Mexican plants, while Mexican managers were brought to New Jersey for training.

INCREASING DISPARITY

Bossidy's NAFTA promises were not confined to U.S. workers. In congressional testimony, he also claimed that NAFTA will benefit the Mexicans; it will improve their standard of living.

Unfortunately for Mexican workers, just the opposite has occurred. The peso devaluation of December 1994 cut the value of their wages by as much as 40 percent, making them far less able to buy U.S. goods today than they were before NAFTA. Interest rates on credit cards have climbed above 100 percent, and the Mexican government reports that retail sales in Mexico's three largest cities have dropped by nearly 25 percent. The continuing crisis is expected to cause the loss of two million jobs this year, and economic desperation is blamed for the 30 percent increase in arrests by U.S. border patrols between January and May 1995.

Workers at AlliedSignal, like those at other Mexican maquiladoras operated by U.S. corporations, have lost significant purchasing power. At the corporation's Monterrey, Mexico plant, workers saw the dollar value of their wages drop from $1.30 to $.82 an hour in January 1995. Laboring 48 hours a week at $.82 per hour, AlliedSignal's 3,800-person Mexican workforce would make approximately $7.8 million a year. By contrast, Bossidy's personal pay last year was worth far more $12.4 million, ranking him among the top eight corporate earners in the country.

AlliedSignal's executive board justifies the salary as necessary to keep Bossidy from being lured away by other corporations. One union leader ironically concurred. "Any CEO who could be the head of USA*NAFTA and then turn around in the first year of the agreement and start laying off people and get away with it he's worth $12.4 million!"

GENERAL ELECTRIC

GE, one of USA*NAFTA's proud captains, made NAFTA history as the target of the first complaint filed under NAFTA's labor side agreement. On February 15, 1994, the United Electrical Workers (UE) charged that GE had fired about 30 employees at its Ciudad Juárez, Mexico plant for union organizing. Workers in the border area report that the GE case reflects common practice. In fact, such violations seem to have increased. After NAFTA became law, companies no longer had to worry about generating bad publicity that might have jeopardized passage.

According to UE, GE officials told one worker that he was being fired for distributing union fliers and for telling a MacNeil-Lehrer News Hour reporter that GE used chemicals in its Mexican plant that are banned in the U.S. The NAFTA agency responsible for investigating labor complaints, the National Administrative Office, dismissed the case, not because it found GE innocent of the charges, but because it could not prove that the Mexican government had knowingly failed to enforce the rights of the GE workers.

Before the Juárez firings, GE management had reportedly warned the workers that the company had come to Mexico to get away from U.S. unions, so if the Mexican workers brought in a union, GE might as well pack up the plant and move it back north. Meanwhile, GE was busily shifting operations from the U.S. to Mexico. In March, it announced plans to cut 271 jobs at its Fort Wayne, Indiana facility. In May, the DoL determined that the layoffs resulted from GE's decision to move jobs to Mexico, and certified 95 of the workers for NAFTA retraining.

Both GE workers and the community of Fort Wayne got swindled. In 1988, the employees had agreed to a $1.20 per hour wage cut to prevent their jobs from being moved to Mexico. Then in 1992, GE managed to squeeze a $485,290 tax cut out of the local government, claiming it was necessary to defray the cost of new machinery needed to preserve jobs. Once NAFTA passed, the wage cuts and the tax breaks were not enough to keep those jobs in Fort Wayne. As one longtime GE employee put it, "You give them all your life, and this is what they give you."

In a cynical recycling of Reagan's failed trickle-down policies, USA*NAFTA predicted that NAFTA itself will improve working conditions by generating economic growth, which will enable all three countries to provide more jobs with higher pay in a better working environment. This theory hasn't held up well for workers at Xerox, another USA*NAFTA member.

XEROX

After taking a loss in 1993, Xerox profits rose to $794 million on sales of $17.8 billion in 1994. Rather than translate this gain into more jobs or higher pay, the corporation began both laying off workers and bargaining down the wages of those it kept. According to the DoL, Xerox has fired 50 workers in Oakbrook, Illinois, and another 13 in Peabody, Massachusetts, and moved the jobs to Mexico. Under the shadow of those job cuts, it's not surprising that Xerox was able to pressure workers at its Webster, New York facility to accept wage concessions by threatening to move to Mexico. Backed to the wall, the union agreed to reduce base pay rates by 50 percent for new employees and cut workers' compensation in exchange for job guarantees through the year 2001.

In a similar move in May 1995, Xerox pressured 700 workers in El Segundo, California, to accept a 20 percent pay cut to save their jobs. The company even demanded the elimination of a paid five-minute break at the end of the day for workers to wash up.

ZENITH

Xerox employees aren't the only U.S. workers who have seen a drop in wages and working conditions. A June 1995 U.S. Department of Labor report revealed that real wages across the country dropped by 2.3 percent between March 1994 and March 1995, even though productivity had risen by 2.1 percent. Economists offer numerous explanations for the declining pay, but the increased power of corporations to bargain down their wages by threatening to move overseas is certainly a major factor. At Zenith's Springfield, Missouri plant, workers accepted an 8.2 percent wage cut in 1987 under threat of losing their jobs to Mexico. However, in spite of these concessions, USA*NAFTA member Zenith has laid off 430 workers in Springfield and another 80 in Chicago after NAFTA took effect, and moved the jobs to Mexico. According to one of the Springfield employees, "If [we] didn't give them the wage concession, they were going to move to Mexico. We just gave more. We just helped pay for it."

South of the border, the TV maker is notorious for its rock-bottom wages. A March 1995 pay stub from one Zenith worker in Mexico showed he was making less than 50 cents an hour. On top of the low pay, Zenith's Mexican workers often face health risks. According to the Coalition for Justice in the Maquiladoras (CJM), thousands of child-bearing-age women work with lead solder in Zenith's TV factories without proper training about its dangers or adequate protective equipment. A 1994 inspection of one Zenith plant in Reynosa revealed that eye protection and gloves were unavailable and unidentified containers of glue sat open on the floor.

ALCOA

NAFTA critics claimed that the agreement would add extra incentive for

U.S. firms in highly toxic industries to avoid expensive safety measures and lawsuits by relocating to Mexico, where they could take advantage of more lax enforcement. A firm like Alcoa, for example, might see the largely unregulated Mexican border area as a pleasant refuge. Ranked by the Environmental Protection Agency as one of the country's top 100 polluters (in terms of toxic releases), Alcoa has been the target of numerous environmental lawsuits. In 1991, it was forced to pay $7.5 million for environmental offenses at its Massena plant in upstate New York. At that time, it was the largest criminal penalty ever paid by a U.S. firm for hazardous waste violations.

As a USA*NAFTA captain, Alcoa dismissed fears of anti-NAFTA environmentalists, claiming that it was a myth that Mexico has lax enforcement of environmental laws and worker protections and that in any case, protections are strict, and getting stricter

During the first year of NAFTA, Alcoa revealed just how seriously it regards these safeguards. According to CJM, in September and October 1994, a series of three unexplained gas intoxications led to the hospitalization of 226 workers at Alcoa's plant in Ciudad Acuña. Community activists and the local press accuse the company of threatening to fire workers if they talked publicly about their experiences. CJM also claims that Alcoa management prevented health officials from inspecting the facilities until it was too late to conduct meaningful air quality tests. Nonetheless, health officials found that the gases had caused sudden spells of nausea, headaches,

dizziness and fainting. So far, these incidents have not resulted in legal action against Alcoa.

BAXTER INTERNATIONAL

The effects of NAFTA in the U.S. are also increasingly toxic not so much to the health of workers (U.S. environmental standards have yet to fall because of NAFTA) but to the health of communities around the country. Last year Baxter International, a medical equipment manufacturer and USA*NAFTA member, laid off 830 workers in Kingstree, South Carolina (population 4,000), after deciding to shift production overseas. About 120 of the workers, who made medical procedure trays, qualified for the NAFTA retraining program because their jobs were moving to Mexico. The rest, whose jobs were destined for Asia, were rejected.

The layoffs dealt a devastating blow to the entire county, which already had the state's lowest per capita income ($10,255) and highest unemployment rate (13.6 percent). The layoffs also contributed to racial tensions in the county, which is 65 percent African American. Angered by the possibility that the loss of so many jobs might drive up local taxes and crime, residents of a small, predominantly white town tried to secede and join a neighboring county that is predominantly white and more affluent. The Justice Department refused the request, but the secession attempt created deep wounds in the community.

Baxter CEO Vernon Loucks, Jr., is far removed from the type of day-to-day economic struggles faced by his company's former employees in Kingstree. A Wall Street Journal article on imperial perks featured Loucks and reported that in 1993, Baxter paid him $79,600 for personal travel by him and his family on the company jet, and kicked in another $33,450 for club membership fees. Loucks was also reimbursed nearly $100,000 for taxes attributable to use of aircraft, a car allowance, a financial counseling allowance, and the maintenance of a home security system. With all those angry unemployed workers out there, the company apparently feels obligated to pay for Loucks' personal security.

USA*NAFTA MARCHES ON

The groups that fought against NAFTA particularly the citizens' coalitions formed by labor, environmental, consumer, family farm and other groups are proud that they took on practically the entire Fortune 500 and nearly won. (The vote was 234 to 200 in the House). At the same time, the experience was a chilling reminder of how things work in Washington.

USA*NAFTA representing more economic clout than many nation-states wrapped its self-serving lobbying campaign in an American flag. During the past two years, that flag has proved to have an exceptionally slick Teflon coating. The group has suffered neither negative publicity nor political disfavor, despite NAFTA's miserable results so far. Nor have USA*NAFTA members drawn fire for the way they contributed to and benefited from the failure of NAFTA to fulfill its stated promises. Their star-spangled report, NAFTA: It's Working for America, opens with a

quote from USA*NAFTA Chair and AlliedSignal CEO Lawrence Bossidy. "Today, it is clear that NAFTA is a success," he proclaims. "Exports to Mexico and Canada are up, and we've been able to create thousands of new jobs here in the United States. By any standards, NAFTA is surely a winner."

As Bossidy indicates, U.S. exports to Mexico did indeed increase in 1994. However, what the report fails to point out is that during that time, U.S. imports from Mexico increased at a faster rate and displaced U.S. jobs by muscling out American products. Since the peso devaluation in December 1994, the U.S. trade surplus with Mexico has turned into a large and growing deficit expanding from $885 million in May 1994 to $6.9 billion a year later, and thereby wiping out any basis for claiming that NAFTA is a net job creator for U.S. workers.

The bulk of the USA*NAFTA report is a state-by-state listing of jobs created by NAFTA. However, a careful examination reveals a sleight of hand. Almost all of the job claims are empty statements by USA*NAFTA firms that they intend to hire more workers, not that they have already created actual jobs.

Although USA*NAFTA's work was completed with the passage of the agreement, the coalition continues to play an important political role in supporting the free trade model. When President Clinton was attempting to mobilize congressional support for the financial bailout of Mexico in January 1995, he arranged for lobbyists from 150 USA*NAFTA firms to meet in Washington. *Business Week* reported that Rep. Robert Matsui (D-Calif.), Clinton's chief congressional strategist on NAFTA, told the group, You got us NAFTA. Now you can deliver on this one, too. The article described USA*NAFTA's strategy as two-fold: mobilizing its troops to voice their support for the bailout package, and fear-mongering among border state legislators by claiming that an aborted bailout might trigger a flood of illegal immigrants.

In the end, Clinton did not need USA*NAFTA's help on the bailout, since he opted to bypass Congress with an executive order. However, the administration is clearly confident that the old USA*NAFTA gang can still wield enough influence and con artistry to help push another free trade agreement through Congress. Otherwise, the administration might not have rushed into its latest round of trade negotiations aimed at expanding NAFTA to include Chile. President Clinton reportedly would like to push the expanded NAFTA through Congress before the 1996 election. When that bill comes up for a vote, USA* NAFTA's patriotic neckties will no doubt reappear in the halls of Congress.

Sarah Anderson is a fellow and Kristyne Peter is a research assistant at the Institute for Policy Studies, an independent research institute in Washington, D.C.

This article was reprinted from CovertAction Quarterly, Fall 1995, 1500 Massachusetts Ave., #732, Washington, DC 20005, phone (202) 331-9763. Annual subscriptions in the U.S. are $22; Canada $27; Europe $33. The issue of Covert/Action, containing the full text of the article with footnotes is available from CAQ for $8 in the U.S. and $12 other.

A GIANT SPRAYING SOUND

On a single scorched block in Villa Jua'rez, Sinaloa, Mexico, four young men have leukemia. Another died of the disease last spring.

The cluster of sickness may have nothing to do with the tons of toxic pesticides that flow into every water source available to the residents of this small farm town; it may be unrelated to the four nearby airstrips where farmers load planes with pesticides to spray over the surrounding fields; it may not be linked to the work that brings young men home soaked to the skin with the chemicals they apply to crops.

But while there has been no comprehensive study of the tragedy, you can search far and wide and not find a single doctor who thinks it is anything but the pesticides that are making the young men of this flat, hot valley sick.

"There is no one who works in this clinic who doesn't believe the leukemia is related to the agrochemicals," says Dr. Sonia Leon, an emergency room physician at the government hospital in Villa Juarez. During the growing season, the clinic treats between 50 and 80 cases of pesticide poisoning a week. "When I go home every night, I run away from here as fast as I can," Leon says. "But what of the people who live here? They look up, and the chemicals drift down from the planes into their eyes. They walk to the fields, and they are dusted with chemicals from the leaves. They are surrounded; they have nowhere to run."

In the Culiacan Valley of Sinaloa, it is normal for 3,000 field workers a year to be hospitalized from what is called pesticide intoxication—the racing heartbeat, loss of consciousness, pounding headache, high temperature, nausea, and burning skin that come from overexposure to pesticides. Throughout Mexico's agricultural belt it is common for children to break out with skin rashes that doctors cannot explain. It is considered inevitable to die young from a combination of malnutrition, inadequate living conditions, and chemical inhalation.

On the unnamed street in Villa Juarez where leukemia is the rule, Ubaldina Soto, 35, rocks back and forth on a porch chair. She clutches a photograph of her son, dead this March of the insidious cancer at the age of 16.

"They say it's pesticides that killed him. How should I know?" Soto asks. "I'm just a mother. I want them to investigate, to clear this place of contamination so this doesn't happen to anyone else. A parent shouldn't live to see her children die."

The death of Adrian Allesquita Soto, who worked in the fields on weekends during the school year, is well known to the doctors of Villa Juarez, and so is the intolerable level of pesticide-laced filth that pervades the town. In a September 1993 analysis by a local human rights group of 100 water samples from the drainage canals that meet in Villa Juarez, 95 percent tested positive for 10 organophosphate compounds and 3 organochlorines. Of the 13 compounds, only 4 are permitted for use in Mexico today.

It has been this way for generations in the fruit- and vegetable-growing regions of Mexico. Growers slather their farmland with chemicals to increase production of the tomatoes, cucumbers, bell peppers, melons, and other crops that make up close to half of the fresh vegetables sold in the United States during winter. The indiscriminate use of pesticides in Mexico stretches from the tomato fields of Sinaloa to the tobacco plantations of Nayarit, where Huichole Indians are dying at alarming rates.

Since the danger of Mexican pesticide abuse first received widespread attention a decade or so ago, improved practices by Mexican growers have cut the danger to U.S. consumers of ingesting significant amounts of agrochemicals. Paradoxically, the very steps taken to prevent harm to the U.S. consumer have upped the danger to Mexican field workers. Growers now use fast-decaying organophosphate compounds that leave less residue on produce but are potentially lethal to field workers.

Government officials promised—and environmentalists hoped—that the North American Free Trade Agreement (in effect since Jan. 1, 1994) would reduce the level of pesticides coating Mexico's fields, but so far this hasn't occurred. In fact, the competition that NAFTA has set off between growers may actually increase the amount of pesticides used on Mexican crops.

Responsibility for pesticide use lies not only with Mexican growers but also with their U.S. agribusiness partners. A *Mother Jones* investigation shows that these companies, which supply capital to more than 40 percent of large-scale agribusiness in Mexico, distribute produce that has been sprayed with pesticides not permitted in the United States. Even when Mexican growers limit the use of pesticides to those allowed in the United States, they look the other way as workers apply chemicals without the basic protective gear and precautions mandated around the world.

The Culiacan Valley produced much of the $3 billion's worth of produce exported from Mexico to the United States last year. Since 1988, when Mexico began to open its markets to foreign investment, business in the valley has skyrocketed. About 250,000 acres of vegetables are farmed today, more than five times as many as 10 years ago.

Ninety percent of this acreage is in the hands of large-scale producers, wealthy men who drive Chevy Suburbans equipped with car phones. The valley stretches from the Gulf of California east to the Sierra Madre Occidental Mountains, and its roads and highways are lined with packing plants painted with familiar American brand names such as Dole.

Between December and May, 250,000 workers spray and harvest endless rows of plants, as planes loaded with pesticides zoom low overhead. Most of the workers are Mixtec Indians from Oaxaca, an impoverished state on Mexico's southern edge. Many live in huge migrant farm camps built by growers—long rows of corrugated tin shacks that roast the workers in the valley heat.

Others, not so lucky, camp out in the fields, bathing and washing in the drainage canals that flow by, the water tinted a sickly chemical yellow. At night, the disease-ridden camps are suffused with the strangely sweet scent of pesticides. In the fields, the fumes can be overpowering.

Ever since U.S. growers realized they could capitalize on Mexico's winter warmth to grow fruits and vegetables when U.S. farmland lies fallow, they have been a powerful political force in agricultural valleys such as Culiacan. Until 1992 Mexican law prohibited foreign ownership of land, so U.S. agribusiness created a complex system that allowed it to own Mexican produce. Under a typical arrangement, a U.S. grower, distributor, or supermarket chain forms a legal partnership with a Mexican grower and provides the capital, seedlings, and technology to cultivate crops. The grower provides the land and the field workers. Often the contract specifies the pesticides sanctioned by the U.S. partner and lays out the safety measures necessary to use them.

In practice, the selection and use of pesticides is usually left to the Mexican partner, who is under keen pressure to produce fruits and vegetables of carefully regulated size, color, and shape. Committed to hitting the market at exactly the time when their U.S. counterparts cannot, Mexican growers feel compelled to use agrochemicals to control the growth cycles of their crops.

"In Culiacan sometimes they'll spray tomatoes 25 times before they're picked," says Robert Paarlberg, professor of political science at Wellesley College and an expert on agriculture in developing countries. He is concerned that the number of acres that are over-sprayed will rise with free trade, as more U.S. growers compete in the Mexican market. "The big distributors are down there now trying to convince Mexican supermarkets that these perfectly round, perfectly formed fruits are what their customers want. It's a big step backwards as far as I'm concerned. People used to be perfectly happy to buy oranges that didn't all look alike."

A 1992 Government Accounting Office study revealed that Mexican growers use at least six pesticides that are illegal in the United States, although some U.S. officials say the number has since declined. According to a source in the Mexican Ministry of Agriculture, more than 165 million pounds of pesticides were used in the country in 1993. But the government does not release such figures, making it impossible to tell how NAFTA has affected total pesticide use.

On a single day's visit to a farm near Culiacan, this reporter spotted workers using parathion and methamidophos, two of the most toxic organophosphates on the market. The local growers association claims neither is still used here. One was being sprayed in the field of a grower under contract with Dole Food Co.

The less acutely toxic compounds paraquat, endosulfan, and malathion were also in use that day, but no workers were following the safety instructions on the skull-and-cross-bones labels. The instructions say special gloves and masks should be worn when handling the chemicals. They say the chemicals are toxic and inflame the skin. They say it all in English, which few of the workers understand, or in Spanish, which few can read.

Thankfully, no growers were applying the still more toxic organochlorine compounds that once were the norm here. One grower said, "We use the strongest stuff we need to keep the product coming up on schedule but that won't show up on inspection. The organochlorines are a dead ringer for getting caught."

Most U.S. growers with operations in Culiacan claim they are not responsible for the way their Mexican partners manage their workers. "We just contract with them to buy the product," says one grower who asked not to be named. "We do it precisely to avoid the kinds of hassles you are giving me."

Confronted with the fact that toxic organophosphates were sprayed in a field the company has under contract, Dole Food Co. spokesman Tom Pernice said, "We recognize at the corporate level that this is an issue, and we are working on an approach that can be used in foreign countries. We are going to craft something that could be successful." Pernice says that Dole is involved in pilot programs intended to prevent pesticide abuse, but he did not return repeated phone calls asking him to name the programs.

So far, the efforts of companies like Dole to prevent pesticide abuse have been met with skepticism. "I work for U.S. growers who have operations in Mexico, so I'm the last one to criticize, but this is one area where I think they are terribly out of line," says David Runsten, an agricultural economist and consultant for the nonprofit California

Institute of Rural Studies. "You very often find people walking around with backpack sprayers wearing sandals and no protective clothing. If [the growers] are conscious of the effects on workers, they should be ashamed. Essentially they are using up these workers, using up their health very cheaply."

When Mexican, Canadian, and U.S. officials first discussed creating the world's largest free trade zone, environmentalists hoped the accord would obligate Mexico to enforce its environmental standards. But neither NAFTA nor the Global Accord on Trade and Tariffs is designed to address social inequity. The pacts focus on reducing the danger to consumers from pesticide-tainted produce, and not on protecting workers.

Sandra Marquardt, a spokeswoman for the Washington, D.C.-based environmental group Greenpeace, says the system is structured to "make sure the residues don't show up in the marketplace. The longer this continues, the more we'll have great-looking fruits and vegetables—and dead workers. That is just not a socially acceptable way of buying food."

Since NAFTA went into effect, U.S. producers have dramatically increased their investments in Mexico. According to a source in the Mexican Confederation of Agricultural Producers, U.S. investment in Mexican agriculture is up by $8 million since 1992.

All this is good news for the Mexican economy, which desperately needs foreign investment. It is likewise good for U.S. consumers, since it will probably result in lower prices. Further, backers of agribusiness argue that free trade itself will limit pesticide use. Since pesticides make up as much as a third of the average cost of farm production, Mexican growers claim to be the first to want to bring pesticide use down. By teaming up with U.S. agricultural concerns, they say they can learn the latest techniques for growing produce without heavy pesticide use.

The problem with this scenario is—as always in Mexico—seeing that it comes to pass. In the past six years, Mexico has made hopeful strides toward stricter environmental standards, but its new regulations are undercut by a total lack of enforcement.

For example, despite the 1987 establishment of an elaborate agency to regulate pesticide use, Mexico still does not monitor pesticide residue levels on produce. (The Mexican government leaves that to growers and U.S. border authorities, who inspect an average of 1 percent of all shipments.) And while Mexico has comprehensive occupational-safety laws that mandate extensive precautions for workers who come into contact with toxic chemicals, there are no inspections to see that the laws are enforced.

"The regulations can be very good on paper, but if they don't verify and enforce them, it's as if they don't exist," says Dr. Arturo Lomeli, a prominent Mexican pesticide expert who is a member of the prestigious environmental organization El Grupo de los Cien. "Inspection and enforcement of worker-safety standards are almost unheard of. In all my years traveling to the fields, I've never seen a worker properly garbed for pesticide application."

If there is hope that the Mexican government will tackle pesticide abuse, it lies, advocates say, in NAFTA's torturously complex side accords on labor and the environment. Under the accords, private citizens have the right to complain if a government or industry is violating environmental or labor laws.

But under the pact, carefully worded to preserve the autonomy of the three countries, the person, group, or agency registering the complaint must be able to prove that the government engaged in a persistent pattern of failure to enforce the law effectively. The complaint must be brought first to a national office, which decides whether to set up an intergovernmental dispute-settlement panel. The panel, made up of representatives from all three governments, can recommend fining the offending government or initiating trade sanctions against it.

Unfortunately, environmentalists say, this process puts workers and environmentalists in the position of enforcing standards that the government should.

"It puts the burden on the victims to prove that they have been wronged," says Monica Moore, program director of the San Francisco-based Pesticide Action Network, North American Regional Center. "It's like putting out a little suggestion box in the capital city and calling that policy. It's just not the real world."

Esther Schrader is the award-winning Mexico City correspondent for the San Jose Mercury News. Research assistance by Anna Snider.

THIS MODERN WORLD by TOM TOMORROW

FUTURISM IS A GROWTH INDUSTRY THESE DAYS! MORNING NEWS SHOWS JUST AREN'T COMPLETE WITHOUT A SELF-PROCLAIMED **CYBER-PUNDIT** CHEERFULLY DESCRIBING THE **BRAVE NEW WORLD** AWAITING US **ALL!**

> --AND SOON EVERYONE WILL HAVE COMPUTERS SURGICALLY IMPLANTED IN THEIR **NOSES!**

> WELL I'LL BE! ISN'T THAT SOMETHING!

OF COURSE, THE FUTURE DOESN'T ALWAYS LIVE UP TO ITS **BILLING**... FOR INSTANCE, YOU MAY HAVE NOTICED A DISTINCT SHORTAGE OF **DOMED CITIES, FLYING CARS,** AND **MOON COLONIES** AS WE APPROACH THE MILLENIUM...

> GOSH BIFF-- ISN'T LIFE **WONDERFUL** HERE IN THE YEAR 1995?!

> YES--EVERYTHING TURNED OUT **JUST LIKE THEY PREDICTED!**

AND FRANKLY, WE DON'T SHARE THE POPULAR FAITH IN **TECHNOLOGY** AS A **CURE-ALL**... AFTER ALL, OUR **PRESENT-DAY** TECHNOLOGICAL CAPABILITIES ARE ASTONISHING--AND YET, MUCH OF THE PLANET IS STILL WRACKED BY FAMINE, POVERTY AND WAR...

> YEAH--BUT THERE'S SURE A LOT OF COOL **STUFF** TO **BUY!**

WIRED
WE'RE SO HIP WE COULD JUST PEE

STILL, THE FUTURISTS THRIVE... SERVING AS PROPAGANDISTS FOR A SANITIZED UTOPIAN VISION WHICH-- LIKE MANY BEFORE IT-- FAILS TO TAKE INTO ACCOUNT THE MESSY REALITY OF **HUMAN NATURE**...

> LAPTOP COMPUTERS WILL LEAD THE WAY TO GLORIOUS NEW VISTAS, COMRADES!

> WE MUST SHINE THE LIGHT OF CHAIRMAN GATES' BENEFICENCE UPON ANTI-REVOLUTIONARY LUDDITES EVERYWHERE!

TOM TOMORROW © 9-13-95

How to Nominate a Censored Story

Some of the most interesting nominations Project Censored has received are from people who spot something in the back pages of their newspaper or in a small-circulation magazine they subscribe to and wonder why they haven't seen anything reported about it elsewhere. In the same way, you can help the public learn more about what is happening in its society by nominating stories that you feel should have received more coverage from the national news media. The story should be current and of national or international significance. It may have received no media attention at all, appeared in your local newspaper or some special interest trade magazine, or been the subject of a radio or television documentary, which received little exposure or follow-up. Your nominations, input, and suggestions are important to the success of Project Censored, and we appreciate them. To nominate a *Censored* story of the year, just send us a copy of the story, including the source and date. The annual deadline is October 15. Please send regular mail nominations to the address below and e-mail nominations to: project.censored@sonoma.edu.

NOMINATION
PROJECT CENSORED
Sonoma State University
Rohnert Park, CA 94928

INDEX

About the Author

Dr. Carl Jensen is a professor emeritus of Communication Studies at Sonoma State University and Director of Project Censored, an internationally recognized media research project. Founded by Jensen in 1976, Project Censored is America's longest-running research project which annually explores news media censorship.

Jensen has been involved with the media for more than 40 years as a daily newspaper reporter, weekly newspaper publisher, public relations practitioner, advertising executive, and educator. He spent 15 years with Batten, Barton, Durstine, and Osborn, the international advertising agency, where he was an award-winning copywriter, account supervisor, and vice president.

Specializing in mass communications, Jensen received his B.A., M.A., and Ph.D. degrees in Sociology from the University of California, Santa Barbara, in 1971, 1972, and 1977, respectively.

Since 1973, he has been teaching media, sociology, and journalism courses at Sonoma State University where he developed Sonoma State University's B.A. degree in Communication Studies and the University's Journalism Certificate Program.

Jensen founded the Lincoln Steffens Journalism Award for Investigative Reporting in Northern California in 1981. He also participated in the development of the Bay Area Censored awards program by the Media Alliance in San Francisco in 1989 and in the development of Project Censored Canada in 1993.

He has written and lectured extensively about press censorship, the First Amendment, and the mass media.

Jensen has been cited by the national Association for Education in Journalism and Mass Communication for his "innovative approach to constructive media criticism and for providing a new model for media criticism." The Giraffe Project honored Jensen "for sticking his neck out for the common good" and for being a "role model for a caring society." The Media Alliance presented Jensen with the Media Alliance Meritorious Achievement Award in the "Unimpeachable Source" category. The Society of Professional Journalists in Los Angeles awarded him its 1990 Freedom of Information Award.

In 1992, Jensen was named the outstanding university professor of journalism in California by the California Newspaper Publishers Association and was awarded the 1992 Hugh M. Hefner First Amendment Award in education from the Playboy Foundation for his achievement in defending the First Amendment.

He has been a guest on many radio/television news and talk shows including a Bill Moyers PBS television documentary on Project Censored.

Jensen is married and has four children and three grandchildren. He, wife Sandra, and Danske, their great Great Dane, live in beautiful downtown Cotati, in Northern California.